An Introduction to the Philosophy of Psychology

Psychology aims to give us a scientific account of how the mind works. But what does it mean to have a science of the mental, and what sort of picture of the mind emerges from our best psychological theories? This book addresses these philosophical puzzles in a way that is accessible to readers with little or no background in psychology or neuroscience. Using clear and detailed case studies and drawing on up-to-date empirical research, it examines perception and action, the link between attention and consciousness, the modularity of mind, how we understand other minds, and the influence of language on thought, as well as the relationships among mind, brain, body, and world. The result is an integrated and comprehensive overview of much of the architecture of the mind, which will be valuable for both students and specialists in philosophy, psychology, and cognitive science.

DANIEL A. WEISKOPF is an associate professor of philosophy and an associate faculty member in the Neuroscience Institute at Georgia State University. He has published numerous articles and chapters on concepts and mental representation, the structure of higher cognition, embodied and extended cognition, mechanistic and functional explanation, and modeling practices in the mind/brain sciences.

FRED ADAMS is professor of linguistics & cognitive science and professor of philosophy at the University of Delaware. He has published more than 100 articles and chapters in philosophy of science, philosophy of mind, philosophy of language, epistemology, and other areas of cognitive science.

An Introduction to the Philosophy of Psychology

DANIEL A. WEISKOPF and
FRED ADAMS

CAMBRIDGE
UNIVERSITY PRESS

CAMBRIDGE
UNIVERSITY PRESS

University Printing House, Cambridge CB2 8BS, United Kingdom

One Liberty Plaza, 20th Floor, New York, NY 10006, USA

477 Williamstown Road, Port Melbourne, VIC 3207, Australia

314-321, 3rd Floor, Plot 3, Splendor Forum, Jasola District Centre, New Delhi - 110025, India

79 Anson Road, #06-04/06, Singapore 079906

Cambridge University Press is part of the University of Cambridge.

It furthers the University's mission by disseminating knowledge in the pursuit of education, learning and research at the highest international levels of excellence.

www.cambridge.org
Information on this title: www.cambridge.org/9780521740203

© Cambridge University Press 2015

First published 2015

A catalogue record for this publication is available from the British Library

Library of Congress Cataloging in Publication data
Weiskopf, Daniel A., 1973–
An introduction to the philosophy of psychology / Daniel A. Weiskopf and Frederick Adams.
    pages   cm. – (Cambridge introductions to philosophy)
ISBN 978-0-521-74020-3 (paperback)
1. Psychology – Philosophy.   I. Adams, Frederick.   II. Title.
BF38.W656   2015
150.1 – dc23   2014034058

ISBN 978-0-521-51929-8 Hardback
ISBN 978-0-521-74020-3 Paperback

In memory of my mother, Rene Shaffer Weiskopf (1947–2013), and my aunt, Marti Stelma (1947–2007).

They always gave me books. I wish they were still here so I could give them this one in return.

– DAW

In memory of Fred and Gladys Adams (1924–2012), for letting me pursue things the import of which they did not understand.

– FA

Contents

Figures

Preface

Our topic here is psychology, the self-styled science of the mind. Psychology's aim is to explain mental phenomena by describing the underlying processes, systems, and mechanisms that give rise to them. These hidden causal levers underlie all of our mental feats, including our richest conscious perceptions, our most subtle chains of reasoning, and our widest-ranging plans and actions. Although the phenomena of mind are intimately related to events occurring in the brain, these psychological explanations are, we will argue, distinct and autonomous relative to explanations in terms of neural processes and mechanisms. According to the view we present here, psychology and neuroscience are different enterprises. We certainly wouldn't claim that our ever-increasing understanding of how the brain works has nothing to say to psychology: on the contrary, they are complementary, because neuroscience can provide invaluable input to psychological theorizing (and vice versa, a point that we think is not stressed often enough). But our task will be to give a thorough account of the scope, methods, content, and prospects for a distinctive science of our mental lives.

This book is intended for students in philosophy, psychology, and the more cognitively oriented branches of neuroscience, as well as for readers who are merely curious about what these fields might have to contribute to our understanding of the mind. However, we hope that our professional colleagues will also find much to engage with here. So we've done our best to produce a book that holds interest on all levels – for undergraduates, graduates, and researchers alike. We have tried not to presuppose any significant background in any of the sciences that we discuss, and we hope that this book will serve as a useful companion for many of those pursuing the interdisciplinary study of cognition.

Part of our motivation in writing this book was to show philosophy of psychology to be, first and foremost, a branch of philosophy of science, not simply an adjunct to the philosophy of mind. This has meant making certain tough choices about what gets included and what gets left on the cutting-room floor. Readers hoping for discussions of the merits of the computational theory of mind or naturalized semantics, for example, will not find them prominently mentioned here. We hope that this omission is understandable, given that they have been widely discussed (nearly to exhaustion) elsewhere. However, that does not mean that metaphysical issues as such have been given short shrift. Rather, where they arise, we have tried to emphasize the consequences that they have for how we design studies and think about the broader implications of theories of cognition. Metaphysical questions about the mind, as they appear here, are always grounded in their relation to scientific practices.

In keeping with this theme, the structure of the book attempts to reflect as much as possible the topics that are actively debated among psychologists, as well as the standard research methods and explanatory strategies they employ. The experiments and theories we discuss, and the styles of argument that we use, should accordingly be ones that are quite familiar to those who know the psychological literature. One of our goals in sticking closely to the science is to give philosophers some sense for how arguments among various theoretical positions are actually decided in psychology. We especially hope to convey just how densely packed with details these arguments can be, and how many different empirical and theoretical commitments they must balance. Indeed, there is much more detail than any single volume could possibly contain, so we have provided extensive references to guide those interested in exploring the literature further.

That is not to say, however, that we have aimed to produce merely a neutral summary of the results. Far from it – we have organized and presented these materials in order to draw substantive conclusions. So this book is intended not only to introduce these debates in some depth but also to stake out positions on the issues, where the evidence seems to warrant it. Where we are taking steps beyond the evidence, we have flagged our views as conjectures to be explored further. We have always aimed to be fair to those we disagree with, but where the results seem to favor a particular view, we have said so emphatically. And we further hope that this will encourage those readers who disagree with us to develop their own views more forcefully by giving them something substantial to resist.

This book, then, may be thought of as an evenhanded, but opinionated, guide to how philosophers can get started thinking about the fascinating picture of the mind being painstakingly assembled by contemporary psychology. For reasons of space, and so as not to tax the finite appetites of our readers, we could not cover every topic of interest, nor could we cover the ones we do address in the full depth they deserve. Nonetheless, our hope is that this discussion is both fair and sufficient to introduce any curious and motivated reader to the field.

Acknowledgments

Several years ago, when Hilary Gaskin approached me (FA) about writing this book, I canvassed the existing books under the title "Philosophy of Psychology." There were several. After looking at them carefully, and meeting with Hilary at the APA meeting in Baltimore, I discovered that they were mainly traditional philosophy of mind books under a different title. So I decided that I would produce a genuine philosophy of psychology book – one that took seriously the *psychology*.

I also knew that to do this I would need help. So I considered persons who might join me in the writing of this book. I didn't have to look far. In 2007, Dan Weiskopf and I were giving papers at a conference organized by Shaun Gallagher at the University of Central Florida. Dan went first on the topic of embodied cognition. To my horror, as he was giving his paper I had the thought, "He's giving my talk tomorrow." This convinced me that anyone who thought so much like me would be the ideal colleague with whom to produce this book. And I was exactly right in my choice. Dan was the ideal colleague on such a project.

What is more, during the writing of this book, Dan and I both experienced close personal family loss. As a result, Dan took over many of the responsibilities in producing this book that should have fallen to me. For that, I am forever grateful to him.

We are both deeply grateful to Hilary Gaskin, Gillian Dadd, Anna Lowe, and the entire staff at Cambridge University Press for their patience, encouragement, and help.

Thanks are also due to Shaun Gallagher and James Garvey, respectively, for permission to use small portions of material from Adams, F. (2010). Embodied cognition. *Phenomenology and the Cognitive Sciences, 9*(4), 619–628; and Adams, F., & Beighley, S. (2011). The mark of the mental, for a special volume edited by James Garvey of the Royal Institute of Philosophy, *The Continuum Companion to the Philosophy of Mind* (pp. 54–72). London, England: Continuum International Publishing Group.

FA, Hockessin, DE

The true beginnings of a thing are impossible to know. But the inception of my own interest in philosophy can, officially at least, be dated with some precision. In the first semester of my freshman year of college I enrolled in Richard Wollheim's introductory class, "The Nature of Mind." I recall little of the specific course content, aside from snippets of Freud and Chomsky, but the lectures were enthralling, full of new tools and vocabulary for thinking about the mind, and Wollheim patiently tolerated my many confused questions after class. I had started college with interests in cell biology and literature. In a fit of youthful enthusiasm, I switched my schedule around to accommodate as many philosophy classes as I could, thereby causing my parents no small amount of alarm. Thanks, then, to Professor Wollheim for an introduction that changed my life. Later coursework with John Searle and the psycholinguist Dan Slobin further convinced me that philosophy could be a productive partner with scientific inquiry and deepened my interests in language and mind. Finally, in my senior year, Bruce Vermazen kindly allowed me to take his graduate seminar on mental causation and encouraged my first attempts at extended philosophical writing. This seems like an appropriate place to say that I'm grateful to them, as well as to all of my early teachers, faculty and graduate assistants alike. Without their guidance, none of this would have been possible.

My sincere thanks to Fred for pitching this project to me, and for the comically accurate account of our meeting above. I'd also like to enthusiastically join him in adding my gratitude to the editorial staff at Cambridge University Press, whose generosity and professionalism have been exceptional. Thanks as well to the chair of the philosophy department at Georgia State University, George Rainbolt, for helping to arrange my teaching schedule in a way that gave me ample time for writing. Discussions with Eric Winsberg helped to frame some of the material on scientific explanation, and Muhammad Ali Khalidi offered helpful comments on a draft of the chapter on nativism. My friends and family have had to endure more than the usual amount of crankiness from me during the drafting of this manuscript, and I thank them for their patience and occasional attempts to slap me back in line. Finally, most of the words I write are composed with the assistance of – or, to be honest, over the loud protests of – my cat Sophie. Her endearing but baffling behavior is a constant reminder that some things are meant to be loved, not understood.

DAW, Atlanta, GA

1 What psychology is

1.1 A science of mind

We spend an enormous number of our waking hours thinking and talking about our thoughts, emotions, and experiences. For example, we wonder: Why did the waiter give me that unusual smile? Did my co-worker see me stealing those office supplies? How can I deflect my unwanted admirer's attention – or attract the attention of someone else? In trying to answer such questions, and in interpreting one another's behavior more generally, we make use of a vast body of lore about how people perceive, reason, desire, feel, and so on. So we say such things as: the waiter is smiling obsequiously because he hopes I will give him a larger tip; my co-worker does know, but he won't tell anyone, because he's afraid I'll reveal his gambling problem; and so on. Formulating such explanations is part of what enables us to survive in a shared social environment.

This everyday understanding of our minds, and those of others, is referred to as "folk psychology." The term is usually taken as picking out our ability to attribute psychological states and to use those attributions for a variety of practical ends, including prediction, explanation, manipulation, and deception. It encompasses our ability to verbally produce accounts couched in the everyday psychological vocabulary with which most of us are conversant: the language of beliefs, desires, intentions, fears, hopes, and so on. Such accounts are the stuff of which novels and gossip are made. Although our best evidence for what people think is often what they say, much of our capacity to read the thoughts of others may also be nonverbal, involving the ability to tell moods and intentions immediately by various bodily cues – an ability we may not be conscious that we have.

Although we have an important stake in the success of our folk psychological attributions and explanations, and while social life as we know it would be impossible without folk psychology, folk psychology also has obvious shortcomings (Churchland, 1981). Our accounts of one another's behavior are often sketchy, unsystematic, or of merely local utility. Moreover, they leave out whole ranges of abnormal mental phenomena such as autism or Capgras syndrome. We have no folk explanation for how we are able to perceive and navigate our way through a three-dimensional space cluttered with objects, how we integrate what we see with what we hear and touch, how we are able to learn language, how we recognize faces and categories, how our memory works, how we reason and make decisions, and so on. The explanations of these varied mental capacities lie far beyond folk psychology's province. If we want to understand the mind, then we need to find better ways to investigate its structure and function. The sciences of the mind have developed in response to this need.

Science aims at systematic understanding of the world, and psychology is the science that takes mental phenomena in general as its domain. This definition has not always been uncontroversially accepted. Behaviorists such as Watson (1913) and Skinner (1965) held that the only proper subject matter for psychology was the domain of observable behavior, in part on the grounds that minds were mysterious and inaccessible to third-person methods of investigation. Few today take this position. Mental states and processes may not be directly observable, but they can be inferred by a variety of converging techniques. Cognitive psychology in particular typically proceeds by positing such inferred states. Many of these states such as occurrent perceptions and thoughts are accessible via introspection with varying degrees of accuracy, but many are entirely unconscious.

"Phenomena" is a cover term for the body of noteworthy natural regularities to be found in the objects, events, processes, activities, and capacities that a science concerns itself with.[1] Objects can include such things as whole organisms (white rats, the sea slug *Aplysia californica*), artificial behaving systems (a trained neural network, an autonomous mobile robot), or their parts (the brain, particular brain structures such as the hippocampus or the supplementary motor area, a particular control structure in a computer). Here the relevant phenomena are reliable patterns of organization or behavior in these objects – for example, the predictable laminar organization and connectivity patterns in the neocortex. Events and processes include any changes

---

[1] This usage follows Hacking (1983). See also Bogen and Woodward (1988).

undergone by these objects: the myelination of the frontal lobes in normal development, a rat's learning to run a water maze, a child acquiring the lexicon of her first language, an undergraduate carrying out a motor task in response to a visual stimulus, a patient with dementia retrieving a memory of an event from his teenage years. Activities and capacities include any functions that an object can reliably carry out. Normal humans have the capacity to rapidly estimate quantity, to selectively attend to parts of a complex visual array, to judge which of two events is more likely, to generate expectations about the movement of simple physical objects in their environment, to attribute emotional states to others, and so on.

Mental phenomena encompass attention, learning and memory, concept acquisition and categorization, language acquisition, perception (both accurate and illusory), and emotions and moods, among others. We won't try to be exhaustive. Traditional distinctions among types of mental states have been made along the following lines. Some mental states involve concepts in their formation, expression, and function. These are the types of states associated with higher cognition and knowledge (from which "cognitive" derives its name). Such states include beliefs, desires, intentions, hopes, and plain old thoughts in general. Other sorts of states, such as sensory states, do not necessarily involve concepts in their activation. One can smell a rose without knowing that it is a rose one smells. One can hear a C-sharp on the piano without knowing that it is a C-sharp one hears. Emotions such as fear, love, and anger also form a distinctive class of mental states. Finally, there are moods: general overall feelings of excitement, happiness, sadness, mania, and depression.

Is there anything that all mental phenomena have in common? This is controversial, but one proposal is that they are all *representational*.[2] The higher cognitive states that involve concepts clearly involve representations that can fit into propositional attitudes and generate knowledge of various facts and states of affairs. Sensory states do not necessarily involve the activation of concepts, but they are still a type of representation on at least some views. They represent the presence of a physically perceptible property and the causal interaction of that property with a sensory system of the body. The sweet taste of sugar represents the interaction of the sugar molecules with

---

[2] We discuss the issue of how to distinguish mental phenomena in greater depth in Section 5.4.4.

the taste receptors in the mouth, for instance. Even moods have been portrayed as representations of general chemical states or changes in the body.

One goal of the sciences is to describe, clarify, and organize these phenomena. Consider the changes that the past 50 years have wrought in our understanding of the cognitive capacities of infants and young children, for example. At some point, normal children become able to understand and interpret the behavior of others in terms of their beliefs, intentions, and desires. In a pioneering study, Wimmer and Perner (1983) showed that four-year-olds are able to correctly predict how characters with false beliefs will act, whereas younger children are unable to do so. In one of their now-classic tasks, the child watches one puppet place a piece of candy in a certain location and then leave the room. The other puppet, which was present when the candy was hidden, now moves it to a new hidden location. The first puppet then returns, and the child is asked either where she will look for the candy or where she thinks the candy is. Passing this so-called false belief task involves correctly saying that she will look in the original location, rather in the actual location, since she will be guided not by the candy's actual location, but by her erroneous beliefs about it. Here the phenomenon of interest is the alleged shift from failure to success in this particular test (and related variants). This result was widely interpreted as showing that some components of "theory of mind" – those connected with the attribution of beliefs – are not yet in place prior to age four.[3]

Surprisingly, though, in recent years it has been shown that even 15-month-olds can respond in a way that seems to display understanding of false beliefs (Onishi & Baillargeon, 2005). These infants will look longer at a scene depicting a character searching in a place that she could not know an object is located (because she had earlier seen it hidden elsewhere) than at a scene in which she searched for it in the place where she should expect it to be. Looking time in infants is often taken to be an indicator of surprise or violation of expectancy, an interpretation confirmed by studies across many different stimuli and domains. Thus the 15-month-olds in this study don't seem to expect the characters to have information about the true state of the world; this strongly suggests that they naturally attribute something like false beliefs. Moreover, 16-month-olds will even act on this understanding, trying to help out individuals who are attempting to act on false beliefs by

---

[3] For much more on theory of mind, see Chapter 8.

pointing to the correct location of a hidden toy (Buttelmann, Carpenter, & Tomasello, 2009).

This case illustrates two points. First, what the phenomena are in psychology, as in other sciences, is often nonobvious. That is, one cannot, in general, simply look and see that a certain pattern or regularity exists. Experiment and measurement are essential for the production of many interesting psychological phenomena. Second, phenomena are almost always tied closely to experimental tasks or paradigms. The phenomenon of three-year-olds failing the false belief task and four-year-olds passing it depends greatly on *which* false belief task one uses. If we agree to call the nonverbal Onishi and Baillargeon paradigm a false belief task, we need to explain the seeming contradiction between the phenomena, perhaps in terms of the differing requirements of the tasks (Bloom & German, 2000). Individuating phenomena is intimately tied to individuating tasks and experimental methods.

To see this, consider the Stroop effect. In his classic paper, Stroop (1935) performed three experiments, the first two of which are the most well known. In experiment 1, he asked participants to read color names printed in a variety of differently colored inks. The names were given in a 10 × 10 grid, and no name was ever paired with the color of ink that it named. The control condition required reading the same names printed in black ink. Subtracting the time to read the experimental versus the control cards, Stroop found that on average it took slightly longer to read the color names printed in differently colored ink, but this difference was not significant. In experiment 2, he required participants to name the color of the ink in the experimental condition, rather than reading the color name. In the control condition, words were replaced with colored squares. Here the difference in reading times was striking: participants were 74% slower to name the ink color when it conflicted with the color name versus simply naming the color from a sample. Conflicting lexical information interferes with color naming.

Although this is the canonical "Stroop effect," the term has been broadened over time to include a range of related phenomena. Stroop-like tasks have been carried out using pictures or numbers versus words, using auditory rather than visual materials, using nonverbal response measures, and so on. Further manipulations have involved varying the time at which the conflicting stimulus is presented (e.g., showing the color sample before the word), and the effect persists. Wherever responding to one kind of information interferes asymmetrically with responding to another that is simultaneously presented, we have a Stroop-like phenomenon. Much of the literature on the effect has focused on delineating the precise sorts of stimuli, tasks, and populations that display the effect (MacLeod, 1991). But the effect itself is elusive outside the context of these experimental manipulations – certainly it is not a straightforwardly observable behavioral regularity on a par with wincing in response to being kicked. More esoteric phenomena may be reliant on even more sophisticated experimental setups for their elicitation.

In these cases, what psychologists are primarily aiming to do is to *characterize* the phenomena. This may require deploying new experimental paradigms, modifying the parameters of old paradigms, or refining techniques of data collection and analysis. The phenomena themselves are dependent on these techniques of investigation for their existence. Producing and measuring these phenomena involve discovering how various parts of the psychological domain behave when placed in relatively artificial circumstances, under the assumption that this will be importantly revealing about their normal structure and function. This is perhaps the biggest advantage scientific psychology has over its folk counterpart, which tends to be resolutely nonexperimental.

But beyond producing and describing phenomena – that is, saying *what* happens in the world – psychology also aims to explain *how* and *why* they are produced. Where we are dealing with genuine, robust phenomena, we assume, as an initial hypothesis at least, that they are not merely accidental. There ought to be some reason why they exist and take the particular form that they do. It is sometimes maintained that what is distinctive about scientific theorizing, as opposed to other ways of reasoning about the world, is that it involves positing and testing explanations. As we have seen, this can't be the whole story, because making and refining ways in which we might better describe the world are themselves major parts of the scientific enterprise. But the psychological phenomena we discover often turn out to be novel or surprising. Hence better descriptions of the phenomena naturally tend to pull us toward generating explanations for their existence.

1.2 Explanations in psychology

We shouldn't assume that all sciences will deploy the same explanatory strategies. What works to explain geological or astronomical phenomena may not work for psychological phenomena. So we begin by considering four sample cases of psychological explanation. We should note that these explanations are to varying degrees contested, but the present issue is what they can tell us about the structure of explanations in psychology, rather than whether they are strictly accurate.

1.2.1 Case 1: Psychophysics

Some of the earliest systematic psychological research in the nineteenth century concerned psychophysical phenomena, in particular how the properties of sensations depend on and vary with the properties of the physical stimulus that produces them. Light, sound waves, pressure, temperature, and other ambient energy sources interact with sensory receptors and their associated processing systems to give rise to sensations, and this relationship is presumably systematic rather than random. To uncover this hidden order, early psychophysicists had to solve three problems simultaneously: (1) how to devise empirical strategies for measuring sensations, (2) how to quantify the ways in which those sensations covaried with stimulus conditions, and, finally, (3) how to explain those covariations.

Fechner (1860), following the work of Weber (1834), hit on the method of using "just noticeable differences" (jnd's) to measure units of sensation. A stimulus in some sensory modality (e.g., a patch of light, a tone) is increased in intensity until the perceiver judges that there is a detectable change in the quality of her sensations. The measure of a jnd in physical terms is the difference between the initial and final stimulus magnitude. By increasing stimulus intensity until the next jnd was reached, Fechner could plot the intervals at which a detectable change in a sensation occurred against the stimulus that caused the change.

After laboriously mapping stimulus–sensation pairs in various modalities, Fechner proposed a logarithmic law to capture their relationship formally. Fechner's law states:

$$S = k \log(I)$$

where S is the perceived magnitude of the sensation (e.g., the brightness of a light or the loudness of a sound), I is the intensity of the physical stimulus, and k is an empirically determined constant. Because this is a logarithmic law, geometric increases in stimulus intensity will correspond to arithmetic increases in the strength of sensations.

Although Fechner's law delivers predictions that conform with much of the data, it also fails in some notable cases. Stevens (1957) took a different experimental approach. Rather than constructing scales using jnd's, he asked participants to directly estimate magnitudes of various stimuli using arbitrary numerical values. So an initial stimulus would be given a numerical value, and then later stimuli were given values relative to it, where all of the numerical assignments were freely chosen by the participants. He also asked them to directly estimate stimulus ratios, such as when one stimulus seemed to be twice as intense as another. Using these methods, he showed that the perceived intensity of some stimuli departed from Fechner's law. He concluded that Fechner's assumption that all jnd's are of equal size was to blame for the discrepancy and proposed as a replacement for Fechner's law the power law (now known as Stevens' law):

$$S = kI^a$$

where S and I are perceived magnitude and physical intensity, k is a constant, and a is an exponent that differs for various sensory modalities and perceivable quantities. The power law predicts that across all quantities and modalities, equal stimulus ratios correspond to equal sensory ratios, and, depending on the exponent, perceived magnitudes may increase more quickly or more slowly than the increase in stimulus intensity.

Stevens (1975, pp. 17–19) gave an elegant argument for why we should expect sensory systems in general to obey a power law. He noted that as we move around and sense the environment, the absolute magnitudes we perceive will vary: the visual angle subtended by the wall of a house changes as one approaches it; the intensity of speech sounds varies as one approaches or recedes. What is important in these cases is not the differences in the stimulus, but the constants, which are given by the ratios that the elements of the stimulus bear to one another. A power law is well suited to capture this, because equal ratios of stimulus intensity correspond to equal ratios of sensory magnitude.

Stevens' law provides a generally better fit for participants' judgments about magnitudes and therefore captures the phenomena of stimulus–sensation relations better than Fechner's law, although it, too, is only approximate.[4] However, both laws provide the same sort of explanation for the relationship between the two: in each case, the laws show that these relationships are not arbitrary, but instead conform to a general formula, which can be expressed by a relatively simple equation. The laws explain the phenomena by showing how they can all be systematically related in a simple, unified fashion. Once we have the law in hand, we are in a position to make predictions about the relationship between unmeasured magnitudes, to the effect that they will probably conform to the regularity set out in the law (even if the precise form of the regularity requires empirically determining the values of k and a).

1.2.2 Case 2: Classical conditioning

Any organism that is to survive for long in an environment with potentially changing conditions needs some way of learning about the structure of events in its environment. Few creatures lead such simple lives that they can be born "knowing" all they will need to survive. The investigation of learning in animals (and later humans) started with the work of Pavlov, Skinner, Hull, and other behaviorists. Given their aversion to mentalistic talk, they tended to think of learning as a measurable change in the observable behavior of a creature in response to some physical stimulus or other. The simplest style of learning is classical (Pavlovian) conditioning. In classical conditioning, we begin with an organism that reliably produces a determinate type of response to a determinate type of stimulus – for example, flinching in response to a mild shock, or blinking in response to a puff of air. The stimulus here is called the unconditioned stimulus (US), and the response the unconditioned response (UR). In a typical experiment, the US is paired with a novel, neutral stimulus (e.g., a flash of light or a tone) for a training period; this is referred to as the conditioned stimulus (CS). After time, under the right training conditions, the CS becomes associated with the US, so that the CS is capable of producing the response by itself; when this occurs, it is called the conditioned response (CR).

There were a number of early attempts to formulate descriptions of how conditioning takes place (Bush & Mosteller, 1951; Hull, 1943). These descriptions take the form of learning rules that predict how the strength of

---

[4] For useful discussion on the history and logic of various psychophysical scaling procedures, see Shepard (1978) and Gescheider (1988).

associations among CS and US will change over time under different training regimes. One of the most well-known and best empirically validated learning rules was the "delta rule" presented by Rescorla and Wagner (1972). Formally, the rule says:[5]

$$\Delta A_{ij} = \alpha_i \beta_j (\lambda_j - \Sigma_i A_{ij})$$

To grasp what this means, suppose we are on training trial n, and we want to know what the associative strengths will be at the next stage $n + 1$. Let i stand for the CS and j stand for the US. Then A_{ij} is the strength of the association between i and j, and ΔA_{ij} is the change in the strength of that association as a result of training. The terms α_i and β_j are free parameters that determine the rate at which learning can take place involving the CS and US. The term λ_j is the maximum associative strength that the US can support. Finally, $\Sigma_i A_{ij}$ is the sum of the strength of all of the active CSs that are present during trial n. This is needed because some learning paradigms involve presenting multiple CSs at the same time during training.

The essence of the Rescorla–Wagner rule is to reduce the "surprisingness" of a US. If a CS (i) is not associated strongly with a US (j), then (assuming no other CSs are present), the parenthetical term of the rule will be large, and so the strength of the association between i and j will be correspondingly adjusted. Over time, as its association with the CS increases, the surprisingness of the US decreases, and so less change in strength takes place.

The Rescorla–Wagner rule is one of the most extensively studied learning rules in psychology, and it has some significant virtues: it unifies a large range of phenomena by bringing them under a single, relatively simple formal description; it explains previously discovered phenomena; and it generates surprising and often-confirmed predictions about new phenomena. To get the flavor of this, consider some of its successes: (1) The rule explains why acquisition curves show less change over time, for the reason given in the previous paragraph. (2) Extinction is the loss of response to a CS when it is presented without its paired US. The model explains this by positing that

---

[5] Gallistel (1990, Chapter 12) gives an excellent critical discussion of the assumptions underlying the R-W rule and its predecessors. He notes that the R-W rule is cast in terms of associative strengths rather than directly observable response probabilities, which represents a significant change of emphasis over earlier behavioristic rules. For a review of some important behavioral findings concerning conditioning, see Rescorla (1988).

during nonreinforced trials, the λ_j term goes to zero and the β_j term is lower than for acquisition, so association strengths will gradually decrease. (3) The rule explains the phenomenon of blocking, which occurs when CS A is paired in pretraining with US, followed by training in which the conjunction of CS A and CS B is paired with US. The result is that pretrained organisms show less association between B and US than do those that lack pretraining; in this case, B is said to be blocked by A. (4) The rule also explains overshadowing, which occurs when A and B are presented simultaneously. In this case, reinforcing AB results in B having less associative strength than if it were reinforced without A. Both overshadowing and blocking were significant challenges to earlier learning rules (Kamin, 1969). The rule's further empirical successes are too numerous to mention here, but see Miller, Barnet, and Grahame (1995) for more examples, as well as cases in which its predictions are not confirmed.

1.2.3 Case 3: Visual attention

Visual perception normally presents us with a world of separate and rela-tively enduring objects and events. The brown wooden chair appears separate from the black coat draped over it, and the gray cat appears separate from the orange couch across which she walks. But this division of the world into objects with determinate properties is not obviously given just by the incoming light array itself. It requires some mechanisms of processing and interpretation in order to be extracted. Based on an extensive series of experi-ments, Treisman (1988) proposed an influential cognitive model of how stable perceptions of objects and their properties are produced that give attention a central role.

In Treisman's model, visual processing takes place in a series of "layers." These layers represent the properties that can be represented by the visual system. The layers are internally organized like "maps" of the properties that the visual system can extract from the low-level signals passed on from the retina and other early stages of visual processing. One map simply encodes locations in visual space and records for each location whether a visual feature is present or absent there. This master location map does not, however, specify *what* features are at which locations – it encodes only locations, presences, and absences. A hierarchy of further maps encodes the possible features that can be detected in the visual scene. Color is one dimension along which objects can vary, so one map encodes possible color values an object may have

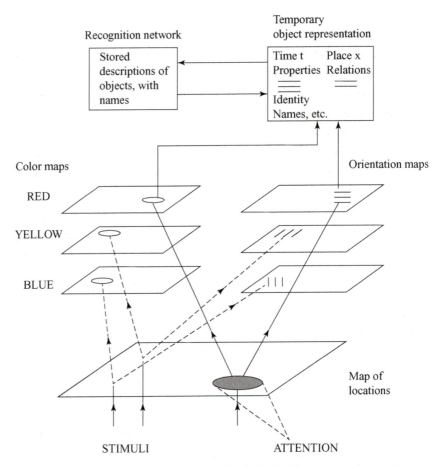

Figure 1.1   (from Treisman, 1988) A model of visual object perception and attention. Objects are represented by features located within maps. An object's location is encoded in a master spatial map, while the color and shape of the object's parts are encoded in separate maps. Attention integrates all of these features into an object file that is then used to identify the object based on what is stored in memory.

(red, orange, blue, etc.). Orientation is another (vertical, horizontal), as are size, motion, etc. The visual qualities that define how a perceived object is represented are distributed across this set of maps.

Attention is the "glue" that binds these separate features together into a unified perceptual representation of an object. When we focus our attention on a region of space, the features that are associated with that region at a time are jointly activated and packaged into an "object file" representation. This representation indicates that there is something at location *l* that has features $f_1, f_2, \ldots, f_n$ at time t. Object files represent objects in terms of their visually detectable characteristics and can be passed on to further systems for elaboration and processing. For instance, an object file that describes a small black fuzzy object moving from left to right across the visual field might be classified as a *cat*, thus making available a stored body of information about cat behavior for the guidance of immediate action. Without attention, however, there is strictly speaking no perception of spatial locations as containing objects with determinate sets of properties.

This model explains a number of surprising phenomena: (1) Searching for objects defined by conjunctive features is a serial process, taking more time when there are more distractor items present; disjunctively defined objects, on the other hand, do not require more time to be located, even when the number of distractors increases. (2) Participants experience illusory conjunctions of features in conditions of divided attention, such as misperceiving a black "X" as a green "X" when they were adjacent to one another. (3) Participants could not reliably identify *conjunctions* of features (e.g., being a red "O" or a blue "X") without accurately finding their location, whereas they could reliably identify individual features even when they could not localize them accurately. (4) When attention is cued to a spatial location, identification of conjunctive targets is facilitated, whereas there is little effect on targets defined by a single feature; moreover, invalid location cues disproportionately affect conjunction targets. These and many other results are summarized in Treisman (1988). Taken together, they suggest that the underlying architecture of object perception depends on an attentional binding mechanism similar to the one Treisman outlines.

1.2.4 Case 4: Reading and dyslexia

Once we have achieved proficiency at reading, it seems phenomenologically simple and immediate, like other skilled performances. We perceive complex letter forms; group them into words; access their meaning, phonological characteristics, and syntactic properties; and then speak them aloud. But the cognitive substructures underlying this performance are complex. Evidence from acquired dyslexias (disorders of reading) has been especially important in providing insight into the structure of this underlying system.

Classifying the dyslexias themselves is no simple task, but a few basic categories are well established. In assessing patients' impairment, three major stimulus categories are typically discussed: regular words (those whose pronunciation conforms to a set of rules mapping orthography onto phonology), irregular words (those whose pronunciation must be learned one word at a time), and pronounceable nonwords (strings that can be spoken aloud according to the phonological rules of the language). Surface dyslexia, initially described by Marshall and Newcombe (1973), involves selective impairment in reading irregular words ("sword," "island") versus regular words ("bed," "rest"). Many of these errors involve overregularization: "steak" might be pronounced as "steek," while "speak" would be pronounced normally. Pronounceable nonwords (e.g., "smeak," "datch") are also read normally – that is, as the rules mapping letters onto sounds would predict for normal speakers. McCarthy and Warrington (1986) present a case study of surface dyslexia, focusing on patient KT. He was able to read both regular words and nonwords, but failed to consistently pronounce irregular words correctly; the maximum accuracy he attained on high-frequency irregular words was 47%. Phonological dyslexia, on the other hand, involves selective impairment in reading pronounceable nonwords versus matched words. There is generally no difference between regular and irregular words. One such patient is WB, whose disorders were described by Funnell (1983). WB was unable to correctly pronounce any of 20 nonwords, but was able to pronounce correctly 85% of the 712 words he was presented with, which included nouns, adjectives, verbs, and functor words. Although there was some effect of frequency on his pronunciation of words, nonwords were unpronounceable even when they were simple monosyllables.

Surface and phonological dyslexia present a pattern of dissociations that suggest that normal reading is not a unitary cognitive faculty. In the former, there is impairment of irregular words relative to regular words and nonwords; in the latter, there is impairment of nonwords relative to regular and irregular words. Although these dissociations are rarely perfect – there is some preserved function in KT's case, and WB is somewhat impaired on infrequent words – they suggest that reading is explained by a set of connected systems that can be selectively impaired. The classic model to explain these dissociations is the dual-route model of reading presented first by Marshall and Newcombe (1973) and revised subsequently by Morton and Patterson (1980), Patterson and Morton (1985), and Coltheart, Curtis, Atkins, and Haller (1993). On this model, reading involves an initial stage of visual analysis, during which visual features are scanned and anything resembling a letter is extracted. These representations of letter strings may then be passed to two distinct pathways. One pathway runs through the lexicon: the internal dictionary in which the semantic, syntactic, and phonological properties of words are stored. A representation of some letter string can access the lexicon only if it matches the visual form of some known word. If it does, then its meaning and phonological properties are retrieved, and the sound pattern it matches is passed to the articulation system, which generates the act of speaking the word.

Aside from this lexical pathway, there is also a pathway that does not involve the lexicon, but rather pronounces strings by applying a set of grapheme–phoneme correspondence (GPC) rules. These rules generate phonemic output for any string in accord with the normal pronunciation rules of the language. Hence they can produce appropriate output for regular words and pronounceable nonwords, but they cannot generate correct pronunciation for irregular strings. It is the presence of both the lexical and GPC routes to reading that give the dual-route model its name.

From the architecture of the model, it should be clear how surface and phonological dyslexia are to be explained – indeed, this is bound to be the case, because the model was developed and refined in part to account for those very phenomena. In surface dyslexia, the lexical reading route is damaged, but the GPC route is intact. This accounts for these patients' ability to read regular words and nonwords – the GPC route can produce the right output for both cases. It also explains the overregularization errors on irregular words, because the GPC route is only capable of presenting regular outputs to letter strings. Phonological dyslexia involves damage to the GPC route with a generally intact lexical route. Hence both regular and irregular words can be pronounced, so long as they have entries in the mental lexicon; however, nonwords that do not resemble any known words cannot be pronounced, because the rule system that could interpret them is unavailable.[6]

1.3 Laws and mechanisms

For several decades of the twentieth century, one conception of scientific explanation reigned virtually unchallenged. This was the idea that explanation in science essentially involves appealing to laws of nature.

[6] The dual-route model has been modified extensively over the years to account for other types of dyslexia, particularly "deep" dyslexia and nonsemantic dyslexia; there have also been single-route models that have attempted to capture the same phenomena (Seidenberg & McClelland, 1989).

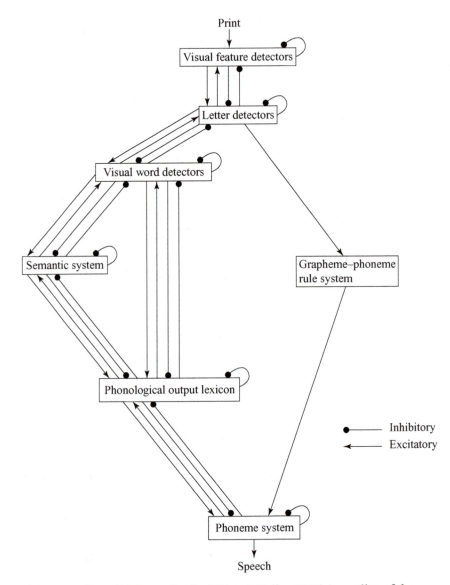

Figure 1.2   (from Coltheart, Curtis, Atkins, & Haller, 1993) An outline of the dual-route model of reading. The model takes visual words as inputs and produces spoken words as outputs. The main components are a lexical system for identifying whole words (left branch) and a nonlexical system for applying general rules of pronunciation to sound out words (right branch). The two routes explain why reading disorders are not all-or-nothing but instead have specific patterns of dissociation.

This conception is known as the covering-law (CL) view of explanation. The long history of this idea is not our present concern, but its outline is easy enough to sketch (see Hempel & Oppenheim, 1948; Hempel, 1965, for original statements of the view; and Salmon, 1989, for a review).

The CL view has three main components. First, scientific explanations are essentially deductively valid arguments in which the existence of the explanandum (the phenomenon to be explained) follows from the explanans (the things that do the explaining). So we explain a particular event such as a monkey's strengthened association between stimulus and response on a learning task, a neuron's firing an action potential, or the occurrence of a solar eclipse at a particular place and time by deducing the existence of that event from a set of premises. This captures the idea that there is a relationship between explanation and prediction: to explain a phenomenon is to have been in the position to predict its occurrence, given foreknowledge of the appropriate facts.

The second component is the requirement that among the premises there must be at least one law of nature. A law of nature is understood to be a generalization linking the occurrence of one event to the occurrence of another (or linking one property to another). To borrow Hempel and Oppenheim's (1948) example, how do we explain the fact that the mercury level in a glass thermometer will rise when it is immersed in boiling water? We can deduce that the mercury rises from the laws of heat conduction and thermal expansion, along with a description of the thermometer itself, the temperature of the water, and other antecedent conditions. These laws themselves describe how events of one sort (e.g., applications of heat to an object) lead to events of other sorts (conduction of heat throughout the object, expansion of the heated object, etc.). This illustrates how a particular phenomenon could have been predicted if only one had knowledge of the appropriate prior conditions and the laws governing how entities in those conditions behave in general.

The third component is that the statements included in the explanans must all be true. Given that explanations take the form of deductively valid arguments, this guarantees that the statement of the explanandum will also be true. The broader idea behind this component is that good explanations should not make essential use of false claims.

This pattern of explanation can be extended to general laws as well as particular events. Although Hempel and Oppenheim (1948) did not take this step, Nagel (1961) proposed that laws and theories at one level could be deduced from – and hence, in his terms, *reduced to* – laws of a lower-level science. In his famous example, the Boyle–Charles law (that the temperature of an ideal gas is proportional to the product of its pressure and the volume of its container) can be deduced from the laws of statistical mechanics (relating pressure and volume to mean kinetic energy) plus a set of supplementary statements he called "bridge principles." Bridge principles (or bridge laws) relate the theoretical terms used in the laws at one level to those used in the laws at another level. These are required because the vocabulary of one theory typically contains terms not contained by that of another. So, in this case, if we add a bridge principle relating mean kinetic energy (a term used in statistical mechanics) to temperature (a term used in thermodynamics), we can deduce, with a few supplementary assumptions, that the Boyle–Charles law holds under certain specified boundary conditions. Hence we can see how at least some thermodynamic laws are explained in terms of underlying statistical mechanical laws.

Not every case in which one set of laws can be deduced from another is clearly a case of reduction: Galileo's laws of falling bodies can be deduced from Newton's laws of motion and gravitation in conjunction with the facts concerning the Earth's mass and radius, but this is less a case of reduction and more a case of showing these laws to be an instance of more general ones. But whether or not all such cases are reductive, Nagel's model shows that both particular and general phenomena can be explained by subsuming the explanandum under some law-involving explanans. We will return to the issue of reductionism in later chapters when we discuss the relationship between psychological and neuroscientific phenomena.

In fleshing out the CL view, we need to say something about what laws themselves are. This question has proven extremely recalcitrant, and philosophers have not converged on a common analysis. For our purposes, we will (to a first approximation) take laws to be true counterfactual supporting generalizations. Saying that laws support counterfactuals means that laws have modal force; they specify not just how things happen to be in the actual world, but also how they would have to be in relevantly similar worlds. So Coulomb's law states that the electrostatic force between two charged bodies is proportional to the product of their individual charges divided by the square of the distance between them. This law makes true other claims about how particular charged bodies *would* behave under different circumstances – for example, if the magnitude of their charges, or the distance between them, were

increased or decreased in various ways. Compare this to the true generalization that all the milk in Dan's refrigerator is past its drink-by date. This does
not similarly entail the truth of the corresponding counterfactual: it isn't
true that if this bottle of unexpired milk were in Dan's fridge now, it would
be past its drink-by date. It is merely accidental that his milk is all expired,
whereas it isn't accidental that charged bodies obey Coulomb's law. Although
the distinction between accidental and so-called lawlike generalizations is
difficult to draw precisely, some such distinction in terms of counterfactual
force is presupposed by the account of laws we are assuming here.

Finally, laws may be either strict or hedged with ceteris paribus conditions.
Strict laws are those that hold without exception: there is no case in which
the antecedent of the law is satisfied but its consequent is not. Hedged laws,
on the other hand, are those that obtain only under certain conditions – they
have force, all things being equal, but they may have exceptions. Philosophers
of science have typically supposed that strict laws, if there are any, are to
be found only in basic physics, whereas the various special sciences that
deal with nonbasic phenomena are more likely to contain ceteris paribus
laws. As with the notion of law itself, explaining what it is for a law to
hold ceteris paribus has proven extremely controversial. One prominent
idea (due to Fodor, 1968) is that nonbasic laws are typically implemented
by complex lower-level structures and processes. The law will hold only in
those cases when these implementing structures are operating correctly or
without interference – that is, when conditions are, in some open-ended and
difficult-to-specify way, "normal." Others have replied that there are no true
ceteris paribus laws and that, where we seem to have one, there is in fact
a concealed strict law operating that just needs to be spelled out in further
detail. We discuss the status of ceteris paribus laws further in the next
section.

In recent years, an alternative view of explanation has been developed as a
rival to the CL view. This new challenger is the mechanistic view of explanation developed by Bechtel (2008), Bechtel and Richardson (1993), Craver (2007;
Machamer, Darden, & Craver, 2000), Glennan (1996, 2002), and Woodward
(2002a).

The mechanistic view takes as its starting point the idea that in investigating many physical systems, especially biological systems, we are interested in
explaining how they come to possess the capacities that they do, or how they
are able to carry out the functions that they do. The lungs are responsible

for enabling us to breathe; what sort of physical facts about lungs makes them able to do this? The hippocampus is implicated in our ability to lay down new memories; what facts about its structure and function make this possible? Pyramidal cells and other neurons produce action potentials: how? These capacities may belong either to entire organisms, as when we ask how humans are able to perceive three-dimensional forms in space, or to their parts at many different levels of organization, as when we ask about how area V5 contributes to motion perception and how the hippocampus contributes to laying down new memories.

A mechanism can be thought of as an organized structure that executes some function or produces some phenomenon in virtue of containing a set of constituent parts or entities that are organized so that they interact with one another and carry out their characteristic operations and processes (Machamer, Darden, & Craver, 2000, p. 3; Woodward, 2002a, S375). This definition has several components. First, mechanisms are always mechanisms for something. There is some function they carry out, some characteristic effect they produce, or in general something that it is their purpose to do. Mechanisms, in Bechtel's (2008, p. 13) terms, are essentially tied to phenomena; therefore we can talk about the mechanisms of photosynthesis, episodic memory, action potentials, and so on. These can be schematized, following Craver (2007, p. 7), as "S Ψing," where S is some entity and "Ψ" is the exercise of some capacity by S, or some activity of S. Mechanisms may also simultaneously be mechanisms for the production of multiple phenomena.

Second, mechanisms are organized structures containing various constituent entities. These entities might be lipid bimembranes, various sorts of voltage-gated proteins, and masses of different types of ions, as in the case of the mechanisms responsible for producing action potentials in neurons. Or they might be larger structures, such as the divisions of the hippocampus into the dentate gyrus, CA1, CA3, the subiculum, and so on. Each of these parts constitutes a causally important part of the overall mechanism, and the mechanism itself depends on these parts being put together in precisely the right spatial, temporal, and causal sequence. Mechanisms are not just bags of parts – they are devices whose ability to carry out their function depends on the parts interacting in the right way. This might be a simple linear flow of control, as in an assembly-line model, or it might be more complex, involving cycles of activity, feedback loops, and more complex ways of modulating activity.

Third, the constituent parts of a mechanism are typically active. They themselves have causal roles to play in bringing about the activity of the mechanism as a whole. The proteins embedded in the cell membrane of a neuron are not passive entities in moving ions across the membrane; many of them play an active role in transport, such as the Na^+ channel, which rotates outward when the cell depolarizes, causing the channel to open and permit ions to flow outward. When the cell's potential reaches a further threshold value, a "ball-and-chain" structure swings into place, closing the channel. The active, organized operations of such component parts explain how the cell membrane produces the characteristic shape of the action potential. This raises a further important point about mechanisms: although some may be active only when their triggering conditions are met and are largely inert otherwise, others may be continuously endogenously active, integrating inputs from the outside into their ongoing operations, as in Bechtel's example of the fermentation cycle in yeast (2008, pp. 201–204).

Mechanistic explanation begins with a target explanandum or phenomenon – say, the ability of some entity to produce some function. These phenomena are explained by showing how the structural makeup of the entity in question enables it to carry out its function. This essentially involves displaying the causal sequence of events carried out by the component parts of the mechanism. It is characteristic of producing mechanistic explanations that one employs various heuristics to discover these components; two of the most important of these are localization and decomposition (Bechtel & Richardson, 1993). Decomposition can be either structural or functional: one might either figure out the natural parts of a mechanism (e.g., isolating the different parts of the cell through electron microscopy) or figure out the functional subcomponents that explain the mechanism's performance (e.g., figuring out the sequence of chemical transformations that must take place to produce a particular substance). Localization involves associating operations or functions with particular structures – for example, assigning the role of carrying out the citric acid cycle to the mitochondrion (Bechtel & Abrahamson, 2005, pp. 432–436).

The structure of mechanistic explanation differs from of CL explanation in a number of ways, of which we will note only two. First, mechanistic explanation is typically local, in the sense that it focuses on some phenomenon associated with a particular kind of entity. Only neurons produce action potentials, and the citric acid cycle takes place either in mitochondria (in eukaryotes) or in the cytoplasm (in prokaryotes). The phenomena that are subject to mechanistic explanation are also typically both "fragile" and historically contingent. Fragility refers to the fact that mechanisms only operate with normal inputs and against a background of appropriate conditions. They are historically contingent in the sense that they are produced by processes such as natural selection that continuously adjust their components and performance. Genuine laws, according to some (e.g., Woodward, 2002a), are usually taken to have "wide scope" – they cover a range of different kinds of physical systems. Moreover, they hold independent of historical contingencies, at least in many paradigmatic cases such as Maxwell's electromagnetic laws. The norms of CL explanation have to do with discovering regularities that unify a maximal range of phenomena, whereas maximal coverage is not necessarily a norm of mechanistic explanation.

Second, the phenomena targeted by each explanatory strategy differ. The CL view in its classical formulation aims to explain the occurrence of particular events and can be extended to explain general regularities at higher levels. The canonical form of these explanations is that of a deductive argument. Mechanistic explanations aim to capture phenomena such as the fact that S can Ψ. They don't aim at explaining particular events per se, and they aim at explaining regularities only insofar as the explanations focus on particular systems, their capacities, and the effects they generate. The mechanistic view is also relatively unconcerned with prediction, at least of particular events. Many mechanistic systems may be so complex that it is difficult to predict how they will behave even under normal conditions.[7]

The CL view and the mechanistic view are hardly the only available perspectives on scientific explanation, but they are the two that have been most widely discussed in the context of psychology. With this background in place, then, we are finally ready to pose the question of which perspective best captures the norms of psychological explanation.

---

[7] However, fully characterizing a mechanism will involve being able to predict under what conditions its activity will be initiated or inhibited, and how its functioning is likely to be affected by "knocking out" various components – for example, producing a lesion in a certain brain region, or blocking neurotransmitter uptake at a certain synapse. This is not the same as predicting what the output of the mechanism will be, because this is already given by the description of the explanandum phenomenon itself.

1.4 Are there laws or mechanisms in psychology?

In keeping with the CL view's historical dominance in philosophy of science, many philosophers have argued that what makes psychology a science is just what makes *anything* a science, namely the fact that its core theoretical tenets are bodies of laws. Science aims to construct predictively and explanatorily adequate theories of the world, and what else are theories but sets of interlocking laws? So, for example, Jaegwon Kim (1993, p. 194) says:

> The question whether there are, or can be, psychological laws is one of considerable interest. If it can be shown that there can be no such laws, a nomothetic science of psychology will have been shown to be impossible. The qualifier 'nomothetic' is redundant: science is supposed to be nomothetic. Discovery, or at least pursuit, of laws is thought to be constitutive of the very nature of science so that where there are no laws there can be no science, and where we have reason to believe there are none we have no business pretending to be doing science.

The view could hardly be stated more boldly. Note that Kim himself claims to be doing no more than expressing accepted wisdom about science. In a similar vein, Jerry Fodor (1968) has influentially argued that theories in the special sciences (those outside of basic physics) are composed of bodies of laws, although these laws are autonomous in the sense that they do not reduce to the laws of any underlying science.[8]

Historically, many psychologists seem to have agreed with this perspective. Hence, from the early days of scientific psychology, we see attempts to state psychological laws explicitly. Our first two cases of psychological explanation, involving Fechner's and Stevens' laws and the Rescorla–Wagner learning rule, were chosen to illustrate this point. If they are true (perhaps within specific boundary conditions), then they could be used to explain the occurrence of particular psychological events. For instance, if there are laws relating the occurrence of sensations to later cognitive states, such as the formation of perceptual judgments or making of perceptual discriminations, then Stevens' law, in conjunction with such laws, would give

---

[8] Fodor in fact hedges this claim somewhat, making only the conditional claim that his view follows only if sciences consist of bodies of laws; he also refers to "the equally murky notions of *law* and *theory*."

rise to generalizations connecting stimuli and judgments. If this system of laws were sufficiently elaborate, it would amount to an outline of all possible causal paths through the cognitive system, from stimulus to behavior. Such is the form of an idealized psychological theory on the CL view.

But how commonly do such laws occur? Cory Wright (personal communication) has produced a Top 10 list of the most frequently cited "laws" in the psychological literature, along with the date they were first formulated. In descending order, the list runs:

1. Weber's Law (1834)
2. Stevens' Power Law (1957)
3. Matching Law (1961)
4. Thorndike's Law of Effect (1911)
5. Fechner's Law (1860)
6. Fitt's Law (1954)
7. Yerkes–Dodson Law (1908)
8. All-or-None Law (1871)
9. Emmert's Law (1881)
10. Bloch's Law (1885)

A notable fact about this list is that it peters out around the middle of the twentieth century. A further fact is that there is a distressing paucity of laws to be found. If science requires laws, psychology would appear to be rather infirm, even accounting for its relative youth.

Philosophers of psychology have sometimes proposed informal additions to this list. So, for example, we have the following: for any p and any q, if one believes p and believes that if p then q, then – barring confusion, distraction, and so on – one believes q (Churchland, 1981). This is supposed to be a predictive principle of folk psychology governing how people will form new beliefs. In a similar vein, we have the "belief–desire law": if one desires q and believes that if one does p, then q, then one will generally do p. Other candidates proposed by Fodor (1994, p. 3) include "that the Moon looks largest when it's on the horizon; that the Müller-Lyer figures are seen as differing in length; that all natural languages contain nouns."

Perhaps reflecting the fact that no psychologists seem to regard these as "laws," however, Fodor hedges and calls them "lawlike." This raises the possibility that psychologists *do* discover laws, but don't *call* them "laws." Indeed, although the psychological literature is law-poor, it is rich in what are called "effects." Examples of effects are the already-mentioned Stroop effect; the McGurk effect, in which visual perception of speech affects auditory perception of phonemes; and the primacy and recency effects in short-term memory, in which the earliest and latest items in a serial recall task are retrieved more frequently than those in the middle. Cummins (2000) argues, however, that it is a mistake to think of these effects as being the elusive laws we seek. Although they are perfectly respectable true counterfactual-supporting generalizations, he claims that they are not laws, but rather explananda – that is, they are what we have been calling phenomena.[9]

The first point to make here is that whether something is a phenomenon is relative to a context of inquiry, namely a context in which it constitutes something to be explained. But in another context the same thing may itself serve to explain something else. Einstein explained the photoelectric effect, but we can also appeal to the effect in explaining why the hull of a spacecraft develops a positive charge when sunlight hits it. Cummins says of the latter cases that these do not involve the effect explaining anything, but instead just *are* the effect itself. But the photoelectric effect doesn't mention anything about spacecraft (or night-vision goggles, or image sensors, or solar cells, or any other devices that exploit the effect in their functioning); it's a general phenomenon involving the release of electrons following the absorption of photons. Further particular and general phenomena, as well as the operation of many mechanisms, can be explained perfectly well by appealing to the effect.

A second criticism of the idea that there are laws in psychology is that they are bound to be at best "laws *in situ*," that is, "laws that hold of a special kind of system because of its peculiar constitution and organization ... Laws *in situ* specify effects – regular behavioral patterns characteristic of a specific kind of mechanism" (Cummins, 2000, p. 121). We have already noted that mechanistic explanation is inherently local; the idea here is that, given that psychology (like all other special sciences) deals with only a restricted range of entities and systems, it cannot be anything like laws as traditionally conceived, for traditional laws are wide-scope, not restricted in their application conditions.[10] Laws in situ, then, are not worthy of the name.

---

[9] This point is also made by Hacking (1983), who notes that the term "effect" also functions to pick out phenomena in physics.

[10] Note that if this criticism holds, it holds with equal force against other special sciences, such as geology, astrophysics, botany, and chemistry; anything that is not fundamental physics will be law-poor, if Cummins' argument goes through.

This is related to a criticism pressed by many against the very idea of ceteris paribus (cp) laws (Earman & Roberts, 1999; Earman, Roberts, & Smith, 2002; Schiffer, 1991). Recall that cp laws are nonstrict: the occurrence of their antecedents is not always nomically sufficient for the occurrence of their consequents. But if these laws are to be nonvacuous, we need some way of filling in these conditions to make them precise and testable; otherwise, we lose any predictive force they might have. And this we have no way of doing. In the case of folk psychological laws such as the belief–desire law, there are indefinitely many reasons why one may not act in a way that leads to getting what one desires. There are indefinitely many reasons why one may not believe even obvious consequences of things one already believes (perhaps it is too painful, or one simply isn't trying hard enough, or . . .). The same worries apply to the laws of scientific psychology: there may be indefinitely many stimulus conditions in which Stevens' law fails to hold, and saying that it holds except when it doesn't is profoundly unhelpful.

There are two possibilities when faced with this challenge. The first is to try to spell out substantive conditions on being a cp law that meet the normative standards of psychology; Fodor (1991) and Pietroski and Rey (1995) pursue this route. This normally involves saying what kinds of antecedent conditions are needed to "complete" a cp law by making its antecedent genuinely nomically sufficient. The second is to abandon the effort at stating such conditions and explain the status of special science laws in other terms. Woodward (2002b) takes this tack; we briefly sketch his approach here.

Although Woodward doubts that there is any way to fill in the conditions in cp laws to make them genuinely nomically sufficient, such statements may still be causally explanatory insofar as they express facts about what sorts of experimental manipulations – what he calls *interventions* – bring about certain sorts of effects. One paradigmatic sort of intervention in science is randomized trials, where we can directly compare the difference between the presence of one putative causal factor and that of another. If the presence of one factor leads to an effect with a greater frequency than the absence of that factor, if this difference is statistically significant and we have controlled so far as possible for all other factors, we can tentatively conclude that we may have located a causal generalization. There are also a host of quasi-experimental procedures for discovering such relationships, many of which are staples of psychological methodology. So Woodward says:

It seems to me that if one wants to understand how generalizations that fall short of the standards for strict lawhood can nonetheless be tested and confirmed, it is far more profitable to focus directly on the rich literature on problems of causal inference in the special sciences that now exists, rather than on the problem of providing an account of the truth conditions for ceteris paribus laws. (2002b, p. 320)

He illustrates this point by reference to Hebbian learning (a process by which neural circuits strengthen their connections as a result of firing together). Although we may not know precisely what circuits obey this rule, or under what conditions they do so, we can still appeal to the generalization that neurons exhibit Hebbian learning because we can show that under certain interventions, neurons do strengthen their connections in the way that the generalization would predict (and fail to do so without such interventions). The same could be said for other putative cp laws in psychology. If one wants to refrain from using the term "law" to describe these statements, it will do just as well for our purposes to call them experimentally confirmable lawlike generalizations that back causal inferences, generate individual predictions, and support counterfactuals.

This brings us back to Cummins' point that psychological laws are only laws in situ. No one expects there to be (in his terms) a *Principia Psychologica* – an "axiomatic system, self-consciously imitating Euclidean geometry" (p. 121) from which all psychological phenomena could be derived. But even for historically contingent and mechanistically fragile systems such as living, cognizing things, there may be robust causal generalizations that can be discovered via systematic manipulations. Modest laws such as these are nonfundamental and hence not fully general, as the laws of physics presumably are. But they are the best contenders for laws in psychology.

All of this, though, is supposing that there really *are* laws in psychology, even of a modest sort. Another possibility is that psychological explanation just isn't law-based at all. This is the preferred interpretation of mechanists. On the strongest interpretation, this view claims that the canonical form of psychological explanation is to start with some function or capacity to be explained, then decompose the system into smaller interconnected functional subsystems that carry out the subsidiary operations required to carry out the larger function as a whole. These subsystems can be further decomposed in turn, and so on, until we reach a point where the mechanistic story ultimately bottoms out – perhaps at the point where we have associated primitive psychological functions with neurobiological mechanisms. This "homuncular functionalist" approach has been championed by Cummins (1975), Dennett (1978), and Lycan (1981). It also seems to lie behind much classic "box and arrows" type modeling in psychology. In such diagrams, one finds boxes labeled with the functions they are supposed to carry out, and various lines connecting them to show the flow of information among subsystems, as well as relations of control, inhibition, and so on.

The dual-route model of normal reading discussed earlier provides a nice example of such functional decomposition. There are pathways for information flow, and boxes for carrying out functions such as visual analysis of images into graphemes, mapping of graphemes onto phonemes, word identification, and lexical retrieval. The precise sequence of operations carried out within each box is rarely explicitly specified, but the existence of distinct functional subsystems is attested to by the partial dissociations observed in lesion patients; this accords with the mechanist strategy of decomposition and localization. The same could be said of Treisman's model of visual attention. Although not "boxological," it does contain several separate constituents, namely the representations of space and various perceivable visual features, as well as a set of control structures, including the mechanisms of attention and binding, which produce representations of unified visual objects as their output. The existence and function of these parts are attested by the experiments describing how people behave in divided attention conditions, how they perceive unattended stimuli, and so on. Presumably both of these preliminary sketches could be filled out into more detailed mechanistic accounts; the elaborate "subway map" model of the macaque visual cortex developed by van Essen and DeYoe (1994) provides a guide to how complex such decompositions may become.

Often in psychology, especially where it interfaces with neuroscience, we do find mechanistic explanations, or sketches thereof. Computational models of cognitive functioning can be regarded as one species of mechanistic explanation, and computational modeling is a common tool in understanding precisely how a physical system might carry out a certain function (Polk & Seifert, 2002).

A final point on the relationship between laws and mechanisms: We've been discussing these two paradigms as if they were adversarial. A more optimistic proposal is that they are complementary. For one thing, psychological

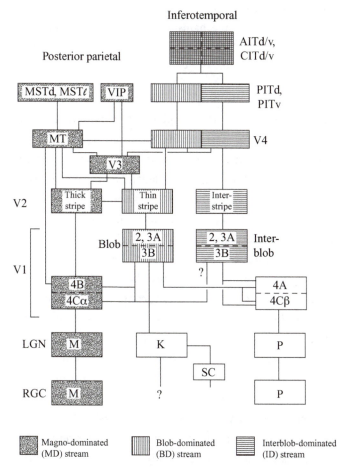

Figure 1.3 (from van Essen & DeYoe, 1994) Subcortical and cortical visual processing streams isolated in the brain of the macaque monkey. Subcortical processing is divided among the magnocellular (M), parvocellular (P), and koniocellular (K) streams, which originate from different populations of retinal ganglion cells. In the cortex, visual processing divides into portions dominated by magnocellular inputs and those that take inputs from so-called blob cells and interblob regions of V1. These inputs are then passed on to higher visual areas for further processing.

laws may entail the presence of corresponding mechanisms. This point has been emphasized by Fodor (1990), who says:

> Nonbasic laws *rely on* mediating mechanisms which they do not, however, *articulate* (sometimes because the mechanisms aren't known; sometimes because As can cause Bs in many different ways, so the same law has a variety

of implementations). Ceteris paribus clauses can have the effect of existentially quantifying over these mechanisms so that 'As cause Bs ceteris paribus' can mean something like 'There exists an intervening mechanism such that when it's intact, As cause Bs.' (p. 155)

This point is correct and important. In nonfundamental sciences where there are laws, there are also mechanisms that implement them. Fundamental laws, by contrast, require no such mechanisms. So nomic explanations in psychology are backed by the promise of mechanistic explanations; certainly this must be true for psychophysical laws, which depend on the mechanisms embodied in our sensory systems, and similarly for laws governing learning, which may involve an array of more complex cognitive mechanisms.

Interestingly, mechanisms themselves may characteristically give rise to corresponding laws, in the modest sense of "law" employed here.[11] Consider: Where we have a mechanism, we have a structure that reliably produces a causal sequence running from its input (initiation conditions) to its output (termination conditions). There may also be effects of the normal functioning of the mechanism that are produced endogenously. So the normal visual system contains systems for producing representations of the relative size, color, distance, and so on, of perceived objects; however, these mechanisms, when functioning normally, also give rise to laws of vision that characterize how objects will be perceived under varying conditions, such as under changes in distance, illumination, or nearby contrasting objects. The Hering illusion provides a nice example – straight lines will reliably appear curved against a background of lines radiating from a central point. Both normal vision and visual illusions involve causal generalizations of this sort; indeed, reliable visual illusions can provide important hints about the rules the visual system follows in constructing representations of what is seen (Hoffman, 1998). Where these satisfy the conditions of being manipulable by interventions, we can regard them as stating rough causal laws that are subject to refinement by later experimental manipulations.

[11] Some mechanists, such as Glennan (1996, p. 52), have proposed that mechanisms themselves *rely* on causal laws to explain their operations. Woodward (2002a) has challenged this employment of the concept of a law, but it nevertheless seems true that the activities and operations of many mechanistic components are best accounted for in terms of lawlike generalizations: consider the role played by laws that describe the passive diffusion of ions, or chemical laws of bonding, in explaining the mechanisms of action potentials.

We are generally pluralists about psychological explanation. Some normatively adequate explanations may involve getting maximally precise descriptions of the causal generalizations that govern some part of the cognitive system. Ultimately, these causal connections will reveal the ways in which we can intervene on and manipulate a system in order to produce a particular outcome. Others may involve delving into the mechanisms that explain how we come to possess some capacity or other. These, in turn, will reveal how these causal levers function to bring about their effects. And there are almost certainly other explanatory strategies at work as well – for example, explaining how we come to have a capacity in etiological or evolutionary terms, rather than explaining how it functions at a particular time. Our present goal has just been to lay out some possible ways of interpreting and assessing research in psychology that aim not just at producing and refining phenomena, but also at explaining them.

1.5 Conclusions

Perhaps nothing could be closer to us than our own minds. But this intimacy does not always bring understanding. We are, in a sense, *too* close to our own minds to truly grasp their workings. Turning our attention inward, we may believe that we can trace the dynamic flow of our own thoughts and perceptions, pushed this way and that by the springs of desire and emotion, ultimately being channeled into actions. And we all become able to report our inner life in cogent sentences for others to consider, freezing and packaging these shifting experiences in a publicly inspectable form. We explain and justify our actions to ourselves and others, and these explanations often take the form of causal statements. At least some grasp of our minds' operations seems built into these practices of everyday life.

Yet, as we have seen, these too-familiar contours conceal surprises and mysteries. In the right sort of experimental situation, subjected to just the right carefully contrived conditions, the mind behaves in unexpected ways, revealing phenomena that are invisible both to introspection and to casual outward examination. Just as the physical and biological sciences needed to go beyond merely observing the natural world in order to uncover its deeper complexity, so understanding the mind requires intervention and systematic observation rather than just spectatorship. And making these phenomena clear is the first step toward explaining how they come about by uncovering the causal regularities and mechanisms that produce them. Scientific psychology gives us a form of self-understanding that only becomes possible once we step backward and take this somewhat detached, objective stance toward ourselves. This is one of the paradoxes of psychology: that the understanding of our inner lives that it promises is available only once we begin to step outside of them.

2 Autonomy and reduction in psychology

2.1 Mind–body relations

Psychology deals with mental phenomena, but these phenomena are intimately related to events in the body and brain. From the inside out, desires lead to plans, which result in intentions, which lead to actions. From the outside in, the environment impinges on us, producing perceptual episodes that lead us to update our beliefs and other models of what is going on in the world. All of these activities, from perception through belief updating, planning, and acting, involve continuous changes to underlying bodily and neural states. How should we understand the relation between these psychological and physical states? This is the mind–body problem as it has traditionally been understood by philosophers. It is the general metaphysical problem of explaining how psychological phenomena are related to physical, biological, and neurophysiological ones.

There are many possible philosophical stances on the mind–body relation, far too many for us to survey here. By far the greatest divide has historically been between dualists, who hold that the world contains two fundamentally distinct kinds of entities, the mental and the physical; and monists, who think that the world is fundamentally one type of thing through and through. Since at least the early twentieth century, dualism in most of its forms has been out of favor, paving the way for the rise of a thoroughgoing materialist or physicalist worldview. The demise of dualism has corresponded roughly with the increasing explanatory scope of the sciences. The more phenomena can be explained in physical and biological terms, the less need there is to posit special, nonphysical substances and properties. There gradually come to be fewer and fewer "gaps" in our understanding where dualistic explanations could carve out a distinctive role for themselves.[1] But rejecting dualism only

---

[1] Perhaps the primary remaining place where substance dualism still seems to have some appeal is in religious contexts, especially where questions of the existence of

puts us on the side of some sort of monism. It does not tell us how we *should* understand the mind–body relation. For this, we need a positive theory.

2.2 Reductionism and multiple realization

The classical Nagelian view of reduction, sketched in Chapter 1, gives us a first pass at such a framework. Recall that Nagel proposes that one theory may be reduced to another by relating the laws and terms of each theory to one another by "bridge principles" or "bridge laws." The idea is that laws of nature couched in the theoretical vocabulary of one science can be reduced to those in another vocabulary, and so on until ultimately all nomic regularities in every science whatsoever can be reduced to those of physics (Oppenheim & Putnam, 1958; Nagel, 1961).

Consider the Garcia effect: when an animal consumes a certain kind of food and then becomes ill (within a certain time window), it will acquire a long-standing aversion to that kind of food. This is a reliable causal regularity, hence a causal law in at least our "soft" sense. To reduce this regularity to a biological regularity, we need to uncover a description of the antecedent and consequent conditions of the law using only the language of biology. That is, we need a description of events in which animals ingest foods that make them ill, and the type of biological and neurobiological state involved in an animal having a food-specific aversion. The relevant biological law would then say that events of the first type cause events of the second type. It would specify a biological process beginning with food ingestion and terminating with acquired aversion. The connection between the psychological descriptions and the biological ones is effected by bridge laws, which function as principles of translation between the two theoretical vocabularies.

Schematically, then, theory reduction starts with laws of the form $P_1(x) \rightarrow P_2(x)$. To these laws are added biconditional bridge principles: $P_1(x) \longleftrightarrow B_1(x)$; $P_2(x) \longleftrightarrow B_2(x)$; and so on. From these we can then deduce biological laws of the form $B_1(x) \rightarrow B_2(x)$. Thus the original psychological (or economic, sociological, etc.) laws are reduced to laws in the "lower-level" science – neuroscience, biology, chemistry, physics, and so forth. The guiding assumption of this form of reductionism is that wherever we find higher-level regularities in

the soul after death are concerned. On the other hand, property dualism still has its advocates, many of whom claim that conscious, experiential properties cannot be reduced to physical ones. See Chalmers (2003) for discussion.

the world, they exist in virtue of such lower-level regularities. Special science laws must be "backed" by corresponding lower-level laws, and higher-level regularities can, ideally at least, be deduced from lower-level ones.

Although the value of theoretical reductions of this sort has been intensely debated, according to one perspective they provide a form of vindication for higher-level theories. To be in a position to reduce one explanatory scheme to another one is to show that the former is at least as scientifically legitimate as the latter and that the categories and regularities enshrined in the former are as real as those in the latter. Because physics is typically taken to be the model of a legitimate science that deals with objects whose reality is unquestioned, the ultimate goal should be to achieve a hierarchy of reductions ultimately bottoming out at the level of physics. Failure of a theory to reduce would be evidence that its explanatory framework was somehow deficient.

Reduction has also been taken to yield ontological benefits. Strictly speaking, reductionism of this sort requires only that higher-level events and laws be *correlated* with lower-level events and laws. If the bridge principles themselves are interpreted as laws, then these correlations are also necessary. But we might wonder why these correlations hold. What explains the fact that psychological occurrences and neurobiological ones go together? If it is not simply a brute, unexplainable fact, a natural explanation is that these higher-level phenomena are *identical to* the lower-level phenomena. This was the sort of inference that motivated the mind–body identity theorists of the 1950s and 1960s such as David Armstrong (1968), J. J. C. Smart (1959), and U. T. Place (1956). According to this view, mind and body are not distinct entities, but rather one and the same. The psychological just *is* the physical.

The identity theory comes in two forms. The *type identity* theory is the stronger of the two. It says that each type of psychological state (or process, event, etc.) is identical to a type of physical state. Consider the ability to smell. Smell depends on a host of neural structures, including the olfactory bulb. Lesions to this structure can result in partial or total anosmia (loss of smell). Given this, then, it doesn't seem implausible to conclude that ordinary olfactory events (such as experiencing the smell of turpentine) are type identical with events in the olfactory bulb. Every time this type of sensory process occurs, the *same* type of physical process occurs – the same neural events, structures, and so on, are present in every creature capable of undergoing that type of process.

Taken in its broadest form, the type identity theory requires that any two creatures that are psychologically similar in some respect must also be physically similar (or similar at the level of the relevant lower-level theory), and vice versa. To many, this has seemed an implausibly strong demand, and it has been the root of objections to the identity theory from philosophers such as Jerry Fodor and Hilary Putnam. Putnam's argument can be put in the form of a challenge:

> [The identity theorist] has to specify a physical-chemical state such that *any* organism (not just a mammal) is in pain if and only if (a) it possesses a brain of a suitable physical-chemical structure; and (b) its brain is in that physical-chemical state. This means that the physical-chemical state in question must be a possible state of a mammalian brain, a reptilian brain, a mollusc's brain (octopuses are mollusca, and certainly feel pain), etc. At the same time, it must *not* be a possible (physically possible) state of the brain of any physically possible creature that cannot feel pain. Even if such a state can be found, it must be nomologically certain that it will also be a state of the brain of any extraterrestrial life that may be found that will be capable of feeling pain before we can even entertain the supposition that it may *be* pain. (Putnam, 1967/1975, p. 436)

Although Putnam does not actually argue that this challenge is unmeetable, he clearly intimates that it is. The very same psychological state can be had even by creatures differing radically in their neurobiological structure; hence that psychological state type cannot be identified with any particular neuro-biological state type. Indeed, these state types cannot even be correlated via bridge laws, so the classical model of reduction would also fail, if Putnam were right.

A similar point was made by Fodor (1965, 1968, 1975) with respect not just to psychology but also to all special sciences.[2] Fodor's argument turns on the analysis of examples such as Gresham's law in economics. If this is a law at all, it governs monetary exchanges. The law says that bad money (commodity currency that is debased, or whose face value is lower than its commodity value) will drive out good money – eventually the circulating currency will be

---

[2] A special science is any science that deals with a restricted domain of entities and phenomena. So while physics allegedly takes everything in the world in its domain (since everything is ultimately composed of physical material), other sciences deal only with, say, hydrodynamical or biochemical phenomena, which are irregularly distributed in the world.

dominated by bad money. Stating Gresham's law requires generalizing across all types of currency and different ways in which currencies can be exchanged. But in practice currencies have been made of any number of different types of physical materials, and in principle there are even fewer limits on what can be used. Similarly, what sort of event counts as a monetary exchange is extremely physically heterogeneous. Reducing Gresham's law would require finding a comparable law at the physical level that describes events involving these massively variable physical objects and their interaction. But it seems unlikely that there is such a law. There is nothing at the physical level that corresponds to Gresham's law because at the physical level, monetary exchanges and other economic events are too unruly and messy to generalize over.

This argument was elaborated on by Block and Fodor (1972), who present three lines of evidence favoring the multiple realizability of psychology. First, neuroplasticity makes it likely that the same psychological function is not routinely correlated with the same neural structure. As an illustration, consider that the neural substrates of their first and second language may be separately localized in "late" bilinguals, but overlapping in "early" bilinguals (Kim, Relkin, Lee, & Hirsch, 1997). Both monolingual Mandarin speakers and early and late bilinguals might have the same competence with Mandarin, but a different neural underpinning in each case.

Second, convergent evolution means that, at times, historically unrelated species will come to have traits that are similar as a result of similar selection pressures, and these traits may well differ in their underlying structural realization. The varieties of evolved visual systems suggests that the same task demands and selection pressures can produce functionally analogous organs that are physically dissimilar (Land & Nilsson, 2002).

Third, artificial systems, especially computers, can replicate human performance on psychological tasks despite having wildly different physical structure. Here the history of research into artificial intelligence may serve as an illustration. Programmed computers have exceeded human performance at chess for years and have recently made inroads into such characteristically human activities as discovering scientific laws (Schmidt & Lipson, 2009). These models typically abstract from certain aspects of human performance, but at some grain of analysis it is plausible that they are instantiating similar capabilities to those of humans despite running on different hardware.

If Putnam and Fodor are correct, there is no guarantee that two psychologically identical creatures are physically identical, contra what the type identity theory claims. Between any two such creatures, their degree of physical similarity would in principle be up for grabs. When a creature is in a psychological state, we will say that some aspect of its physical state at that time *realizes* the psychological state in question.[3] Where creatures differ in their neurobiological structure, the states that realize their psychology will also differ. This is known as the *multiple realizability* of the mental.

Many things are multiply realizable. Canonical examples are artifacts such as computers and corkscrews. There is no unique way to build such things – early computers used vacuum tubes and acoustic drum storage, whereas contemporary ones use magnetic disks and flash memory; the DEC PDP-8 was a 12-bit machine, but modern desktop systems are 64-bit; and so on. Early calculators were mechanical, then electromechanical, then electronic, and now many run exclusively as software. Different physical structures are involved, but the function of performing arithmetic is the same. Corkscrews may use wings and levers to withdraw corks, or they may not. To be an artifact of a certain kind is to be multiply realizable, and if the general argument is correct, the same goes for all of the objects of the special sciences, including biological and psychological systems.

Finally, multiple realizability is compatible with a weaker form of identity, namely *token* identity. This says that every time a creature is in a certain sort of psychological state, it is in *some* sort of physical state or other, and this particular (token) psychological state is identical with this (token) physical state. There must be *some* physical event or other that takes place, but there is no requirement that the same psychological process and the same physical process co-occur across species, within species, or even within individuals. Jane's present intention to move her arm is identical with a certain state of her motor cortex, but John's present intention to do the same might be identical with a different sort of motor state. Token identity preserves materialism – there is nothing nonphysical in the world – but is consistent with the denial of reductionism.

---

[3] Realization is a relation that is intended to be looser than identity. If a state N(eural) realizes a state P(sychological), then N makes it the case that P obtains. That is, N is sufficient for P. However, it need not be the case that P is also sufficient for N. In identity, because N = P, each is sufficient for the presence of the other. A further caveat: not every aspect of a creature's physical state realizes its psychological state. A realizer is the *minimal* physical state that is sufficient for being in the relevant psychological state.

2.3 Functionalism and the autonomy of psychology

Metaphysical views about the mind can have methodological consequences for psychology. If the type identity theory is correct, we could in principle confirm that a creature has a particular psychological capacity using only neurobiological evidence. Having found the physical basis for a cognitive capacity in one creature, we could confidently project it to others. If multiple realizability is true, on the other hand, we have no such guarantee. But that does not mean neurobiological evidence will not be relevant to confirming psychological hypotheses. For one thing, there are general constraints on the ways one can build psychological systems. A creature that is completely homogeneous inside (e.g., full of Jell-O) cannot support psychological states. Even if type identity is false, there may be constraints of this sort.

Functionalism is a view about the nature of psychological phenomena that is closely allied with multiple realizability. Functionalism says that psychological states, processes, and mechanisms are defined functionally. Functional definitions refer to what a thing does, what sorts of capacities it possesses, what sorts of events bring it about, what sorts of effects it has, and how it fits into an interlocking system of entities also defined by their functional and causal roles. In particular, functional definitions do not inherently refer to facts about something's physical makeup (what material it contains, how it is organized, etc.). They only require that the physical organization must be sufficiently stable and complex to carry out the relevant functions.

Functionalism is an ontological claim about psychological entities. To be in a psychological state or to undergo a psychological process or to possess a psychological mechanism is just to be in a certain functional state. For instance, a belief is a kind of state that represents certain information about the world, is capable of entering into inferences with other beliefs, is capable of being formed on the basis of perceptual evidence, is capable of interacting with desires to produce actions, and so on. This sketches part of what beliefs *do* – part of their *functional role*. Functionalism requires that there be a distinction between such roles and what realizes them.[4]

---

[4] There is debate among functionalists whether psychological states should be taken to be identical with these roles or with the states that realize them; hence, there is a distinction in the literature between "role" and "realizer" functionalists. Some enthusiasts have even held that the role–realizer distinction is ubiquitous, and that functionalism itself is a completely general doctrine that applies to all sciences, not just psychology (Lycan, 1987).

The crucial point about these role specifications is that they are independent of the underlying material constitution of the system that realizes them. To say that something is a face recognition system, for instance, is to describe part of its functional profile. It is a system that takes visual representations as input, and its outputs sort them into those that are faces and those that are nonfaces. There are many possible ways to implement this function, and many different kinds of physical device that can realize it. What it is to be a face recognizer – or to be a belief, or an emotion, or anything else in the domain of psychology – is just to have the appropriate kind of functional organization.

The functionalist perspective is implicit in vision scientist David Marr's famous three-level account of how we can analyze what goes on when a creature or artificially designed system faces an information-processing task. Marr's levels of analysis are:

> *Computational theory:* What is the goal of the computation, why is it appropriate, and what is the logic of the strategy by which it can be carried out?

> *Representation and algorithm:* How can this computational theory be implemented? In particular, what is the representation for the input and output, and what is the algorithm for the transformation?

> *Hardware implementation:* How can the representation and algorithm be realized physically? (Marr, 1982, p. 25)

A computational description of a system specifies what function it is aiming to carry out. Is it an adding device, a face recognizer, a device for guiding arm movements on the basis of visual inputs? These are all distinct computational functions. The algorithmic description of a system specifies the types of representations used by the system and the exact sequence of operations and transformations that they undergo in order to carry out the system's computation. There are many different ways to represent the same information (e.g., different base systems for numbers) and perform the same computational tasks (e.g., different ways of doing long division). Finally, the implementation description tells us how these representations and processes are realized in the underlying material structure of the system.

In this scheme, the mapping from computational to algorithmic description is one-many, since for any computational function there are many possible algorithms by which it might be carried out; and, moreover, there is a one-many mapping between algorithm and implementation for precisely the same reasons. Marr's levels of description, then, imply that the computational functions characteristic of cognition will be multiply realizable in at least two separate ways.

Each level provides a distinctive explanatory contribution. In order to properly understand *why* an information processor is doing what it does, Marr argues, we need to understand the computation it is carrying out. Algorithmic and neural descriptions of the system can tell us *what* a system is doing – what representations it processes, how various neural structures behave – but they cannot illuminate these why-questions. As he puts it, "Trying to understand perception by studying only neurons is like trying to understand bird flight by studying only feathers: It just cannot be done. In order to understand bird flight, we have to understand aerodynamics; only then do the structure of feathers and the different shapes of birds' wings make sense" (Marr, 1982, p. 27).

Marr's argument for the necessity of his three levels of understanding, as well as the Putnam–Fodor arguments, have persuaded many philosophers and psychologists that minds are in fact multiply realized. Functionalism was also bolstered by the rise of computational modeling in psychology, as well as by the computational theory of mind, which holds that cognition itself is just a species of computation (Fodor, 1975; Newell, 1980; Pylyshyn, 1984). Computers are ideal examples of multiply realizable systems, because there are many different ways to arrange a physical system to compute a mathematical function.[5] Functionalism makes room in principle for multiple realizability, since psychological capacities can be described functionally at a level of abstraction that permits them to have many possible physical realizers. This relationship is weaker than entailment, because there may be only one physically possible way to realize a given function if it is sufficiently fine-grained.

---

[5] To avoid confusion here, note that "functions" in the functionalist sense are not identical with functions in the mathematical sense. A mathematical function is a mapping from a domain to a range such that no element in the domain corresponds to more than one element in the range. There are several ways of unpacking the notion of function at work in functionalism, and each one of these gives a somewhat different notion of the doctrine. The most general notion is of something that a system or state does – some aspect of its causal role. This causal role might be pinned down by the developmental or evolutionary history of the system, by certain aspects of its functioning at a time, or in many other ways.

Even so, since functionalism makes multiple realization possible, observing multiple realization provides some evidence in favor of functionalism.

This can be put as an argument:

(1) Biological cognitive systems are multiply realizable (physically heterogeneous but psychologically homogeneous);
(2) Artificial computational systems can often match biological cognitive systems' performance, despite being physically dissimilar from them;
(3) Functionalism explains how (1) and (2) could be true, whereas the type identity theory does not;

Therefore, (4) the likelihood that functionalism is true is greater than the likelihood that the type identity theory is true.

The facts given in (1) through (3) do not straightforwardly entail functionalism. But they do make it more likely than its most prominent competitor. This *likelihood argument* gives us an inference to the best explanation in favor of functionalism.

If psychological kinds are functional, everything essential about them can be captured without reference to any underlying realizing or implementing structures. There would invariably be more to say about how they are implemented, but these facts would not be important to psychology as such, any more than metallurgy would be relevant to economics in the case of Gresham's law. To say that psychology is *autonomous* is to say that psychological kinds and the descriptions, theories, models, laws, and explanations that refer to them are potentially independent of what underlies them and independent of any other discipline's modes of classification and explanation.

It is important not to overstate the claims of autonomy, however. In a famous example, Putnam (1975) argues for the irrelevance of lower levels of description and the explanatory superiority of higher-level taxonomies. Suppose we have a board with a 1-inch square hole in it and a 1-inch diameter circular hole in it. A square peg 15/16ths of an inch across will pass through the square hole but not the circular hole. We might explain this fact by appealing to the macrolevel facts about the peg and board, such as their solidity and relative dimensions; or, alternatively, we might explain it by appeal to their microproperties, such as the precise positions of the atoms that make them up. The macrofacts in this case could be realized by different microfacts, since macro-identical pegs and boards could be made of different materials arranged differently. But Putnam holds that the macrofacts provide a sufficient explanation for the peg's passage. Indeed, he makes the stronger claim that the microfacts are *not explanatory* here. They bring in a welter of irrelevant detail that fails to capture the higher-level or organizational properties at the macrolevel. So it is with multiply realized systems: their higher-level characterizations, in virtue of eliding this detail, enable us to state explanations that are invisible at the microlevel.

Elliott Sober (1999a) notes, however, that this is a false dichotomy. There are explanatory trade-offs involved in moving from one level to another, but which one is better depends on the explanatory context. So macrolevel explanations that employ multiply realizable categories may be more unifying in that they subsume systems that have widely divergent physical makeups. In some contexts, unification may be what is desired. On the other hand, microlevel explanations may be more detailed and enable more accurate predictions. They may also be able to describe breakdowns that cannot be captured in macrolevel characterizations. For instance, so long as an integrated circuit is functioning properly there is no need to mention the physical facts about its makeup, but if it malfunctions, this fact is best explained by a microlevel account of how small fractures are causing it to perform imperfectly under certain conditions.

The moral of Sober's argument is that while higher-level explanations might be indispensable for certain purposes, this does not preclude us from giving lower-level explanations of how those systems behave. Where we prize fine-grained predictions, or where we are trying to explain why a system fails to display some higher-level pattern of behavior, lower-level categories are the appropriate ones to use. The case of Putnam's peg, properly interpreted, shows that there is no essential competition between these two explanations. One does not exclude the other.

Two distinct autonomy theses can be teased apart:

Explanatory autonomy: Psychological models and theories do not depend for their explanatory legitimacy on those of any other discipline.

Methodological autonomy: To confirm the explanatory claims made in psychology, we do not need to appeal essentially to the methods or results of other disciplines.

In what follows, we elaborate on each of these and consider to what extent they are defensible.

Explanatory autonomy says that how psychological explanations measure up to the standards of good explanations is something that can be assessed independently of other, nonpsychological explanations that are available. To illustrate this, imagine for a moment that the classical reductionist picture turned out to be true, and the laws of psychology turned out to reduce smoothly to those of physics. Would it follow that to give a psychological explanation one would have to be in a position to state an explanation of the system's behavior in terms of its quantum-mechanical description? Hardly so. If I describe the process by which a foraging creature decides, based on information about local cues, where to seek food, the *explanatory force* of that psychological story does not depend on our having an explanation for the creature's behavior in any other terms. It turns only on whether the model itself satisfies the kinds of local, discipline-specific explanatory standards that are at play here. For instance, does it adequately predict what the creature will do? Does it break down or fail in the appropriate circumstances? Does it support the appropriate sorts of manipulations of and interventions into the creature's behavior? Does it mesh with the other explanations of the creature's psychological capacities that we have? And so on. These questions have to do with the explanatory standards for psychological theorizing, which do not themselves make reference to the availability of any other kinds of explanation.

Methodological autonomy has to do with how these models and theories are confirmed or disconfirmed, and with what kinds of evidence lead us to adopt one or another psychological explanation. Sciences characteristically develop their own equipment, laboratory methods, experimental and observational techniques, devices for data recording and analysis, and so forth. Psychology is no different in these respects, and the development of psychological methods has gone hand in hand with the production of new phenomena. We have already commented on studies of response times in Stroop-like tasks (see Chapter 1). For examples from the domain of memory, consider Ebbinghaus's pioneering investigations, which involved combining serial learning techniques with the use of nonsense stimuli (letter trigrams) to minimize the effects of prior knowledge, as well as his use of savings on relearning as a measure of retention (Ebbinghaus, 1964; Roediger, 1985). Serial position curves and relearning curves are phenomena that have spawned entire industries of methodological refinement and modeling. These methods and others like them rely on behavioral measures of various sorts. These methods also typically carry with them certain assumptions about how they are to be interpreted that guide the process of constructing models and theories. Methodological autonomy claims that psychological theories are supported by a set of methods that are proprietary to psychology and are not dependent on the methods of any other discipline.

2.4 Eliminativism and the replacement question

Let us return now to the question of reduction. Suppose that multiple real-izability undermines classical, Nagel-style reductionism. Suppose that it also supports the autonomy of psychology, for two reasons: first, psychological explanations will be couched in abstract terms that involve no reference to particular types of physical structures; and, second, there will be no lower-level generalizations that can replace those used in psychological explana-tions. Anti-reductionism says that the categories of the special sciences do not map smoothly onto the categories of lower-level sciences. Autonomy says that these high-level categories and theories nevertheless belong to a domain that can support deep, scientifically interesting inquiry. The philosophical problem of the special sciences is about how to reconcile these two claims.

Some have argued that they cannot be reconciled. *Eliminative materialists*, or *eliminativists* for short, believe there is something inherently defective in our psychological taxonomies and theories and that we would be better off in terms of explanation and prediction if we simply dropped them altogether. Eliminativists argue that the failure of mental categories to track deeper neurobiological ones shows only that the mental categories are illusory and cannot bear the weight of serious scientific study.

This line of argument has been pursued most aggressively by Paul and Patri-cia Churchland (P. M. Churchland, 1981; P. S. Churchland, 1986).[6] The target of their attack is folk psychology (FP). Considered as a theory, an attempt to construct a coherent framework to account for psychological phenom-ena in general, FP is alleged to be radically defective. Patricia Churchland (1986) raises several criticisms of FP. First, it is incomplete: there are many phenomena that it simply does not capture (see Chapter 1). Second, it is a stagnant research program. Its fundamental categories and principles have

---

[6] Eliminativism about the mental has also been argued by Feyerabend (1963), Quine (1960), and Rorty (1965), although we will not deal with their arguments here.

not changed in millennia and show little sign of evolving in response to new evidence. Third, there exists, in embryonic form, a theory that can capture all of the phenomena that FP purports to and more as well. Churchland has sometimes taken this theory to be completed neuroscience, and sometimes the computational theory of artificial neural networks. But, either way, the point is that this new theory, by virtue of its greater explanatory scope, more fine-grained predictions, and superior integration with the other biological sciences, will displace FP entirely, relegating its categories to the realm of fiction.

Since our concern here is scientific psychology, not folk psychology, these arguments against FP do not necessarily carry over.[7] Scientific psychology has significant explanatory scope, as the chapters to follow will show in detail. Moreover, it revises its core theories and constructs in response to the evidence. So if Churchland's objections are to be sustained, the challenge will have to be of roughly this form:

(1) Neuroscience is a research program that is in competition with psychology and has greater explanatory and predictive scope than the latter does;
(2) Generally, we should prefer theories that allow better prediction and explanation;

Therefore, (3) we should prefer neuroscientific explanations to psychological ones.

If this argument is sound, psychological theories will be superseded by the superior explanatory framework of neuroscience. Call this the *replacement thesis*.

The argument is speculative at this point. In terms of their explanatory power, it is difficult to assess the comparative strength of neuroscience and cognitive psychology, taken in their current forms.[8] For some phenomena,

---

[7] However, one might argue that there are similar problems of incommensurability and displacement in relating folk psychology to our more systematic scientific psychology.

[8] In fact, it is particularly difficult – perhaps even senseless – given that "neuroscience" and "psychology" are not names of single, unitary disciplines. Social and developmental psychology are rather distinct in their theories and methods; similarly, molecular and systems neuroscience are equally distinct enterprises. It is more plausible to see these fields not as unified theories but as overlapping mosaics of models, methods, explanatory frameworks, and so on. What are being compared, then, are the explanations provided for the same phenomena by these two loosely connected mosaic-fields.

psychology displays a clear advantage: studies of the neural underpinnings of reasoning and inference, categorization, and decision making are underdeveloped relative to our understanding of other faculties. Some areas show impressive mutual development: sensory perception and some aspects of memory provide examples. The physiology of sensory receptors, the structure of transduction, and early sensory processing are highly active research areas in neuroscience, and the psychology of sensory perception is similarly well developed. In the domain of episodic memory, especially the formation and encoding of episodic memories, we have the beginnings of neural theories dealing with the role of long-term potentiation in effecting changes to the hippocampus and associated structures. Here, too, we have consilience with psychological research. And there are some areas where neuroscience has greater explanatory scope than psychology, most notably the study of sleep and dreaming. *Overall* comparisons between the disciplines, however, are impossible to make.

We can consider the hypothetical case in which some futuristic ideal and complete versions of cognitive psychology and neuroscience square off against one another. Is there any reason to think that the neuroscientific theory will invariably win? If Churchland's argument generalizes, we would expect:

(1) Everything in the explanatory domain of psychology will also be in the domain of neuroscience;
(2) Neuroscience will also include *more* in its domain than psychology;
(3) The predictions of neuroscience will be more fine-grained than those of psychology.

These three points flow from the fact that neuroscience *realizes* psychology. So reasons to prefer theories with greater explanatory power are ipso facto reasons to prefer neuroscientific explanations.

However, (1) is arguably false and (2) and (3) do not support the replacement thesis. That (1) is false follows from the fact that psychology is multiply realizable. Nothing in the argument so far has challenged this fact (though see the next section for arguments in this vein). If psychology is multiply realizable, its domain covers a wide range of physical structure types, of which human neurobiological systems are only one example. Neuroscience would have a wider domain than psychology if the only realizers for psychological systems were neurobiological. But multiple realizability says the opposite of this.

If we focus only on explaining phenomena connected with human behavior, however, neuroscience *does* seem to have the potential to explain more than psychology. This is because for every psychological occurrence, there will be a corresponding neurobiological occurrence, and hence a corresponding neurobiological explanation. Moreover, there will be many neurobiological occurrences that simply do not correspond to psychological occurrences. Many cellular, molecular, and genetic events in nervous systems have no direct psychological consequences, and there may even be neural events that are behaviorally relevant that are outside of the domain of psychology. These events will often allow fairly fine-grained descriptions and predictions of what an organism will do. Knowing that a creature intends to move its limb a certain way will help to predict that it will make a certain type of motion, but knowing the firing pattern in the motor cortex, how the motor neurons synapse with the muscles, and what the kinematic and dynamical properties of the limbs are will provide much more information.

But neither of these points undermines the utility of psychological explanations. Or, if they do, they also undermine similar explanations in neuroscience, in biology, in geology, and in every other nonfundamental science. The reason is that these points hold for *any* science that is realized by another. Neuroscience is to more fundamental branches of biology as psychology is to neuroscience, and so precisely the same arguments should apply. And so on, until the only legitimate explanations are couched in the language of the most fundamental sciences (quantum mechanics or its descendants, perhaps). This strikes us as a reductio of the argument. The special sciences exist and seem to provide valuable explanatory leverage. Even if there is something defective about psychology in particular, we should be suspicious of such a sweeping conclusion.

This first argument for the replacement thesis does not claim that psychological explanations are false, only that they are not best able to meet our explanatory demands. Whether an explanation is a good one depends on how well it conforms to general norms for scientific explanations and the specific norms of its discipline. Another threat to autonomy comes from the existence of competing explanations. The first argument considered competition between psychological and neuroscientific explanations, where both were assumed to be true. But competition can also involve *falsifying explanations*. Perhaps psychological explanations are not autonomous because they can be *trumped* in certain ways by neurobiological explanations.

Suppose we model a psychological process by decomposing it into three subprocesses that occur in a fixed order and have a certain direction of causal flow, involving the transfer of a specific type of information. Now suppose that in trying to map this model onto the brain, we cannot locate any sequence of neural processes that corresponds to this model – perhaps the connectivity among regions is wrong, so that one type of information would be unavailable to later processes at the time that the model predicts, or what appears as two components in the model is functionally aggregated within a single neural region. The models make incompatible claims about causal structure. This looks like a case of one explanation trumping another one, and we might well take the conflict to be decided in favor of the neurobiological explanation.

There are several things to note, however. First, it is not always clear that the thing to do is to reject the psychological model. The relationship between psychological models and neurobiology may be complex and indirect, and integrating these two perspectives requires care. Failure to find a discrete neural region that corresponds to a particular stage of a psychological model is only negative evidence if we assume that psychological functions must be localized (Bechtel & Richardson, 1993). An alternative to localization is that the psychological functions that are assigned to a single functional component of the model are distributed over a set of neural regions. Heuristic assumptions such as localization may guide the search for realizers but are not essential.

Setting this aside, though, do these cases of trumping actually show that psychological explanation is not autonomous? In this case, we have a psychological model that is *falsified* by a neurobiological one. But autonomy does not require that psychological theories be immune to falsification from any extra-psychological sources of evidence. No science is autonomous in this sense, because theories from every science are potentially open to falsification from any source of evidence. So just the falsity of a theory is not enough to show that it is nonautonomous. By the same token, neurophysiological evidence can also *confirm* psychological models and theories, by displaying that the causal patterns in the underlying realizing structures correspond to those that the models posit. But a psychological explanation of a creature's behavior has force independently of our knowing these facts about realization.

To sum up this lengthy discussion, neither the argument from the greater explanatory power of lower-level explanations nor the argument from the falsifiability of higher-level theories by lower-level ones undermines the autonomy of psychology. In this debate, it is important to bear in mind the following distinction. It is one thing to ask what *confirms* or *disconfirms* a model. This has to do with how well-supported the model is by the evidence. Psychological models can be confirmed or disconfirmed by neuroscientific evidence, although doing so is a complicated matter. It is another thing, though, to ask whether a model has genuine *explanatory force*. This has to do with whether or not the model satisfies the criteria for being a good explanation: is it true, does it unify many different phenomena, does it allow predictions and interventions, and so on? It is one thing to ask whether a psychological model could be falsified by neuroscientific data. It is another to ask whether, considered in itself, it provides a good explanation of a creature's behavior. Even if psychology can be supported or undercut by evidence from neuroscience, psychological theories and models can have independent explanatory force.

2.5 Against multiple realizability

Multiple realizability is not the only piece of evidence in favor of functionalism, but it is an important one. Bechtel and Mundale (1999) launched an influential attack on multiple realizability, or more specifically on the claim that psychological states are *actually* multiply realized (call this the claim of multiple realization). Multiple realization (MR) entails that the taxonomies of psychology and neuroscience have a one-many relation. But Bechtel and Mundale argue that neuroscientists construct taxonomies of brain regions in ways that are in tension with what MR predicts.

The oldest attempts to subdivide the brain created major divisions into roughly defined lobes, and groupings that rely on the placement of gyri and sulci (bulges and fissures in the surface of the brain). More sophisticated neuroanatomical maps were made possible with the emergence of staining techniques, and the still-canonical maps of distinct anatomical regions were published by Korbinian Brodmann in 1909. Brodmann's maps relied largely on architectonic features: regions were defined anatomically by the types of neurons present in each region and the laminar organization of cortex in that region. A second type of organization of brain regions is topographic: this refers to the maplike preservation of spatial relations within a region. The retinal surface is a map of spatial locations, and higher visual areas are made up of similar maps corresponding to the location of various features in space. A third type, which has been the focus of intensive research in recent years, is connectivity, or the ways in which regions are connected to one another across long and short distances, and in which parts of regions are interconnected.

These attempts rely on cell types, organization, and wiring. However, brain regions may also be categorized in terms of their function, specifically the types of psychological functions that they are involved in. For example, the temporoparietal junction, especially in the right hemisphere, has been thought of as both a "theory of mind" region and a region involved in modulating attention (Young, Doddell-Feder, & Saxe, 2010). If it is in fact selectively involved in making theory of mind judgments (and not in attention more generally), it might be appropriate to call this a theory of mind region. Brain regions might be classified by their psychological role rather than architectonics, topography, or connectivity. Similar function-based taxonomies have been applied to visual processing regions and memory systems.

Identifying brain regions by their psychological functions is part of the project of localizing these functions. Once a system or a task has been decomposed into its subparts or subtasks, localization is the attempt to assign functions to parts of the system, or locations to various processes that make up the ability to carry out a task. Decomposition and localization are two heuristics that are widely used to make sense of the behavior of complex systems (Bechtel & Richardson, 1993). However, this use of functional criteria undermines MR insofar as it ties the taxonomy of brain regions to psychological taxonomy. Multiple realization requires that these two be independent parameters: it should be possible to vary underlying brain structure and get the same psychological state, and vary the psychological state and keep the brain structure constant.[9] But when regions are taxonomized by their functions in this way, we lose this independence. The lower-level taxonomy becomes subservient to the higher-level one.

Their second argument rests on how brain regions are named in comparative neuroanatomy. We often say that "the same" region can be found in two distinct species: so we can talk about BA5 existing in both humans and macaques, despite the fact that our brains are rather different from theirs. The criteria for identifying the same region across species are various, but

---

[9] In case this latter point is not obvious, remember that whether a particular neural region realizes a psychological function may depend on how it is connected to other regions, not just on its intrinsic characteristics. Causal and functional roles are often *relational*.

whatever differences there may be, neuroanatomists often feel comfortable in designating regions as the same in spite of them. This practice seems to undermine the idea that cross-species differences will inevitably support MR.

Bechtel and Mundale offer a diagnosis of why so many have found claims of multiple realization tempting. They suggest that proponents of MR have implicitly been using taxonomies of different grain in deciding whether some property is multiply realized. So Putnam takes there to be a common property *pain* that is shared by mammals and cephalopods. This is a coarse-grained property, since pains can vary widely in their intensity and character; stabbing pain is not the same as burning pain, superficial and deep pain have different phenomenology, and so on. Proponents of MR assume that all of these have something in common, and that this common trait can be projected across species. They then draw attention to the fine-grained details at the level of neuroanatomy and neurophysiology such as having certain types of neurons, using certain neurotransmitters, having a certain kind of laminar organization, having certain response profiles, and so on, and argue that these differences establish MR. The one-many mappings found in MR, then, are the result of choosing *mismatched taxonomies* of the coarse-fine sort.[10]

Do these arguments undermine multiple realization? Not clearly. One way of identifying brain regions is by psychological functions. But while this method aligns functions and underlying neural structures by fiat in the organism being studied, the same way of individuating brain regions need not be carried over to other creatures. The fact that one mechanism underwrites this function in humans does not imply that the same mechanism is at work everywhere.

What about the point that comparative neuroanatomists often ignore many structural variations? There are two possible interpretations of this practice. One is that neuroanatomical taxonomies that are constructed for the purpose of cross-species comparisons are often coarse-grained. That does not rule out individuating these regions in more fine-grained ways for other

---

[10] We should note that putting things in terms of coarse and fine here does not quite get at the heart of the issue. A coarse-coarse taxonomy can still be one-many if there are several possible coarse-grained lower-level realizers, and the same goes for a fine-fine taxonomy. MR strictly speaking relies only on mismatching taxonomies of the one-many sort. Coarse-fine mappings are one way in which this can happen – perhaps the way that MR advocates have historically fallen prey to – but not the only way.

purposes – for example, the same Brodmann area in humans and macaques may have a very different functional profile. Another interpretation is that neuroanatomical taxonomies are themselves made on the basis of coarse-grained functional characteristics. This opens up the possibility that properties such as *being BA10* are multiply realized as well. So it might be that a psychological function is realized by a single coarse-grained brain region that is, in turn, realized by a variety of networks that can be taxonomized in more fine-grained ways.

There is evidence that cross-species classifications are somewhat coarse-grained. In a recent survey, Semendeferi, Armstrong, Schleicher, Zilles, and Van Hoesen (2001) carried out cytoarchitectural comparisons of the frontal pole, location of the putative Brodmann area 10, in humans, chimpanzees, bonobos, gorillas, orangutans, gibbons, and macaques. They conclude that there are sufficient similarities to say that area 10 exists in all species except gorillas, but there is still variation along many of the dimensions that they use to classify the region. The relative laminar widths are similar across species, for instance. But area 10 in humans is far larger than in other species, both absolutely and relative to total brain volume, while the relative volume for other species is variable. Similarly, there is variation in density of cell bodies at various cortical depths across species, leaving room for more intraneuronal connections as this density falls off. These differences may be expected to have functional consequences as well. So by some criteria there is the same area across species, but other criteria might yield a different verdict, and there is no guarantee that this area will have a common function.

In short, none of these arguments establishes that there is not multiple realization. The heuristic positing of identities in neuropsychological studies, especially lesion and imaging studies, can be taken to show only species or population-specific identities; that is, only *local* realizations are established by such studies. And cross-species similarities among regions may just as well show that brain regions themselves are multiply realized. Although Bechtel and Mundale draw attention to important facts about the practice of taxonomy in neuroscience, these do not undermine the MR thesis.

Larry Shapiro (2000, 2004), however, makes a more direct attack on the notion of multiple realizability, arguing that proponents of the notion have been altogether too casual in deploying it. Once the thesis is properly clarified, he holds that it is likely false that minds are either multiply realizable or multiply realized. Shapiro focuses on our criteria for individuating realizers. What, he asks, makes two structures the same or different realizers of a particular psychological state? Call the properties that make something eligible to realize a certain functional state its R-properties. The R-properties of an AND-gate in electrical engineering, then, are whatever enables it to turn on when and only when there is current active on both of its inputs. Different materials may perform this function; hence there are many sorts of AND-gates, and hence AND-gates are multiply realizable.

Shapiro challenges this inference. We cannot conclude that that being an AND-gate is *multiply* realizable unless its realizers are *substantially* different; that is, they need to belong to theoretically distinct kinds. But this poses a dilemma. For a functional category F with two possible realizers A and B, either A and B will be similar in their R-properties, or they will not. *First horn*: if they are similar in their R-properties, then they cannot belong to theoretically distinct kinds, since they just belong to the category determined by possession of those R-properties. So there is no multiple realization. *Second horn*: if they differ in their R-properties, then even if they both satisfy the functional specification F, they do not belong to a common kind, since by hypothesis they differ in their underlying causal features, and kinds are defined by the possession of *common* causal features. So either they do not realize the same functional category, or they do, but not in virtue of belonging to different kinds.

A number of examples bolster this point. In the realm of artifacts, consider corkscrews and watches. There are many types of corkscrew, all of which ultimately serve to remove corks from bottles. But they do so in markedly different ways: using double-levers and a double-sided rack, using a single lever as in a waiter's corkscrew, using an injected burst of CO_2, or the like. Because these differ in their lower-level properties, they cannot belong to a single kind. So there will be no interesting generalizations to make about corkscrews as such. Similarly for watches: analog and digital watches both tell time, but at the level of their detailed implementation, they are so unlike that there is no general account covering both of them – springs and gears have nothing in common with printed circuits beyond being timekeepers; hence being a timekeeper is not interesting as an artifact kind.

In the realm of neuroscience, consider a case of surgically induced neuroplasticity. Von Melchner, Pallas, and Sur (2000) rewired (what would normally be) the auditory cortex of ferrets to receive input from the retina, severing their ordinary connections to visual cortex, and then measured their visual acuity. Postoperatively, these ferrets can in fact see, which might suggest that this should be seen as an example of multiple realization: the "auditory" cortex is capable of altering its structure to support vision as well. But Shapiro argues against this, noting first that the visual acuity of these ferrets is in fact inferior to and different from that of regular ferrets, and second that the structure of the altered "auditory" cortex strongly resembles that of ordinary visual cortex. This latter point is particularly important, because if true it would show that there is no genuine difference in the realizers in this case – merely the same R-properties instantiated in a physically and spatially distinct region. And this would disqualify it from being a case of genuine MR.

These examples seem to show either there are no genuinely distinct realizers for a single kind, or else there are distinct realizers but there is no common kind to which they belong. So arguments for multiple realization are Pyrrhic, because what is realized can never have the causal unity and integrity necessary to scientific kinds. Shapiro's cautionary point here should be conceded: in deciding whether we have a case of MR, we need to be sure that the realizers really belong to distinct kinds. Many standard examples do not fit this template: just as being differently colored or made of different metal does not make corkscrews belong to different kinds, so merely being made of different materials does not automatically guarantee differences in the realization of psychological kinds.

However, Shapiro's dilemma itself seems to be a false one. The reason is that one cannot infer from the fact that A and B belong to different kinds that they do not also belong to a further common kind F, defined functionally. Hierarchically nested kinds are commonplace in nature, particularly in the biological world. Biological species are a particularly nice example, since they belong not just to their own narrow class but also to larger classes that have distinctive features despite subsuming these otherwise heterogeneous subgroups – for example, *animalia* are heterotropic, multicellular, motile eukaryotes; both chordates and arthropods are types of animals, despite their large dissimilarities. We cannot decide a priori whether entities belonging to two different kinds will also belong to a common overarching kind. Whether this is so depends on there being an appropriate overlap in causal powers between these two otherwise dissimilar things.

There is another issue lurking in the background of Shapiro's discussion, however, which concerns kind-splitting arguments more broadly. A *kind-splitting argument* is one that aims to show that a category lacks the requisite unity and integrity needed to support scientific explanations. Categories may fail to be useful by being empty (e.g., the luminiferous aether in pre-relativistic physics), but more frequently they simply fail to line up properly with causally unified groupings of entities – groupings that have similar underlying structure and concomitant causal powers or similar functional organization, or that support similar ranges of inductive generalizations. When we lump together two phenomena that are sufficiently causally distinct, discovering this may motivate us to split the putative kind. An example of this is the fragmentation of the folk concept of "memory" into many distinct subtypes. It is standard to distinguish declarative and procedural memory from one another; within declarative memory, episodic and semantic memory are distinguished; and so on.[11] Since these systems have substantially different properties, memory itself is not a unified kind for psychology.

Shapiro is arguing that apparent cases of multiple realization should really be seen as opportunities for kind-splitting. We've suggested that this is overly hasty, but some kinds are in fact ripe to be fragmented into several more useful successors. There may be no generalizations about memory per se in a well-developed psychological theory. Where there are different psychological generalizations about two types of memory, this may owe to some differences in the underlying mechanisms that realize each type; and we do in fact find that declarative and procedural memory are realized by different neural structures. The mere fact of these differences, though, is not what nudges us toward splitting memory as a kind: if we just discovered that memory functions are realized by different sorts of neural regions, that alone would not motivate splitting memory. We could simply conclude that memory is a single thing, but not neurally localizable. What matters is whether the *functions* carried out by these regions are so dissimilar that, on balance, there is no explanatory gain to be had by grouping them together.

This point reinforces, rather than undermines, the autonomy thesis. Discovering neurobiological mechanisms is important for answering the question of *how* a system performs its function. It may turn out that one system does so in many ways, or that many systems do so in their own ways. But as long as these ways do not differ in the essentials of the function they

---

[11] One commonly used taxonomy, that of Squire (2004), actually separates systems into declarative and nondeclarative, with the latter comprising a grab bag of processes such as procedural learning, perceptual priming, and classical conditioning. What these have in common is not clear, aside from just not being declarative systems.

perform, there is little justification for kind-splitting. On the other hand, if these different mechanisms are mechanisms *for* carrying out interestingly different functions, then we do have such justification. This illustrates the oscillation between top-down and bottom-up methods that is characteristic of attempts to integrate two separate fields. We will discuss this integrative picture further in Section 2.7.

2.6 A reductionist revival

Some, however, continue to pursue the reductionist agenda. Most prominently, John Bickle (2003, 2006) has proposed a view he calls *ruthless reductionism*, which states that some mental or psychological kinds can be reduced all the way to the level of molecular biology, with reductions to biochemistry looming in the near future. His view is of interest because of its radical nature as well as his claim that it fits a new style of reduction. Its radical nature comes from the proposal that the mind can be understood in *directly* molecular terms, and thus we can leap immediately to very low levels of reality to identify and explain cognitive kinds. This forms part of an ongoing research program that the neuroscientist Alcino Silva (2003) calls molecular and cellular cognition.

What makes this form of reductionism new is that it bypasses all higher or intermediate levels of the reducing science. This puts it at odds with both the classical model of deduction of higher-level regularities via bridge laws and the mechanistic model of reduction. The classical model supposes that there are many intermediate stages involved in reducing a high-level science like psychology to fundamental cellular neuroscience. The mechanistic model also envisages a hierarchy of explanatory levels, each involving its own distinctive mechanisms. Following in the footsteps of neuroscientists such as R. D. Hawkins and Nobel Prize winner Eric Kandel (Hawkins, 1984; Hawkins & Kandel, 1984), Bickle believes that the explanation of intelligent behavior, including perception, action, thought, and memory, are now actually being given by practicing neuroscientists, not only at the level of the cell physiology of the neuron but also at the intracellular molecular level.

Bickle's method is to find a link directly from the molecular and chemical level of the brain's mechanisms to behavioral pathways and skip the intermediate or higher levels of what functional or psychological states the cellular- and molecular-level states might realize. The practices of studying the molecular basis of mind allow us to "intervene directly at the cellular or molecular levels and track specific behaviors in well-accepted experimental protocols for studying the psychological kind at issue" (Bickle, 2006, p. 414). An *intervention* is any experimentally produced change in a system that predictably and reliably changes its state. Intervention-based methods are common in neuroscience, including the production of lesions, direct stimulation of cells using microelectrodes, chemical blockade of synapses or alteration of metabolic pathways, and use of genetically engineered "knockout" organisms.

The logic of radical reductionism involves making specific genetic, cellular, or molecular interventions; observing the resulting changes to a creature's cognition and behavior; and inferring that the microscale component that has been intervened on is the basis for the relevant cognitive capacity. Bickle cites numerous examples of low-level biochemical explanations of the neurochemistry of fear conditioning in mice or memory consolidation in a range of organisms. If ordinary memory behavior is altered or destroyed on adding or removing a certain neurochemical, then Bickle would say the scientist has identified part of the molecular or cellular basis of memory. If the presence of the appropriate neurochemical affects fear responses of the organism, then Bickle would say the cellular biologist has identified fear in the animal. This process can be summed up as "intervene molecularly, track behaviorally."

Consider Bickle's example of long-term potentiation (LTP) in mice. LTP is one of the most heavily studied neurophysiological processes. When strong electrical stimulation is delivered to a tract of neurons, they fire intensively, producing correspondingly high levels of activity in the neurons that they synapse with. When this stimulation is repeated with high frequency, the activity in the postsynaptic neuron becomes "potentiated," so that the same level of stimulation will produce a large postsynaptic effect that often persists for a relatively long time. LTP is the phenomenon of long-term change in the response properties of postsynaptic neurons following high-frequency stimulation.

Although much attention has been paid to the physiology underlying the induction and maintenance of LTP, there are also intriguing links between LTP and behavior. For example, mice that have genes connected with building molecules crucial for normal LTP knocked out also suffer from highly specific memory disruptions. Their long-term conditioned responses to fear are abnormal, as is their long-term social recognition memory. These interventions underwrite explanatory claims: "The behavioral data is fully explained by the dynamics of interactions at the lowest level at which we can intervene directly at any given time to generate behavioral effects, along with the known anatomical connectivities throughout neural circuits leading ultimately to effects on muscle tissue attached to skeletal frames" (Bickle, 2006, p. 429).

We may wonder, however, whether the radical reductionist picture can really provide us with explanatory reductions of psychological phenomena. One worry is a familiar one about multiple realization: there is no guarantee that there are not other types of chemicals that might produce the same behavior. However, Bickle has argued that even across widely diverse biological species, the molecules known to be involved in these pathways are virtually identical. If they emerged sufficiently early in the evolution of terrestrial nervous systems, it is possible that they might have been conserved throughout the lineage. Conserved traits such as these have a single realizer as a matter of historical contingency.

A second worry has to do with whether molecular causes can capture cognitively guided behaviors. For something to be an *action*, as opposed to a mere bodily motion, it must be appropriately produced: some cognitive state has to figure in its cause. If my finger moves, it may be because you supplied an electric shock, or a brain tumor pushed on a motor area. But for its movement to be *my* act, a kind of behavior that is interesting and intelligent, it must be produced by a cognitive cause. The same is true for the behavior of the mice. If we are really giving neurochemical or cellular level explanations of intelligent behavior, then, despite what Bickle says, there must be a level of description available at which the events constitute cognitive states of the mice, and therefore we would expect something that looks a lot more like the traditional multilevel models of reduction.

A third worry is that the ability to intervene and disrupt a capacity is not sufficient for either reduction or explanation. Suppose that an intervention on a component C at the microscale produces a certain macrolevel effect on a system. This may show that C is *explanatorily relevant* to the system, in a broad sense, since it requires C for its normal functioning. But it hardly shows that C itself explains the system's functioning, even if it is part of such a complete explanation. Even if we had a complete understanding of the genetic and molecular basis of LTP, we would not yet have an understanding of how memories are formed and stored. LTP is a phenomenon occurring at specific synaptic junctures, whereas forming memories is something done at the level of the whole organism, or at least a large part of its brain. To understand LTP's contribution to this much larger and more complex event, we need to situate it properly within the system, and this requires knowing about much more than LTP itself. Microlevel facts and phenomena can contribute to the explanation of systems-level phenomena when they are appropriately slotted into this wider causal and mechanistic context. And if these microlevel facts are not by themselves explanations of systems-level facts, we cannot say that the systems-level facts have been *reduced* to the microlevel facts, either, because being able to explain something's properties and characteristic phenomena is a necessary condition on a successful reduction.

So we may turn the tables on Bickle. He has argued that sciences will still look for higher-level laws and descriptions as mere heuristic tools, useful but dispensable. They will be heuristic because in the end the real explanations will involve only the lower-level mechanisms Bickle cites from molecular biology. However, it may be that the discovery of direct manipulations of the sort Bickle describes are themselves the heuristics that will be followed by wider causal laws and larger mechanistic analyses that give the complete explanation of what lies behind the success of the manipulations at the neurochemical level.

2.7 Autonomy and theoretical co-evolution

If reductionism turns out to be untenable, how should we think about the relationship between psychological processes and neurobiological ones, particularly if we want to defend the autonomy of psychology? One approach is to posit a co-evolutionary relationship between the disciplines such that they develop in tandem, refining their categories, models, and generalizations in response to each other. This relationship is emphasized by Churchland (1986), who notes that functional analyses of psychological capacities can be revised by neuroscientific discoveries about the disunity of their underlying mechanism (the same kind-splitting that we saw at work in Shapiro's argument). There is nothing inviolate about these categories, and we cannot assume that there will always be a top-down direction of influence on the development of our theories. Rather, "psychology and neuroscience should each be vulnerable to disconfirmation and revision at any level by the discoveries of the other" (p. 376).

Is this a threat to autonomy? Churchland caustically, but correctly, observes that "it would simply be boneheaded for a cognitive psychologist working on learning and memory to refuse to care about animal models, pathway research, clinical cases, imprinting in chicks, song learning in canaries, and habituation in *Aplysia*" (p. 373). We would be surprised to find any psychologists who would argue the contrary. To the extent that these are all potential sources of data about the structure of human learning and memory, or about memory mechanisms in general, psychologists *should* care about such things.

However, this conflicts only with our methodological autonomy thesis. This was the claim that psychology possesses a set of distinctive methods for designing and running experiments, tasks, and procedures; for collecting and analyzing data; and for constructing models that are not possessed by other disciplines and that have an epistemically special status in supporting (confirming or disconfirming) psychological explanations. Their special status involves the fact that they are the *proprietary* data for psychology.

But there are no such proprietary data. To maintain that there are would be as perverse as a cell biologist arguing that only evidence collected via light microscopy could confirm her hypotheses, thus ruling out evidence collected by centrifugally separating cells into their components, or through electron microscopy. This point has been made repeatedly in the history of psychology. Critics of behaviorism noted that by focusing only on third-person phenomena, behaviorists were neglecting the rich sources of introspective information that people have about their conscious experience. In a landmark article, John R. Anderson (1978) argued that the choice between competing cognitive models might be underdetermined by any set of behavioral evidence that we choose. Illustrating his point with reference to the debate over the format of visual imagery, he noted that the same behavioral data can be accommodated by either a pictorial (image-like) format or a propositional (sentence-like) format, depending on what sorts of processes one adds to the system. So the choice between two incompatible models needs to be made by appeal to other evidence. And, indeed, the imagery debate is now an ideal case of theoretical co-evolution, with lesion studies, neuroimaging evidence, and behavioral data all playing a role (see Chapter 6 for more discussion).

Anderson's conclusion is a strong one: resolving debates among cognitive models will eventually *require* nonbehavioral sources of evidence. One need not endorse this strong claim to reject methodological autonomy.[12] But this rejection cuts both ways. If psychology can be informed by neuroscientific evidence, neuroscience can similarly be informed by psychology.[13] A mechanistic picture of explanation gives us particular reason to think that this will happen. Recall that mechanisms are always tied to functions such as S's Ψing. Where Ψ is a psychological function, the appropriate taxonomy at the neurobiological level will be dictated by the search for whatever structures constitute the mechanism of *that* function. In a co-evolutionary picture, we have no guarantee that either the higher- or the lower-level theory will dominate when they disagree.

Rejecting methodological autonomy, then, does not show that psychology will eventually be absorbed by neuroscience. If there is a convergence between the fields, it is just as likely to be a convergence that *preserves* cognitive properties and processes as one that eliminates them. And rejecting methodological autonomy does not, as we have argued earlier, require rejecting explanatory autonomy. Explanations are successful when they account for the relevant phenomena and mesh with other well-confirmed theories and models. The explosion in interdisciplinary modeling has produced more data that bear on the evaluation of these models, but this does not undermine the notion of an autonomously explanatory psychology.

2.8 Conclusions

We can now draw together the threads laid out in this chapter. First, reductionism and eliminativism about cognition are logically independent positions. One might be both a reductionist and an eliminativist. On this view, it is the very fact that mental phenomena can be correlated with neurobiological (or lower-level) phenomena that makes the realm of the mental

---

[12] In fact, we are not sure we endorse it, either. To think this requires thinking that there can be neurobiological differences that are relevant to cognition but in principle cannot be revealed in any sort of behavioral context. This is a strong claim, and it's not clear that even Anderson's examples of purportedly behaviorally indistinguishable cognitive models establish it.

[13] This point, in a way, is implicit in Bechtel and Mundale's critique of multiple realization. If functional criteria drive decisions about how to taxonomize brain regions, and the functions in question are psychological ones, advances in neuroscience will depend on having an adequate psychological theory just as much as the other way around.

ripe for elimination. The existence of successful reductions shows that the reduced theory or domain is ontologically and explanatorily redundant. A contrary position says that reductionism supports anti-eliminativism. Successful reductions can be seen as a kind of *vindication* of a higher-level theory, a demonstration that the states and processes mentioned in the theory are independently certified as real. This position was held by many of the original type-identity theorists. Smart and Place, for example, did not think that identifying consciousness with brain processes entailed that there was *really* no such thing as consciousness.

On the other hand, anti-eliminativism has often drawn its strongest support from anti-reductionism. The functionalists' arguments that psychology is irreducible were meant to show that psychological explanations are autonomous and, indeed, indispensable. But anti-reductionism can also be seen to have eliminativist consequences. Anti-reductionism implies that psychological taxonomies do not line up neatly with underlying neuroscientific taxonomies. Because the neuroscientific taxonomies, by hypothesis, track kinds and other causal mechanisms, we should see the psychological taxonomies as defective and ripe for splitting and replacement.

So there is no simple relationship between (anti-)reduction and (anti-)elimination. Which of these pairings obtains in any particular situation depends on the details. What of the case for anti-reductionism itself? As we have presented it, the phenomenon of multiple realizability is its main support. In turn, multiple realizability helps to motivate the functionalist view of psychological states and processes. We have argued that there is robust evidence that many psychological states are multiply realizable and that the arguments against this are not, on the whole, compelling. On the other hand, there is not likely to be a universal answer to the question of whether psychology is multiply realizable. Although some psychological functions might seem realizable only in one kind of physical architecture, claims about multiple realizability in general are always relative to how the functions themselves are being described.

3   Modularity and cognitive architecture

3.1 The mind as a complex system

Brains and bodies are obvious examples of *things* – physical entities or objects. Like other paradigmatic physical objects, they have stable spatial boundaries and a host of other properties such as mass, density, and internal composition and organization. But are minds, or the ideas that fill them, also things? Are they object-like in these ways? Cartesian substance dualism, while it denied that the mind was something physical, nevertheless took it to be a kind of object or entity. Descartes argued further that the mind was not only a nonphysical object, but that it was also an indivisible object: it could not be decomposed into parts in any way whatsoever.

Ontologically, minds are *systems*, and some systems can also be object-like or entity-like. Atoms, solar systems, biological organisms, and hurricanes are all examples of entity-like systems. As systems they are decomposable into component parts and operations, but like many objects, they are also relatively persistent, coherent, and spatially circumscribed. Given the complex psychological and behavioral phenomena they give rise to, minds must be systems of extreme complexity. Like other complex systems, they have an internal design plan. For artificial computing devices, this plan corresponds to their circuit diagram – the description of their central processors (e.g., their instruction set), memory, system bus, various sub-controllers for storage, networking, audiovisual output, and so on. For biological organisms, this plan corresponds to their overall anatomical organization, their breakdown into organ systems (circulatory system, respiratory system, immune system), into individual organs and other active components (airway, lungs, diaphragm, etc.), and still further into specific types of specialized sub-organs, tissue and cell types, secretions and fluids, and so on.

3.2 Discovering cognitive architecture

By analogy with artifacts and organisms, understanding the mind as a complex system also involves delimiting its relatively stable components and organization, or what is known as its *cognitive architecture*. Specifying this architecture involves decomposing the mind into its subsystems and enumerating the ways in which they can control and pass information to one another. The result often takes the form of a map or diagram depicting these subsystems and their relations. A more detailed map would also describe the internal workings of these subsystems, especially the kinds of representations they contain and the cognitive processes that they can execute. Debates over cognitive architecture therefore focus on what component systems the mind has, how these systems are related to one another, and what kinds of representations and processes these systems use in carrying out their functions. In the remainder of this chapter, we discuss some differences among various architectural plans and the empirical and theoretical arguments that favor one plan over another.

Discovering mental architecture requires carrying out *functional analysis*, which can be regarded as a set of mutually constrained inquiries. First, there is the process of *task analysis*, in which we speculate about how a single complex capacity might be analytically decomposed into a series of less complex or less demanding tasks. The capacity to play a decent game of chess involves the ability to remember many possible board positions, to recall a range of stereotyped opening moves, to calculate many moves ahead, to take on the strategic perspective of one's opponent, and so on. Even capacities that are executed practically instantly can be highly complex. Understanding a sentence is a prime example, since it requires phonological or graphemic analysis, syntactic and morphological parsing, lexical retrieval, and integration of the sentence's meaning with general world knowledge. The capacity itself can be regarded as involving the exercise of various sub-capacities, of the sort that might be modeled using a flowchart or other abstract diagram. There is no unique way to decompose most tasks and capacities. Task analyses are initially put forward as tentative hypotheses about how the mind *might* carry out a certain operation, guided by intuitive judgment or speculation based on what is already known about the available set of cognitive capacities.

Second, there is *systems analysis*: a mapping of tasks onto functional "boxes" in the actual system itself. This is accompanied by a diagram or description of how these systems relate to one another and how information and control flow through them. A cognitive system is a set of processes and components that are interactive and highly integrated. The parts of a system are capable of exercising more control over one another than they are over things not in the system, and more than things not in the system can exercise over them (Shallice, 1988). Finally, the interactive integration of these parts serves a particular function. There is a set of things that the system routinely or normally does, and that it is (in some sense or other) *supposed* to do. The function of the system can be thought of as being located at Marr's computational level of analysis (see Section 2.3).

Specifying a complete cognitive architecture requires describing how the mind's systems are related to one another. Systems can include other systems as parts, which means they can be recursively decomposed into nested subsystems. For instance, a system that multiplies natural numbers may be decomposed into a subsystem that repeatedly adds natural numbers. A gaze detection system would require subsystems for detecting facelike stimuli by their characteristic display of two dark dots (eyes) above a single dark dot (mouth), for computing the direction in which the pupils are aimed, and for locating the most plausible object in the surroundings that could be the target of the gaze. Where one system is not a component of the other, they may still be intimately related, however. Two systems may be separate, but one may call on the other routinely in the course of its operations. Imagine a computer that has a variety of special-purpose chips for different operations. A graphics chip may outsource certain computations to a math processor, thus making its operation dependent on the external processor even if the two are functionally distinct components.

Third, there is *state and process analysis*. Once a system is decomposed into subsystems, their internal operations need to be determined. This requires describing the mechanistic organization of each system by unpacking the representations, processes, storage, and other resources that allow it to carry out its functions. Different types of representations are often better suited to carrying out one type of task than another, so where the function of the system differs, so do the information processing methods used to produce it. This type of analysis involves specifying what goes on at Marr's representational and algorithmic level (see Section 2.3).

State and process analysis separates mechanistic explanation from "black box" psychology. In the early stages of theorizing, we may posit mental components to carry out certain functions without knowing precisely *how* they do so. But a more complete explanation involves looking inside these boxes and describing their functional organization. So, for instance, we know that infants and certain animals can rapidly estimate small numbers and quantities. We might assign this function to a hypothetical "small number system" without knowing how it actually works inside. To go beyond positing such a black box, we need to describe the representations and processes that underlie this ability. Each subsystem is decomposed until the psychologically primitive or basic level of analysis is reached. This is the point at which there are no further psychological components and activities to which one can appeal in explaining the system's behavior. Any explanation of how these ultimate components function will have to appeal to the properties of the underlying neurobiological machinery that realizes them.

Fourth, there is *implementation analysis.* Implementation analysis involves finding a physical structure that realizes a cognitive capacity, system, or operation. Arguably the greatest progress in discovering mental architecture within the past several decades has come from new and massively powerful tools for studying the structure and dynamics of living neural systems. Cognitive neuroscience and neuropsychology are the disciplines that have made the greatest contributions to this sort of analysis, particularly where they rely on methods such as functional neuroimaging (PET, fMRI), lesion studies, and electrophysiological measurement and intervention (EEG, transcranial magnetic stimulation, single-cell recording). Various computational techniques may also be used, such as correlating the activity of neurons with the computational operations required to carry out a system's hypothesized function. Such correlations may provide evidence that the function in question is localized to neural regions having those properties. These techniques aim at linking cognition with neural structures and, where possible, localizing cognitive function in particular neural regions.

3.3 The classical model

One proposal about cognitive architecture that has been widely discussed is Jerry Fodor's (1983) suggestion that many subsystems of the mind, particularly the perceptual (input) systems and the action (output) systems, are *modular.* The functional demands of carrying out perceptual analysis, providing input to belief-formation and desire-regulation systems, and translating those beliefs and desires into action schemata mandate that input and output systems be specialized in a way that other cognitive systems are not. *Modularity* is the name that Fodor gives to the cluster of properties that these systems purportedly have in common.

Fodorian modules are systems that are (1) domain-specific; (2) mandatory; (3) cognitively impenetrable in their operations; (4) fast; (5) informationally encapsulated; (6) shallow in their outputs; (7) associated with fixed neural structure; (8) associated with stereotypical patterns of breakdown; and (9) associated with a stereotypical developmental trajectory. Properties (1) through (6) are the most central ones in this cluster and the ones we will focus most of our attention on here.

Modular input systems are evolutionarily designed to work on distinct classes of inputs. That is, there will be something distinctive about the inputs that "activate" the modules. A speech perception module would be tuned to human utterances specifically and would not respond (or would respond quite differently) to physically similar inputs that were not human utterances. There is some speculation that it is the *eccentricity* of the domain that requires modularity in the first place: more homogenous and non-eccentric domains would not require a specialized input module. Sentences of human languages are, compared to all possible auditory stimuli, an arbitrary-seeming collection of noises, which makes any device that detects and processes them special-purpose, in the sense that being tuned to just that strange class of inputs is unlikely to render such a device suitable for processing other sorts of input. Similar points have been made about face processing. This is an ethological point that can be strengthened by comparing the kinds of properties that human senses can detect to those of other terrestrial creatures.

Input modules are also mandatory and not cognitively penetrable or alterable. You can't help hearing a sentence that contains your name as a sentence containing your name (no matter how hard you may try not to or try to concentrate on merely the sounds of sentences rather than their content). You can't help see your mother's (daughter's, spouse's) face *as* her face.[1] Mandatoriness just means that once an appropriate input is presented, the operation of the system is automatic and not under voluntary control. In this way, modules

---

[1] Unless, of course, you have a disorder such as prosopagnosia. The existence of conditions like this give credence to the idea that some systems are modular: face recognition represents an eccentric domain that is rapidly processed and can be selectively impaired.

are like reflexes. What is more, other cognitive systems seems to have limited access to the internal processing of modules, and the central systems mainly have access to the outputs of these systems. Cognitive impenetrability refers to the fact that the representations and processes that mediate between the input and the output of a module are not usually externally accessible. What is going on inside the system does not typically "leak out" to other systems. This helps to explain why we are aware of *what* we are seeing, but not *how* the internal mechanisms of seeing actually work.

Processing in input modules is not just automatic but fast – on the order of milliseconds. As Fodor (1983, p. 80) puts it, "what encapsulation buys is speed, and . . . it buys speed at the price of unintelligence." It does not require executive decision making on the part of the subject to decide whether one hears a sentence containing one's name or see's one's mother's face.

Crucially, modular systems are also *informationally encapsulated*: the information and processing resources for the module come from within the module and do not, for the most part, recruit information from systems outside the module. For a simple demonstration, pressing on your eye with the other eye closed makes the world appear to move. Though you know better, the perceptual module does not have access to what *you* know. It only has access to what enters the eye and is processed in the visual perceptual modules. So the world appears to jump and move, despite your firm conviction that it is standing still.

Input modules also process information to a shallow level of output. That is, a visual module can identify the properties of shape and color of a stop sign. But it would not output the property of being a stop sign. The visual system knows about colors and shapes, not about stop signs as such. Or to take another example, your visual module delivers the visual information about the limping of the spy, but not the information that it is a spy who is limping. The property of being a spy is not one that the visual system is in the business of detecting. That is reserved for processing further up in the central system, according to the modularity of input systems.

Central systems, on Fodor's view, differ importantly from the modular periphery. They have the ability to compare, combine, and integrate information from many different cognitive domains. Therefore, they fail to be encapsulated and cannot be modules. Central cognition has two key properties that exemplify its lack of encapsulation. The first is *isotropy*. A system is isotropic when, in deciding whether a particular belief is true, it may draw on any piece of information that it regards as already being established. That is, there is no a priori limitation on what is or may be relevant to whether a particular claim should be believed or not. As Fodor vividly puts it, "our botany constrains our astronomy, if only we could think of ways to make them connect" (1983, p. 105).

The second property is being *Quineian*.[2] A system is Quineian when, in deciding whether a particular belief is true, the system is sensitive to global or collective properties of all of the information that the system has access to. For example, a theory might be simple and fit well with much of the available evidence, but when taken in combination with the rest of what we know it makes for a more complicated or less plausible overall model of the world. Consider: In trying to explain how a suspect escaped from a locked room, it would be simplest to assume they have a teleportation device. But the existence of teleportation devices would significantly complicate many of the other things that we believe about the world – we would have to rewrite large parts of our physics, at the very least. These qualities can only be assessed by looking at the theory's coherence with the rest of our information, which is not a merely local matter.

Both of these properties are *global* or *holistic* ones. To determine whether a proposition should be accepted or rejected, we may need to draw on an unbounded range of possible evidence, and even having done so, whether we ultimately accept it or not also depends on how much deformation of our other beliefs would be required. These are characteristics of many inferences made in the process of confirming scientific theories, and Fodor relies here on an analogy between scientific reasoning and belief fixation in ordinary individuals. Although there is surprisingly little empirical study of the degree to which individual cognition is isotropic and Quineian, it seems undeniable that it displays at least some elements of these properties. Each property individually requires that the systems of belief fixation be unencapsulated, since they need access (potentially) to any piece of information that one believes in order to compute the appropriate degrees of evidential support and coherence that propositions should be assigned.

We will refer to this overall architecture as "classical," since it serves as the point of departure and criticism for many that followed. Moreover, it

---

[2] After the philosopher W. V. Quine, whose paper "Two Dogmas of Empiricism" (1953) is the inspiration for the property that Fodor names for him.

enshrines many traditional tenets of philosophical theories of knowledge: for instance, there is a sharp division of labor between systems that aim to present a veridical picture of the perceived world – the world as it seems here and now to a creature – and those that aim to determine what should be believed about the world. Perceiving and believing are not merely distinct systems, but distinct *kinds* of systems; and while information flows from perception to belief, it does not flow in the other direction. How we perceive the world is in principle insulated from our beliefs about the world (Fodor, 1984; Churchland, 1988). On the classical view, then, divisions between cognitive systems recapitulate distinctions made in normative epistemology.

We should pause here to distinguish *intentional* modules from *Fodorian* modules. The notion of an intentional module was introduced into cognitive science by Chomsky (1980) in his arguments concerning the origins of our linguistic competence.[3] Chomsky proposed that normal speakers possess an innate body of information that, when combined with the right environmental inputs, would be sufficient to produce the grammar of any possible human language. This body of information takes the form of an unconscious or implicit theory of the language in question, and possession of this information explains how speakers can produce and interpret the sentences of their language, as well as reach judgments about whether particular constructions are well formed or permissible in that language. Finally, this information is largely inaccessible or isolated from other, similar databases as well as the person's own beliefs. Any self-contained, possibly innate body of information such as this is an intentional module.

Intentional modules differ from Fodorian modules in several ways, the primary one being that they are *databases* rather than *processing systems*. Fodorian modules may often contain proprietary databases, but they need not, and so intentional modules are not just a variety or subset of Fodorian modules.[4] Other senses of modularity will be distinguished in the sections to come.

---

[3] Fodor (2000) refers to these as "Chomskian modules," but we will follow Segal's (1996) coinage here and call them "intentional modules." The name "intentional" in this context means roughly "representational" or "informational"; it derives from the term "intentionality," which is a philosophical way of referring to the representational properties of mental states.

[4] Fodorian modules may be encapsulated without having private databases in the limiting case where their operations do not require any stored information to produce the appropriate outputs. This is a kind of "limiting case" of informational encapsulation in which a cognitive system is maximally reflex-like.

3.4 Massive modularity

Many have noted that Fodor's title, *The Modularity of Mind*, is misleading: input and output systems are modular, but the central core, the seat of distinctively higher cognition, remains nonmodular. Others have proposed taking the title more seriously, advancing the claim that modules are essentially the only building blocks of the mind. The hypothesis of *massive modularity* states that the mind is *entirely* composed of modular subsystems.

The most controversial claim that massive modularists make is that there is no single faculty of central cognition. The tasks of reasoning, planning actions, constructing theories, and so on are no longer the job of the belief/desire/intention system that Fodor posited. Instead, there are separate subsystems for reasoning about mate selection, about the biological world, about the minds and intentions of others, and so on. Similarly, plans and intentions are the property of various special-purpose practical reasoning systems, rather than a general decision-theoretic mechanism; and the same goes for all other higher cognitive processes. The mind is not a single all-purpose reasoning tool, but rather a Swiss Army knife, containing specialized tools for different jobs.

Massive modularity comprises two complementary claims. First, there is an *existence claim*: there are many distinct, modular specialized systems for reasoning about different sorts of content. So we have a module for social cognition, a module for physical object cognition, one for biological reasoning, and so on. Second, there is a *nonexistence claim*: there is no distinct system whose function it is to reason about all of these different sorts of content. The requirement that this system be *distinct* is important, as we will see later. Bear in mind that without the nonexistence claim, it is perfectly possible that we could have an architecture in which there are many specialized reasoning systems that are allowed a "first pass" at drawing inferences about a domain, then pass those results to a centralized general-purpose reasoning system that coordinates, integrates, and evaluates the results of these specialized cognitions. The nonexistence claim is meant to rule out this kind of arrangement.[5]

---

[5] Notice that massive *intentional* modularity would not pose a threat to the existence of a Fodorian central cognitive system. There could well be a single belief–desire reasoning mechanism that nevertheless contained distinct proprietary databases for various topics. These might even be innate. Samuels (1998) calls this the Library Model

Beyond this point there is disagreement about what massive modularity requires, centered on how strong a notion of modularity is required. Few maintain that the full Fodorian cluster should be accepted, but some partisans hold that these systems must at least be domain-specific, others that they should be informationally encapsulated, and still others that they should be neurally localized. In order to simplify the discussion, we will assume that these systems are domain-specific and encapsulated. As we will see, this is central to many of the arguments behind massive modularity.

3.4.1 The computational tractability argument

This argument aims to show that overcoming the kinds of computational challenges that human reasoners can meet requires that the mind be massively modular. The central problem here is a version of what is known as the "Frame Problem." This problem – or, more accurately, family of related problems – was first raised in early artificial intelligence research. In a landmark paper, McCarthy and Hayes (1969) were concerned with how to apply logical formalisms to the problem of modeling the results of ordinary plans and actions. Actions change certain parts of the world, but not others: rolling a ball across the floor changes only the ball's location, not its color, and, unless it knocks something over, nothing else in the room either. Moreover, the world often exhibits a kind of inertia: if someone gives me an address over the phone and I write it down on a piece of paper, I continue to have the paper and the address once the conversation is over. Formalizing these facts about change and persistence within an automated reasoning system turns out to be fiendishly difficult. Early attempts to do so often wound up either ignoring real changes, or else becoming lost in the infinite problem of how much should be ignored as irrelevant and unchangeable in the present context.

The problem of modeling change that gave such grief to early AI systems was the original Frame Problem.[6] But the problem covers a whole family of difficulties facing automated reasoning systems, all connected with issues

---

of cognition. The thesis of massive modularity is usually read to involve modules understood as processing devices rather than bodies of information, and we will interpret it that way here.

[6] We won't take a stand here on what the "true" Frame Problem is. For discussion, see the papers in Pylyshyn (1987) and Boden (2006, pp. 769–757).

of computational tractability. Human beings, however, routinely seem to solve the tractability problem (or, rather, the problem never arises for us in the first place). This suggests the following argument: completely domain-general systems cannot overcome the tractability problem, but humans can overcome it. Because no completely domain-general system can solve the tractability problem, human cognition must not essentially rely on such a system. But modular systems *can* overcome the tractability problem. So the best explanation of human cognitive performance is that the mind is entirely modular.

The tractability problem can be posed with respect to a range of activities. Consider different types of reasoning: formulating a plan, constructing a theory, or simply updating one's beliefs in response to a perceived change. To carry out any of these processes requires an interaction between a memory store, processes that retrieve relevant and useful pieces of information from that store, and processes that draw inferences to new and relevant pieces of information that go beyond what is already stored and combine them into larger units of knowledge that can be integrated with what is already known. Retrieval and inference must succeed within temporal constraints: to live requires timely action, not interminable contemplation.

Temporal considerations enter in various ways. First, search is costly: if the database of information is too large, search times may be prohibitive. There is no easy way to measure the actual amount of information stored in the typical human's memory, but on any account it must be vast. Search must somehow be constrained if it is to be practical. Second, inferences are also costly. Making any inference takes time, as does assessing the plausibility of candidate hypotheses that one generates. So efficient reasoning requires some sort of restriction on the space of hypotheses that are considered, since there are always indefinitely many conclusions that one is permitted to draw from any set of information, only a few of which will be reasonable in the circumstances.

Tractability, then, requires that retrieval and reasoning processes be both *speedy* and *relevant*. But this is a challenge for an informationally unencapsulated system. Unencapsulation means that potentially any piece of information in the system may be accessed and used for any purpose. However, in a large enough database, this means that total search will rapidly become impractical. Some way needs to be found to constrain the amount of information that is searched, and encapsulation provides a natural way to do this.

The problem of relevant retrieval under temporal constraints is effectively solved in modular systems by constraining the available database.

The problem of inferential relevance is more challenging, but here the problem may be solved by appealing to the constrained or reflex-like nature of modular computations. Modules have a limited number of inferences that they can carry out, and (in the Fodorian tradition) they do so in a restricted, stereotypical fashion. This property might be thought of as a processing analogue of informational encapsulation. Domain-general or nonmodular systems, on the other hand, have a larger and more open-ended set of inferential moves open to them at any stage. Inferential relevance, then, is also achieved by restricting the range of processes in the architecture itself, just as retrieval relevance is solved by restricting the database.

So it seems that modules can solve the tractability problems that plague nonmodular systems. Is the argument convincing? First we should note that it has a negative and a positive component. The *negative* component claims that completely nonmodular systems face certain intractable problems. The *positive* component claims that a massively modular system will not face those problems. We will assess these components separately.

The negative component divides, as we have seen, into the search argument and the processing argument. The search argument *does* show that a system with a sufficiently large database and a sufficiently inefficient search procedure will fail to retrieve information in a timely and useful way. But we also know of automated search algorithms (e.g., those used by major Internet search engines) that can retrieve information with impressive speed. Although they all employ some sort of automated processes that organize information for efficient retrieval, it is widely thought that human memory contains automatic processes that consolidate information in various ways, so this is not implausible. There is accordingly no reason to assume that unencapsulation per se entails intractable search.

A more subtle issue concerns how *relevant* information can be retrieved. There is no guarantee that rapid searches will retrieve mainly relevant results, of course (as anyone who has been frustrated with a Google results page can testify). But the general topic of how relevance relates to encapsulation we will treat alongside worries about relevant processing more generally.

The processing argument is supposed to support encapsulation in the following way. If a system has an indefinitely large range of possible moves that it can make, there must be some tractable procedure by which it focuses on the *right* moves, where the right moves here are the ones that make the most relevant inferences. In classic discussions of the Frame Problem, it is often noted that there are infinitely many deductively valid inferences that can be made given any change in the world's state. Most of these are of absolutely no interest, however, and it would be a waste of time and resources to pursue them. A system that is "process unencapsulated" has too many possible inferential moves available to it, whereas one that has only a restricted set of moves, or that operates under relatively tight constraints, does not face a similar decision problem. Hence no inference engine that is both timely and relevant can be *completely* unconstrained in terms of its ranking of what inferences should be drawn in any particular circumstance. By the same token, processes that retrieve information for use in reasoning also need a way to rapidly rank that information for relevance.

These points are correct as far as they go. Successful cognition requires a sense of what is relevant, and the great challenge for theorists and engineers is to understand what this sense of "relevant" might amount to, and how it might be mechanically implemented. This is one of the most significant descriptive challenges facing psychology – indeed, we have barely made a start in describing the phenomenon of something's appearing relevant to us (Wilson & Sperber, 2012).

But this argument does not support the conclusion that central cognitive systems must be encapsulated. All that it requires is that there be *some sort of system* that prioritizes certain inferences over others, that ranks certain processes according to their order of precedence, and that decides which are most important in the current context. The facts that need to be explained are that humans can carry out relevantly context-sensitive thought, and so there must be some mechanism that orders and schedules processes according to relevance. Taking a page from computer science, we can call such a system a *scheduler*. These scheduling procedures function as a constraint on the kind of processing that takes place in the system. But precisely because every system whatsoever requires some kind of scheduling procedures like this, the existence of a scheduler cannot make the difference between an unencapsulated cognitive system and a massively modular one. Any system that has more than one possible path through the space of possible processes it can execute needs a scheduler. To claim that an unencapsulated central cognitive system must completely lack any kind of constraint on how it processes information is just to caricature the nonmodular position.

In fact, when massive modularity theorists come to specify the procedures that their systems use to solve the computational tractability problem, it turns out that their solutions can just as easily be adopted by nonmodularity theorists. Consider a proposal made by Peter Carruthers (2006). Carruthers distinguishes between two forms of informational encapsulation: "narrow scope" and "wide scope." A system is *narrow-scope encapsulated* when most of the information in the mind is such that in the course of the system's processing it does not have access to that information. That is, there is a particular restricted portion of that information that the system is able to access, and the rest is off limits. This notion corresponds to the classic notion of encapsulation, which is implemented by modules having access only to their proprietary database. A system is *wide-scope encapsulated*, on the other hand, when in the course of the system's processing it has access to only a portion of the information stored in the mind – but not any specific, fixed, or determinate portion. The operation of the system is informationally frugal, but not in virtue of being tied to any particular database. Instead, its operations retrieve only some portion of the total information available, and query only a subset of the available systems.

Carruthers holds that modularity theorists should adopt wide-scope encapsulation. Although both forms provide a way for cognitive processing to be appropriately frugal, wide-scope encapsulation places no arbitrary limits on the *type* of information that can be retrieved by a module. Proprietary databases, on the other hand, require modules to be informationally self-sufficient. Yet many of the tasks that alleged central modules perform seem to require more information than any single, simple database could contain. If proprietary databases are inadequate to the tasks carried out by central modules, this suggests that the right conception of encapsulation to adopt is wide-scope.

However, it should be clear that wide-scope encapsulation is *perfectly compatible* with a nonmodular architecture. A single general reasoning system or unified inference engine might employ *only* processes that are frugal in this way: that is, processes that selectively employ only a portion of the total information store that is potentially available to them. Indeed, this is part of the very notion of these processes being tractable. If there can be such processes that belong to a functionally dedicated (modular) processing system, there is no reason that there cannot also be such processes belonging to a less dedicated or special-purpose system. The literature on the computational implementation of heuristic processes provides a rich source of examples of just this kind (Gigerenzer, 2008).

So the same steps that massively modular architectures can take to avoid intractability can equally be implemented in nonmodular systems. If this is correct, the negative arguments that are supposed to show that nonmodular (specifically, unencapsulated) systems cannot solve the tractability problem are inconclusive.

A further point can be made, however. Tractability is one feature that cognitive models need to accommodate. The other is relevance. It is not at all clear that the mechanisms proposed by massive modularists solve the relevance problem. Classical modules solved the relevance problem by using exhaustive search through a restricted database. But wide-scope encapsulation does away with this idea, instead putting the burden on heuristics and other processes to query and retrieve the appropriate information. Something's merely being a wide-scope encapsulated process does not guarantee that it will retrieve only relevant information. Any process that does this would be an add-on to the theory, and any such add-on that massive modularists propose could just as easily be incorporated in a nonmodular system. So there appears to be no *general* reason why massively modular systems can accommodate frugality and nonmodular systems cannot.

The negative component of the argument from tractability fails to establish its conclusion, then. What about the positive component, which aimed to show that a massively modular system *can* be frugal and relevant? We have just seen that there is nothing in the idea of massive modularity itself that enables such systems to be tractable and relevant. The same problems of information retrieval carry over, and problems of process scheduling simply reappear as problems of controlling information flow among modules.

This point should, in fact, have been anticipated from the beginning. That is because there is a subtle error in the argument from tractability. It may be correct that a *single* classical Fodorian module does not face the retrieval and relevance problems, because it has a proprietary restricted database and a highly rigid order of processing. This considerably reduces the scope for these problems to arise. There is therefore no *intramodular* tractability problem. However, it does not at all follow that a massively modular mind would not face this problem. Whether there is an *intermodular* tractability problem is an open question. Even if the modules that make up such a system can overcome the problem when taken individually, the issue is whether the architecture *as a whole* can overcome it.

It is generally well understood that one cannot infer from properties of parts of a system to properties of the system as a whole. Yet that seems to be the precise structure of the positive argument in favor of massive modularity: a single module does not face the tractability problem, therefore a massively modular system does not either. But that is simply a non sequitur.

3.4.2 The no-general-mechanisms argument

The no-general-mechanisms argument starts from some very broad evolution-ary considerations. Using these, massive modularists aim to show that there is something incoherent in the idea of a truly domain-general cognitive mech-anism, and thus a massively modular design is the only one consistent with the empirical facts about evolution. Cosmides and Tooby put the argument in its strongest form: "It is in principle impossible for a human psychology that contained nothing but domain-general mechanisms to have evolved, because such a system cannot consistently behave adaptively: It cannot solve the prob-lems that must have been solved in ancestral environments for us to be here today" (1992, p. 90).

The argument starts from a truism: a learning system needs some crite-rion of success and failure to do its job. But what counts as success and failure differs from domain to domain. A principle that leads to successful action or accurate cognition in one domain may lead to failure and falsehood in another. If you are about to get into a fight, it pays to stick close to the largest, most powerful fighter in your group. On the other hand, if you're trying to mate with his partner, you're best served by being as far away from him as possible. Whether you approach or avoid depends on what your aims are, and thus on what the domain is, in some broad sense. Hence, "because what counts as the wrong thing to do differs from domain to domain, there must be as many domain-specific cognitive mechanisms as there are domains in which the definitions of successful behavioral outcomes are incommensurate" (Cosmides & Tooby, 1994, p. 92). So, they conclude, there can be no such thing as a mechanism that is generally prepared to deal with any adaptive contingency. Any such mechanism would have to, at least initially, treat all situations and contexts identically, and thus would lead to maladaptive out-comes, in effect eliminating itself as soon as it emerged.

That argument makes massive modularity virtually compulsory, given cer-tain minimal assumptions. But an argument that seems to entail such a strong conclusion about cognitive architecture using such relatively weak assumptions should be questioned closely. And, in the present case, the contentious claims about how a domain-general reasoning system would have to work cannot be supported.

The first point is that domain-general mechanisms may be coupled with domain-specific bodies of information. Recall the distinction made earlier between intentional and Fodorian modules (modular *databases* vs. modular *processors*). A domain-general inference system may have access to an intentional module containing a host of domain-specific information that will prove useful in generating hypotheses that are highly tuned to the adaptive problem in question. The strongest inference that can be made, then, even assuming that the argument is on the right track, is that there should be *something* domain-specific about how learning takes place. Whether this is a kind of processor or a body of information cannot be settled without further investigation.[7]

The second point concerns whether domain-general systems can learn domain-specific definitions of error. A system that has absolutely no information about particular types of objects or situations would have no reason to treat them differently, and hence might initially apply the same policies across domains. Although this might lead to maladaptive behavior, as long as the system can also *detect* error signals, there is no reason that these behaviors would persist long. Humans are shielded from many of serious adverse consequences of their initially flawed reasoning by the fact that they are social animals with a long developmental period, during most of which they are protected by their parents and other caregivers. There is a long period that allows developing children to make mistakes without immediately perishing. Cosmides and Tooby simply insist that domain-general mechanisms must *overgeneralize*. A system that overgeneralizes incorrigibly will obviously lead to improper and maladaptive behavior. But to assume incorrigibility is just to assume that domain-general systems must be *stupid*, and this is surely a straw man.[8]

---

[7] As a matter of fact, it is extremely difficult to empirically distinguish between two possibilities: (1) there is a domain-specific processing mechanism at work; or (2) there is a domain-general processor that has access to a domain-specific and encapsulated body of information.

[8] This is, in fact, something of a tradition among strong advocates of domain-specific processing. Chomsky's early arguments in favor of linguistic modularity and nativism sometimes proceeded by trying out a few candidate domain-general rules of an exaggeratedly simple nature on a particular linguistic construction, and then inferring

The third point is that even domain-general learning mechanisms may produce correct domain-specific results in the right circumstances. David Buller (2005, pp. 145–146) offers the example of social learning, or learning by imitation. In this practice, one first observes a particular kind of behavior carried out by a teacher, and then later imitates it. One observes, for example, one's older sibling or young adults in the community choosing a certain type of mate and one then imitates this sort of mate choice behavior, that is, selects a mate with relevantly similar characteristics. Similarly, observing a group of adults making kayaks can be a way of learning how to make a good kayak. What makes a good kayak is different from what makes a good mate, and those are the qualities that are detected and mimicked in each context. Mechanisms for careful observation of behavior plus imitation of that behavior are arguably domain-general, but there is no reason to think that the "same outcome" is produced in each case.

What these points show is that the broad-brush argument against domain-general learning systems fails to show that they cannot learn domain-specific information. Obviously this leaves the actual structure of the relevant domain-general learning mechanisms unspecified in many respects. But this is no worse a situation than we began with: our goal here is only to block an a priori argument against the existence of such mechanisms.

We will make one last point before leaving the topic of learning. To foreshadow an objection we will raise in Section 3.4.3, a mind that contains only domain-specific learning mechanisms will face difficulties accounting for behavioral and cognitive flexibility. On massive modularity, we have, initially at least, as many domain-specific learning systems as there were adaptive problems to be overcome in the human ancestral environment. But it is equally clear that we can learn indefinitely many things that correspond to no adaptive problems at all: playing chess, taking photographs, programming a computer, teaching a child to ride a bicycle, and so on. Massive modularists face several possible choices here. They might say: (1) that these activities all belong to some common higher-order adaptive domain; or (2) that they are somehow assembled from other, pre-existing modular learning systems; or (3) that they are themselves learned or otherwise acquired. None of these are appealing, however.

that no domain-general mechanism could learn that construction. More sophisticated domain-general mechanisms have since proven capable of learning many of these constructions under relatively realistic conditions, however.

The higher-order domain option runs the risk of making adaptive domains fanciful and unconstrained. Massive modularists might concede that playing chess is not an adaptive domain, but game-playing or strategic thinking and planning might be, and these subsume chess-playing. If making artworks is an adaptive domain, then taking photographs might be learnable as a special case. But these domains are plainly being invented to cover the cases at hand. There is no independent evidence that playing games or making art are adaptive problem domains in the evolutionary history of our species, or that they form natural domains of cognitive functioning. This is a perennial danger one courts when hypothesizing about adaptive functions.

The assembly option may have merit, if the relevant notion of assembly can be cashed out. For example, some capacities may result from the sequential or coordinated use of various systems. Hitting a baseball results from the use of visual object tracking systems and motor planning systems that are not adaptations for that purpose. Rather, these systems have their own adaptive functions, but can be combined online to produce new behaviors and underlie new capacities. It is an open question whether all of our novel capacities are explicable as the exercise of assembled arrays of modules. Progress here can only come with a better understanding of what modules we come equipped with, and what grain their domains are. Some theorists maintain that domains are roughly the size of commonplace daily challenges such as social reasoning, mate choice, detecting cheaters, and so on. Others maintain that they are much, much more fine-grained, being constituted by microcircuits that compute problems having no simple description in natural language (Anderson, 2007, 2010; Bechtel, 2003). While the latter type of "microdomain" comports most naturally with the assembly picture, in the absence of more evidence we can conclude only that the possibility of an assembly-based solution has not been foreclosed.

The final possibility, that new modules might themselves be learned or acquired, has been proposed several times in the literature. Despite this, it seems in tension with several core commitments of massive modularity. The idea behind this approach is that rather than new capacities being produced by the coordination of already existing modules, *entirely new* modules might be added to the mind's architecture. Just how this process takes place requires careful spelling out. A process that produces new modules takes the mind from a state where there is no domain-specific processing system of a certain kind to one in which there is. But it is hard to see how any process that implements this function could fail to be a domain-general learning system; or, more cautiously, it would have to be significantly *more* domain-general than most massive modularists are comfortable with. So learned modules are in tension with the rejection of domain generality.

In fact, this almost falls out of the task description itself. If the end product is to be an "exquisitely tuned" device capable of reaching adaptively appropriate solutions to domain-specific problems, then any system capable of constructing that device either will *itself* need to have access to the information necessary to reach those solutions, or will need to be capable of *constructing* the right sort of device by, essentially, repeated trial and error. The prespecified design possibility has, unsurprisingly, not been taken seriously. Rather, proposals concerning module construction appeal precisely to properties of neural populations that resemble natural selection – that is, processes that achieve complex designs and arrangements in an *unguided* fashion, without prior information about the appropriate shape of the functional structures that they produce (Calvin, 1996; Edelman, 1987). These Darwinian mechanisms of neural plasticity are as domain-general as it gets. They apply widely across brain structures and underlie learning and development in many different areas, and they achieve their ends using the same processes regardless of what kind of module is being constructed.

If this line of argument is correct, any new modules that the mind possesses come about from a domain-general system that is capable of constructing systems that can perform adaptively under a wide range of (possibly highly variable) error conditions. But this is much like what the no-general-mechanisms argument claims *cannot* be the case. Because success and error are domain-dependent and also adaptively significant, the argument went, any putative domain-general system could not learn what an organism needs to survive. If this is so, the argument should equally apply to the learning systems that produce new modules. It is not just the learning of entirely new modules that raises this difficulty, but also the ability to combine pre-existing modules in adaptive ways to produce new capacities as the assembly option proposes. Learning to *combine* several modules, like learning to construct new modules, cannot be the property of any pre-existing modular system, because it necessarily involves crossing domains. If domain-crossing processes are ruled out, then massively modular minds will be unable to amplify their cognitive capacities beyond the resources given by the initial set of modules. But this seems inconsistent with the patent open-endedness of human cognition.

3.4.3 The objection from content flexibility

We turn now to an objection to massive modularity that focuses on this flexible open-endedness, specifically the fact that human concepts can be freely recombined in ways that arbitrarily cross the boundaries of cognitive domains (Weiskopf, 2010a). Generally speaking, if we are capable of thinking about F, and also capable of thinking about G, then we are capable of combining these thoughts and thinking about both of them together, of comparing and reasoning about the relationships between Fs and Gs, and of drawing (dis)analogies between Fs and Gs. All of these capacities require cognitive mechanisms that are not just specialized for reasoning about Fs or Gs, but which can reason about the relationships between the two, and which have as their domain something having scope over Fs and Gs together. Given that this ability is a general one, not one restricted to any particular choice of F or G, it seems that we need to posit the existence of a cognitive system that subsumes these various modular domains and potentially integrates information across all of them. This, though, is just the classical function of central cognition itself. The *content flexibility* of human cognition strongly suggests the existence of just such a system.

Content flexibility can be illustrated with respect to two kinds of processes: conceptual combination and analogy-making. Concepts represent particular categories and hence can be seen as domain-specific. So the concept *zebra* is the concept of a certain type of animal, perhaps belonging to the realm of folk biological understanding. The concept *blanket* is the concept of a certain type of artifact. Having these concepts, we can also conceive of a *zebra blanket*. While you may never have encountered this combination before, you may be able to generate several plausible features that the concept possesses. For example, if a zebra blanket is understood to be for keeping zebras warm at night, it might be understood to be especially large and heavy (and, for that matter, to smell like zebra). If, on the other hand, it is understood to be a zebra-patterned blanket, it plausibly would have black and white stripes on it. There might be systems for reasoning about zebras, and perhaps for reasoning about artifacts like blankets, but it is unlikely that either of these systems could generate these features, the production of which depends on being able to reason either about the needs that zebras might have for blankets or the aesthetic qualities of zebras that might be transferred to commercial products like blankets. Neither are these qualities likely to be the property of any further system of the mind. Conceptual combination often results in the production of emergent features such as these that belong to neither of the original concepts.

Examples of such features abound. An *arctic snake* is usually taken to be white, since that would explain its ability to camouflage itself in the snowy environment. Generating this feature requires a bit of informal causal-ecological reasoning, but this reasoning is not the property of any system for thinking about the arctic or snakes per se. A *Harvard carpenter* is plausibly nonmaterialistic, but although this might not generally be true of Harvard grads or carpenters, it would explain the Harvard grad's choice of profession. While the properties that govern emergent feature construction are not well-understood, both the choice of a feature to transfer from one concept to another and the construction of genuinely new features seem to be guided by general causal-explanatory principles. Since it is unlikely that there are any such principles that are specific to the intersection of these particular domains, this appears to be an instance of broadly cross-domain reasoning.

Analogical reasoning provides numerous examples of domain crossing. Kepler initially explained the unknown force that keeps the planets in uniform motion around the sun by an extended analogy with light, and various other aspects of their motion were explained by analogy with the way a boatman steers his ship (Gentner & Markman, 1997). Development economist Barbara Ward coined the notion of "Spaceship Earth" to remind us that we all inhabit a fragile, resource-limited ship in a forbidding sea of space, and politicians (fallaciously) analogize the nation and its finances to individual households and their budgets. A relationship or marriage may be analogized to a war or journey, one's love to a rose, and one's feelings of grief, loss, or estrangement to the distance between stars. Analogy is omnipresent and compelling, drawing our attention to hidden similarities and facilitating the generation of new inferences about a domain (Gentner, 1998). But analogy is precisely a process that can cross more or less arbitrary domains – hence when pressed by an experimenter to compare, say, a magazine and a kitten we resort to listing *disanalogies*. The processes that underlie this ability seem to be quite domain-general.

If these examples are on the right track, there are empirical grounds for thinking that Fodor was correct that higher cognition is typically isotropic: information from one domain may freely be brought to bear on another. This poses a challenge for massively modular architectures, since it is central to their view that there is no system that has the function of integrating all of this information. Of course, causal reasoning, analogical reasoning, creative conceptual combination, and abduction more generally are among the least well-understood of our cognitive processes. It may be that there are ways for massively modular systems to implement this kind of isotropic content flexibility. But doing so remains a serious problem for these models.

3.5 The critique of modularity

So far we have been proceeding as if the notion of a cognitive module will play an explanatorily central role in our theories of cognitive architecture. But this view has come under fire in recent years. Few theorists these days endorse the full-blown notion of a Fodorian module, although many continue to believe in modules in a weaker sense: either as domain-specific or informationally encapsulated processors. We now raise some criticisms of these weakened notions of cognitive modularity.

3.5.1 Against domain specificity

Max Coltheart (1999) has argued that the defining trait of a module is simply domain specificity, with all the other Fodorian characteristics being optional. But there are several different notions of domain specificity to be teased apart.

By domain specificity, Coltheart means that a module responds only to stimuli of a particular class. Call this *input domain specificity*. If a system takes as its inputs only representations *of* a certain kind of thing, then the things that are the content of the input representations are also the domain of the module. A face recognition module is not activated (except accidentally) by trees or desks. It takes faces as input and produces judgments that they are either recognized or not recognized. But how a module operates once activated is left open: it may compute rapidly or slowly, mandatorily or optionally, and in an encapsulated or unencapsulated way.

A second notion of domain specificity pertains not to a system's inputs but to its function. A system is *functionally domain-specific* just in case its function is to process information about a certain kind of thing, carry out a specific task, or address a specific problem, particularly an *adaptive* problem (Buss, 1995; Carruthers, 2004). This conception places no restrictions on the sorts of input that a module may take. Potentially anything may activate a functionally domain-specific system, but its operations are aimed at solving only a certain narrow type of problem or executing a specific type of task.

There are many different notions of function that can be employed in delimiting what the domain of a cognitive system happens to be, and we won't canvass them all here. We will briefly mention the notion of *adaptive function*, derived from evolutionary theory. Following Cosmides and Tooby (1994), "An adaptive problem can be defined as an evolutionarily recurrent problem whose solution promoted reproduction" (p. 87). These problems included finding and successfully courting mates; communicating with and manipulating conspecifics; hunting and foraging for food; seeking shelter from dangerous weather; navigating varied terrain; gathering and shaping local materials to make tools, weapons, and clothing; and so on. An *adaptive domain* refers to a problem of this kind: one that was faced in the evolutionary past of the species to which an organism belongs, and which the cognitive system in question is adapted to solve.[9]

Taking stock: domain specificity can be thought of either in terms of the inputs to a system or in terms of the system's function. Either way, a notion of modularity must be able to distinguish between modular and nonmodular systems. Even if one claims that there are *in fact* no nonmodular systems, being able to make the distinction matters so that modularity is not trivialized. The question is whether these notions of domain specificity can do this job adequately.

Consider input domain specificity first. For one system to be more general than another on this view is for the content of the representations that activate it to be a *superset* of those that activate the other. Where one system might be activated only by equilateral rectangles, another might be activated by rectangles with sides having any length ratio, or one system might be activated by representations of family members while the other is activated by representations of any conspecific. In these cases, the latter system is more general than the former one.

---

[9] An adaptation here is meant in the sense of evolutionary biology. Adaptations are traits that increased the fitness of past organisms and that persisted in virtue of this contribution to overall fitness. For a trait to be adapted for a certain task or purpose is for it to be to be such that (1) the past instances of that system carried out that task or causally contributed to that purpose, (2) their doing so increased the overall fitness of their possessors, and (3) their contribution to fitness explains their presence in present-day organisms.

But this condition will not properly distinguish modular from non-modular systems even in the canonical cases. Perceptual systems take as input various physical magnitudes arriving at their transducers. The content of their input is these magnitudes and quantities. The output of perceptual systems, though, is not couched in terms of those same input properties. Instead, these systems produce representations of, for example, three-dimensional visual scenes populated with objects. The vocabulary needed to specify the output is different from that in which the input is given. And because these outputs form the input to later stages of processing, these more central processors which they feed into will *not* be more domain-general than the perceptual systems. Rather, they will simply have a *different* content domain, not a domain that is more general in its content than those of the peripheral systems.

Functional domain specificity also proves inadequate in defining modularity. Consider what it means for one device to be more functionally domain-general than another. A visual processor might have the function of transducing ambient light and producing spatial representations of various objects in the local environment. Compare this single device with three other devices: one that only represents the *form* of visual objects, another that represents their *motion*, and the last, which represents their *color*. If the original device represents these objects in terms of form, motion, and color together, in an intuitive sense it should be more domain-general than any of these three, since its function includes theirs. A device that categorizes creatures as to whether they are Siamese cats or not is similarly less domain-general than a device that categorizes them as to whether or not they are cats. Domain generality involves a system carrying out a superset of the tasks that others carry out.

But this will not help to define the notion of domain generality as it is applied to central cognition. The reason is that the function of the central cognitive system is *not* a conjunction, union, or superset of these various domain-specific systems. Take the classic input systems as an example: the function of these systems is to map transduced physical stimuli of many kinds (pressure, heat, light, sound, various chemical signals, etc.) onto representations of objects, properties, and events. More specifically, their function is to generate *percepts* of those things. A percept is a representation of part of the environment in terms of sensible categories and qualities that plays a distinctive functional role, namely being the input to processes of belief fixation.

Central cognition, on the other hand, does not function to generate percepts, but to carry out higher cognitive processes such as deductive and inductive reasoning, categorization, analogy-making, planning and practical reasoning, abstract theorizing, and so on. These processes may be initiated by percepts or by other higher cognitive states (judgments, desires, plans, etc.), and their output may be further higher cognitive states or instructions to other systems: plans for motor systems to engage in behaviors, or instructions to visual systems to generate images or language systems to generate sentences. None of these functions are *generalizations* of more domain-specific processes. They are, once again, simply *different* functions.

Although this argument is pitched in terms of functions construed broadly, it applies to the notion of adaptive functions as well. One system may have a more general adaptive domain than another. A system that is adapted to detect cheaters in social exchanges who are also members of one's own extended family is less domain-general than one that detects cheaters across the board. But a system that is adapted to carry out inferences characteristic of formal logic is *not*, by this criterion, more domain-general than one that is adapted to detect faces, because the adaptive "problem" or task of deductive reasoning is not one that is a superset of the task of detecting faces. They have different input conditions, operate according to different rules, and have different success conditions. Moreover, they emerged historically under different sorts of evolutionary pressures: the circumstances that led to the development of perceptual systems are not the same as those that led to the development of higher reasoning systems. Because central systems and input/output systems target *different* adaptive problems, their adaptive domains are not related in the way that general domains are to more specific ones.

We have been pursuing the question of whether modularity can be defined in terms of input or functional domain specificity. The conclusion we have reached is a negative one. We can compare systems in terms of the types of representations they take as input, or in terms of their functions (adaptive or otherwise), and we may find that some are more general than others in these respects. But there is no way to use these properties to define a notion of domain specificity that can draw the modular/nonmodular distinction. The idea of domain specificity has intuitive appeal, but on closer examination it simply dissolves as a useful way to categorize cognitive systems.

3.5.2 Against encapsulation and impenetrability

Many theorists have taken informational encapsulation rather than domain specificity to be the heart of modularity. In his most recent official pronouncement, Fodor himself says that "a module *sans phrase* is an informationally encapsulated cognitive mechanism, and is presumed innate barring explicit notice to the contrary" (2000, p. 58). But informational encapsulation may fare no better than domain specificity in defining modularity.

Encapsulation as a criterion for modularity has been challenged on the grounds of *vacuity*: no systems display it to any interesting degree. There is psychological evidence that some cognitive systems are unencapsulated. In perception, there is most famously the McGurk effect: hearing an ambiguous phoneme pronounced while watching a mouth silently saying one of its possible nonambiguous pronunciations can lead to hearing the sound as being that phoneme (McGurk & MacDonald, 1976). Other effects are more complex and striking. Phantom limb pain is an unpleasant sensation experienced "in" an amputated arm or leg. This pain is difficult to treat, but can be managed by using a mirror array to maneuver the remaining intact limb into a visual position that would be occupied by the amputated limb. If the intact limb is then massaged or manipulated, the phantom pain lessens (Ramachandran & Rogers-Ramachandran, 1996). The brain appears to interpret the soothing sensations delivered to the intact limb as if they were being delivered to the phantom, on the basis of the visual information provided. Thus pain sensations are not encapsulated with respect to visual input.[10]

In fact, a large body of research suggests that perception is *inherently* crossmodal or intermodal, and that the notion of sharply distinct sensory processing regions needs to be abandoned. Examples of these crossmodal interactions abound (Driver & Spence, 2000; Shams & Kim, 2010; Shimojo & Shams, 2001). Consider the sound-induced flash illusion: a single flash of light accompanied by two or more beeps can be perceived as two or more flashes. These percepts correlate with event-related potential (ERP) recordings of activity in primary visual cortex, suggesting that the effect occurs early in the stream of processing and is not a later, more cognitively interpreted phenomenon. In addition,

[10] We should note that phenomena involving phantom limbs may reflect reorganization of areas of sensory cortex that occurs after the initial injury. It is therefore unclear whether we should conclude that normal limb perception is unencapsulated on the basis of these studies (Ramachandran & Hirstein, 1998).

the effect is initiated rapidly (within 35–65 ms of the stimulus), suggesting it is not produced in lower-level areas by top-down feedback.

Another example involves the resolution of ambiguous motion displays. If two silhouetted objects appear to be moving toward each other, the paths they follow after making contact can be interpreted as either the objects passing through one another and continuing on their original paths, or as the objects bouncing off each other and moving in the opposite direction. How the visual display appears can be influenced by whether a sound is played within a certain temporal interval of the objects' making contact (Sekuler, Sekuler, & Lau, 1997). If a sound or a tactile vibration is presented around the moment of contact, the objects will appear to rebound off each other; otherwise they will appear to pass through each other. Sensory systems may make use of multimodal cues like these in constructing a conscious picture of the world. This arrangement would make sense, given that many events in the world can best be detected multimodally.

Finally, a number of studies seem to challenge the *impenetrability* of perceptual processing. Perceptual impenetrability means that there is no direct effect of beliefs, desires, and other higher intentional states on perceptual states. Roughly speaking, if perception is impenetrable, then merely wanting or believing something does not in and of itself produce changes in how the world *appears* to us. These sorts of top-down effects are inconsistent with modularity insofar as they are forms of interference with modular processing by other cognitive systems.

For a striking example, consider the phenomenon of "wishful seeing" (Balcetis & Dunning, 2010). People who were thirsty after consuming a bowl of pretzels tended to perceive a bottle of thirst-quenching water as being closer to them than did people who were not thirsty. This was measured by asking the thirsty participants to make numerical estimates of the distance to the bottle, and also by using action-based measures such as tossing a beanbag the estimated distance toward the object. People not only rated the desired object as closer, but tended to "undertoss" the beanbag, suggesting that they saw the target object as being nearer to them. These results hold across a range of targets having different kinds of value, including chocolates, $100 bills, and gift cards. Negative targets such as pretend bags of dog feces were also perceived as being further away. These results suggest that desire modulates perception. We not only tend to judge desired objects to be closer (and undesired ones to be further away), but also we tend to *see* them as closer.

Perceptions of other spatial qualities and relations can be distorted in similar ways. For example, people often overestimate how steep an incline is, but those standing at the top of a hill looking down make greater errors than do those standing at the bottom looking up (Proffitt, Bhalla, Gossweiler, & Midgett, 1995). A hill with an incline of only 7 degrees may be perceived to have a 25-degree incline when viewed from the top. These perceptual errors may correlate with fear of heights and awareness of the possibility of tripping downhill. When people were asked to look downhill in slightly worrying conditions such as standing on top of a skateboard, they made greater estimation errors than while standing on a fixed object such as a box (Stefanucci, Proffitt, Clore, & Parekh, 2008). These conditions also correlated with self-reports of fearfulness. So either fear itself or the cognitive awareness of being near a hazardous descent may affect how steep something looks.[11]

The affective content of a stimulus can also affect its perceived size. Van Ulzen, Semin, Oudejans, and Beek (2008) presented people with pictures of circles containing symbols that have different emotional associations: positive (kittens, flowers), negative (aimed gun, skull), or neutral (bird, mushroom). Some targets were also blank. Their task was to match the size of the target circle with an adjustable comparison circle. Blank circles were matched correctly. Positive and neutral circles, however, were underestimated in size relative to the blank circles, while negative circles were underestimated by less. So there is a general tendency to underestimate the size of circles containing any sort of image, but there is nevertheless an effect based on the associative emotional content of the type of image. If these size-matching judgments reflect the perceived size of the circles, we have yet another example of cognitive states penetrating perception.

As a final example, a number of studies have pointed to the role of effort in shaping perception. When people are encumbered by a heavy backpack,

---

[11] However, not every way of eliciting estimates of an incline's steepness produces errors of the same magnitude. Verbal estimations and visual matching of the incline are more incorrect than measurements made by using a palmboard to estimate it. This suggests that information for the purposes of guiding action may be more accurate than information that influences conscious perceptual awareness. This dissociation between perception and action is a theme that we will return to in Chapter 6. In addition, whether fear is actually responsible for the misestimates in these cases is unclear; see Stefanucci and Proffitt (2009) for some more equivocal results and discussion.

there are changes to their estimations of both the steepness of an incline (Bhalla & Proffitt, 1999) and the distance to a target (Proffitt, Stefanucci, Banton, & Epstein, 2003). Wearing a backpack produces judgments that inclines are steeper and targets farther away, correlating with the effort that it would physically take to scale the hill or reach the target. In addition, skilled performance also affects perceptual judgments: lower-scoring (better) golfers tend to judge that the hole actually looks bigger, while higher-scoring (worse) golfers judge that it looks smaller (Witt, Linkenauger, Bakdash, & Proffitt, 2008). This suggests that the ease or difficulty with which they are able to sink the ball correlates with the perceived size of the target. Once again, a higher cognitive state such as awareness of skill or effort seems to penetrate to lower-level perceptual representation.

None of these studies is without its difficulties, and the results are no doubt open to alternative interpretations. Whether and to what degree perception is penetrable is an unresolved question. However, the evidence raises a serious challenge to the classical model of perceptual systems as informationally encapsulated and impenetrable to direct influence from higher cognitive states. The traditional idea of informational encapsulation may not even apply to the cases for which it was originally intended. So if modules are defined by encapsulation, there may turn out to be very few of them – possibly even none.

3.6 Conclusions

We have contrasted two broad pictures of the mind's functional architecture: the classical model and the massively modular model. These hardly exhaust the possible ways that the mind might be organized, of course, but they do capture two widely discussed options. Either there is a single, unitary central system where most of higher cognition takes place, surrounded by a modular sensorimotor periphery, or else the mind is interconnected modular systems all the way through. The principal arguments we have surveyed have focused on how much of the mind is modular, and what sense of modularity is most appropriate for understanding the mind's structure. Both the massive modularity view and the classical view seem unsatisfactory.

Assumptions about modularity are best seen as having a heuristic role. When we make an initial sketch of how a complex system works, it can be useful to assume that it is modular in some particular respects. But this assumption is one that can be discarded once its limits are realized. Heuristic modularity claims can help us to get a grip on how cognitive systems operate when considered as isolated components, but understanding the mind as a whole requires stitching those components together in a way that preserves the pervasive holistic unity of mental functioning.

4 Nativism, development, and change

4.1 Explaining development

Minds, like living creatures, are born, grow, and change. Developmental psychology aims to describe these processes of change, and to characterize what the initial state of the mind is and how it gets from that initial state to its relatively stable and enduring mature form. The task for developmental psychology is to understand the factors that produce the normal initial state of the mind, and that take it from that initial state to its mature state, in much the way that developmental biology considers how new organisms are produced (e.g., as zygotes) and develop from embryos to reproductively mature adults.

In biology, early thinking about the origins of form involved *preformationism*, the doctrine that the form of a new organism somehow already existed, complete and entire, before its coming into material existence as an autonomous being. Where else could the form of a new, complete human being come from except from a tinier version of the same form, presumed to be curled up inside the parent cell, waiting until it could grow and be nourished in the womb? The theory, of course, only pushes the explanatory question back a step, since it fails as an ultimate explanation for the origins of biological form. This illustrates a common explanatory strategy: if there is no other plausible explanation for the existence of a certain form that appeals to known principles of assembly, then that form must not have been assembled at all. It must have already been present but hidden, just waiting for the right conditions to emerge.

Preformationist accounts, then, arise when there is no known mechanism of development that could produce the mature structure in question. Their reign in biology eventually ended with the discovery of epigenetic mechanisms for assembling complex structures, but they have also enjoyed a long history in psychology. Leibniz refers to a "preformation which determines our soul" in discussing the origins of mental structures, and this sort of language survives down to Piaget, who opposes his constructivist theory of development to those grounded in preformation.[1] But whereas preformation has a literal interpretation in the case of organisms – the whole thing is truly there from the beginning, just much smaller – it is less clear how to interpret it for minds. The analogy of containment and growth, in particular, needs to be explained.

Modern-day nativists, the intellectual heirs of the preformationists, have tried various ways of spelling out the sense in which mental characteristics might be present from the start in something like their final form, hidden somehow from overt observation. Part of the task for nativists is to explain what it means for a mental characteristic to be innate at all. A further question is whether there is reason to think there *are* any innate mental characteristics.

4.2 Case studies in nativism

The notion of innateness has played a key role in cognitive science, most famously in Noam Chomsky's argument for linguistic nativism, and Jerry Fodor's argument for concept nativism. Although these arguments turn on different conceptions of innateness, unpacking them will give a sense of how such arguments typically proceed.

4.2.1 The poverty of the stimulus

Linguistic theory aims to describe the structure of language: the system of rules that determine what sounds are part of a language's phonetic inventory, how words can permissibly be formed, what strings of words constitute well-formed sentences, how sound-meaning correspondences are established, what sorts of things words can and cannot mean, and so on. The set of these rules describes what a competent speaker of the language must know in order to use and understand it. Consequently, learning a language involves somehow acquiring knowledge of these rules, on the basis of the information available in the normal environment.

---

[1] For historical texts and discussion, see the papers in Stich (1975) and Cowie (1999, Chs. 1–3). Pinto-Correia (1997) is an excellent history of preformationism in biology.

However, the case of language is exceptional in certain ways. It is universally acquired, at least in normal humans (a caveat we omit from here on). It is also acquired comparatively rapidly. Newborns display sensitivity to the sound patterns of their own language, having been exposed to them in the womb. Children are sensitive to pauses at clause boundaries in spoken language by 5 months, and to pauses at phrase boundaries by 9 months (Boysson-Bardies, 1999, p. 103). Production of single words begins between 11 and 14 months. By contrast with many other cognitive capacities, particularly those that depend on more general world knowledge, this development is impressive. But it also appears to be capped: the critical period for language acquisition terminates around early adolescence, after which normal acquisition of a first language becomes difficult to impossible, and further languages also become much more effortful to learn. Importantly, this rapid acquisition takes place despite the fact that infants and children are exposed to only a fragmentary and degenerate sample of their language, one that omits many possible constructions and contains many "false positives": utterances that pass as part of the ordinary stream of speech despite not being well formed.

The argument from these facts to linguistic nativism takes the form of a reductio ad absurdum known as the *poverty of the stimulus* (POS) argument.[2] Suppose that learners had available to them only a kind of general-purpose set of principles for formulating and projecting hypotheses about the structure of the language in their environment; moreover, suppose that they had no particular information about the language itself (or about languages as a domain more generally), and no special rules for making generalizations on the basis of linguistic data. This kind of language learner would be *minimally equipped*, having no special information or mechanisms that are attuned to the task of learning language. The available data, however, are consistent with indefinitely many possible sets of rules. This follows from the fact that from any finite set of instances, there are always indefinitely many ways to generalize to unobserved instances. In the case of language, the correct generalizations

---

[2] There have been many attempts to extend the POS argument to domains besides language. We should be cautious about such attempts, however. In the case of language, we have a range of extremely detailed descriptions of the phenomena, namely the various grammars of English and other languages. We have nothing comparable for most other domains (the rules of the visual system may be an exception). Without a description of the complexities underlying the phenomena, as we will see, we cannot argue from the POS to nativism.

themselves are not necessarily the "simplest" ones that could be made from the data – linguistic rules are often convoluted or arbitrary-seeming compared to the generalizations that apply in other domains, and they employ categories that are often not manifest and marked in the data. And given that the data available are fragmentary and degenerate, there is not enough information available to choose the correct set of rules and block the learner from picking a grammar from the infinite set of erroneous generalizations available.

So the right linguistic rules are *underdetermined* by the data, *unnatural* by ordinary standards, and more or less *inaccessible* given the evidence. These traits can be summed up by noting that the available linguistic data are highly impoverished relative to the mature state of linguistic knowledge – hence the "poverty of the stimulus." Given these empirical claims about the linguistic data, and given the assumptions about how general-purpose learning systems work, a minimally equipped learner could not acquire language on the basis of the available data. But since we do converge rapidly and in a surprisingly error-free way on the same language that is spoken around us, we must not be minimally equipped learners. We must in some sense or other come with either language-specific information or principles for generalizing from data to correct grammars. That is, we must be *richly equipped* learners.

Both minimally equipped and richly equipped learners have some innate competence; the difference between the two does not center on the acceptance or rejection of nativism per se. The difference lies in how much innate structure there is, and in whether it is functionally domain-specific. Linguistic nativists who advance the POS argument have traditionally thought that (1) there is a rich innate body of knowledge about language (an intentional module in the sense of Section 3.3); (2) this body of knowledge is part of a functionally distinct mental system; and (3) this system has a proprietary set of processes for interpreting linguistic information. What is innate, then, is a functionally domain-specific system equipped with a proprietary database.

Further evidence for such a distinct system, apart from the precocious learning trajectory language normally follows, comes from developmental disorders such as specific language impairment (SLI). As the name suggests, this involves a primary deficit in developing language, accompanied by largely spared nonlanguage cognitive capacities, including normal intelligence. Acquired disorders of language such as the various aphasias also indicate that language develops into a functionally distinct system.

The POS argument qualifies as a nativist argument insofar as it makes an explicit claim that certain cognitive structures are innate, and insofar as it implicitly carries a notion of what it means to make such an innateness claim. What is innate in this case is a capacity for acquiring language in particular – that is, both a body of information concerning how languages in the environment are likely going to be organized (a "universal grammar"), and a set of processes and mechanisms that ensure that any of these languages can be rapidly detected and acquired. These mechanisms themselves embody assumptions about language, which accounts for the fact that such an eccentric stimulus domain should so rapidly be mastered. To say that all of this is innate means, to a first approximation, that it is present or acquired independently of exposure to or experience with language. That isn't to say that children can understand language without any exposure to it, since exposure is clearly necessary. Rather, the role of experience is not to *teach* language. The pattern of errors – or rather, the pattern of errors *not made* – is inconsistent with teaching, as is the speed with which correct generalizations are made on the basis of limited and open-ended evidence. In other domains, we would expect to find (and do find) a different developmental trajectory. Hence, whatever is going on, it is not much like a traditional learning process, but something more like a process of *evoking* linguistic knowledge.

A thorough assessment of the POS argument is well beyond our present inquiry (see Laurence & Margolis, 2001). However, a few responses are worth noting. First, one might claim that the data are actually much richer than has been assumed. Early discussions of the POS argument did not generally have the benefit of massive searchable databases of child-directed speech and other corpus sources. If there is more information in the environment than the argument assumes, this undermines the argument against minimally equipped learners.

Second, one might attempt to refine the characterization of what minimally equipped learners know. Various connectionist models of language acquisition have been developed along these lines. These networks employ complex techniques of statistical data analysis to converge on the ability to correctly sort grammatical from nongrammatical sentences, and they do so without substantial initial information (they are "randomly wired" and equipped with no language-specific learning rules).

Third, one might define down the complexity of the task by adopting a different theory of the structure of language itself. The seminal arguments for linguistic nativism have been made by Chomsky and those working in the broad paradigm of modern generative grammar – that is, the tradition that runs from the early Standard Theory through the Extended Standard Theory and the Principles and Parameters approach. To this day, many informal presentations of the argument rely on the complex analyses these theories propose for even the simplest sentences. Even a sentence like "Jill likes cats" may contain a dozen "empty" or unpronounced elements that nevertheless are needed by various rules. This hidden complexity is part of what justifies the claim that no minimal learning system could master language. But there are now a number of alternative grammatical theories that do away with much of this complexity in favor of simpler structures. It is unclear how successful these grammars will prove in the long run, but by the same token it is important not to overestimate the descriptive successes of more mainstream generative approaches. Ironically, even the most recent descendent of the Standard Theory, the Minimalist Program, posits almost no sophisticated language-specific rules. The less eccentric language turns out to be, the less need there would be for rich innate structures.

These three approaches all involve simplifying the task of the learner in various ways. Even if they are successful, however, there is a residual challenge: language is undeniably acquired rapidly and universally, with a high degree of convergence across environments. Why is language so unlike other cognitive capacities in this respect? The *specialness* of language might remain mysterious even if the learner's task is less overwhelming than the POS argument maintains. One point worth noting is that children are highly motivated to learn language, in a way that is true of few other capacities (Sampson, 2005). Language is essential not only for speaking their thoughts and interpreting the behavior of others, but also for manipulating the world in ways that go beyond their own abilities. Children's early language is full of requests, complaints, and orders. Differences in motivation may go some distance toward explaining this unique acquisition profile.

A second, more significant point has to do with the nature of learning systems more generally. The POS argument pits a particular type of general learning rule (a minimal rule) against a rich, innate system that hardly needs to "learn" at all (hence Chomsky's famous comment that children no more learn their language than birds learn their feathers). But this comparison crucially depends on having explicit, well-defined models of the relevant learning systems in hand. Otherwise the comparisons are likely to be hopelessly impressionistic, if not outright unfair. Connectionist models have advanced this debate significantly by illustrating the power of minimally equipped learning devices. Recent results in both formal learning theory and automated learning have shown the surprising power of minimally equipped systems in general (see Clark & Lappin, 2011, for extensive discussion).

At the same time, there have been almost no formal models of richly equipped learning. Lacking these, fairly assessing the POS argument becomes challenging. Doing so would require comparing the precise abilities of well-specified models from each camp against the known developmental data. The tide in recent years appears to have turned, however, and it can no longer be assumed that minimally equipped models are, as a class, too weak to answer their critics. The POS argument can set a *lower bound* on the structure a language learner must bring to the task by ruling out certain systems as too minimal to succeed. But whether the POS argument is ultimately convincing depends on making comparisons of real models – the best existing instances of the minimally and richly equipped approaches – rather than battering away at "straw models."

For the moment, we let our critical assessment of the POS argument rest. We will discuss some of these issues connected with learning theory more in Section 4.5, when we lay out the notion of innateness it presupposes.

4.2.2 Radical concept nativism

A second argument for nativism focuses on how we are able to acquire our incredibly rich and varied conceptual system. Concepts, as they are understood by most cognitive psychologists, are mental representations of categories that govern behavior and guide various forms of higher reasoning, planning, and inference. They are, in other words, the mental representations that are deployed in central cognitive systems. The ability to discriminate, sort, and appropriately interact with objects involves, in part, deploying our concepts of those sorts of things. The ability to form beliefs, desires, and intentions, and in general to think about a category at all, also involves having concepts: lacking the concept *refrigerator*, I cannot wonder whether I left my keys in the refrigerator, and lacking the concept *gin*, I cannot intend to mix a gin and tonic. Human concepts extend from obvious perceptually manifest categories (red things, round things, things that can be gripped) through middle-sized everyday entities (tables and glasses, skyscrapers, diet foods, money), and finally to the most theoretical and abstract categories (genes, Hilbert spaces, quantum entanglement). For us to be able to think about such things entails that we have concepts of them.

One of the more enduring questions in psychology concerns the origin of this vast array of concepts. According to one view, most of the concepts that we can entertain are complex constructions out of simpler ones. Ultimately, all of our concepts are built up from combinations of the relatively small set of primitive concepts.[3] In the classical empiricism of Locke and Hume, the primitive concepts are entirely perceptual (or sensorimotor). We start with ideas of whiteness, roundness, hardness, and so on, and we build up ideas of complex qualities, middle-sized objects, events, and so on out of these. So the idea of a snowball would be something round, white, cold, and hard; the idea of a cat would be a furry, meowing quadruped; and so on. If concept empiricism – or some other combinatorial theory of concepts – were correct, the acquisition problem would seem to be solvable in principle, even if hard to carry out in practice.

Of course, concept empiricism has also had its historical detractors, among them the classical nativists such as Descartes and Leibniz, who have argued that there are innumerable concepts that cannot just be combinations of perceptual concepts. These include theoretical concepts (*quark, gene*), mathematical and logical concepts (*addition, integral, disjunction*), moral and aesthetic concepts (*justice, beauty, modernism*), philosophical concepts (*cause, truth, reason*), and so on. How would one reduce any of these to a perceptual description? There is nothing that *justice* or *addition* look, sound, or feel like. Even many everyday concepts like *diet, scandal*, or *recession* seem hard to pin down to sensory manifestation. This sort of argument is historically popular with rationalists, who hold that our ideas have their origins not in sensory experience, but in the faculty of reason. Experience may activate these concepts under certain conditions, but the concepts thus activated are not complex copies made from experience.

One way of framing the debate between concept empiricists and concept rationalists is in terms of the size of the primitive conceptual basis that they presuppose. Empiricists hold that the basis consists entirely of sensorimotor

---

[3] To call a concept "primitive" here is just to say that it cannot be further broken down into other concepts. A primitive concept is a simple unstructured symbol. This sense should be kept separate from the use of the term "primitive" in Section 4.4, where it refers to psychological structures that are acquired by nonpsychological means.

concepts. Rationalists hold that it is potentially much larger: it may include various abstract notions (*cause, force, space, time*), mathematical ideas, and theological/philosophical concepts, among others. This gives rise to two different acquisition stories for most of our everyday concepts. For empiricists, they are acquired by combining perceptual concepts in new ways, whereas for rationalists, they are acquired by experiences that "awaken" these concepts in the mind.

However, there is a general argument, owing to Jerry Fodor (1975, 1981, 2008) that on either of these views, more or less all of our ordinary concepts are going to turn out to be innate.[4] That is, not only are concepts such as *red* or *square* innate, which some might be willing to grant, and not only are concepts like *cause* and *God* innate, which have also not seemed completely out of bounds to classical rationalists, but also concepts like *curry* and *rutabaga*, *quark* and *drywall*, *mitochondria* and *debt*. This radical form of concept nativism has been greeted with almost universal derision by cognitive scientists.[5] The very idea that human beings are innately equipped with such concepts can seem absurd – how could evolution know that we would someday need to construct theories concerning isotopes, and thus provide us with an innate concept of them? Incredulity aside, Fodor maintains that radical concept nativism is unavoidable no matter *what* view of concepts one adopts.

The argument for radical concept nativism (RCN) begins with an assumption about what learning a concept involves. In many standard experimental paradigms, a child or adult is being taught some artificial concept, usually one defined by a set of relatively simple stimulus parameters. The ultimate

---

[4] It is hard to pin down exactly what is meant by ordinary, commonplace concepts here. As a rough guide, we are talking about our "lexical" concepts: those that are expressed by monomorphemic words. This is problematic in various ways – for one thing, morphemic inventories differ across language, whereas it's not clear that concepts do – but we will not attempt any further clarification here. As a heuristic, we can take "concepts" to be "word meanings," or at least the meanings of *simple* words, even if the true relationship is considerably more complex.

[5] In fact, the reception of Fodor's nativist argument has been *much* worse than that of Chomsky's. It is interesting to reflect on the reasons that this might be true, especially since much of Fodor's work has been enthusiastically adopted by practicing cognitive psychologists – his notion of modularity revolutionized the debate over cognitive architecture, and his arguments for the supremacy of symbolic models of cognition over connectionist models have spawned a sizeable literature. Confusions over what is meant in calling something "innate" have been partially responsible, as, we think, has some of Fodor's own rhetoric.

task of the learner in this situation is to acquire the correct concept in order to perform some later task: making inferences concerning the category, projecting the category to cover new instances, and so on. So there are a range of examples of Category A presented, followed by a later task that depends on properly learning about As. What must happen in order for learning to take place, according to Fodor, is that the individual must formulate a hypothesis about the sorts of things that fall under the concept A, along the lines of: things that are A are F, G, H, and so on, where F, G, and H are concepts already in the learner's repertoire. Without such a hypothesis, the learner would not be in any position to draw any sort of line separating the As and the non-As, and hence would not be able to project A to new instances, or draw inferences concerning As as such. The same is presumably true in more naturalistic situations: a child who does not yet have the concept *dog* who is presented with a number of dogs may notice certain similarities among these individuals that prompt her to formulate hypotheses about how those animals are grouped together. With such a hypothesis, the learner can then go on to confirm or disconfirm it – that is, to seek out evidence that she has drawn the proper lines around the category to be learned. In an experimental situation, later tasks can confirm the degree to which she succeeds; in ordinary life, success in practical tasks and convergence in her judgments with her teachers and peers will decide the issue.

Learning a concept, then, is a kind of inductive exercise in which one projects and confirms hypotheses concerning the extension of the target concept. Doing this requires being able to represent these hypotheses, as well as the relevant data (in this case, descriptions of the various instances one encounters) and having in hand a mental inductive logic, that is, a mechanism for deciding whether the data confirm the hypothesis, and to what degree. However, this already gives the nativist all he needs. To learn a concept requires formulating and projecting hypotheses concerning that concept. As suggested earlier, these might have the form "Things that are A are F, G, H, and so on." This hypothesis, though, already involves the concept A itself, which is the target concept to be learned.[6] So if learning a concept involves hypothesis

---

[6] Moreover, it also involves concepts F, G, and H that are (if learning is successful) coextensive with A itself. Thus Fodor also holds that it is impossible to learn a concept that truly *extends* the representational power of one's existing conceptual repertoire. Any allegedly new concept A could only represent something that one could represent using concepts that one already possesses.

testing, and hypothesis testing involves representing one's hypotheses, and if the hypotheses in question have something like the form described here, then concept learning requires already having the target concept. That is, concept learning is not *learning* at all. "Learning" a concept turns out only to be possible if one already has the concept. If these concepts are not really learned but somehow present or presupposed already, then they must have been acquired without being learned. And on one prominent conception of innateness (see Section 4.5), an innate structure is exactly one that has this property – one that is present without having been learned from experience or the environment. As rationalists have always suspected, it turns out that concepts are evoked or triggered by experience, not learned from it.[7]

Putting all of this together, the argument for RCN supposes not only that this is the correct story about what learning is in general, but also that there is really nothing else that we could coherently mean by "learning a concept." Anything else that we might pick out would have to, ultimately, reduce to something like hypothesis confirmation, in which case the same line of reasoning applies. Because there is no alternative view on offer, we conclude that all of our concepts must be unlearned, that is to say, innate.

To say that we possess concepts innately isn't to imply that they are present at birth, clearly, since infants clearly have relatively few concepts. Most of these innate concepts will *never* be activated in us. The argument, after all, implies that every primitive concept is innate, and most of these may never be activated in most people. What this illustrates is that it would be a mistake to infer from the fact that we have F innately to the fact that we now actually have F. To possess a concept innately means, in the context of RCN, that we have an innate *disposition* to acquire the concept by a nonlearning process. But it may be much less dramatic to say that we are innately disposed to acquire *quark* than to say that *quark* itself is innate, particularly when "innate" itself is glossed as "not learned."

Many critics are not mollified by this clarification, however, because a lot of what goes on in concept acquisition looks an awful lot like learning. To acquire *credenza*, *limburger*, or *punk rock*, one typically needs to be exposed to a range of instances and non-instances and have feedback from more expert concept users in the category's salient characteristics as well as central and marginal

---

[7] In Leibniz's words, these innate ideas are "living fires or flashes of light hidden inside us but made visible by the stimulation of the senses, as sparks can be struck from a steel" (1765/1996, p. 49).

cases. The required sensitivity to experience, including negative feedback, certainly suggests that this is learning-like. The nativist needs to show that the mechanisms underlying the disposition to acquire these concepts are ones that are somehow (1) sensitive to the right range of triggering conditions, but (2) not so richly structured as to count as learning mechanisms.

This problem is especially acute because, as Fodor (1981) points out, the relationship between a trigger and the state that it produces is potentially arbitrary. In ethology, any local sign may be co-opted to produce a cognitive trait or behavioral outcome. However, the relationship between concepts and the stimuli that trigger them does not seem to be arbitrary in this way. Some explanation for this peculiar "fit" between the circumstances of acquisition and the concept acquired seems to be required for nativists to discharge their explanatory burden.[8]

Responses to Fodor's argument have typically involved arguing that the conception of learning as hypothesis projection and confirmation is too restrictive. Doing this requires saying what else learning might be, and sketching a mechanism for producing new concepts that satisfies this description. We learn many things. Some of these are facts, others are skills or abilities. It might be that concept learning is more like learning an ability: the ability to represent and think about a new category. Learning this ability may not require that we already have the concepts required to formulate hypotheses about the category (Margolis, 1998; Laurence & Margolis, 2002; Weiskopf, 2008a).

Again, extensive discussion of the merits and failings of the RCN argument is beyond the scope of this chapter. The main point for our purposes is that the RCN illustrates another line of nativist argument in cognitive science, and it embodies its own assumptions about what nativism itself is. We turn now to unpacking several analyses of the innateness concept and its distinctive role in psychology.

4.3 Invariance accounts

A cluster of prominent analyses of innateness tie the concept to its roots in developmental biology, ethology, and evolutionary theory. These ties reflect

---

[8] Fodor (1998) calls this the doorknob/DOORKNOB problem: the problem, roughly, of explaining why experience of stereotypical doorknobs typically leads to the acquisition of the concept *doorknob*.

the fact that innateness claims arise in a number of different disciplines besides psychology. The hope of these analyses is that a single, unitary account of innateness can be crafted that will apply across the biological and psychological domains.

4.3.1 Canalization

One biologically inspired account draws on the concept of *canalization* as presented by the developmental biologist C. H. Waddington in 1936. Waddington noted that some traits of organisms developed under a range of disparate conditions and seemed to depend on no specific triggers for their unfolding. He imagined that development took place in a kind of "epigenetic landscape" consisting of many branching pathways, each leading to a certain endstate. Once an organism starts down one of these pathways, it becomes more difficult to dislodge it from its course and lead it to a different outcome. Once a pathway is entered into, development is to some extent buffered from environmental influence. This buffering of development against the environment is canalization.

Canalization as a biological phenomenon does much of what we want from an account of innateness. Canalized phenomena tend to be environmentally stable, they emerge in development in a predictable way, and their emergence in populations is explicable by appeal to natural selection. This suggests a bold identification, made explicitly by André Ariew: perhaps innateness just *is* canalization (Ariew, 1996; 1999). The identification proceeds as follows:

(IC1) For individuals possessing a certain genotype, the degree to which a biological trait is innate is the degree to which the developmental pathway for that trait is canalized in individuals with that genotype; and

(IC2) The degree to which a developmental pathway is canalized is the degree to which the development of a phenotypic endstate is insensitive to a range of environmental conditions.

(IC1) establishes a link between innateness and canalization for traits relative to genotypes, and (IC2) establishes the link between canalization and invariance in the face of a range of environments.

Canalization provides a plausible account of the innateness of many biological and ethological phenomena. Birdsong and mating behaviors are examples. Whereas some birds only develop their normal, species-typical song when they are exposed to it, others do so whether they are or not. Similarly, as Lorenz noted, female mallards raised exclusively in the company of pintail ducks display no attraction toward pintail drakes, but will immediately display attraction toward mallard drakes once exposed to them. Song and mating behavior appear to be canalized, in that they appear in a wide range of environments. The degree to which the pathways that develop these traits are canalized is just the degree to which these traits are innate in these species.

Canalization gives us a way of explaining innateness in terms of the relative *invariance* of traits across development environments. Accordingly it can be viewed as falling into a general family of invariance-based accounts. A chronic problem for this type of analysis is that it tends to be too liberal: that is, it classifies traits as innate that we would not, prima facie, think should count. For instance, take many commonplace beliefs such as the belief that the sun is hot, or that water quenches thirst. It seems fair to say that almost every human develops these beliefs, with the exception of those who live extremely short or deprived lives. These beliefs, then, arise as part of cognitive development in an extremely wide range of environments. But it seems odd to count them as *innate*; rather, they seem to be paradigms of empirically acquired beliefs.

Proponents of canalization might respond that there are environments where these beliefs are not in fact acquired – for instance, because the environment does not contain the resources to form the relevant concepts. Those raised in sufficiently impoverished environments may not come to know about water or the sun, and hence cannot have the beliefs. But even so, canalization is a graded notion, and so is innateness. These beliefs will still turn out to be highly innate, if not perfectly so, since in most life-supporting environments, beliefs about water and sunlight are part of the normal cognitive repertoire.

Broadening the range of allowable environments also leads to a further problem, namely that traits become less canalized as the range becomes broader. There may be a range of conditions consistent with life that nevertheless promote monstrous and nonstandard forms of development: being bathed in teratogenic chemicals or lightly irradiated need not be fatal, but both clearly interfere with the production of normal physical and cognitive traits. The problem for canalization accounts, then, is to provide a way of specifying the relevant range of environments in a way that rules in the paradigm innate traits but rules out paradigm learned traits such as empirical beliefs.

A further worry is that canalization as such may not capture the sense of innateness at work in the poverty of the stimulus and radical concept nativism arguments. This is especially clear for RCN. Although some developmental psychologists seem to think that the early and more or less universal possession of certain concepts shows that they are innate, what Fodor himself means by the nativist claim is *not* that all of them emerge across a wide range of environments. This claim isn't even true, since many concepts have only come to be possessed in comparatively recent history, by a well-educated minority of the population. Moreover, these concepts are individually tied to relatively specific triggering conditions, at least in Fodor's (1981) conception. Exploiting an ethological analogy, Fodor comments that concepts may require relatively specific stimulus conditions to be "released." But the more narrow these conditions are, the less invariant possession of the concept becomes. Finally, what the argument itself turns on is not the fact that all of our concepts are possessed invariantly, but rather the fact that these concepts cannot be acquired by a certain type of learning process. It is the impossibility of learning concepts that matters here, not their distribution across possible developmental pathways.

The POS argument may seem to be a better case for the canalization account, because it emphasizes the stable emergence of language across a range of conditions that are degenerate and impoverished in various ways. The wider the range of environments that is compatible with an endstate that includes language as part of the cognitive phenotype, the more canalized (thus more innate) language itself becomes. However, we should separate the evidence that is part of the argument for linguistic nativism from what is meant by linguistic nativism itself. The argument does depend on facts concerning canalization. But the conclusion is not just that language is canalized; that would just restate the premises. Rather, the conclusion is that a certain specific kind of mental structure exists, namely a device that already has some domain-specific information or biases that conduce to rapidly acquiring language under those variable and degenerate conditions. The content of the linguistic nativist claim seems to be that such a device is part of the species-typical endowment for humans (see Section 4.5 for more discussion). This claim about possession of a mechanism with a certain structure goes beyond the canalization claim, and so, although canalization plays a role in the POS argument, it is not an adequate gloss on what linguistic nativism itself means.

4.3.2 Closed-process invariance

Canalization, however, is not the only invariantist position on nativism. An alternative view, developed by Mallon and Weinberg (2006), analyzes innate-ness as *closed-process invariance*. This view supplements a standard invariance view of innateness with a constraint on the kinds of developmental processes that are involved in the emergence of phenotypic traits. Developmental processes normally result in a certain range of possible outcomes. For some processes this may be a fairly restricted range, possibly even a unique outcome, whereas for others it may be a rather wide or possibly open-ended range. A *closed* developmental process results in a relatively restricted or nondiverse set of endstates; *open* processes result in a wider range, in a way that depends on the organism's environment. Canonical closed processes include those that produce a bilaterally symmetrical bioplan, those that guide neural development and organize the gross anatomy of the brain, and so on. Open processes include those that operate in semantic memory to learn new declarative information, or that underlie significant neuro-plasticity (e.g., Hebbian learning or experience-guided synaptic growth and pruning).

Closed-process invariance assembles these claims as follows. A trait is innate in an organism just in case:

(CPI1) That trait would develop across (is invariant across) a range of normal environments; and

(CPI2) The proximal cause of the trait's development is a closed process (or closed processes)

Closed-process invariance thus relies on two potentially contentious notions: that of a normal developmental environment and that of a closed process. Both are potential sources of objections to the view.

As noted in the case of canalization, all invariance accounts assume some-thing about what counts as a normal background for an organism to grow in. What qualities are part of this background, however, is often unclear. Basic physical conditions for survival in a terrestrial environment should surely be counted. Beyond this, though, almost everything seems up for grabs. Human history has covered an incredibly diverse range of physical, nutritional, social, and cultural-technological conditions, all of which potentially have an effect on development. Extracting the "normal background" from this messy web depends on a variety of pragmatic factors that resist easy systematization (Sober, 1999b).

More serious worries concern what should count as a "process." In particular, as Mallon and Weinberg (2006) point out, if we are allowed to individuate processes freely, we can easily find open processes wherever we look. Every individual person is the unique product of countless overlapping causal processes. Take the set of processes that produced Barack Obama and call that a single complex process called "Obama's developmental process." This process produced Obama as he is in the actual world, but had the world been different, that process would also have produced someone with different traits. So there are many possible endstates for Obama, given various possible environments he might have been in. This makes Obama's developmental process an open process, which in turn suggests that none of his characteristics are innate.

This is a highly suspect route to anti-nativism. The response is to appeal to some independent standard for what counts as a developmental process. Processes are determined by the structure of the underlying physical, biological, neural, and cognitive system. We cannot simply lump together any set of causal factors and call them a "process." Processes are recurrent causal sequences that are executed by an underlying system, or by an organized collection of such systems. There is no system, or collection of systems, that is responsible for executing Obama's developmental process *as such*. So picking out such fictitious "processes" is no threat to the coherence of closed-process invariance.

Whether a trait is innate or not depends heavily on whether the endstate is characterized as open or closed. Take the case of language acquisition: is this an open or closed process? It depends on the target endstate. If we take the endstate to be competence in English, or French, or Urdu, or Dutch, and so on, then there are many possible endstates and many possible developmental routes to them. This makes language acquisition look relatively open, since it is uncontroversial that the particular language learned depends closely on experience. On the other hand, if the endstate is just "possession of a human language," this looks like a closed process, because that endstate is achieved for many possible pathways.[9]

---

[9] Notice that the processes that lead to knowing English, French, and so on are not *arbitrary* processes, since they involve the operation of the underlying language faculty. Hence there is (assuming nativists are right) a real cognitive system to ground their reality as processes.

So, is linguistic competence innate or not? Presumably the answer is that the capacity for human language is innate, because the processes of acquisition map a wide range of developmental trajectories onto a single common, though highly general, endstate. But knowledge of particular languages is not innate, because the language acquisition system can also be viewed as a learning device that produces these various endstates in response to different linguistic environments. We need to be clear about which capacity we have in mind; distinguishing these ways of typing the endstates removes the paradox.

Closed-process invariance does not, however, overcome canalization's problems in capturing the sense in which concepts are supposed to be innate. Although the mechanisms that trigger particular concepts are, presumably, maximally closed processes, most concepts fail to be sufficiently invariant across environments. Adding the closed-process restriction does not overcome the problems that the canalization account had in explaining what sense of nativism is at work in the radical concept nativism argument. Non-invariance accounts, however, may fare significantly better.

4.4 Primitivist accounts

A different approach to the analysis of nativism shifts the focus away from the invariance of a trait across environments and focuses instead on the kind of mechanisms that produce the trait. Rather than beginning from the near-universal emergence of an innate trait, this approach begins instead with the contrast between innate and learned characteristics. In particular, it makes central the principle articulated in Section 4.2.2 that if something is learned, it cannot be innate, and (contrapositively) if it is innate, it is not learned. The nativist arguments canvassed so far give some support for the important role of this principle. Further support is given by the following commonplace inference made by developmental psychologists: if something emerges early in development, then it is likely to be innate, which turns on the prima facie plausible claim that learning, whether passive or active, takes a certain minimum amount of time.

The link between innateness and being unlearned is widespread. But although learning is one form of building new psychological structures, it may not be the only one. Structures can be acquired from experience in a number of ways, including simple copying and abstraction. Perceiving a lion may lead to storing a visual representation of that creature in memory, which can be retrieved and used in future recognition tasks. There may be a host of similar perceptual storage and generalization mechanisms beyond the higher cognitive forms of learning. We would clearly not want to count the products of such complex, environment-involving psychological processes as innate.

Generalizing this idea, Richard Samuels (2002) proposes a *primitivist* analysis of nativism. On this view, a mental structure is innate in the event that it is a psychological *primitive*, and a structure is primitive just in case:

(P1) That structure is posited as part of a correct psychological theory; and

(P2) There is no correct psychological theory that explains the acquisition of that structure.

According to primitivism, innateness is the claim that a representation, belief, system, module, mechanism, or any piece of psychological apparatus at all, is acquired by some *nonpsychological route*. The story of how these characteristics emerge in development has some explanation or other, but telling that story is outside the explanatory ambit of psychology proper.

Primitivism is an analysis of nativism tailor-made for psychology, rather than a more general account pressed into service to cover many domains, as should be clear from the fact that the thesis itself makes explicit reference to psychological theorizing. In this it differs from invariance accounts, which purport to cover biology, ethology, psychology, and so on. However, while the thesis is narrowly tailored, and although psychology only became historically differentiated fairly recently, primitivist notions have a long pedigree.

In her extensive historical study of nativist thought, Fiona Cowie (1999) argues that Leibniz and Descartes can both be productively read as endorsing a form of primitivism. Both thinkers were deeply skeptical about the prospects for providing an explanation of how our minds come to be furnished with ideas, beliefs, and other mental structures. Whereas the classical empiricists had an outline of a story about how experience could give rise to such structures, nativists have been doubtful that any explanation along these lines will pan out. She dubs this skeptical outlook the "Mystery Hypothesis," and takes it to be the expression of a kind of nonnaturalism about the acquisition of new psychological materials. The Mystery Hypothesis is nonnaturalistic insofar as it forecloses any possibility of giving a scientific explanation for how psychological acquisition and development takes place, and specifically for how new mental structures can be acquired via experience.

Primitivism itself, however, is more narrow than the Mystery Hypothesis. As noted, it claims only that there is no distinctively *psychological* explanation for acquisition, not that there is no (scientific) explanation at all. Nativism entails only a limited kind of inexplicability. But since psychological structures are themselves realized in neural structures, there may be any number of nonpsychological reasons why a feature is present. Environmental interventions or normal developmental processes can cause reorganization of the underlying neural architecture in ways that produce new psychological structures, without those processes of acquisition themselves having a psychological description. When this happens, the emerging structures are primitive, and hence innate, from the point of view of psychology.

Primitivism fares well in accounting for some allegedly innate psychological traits. On any naturalistic account, the first elements of the mind must be assembled from nonmental materials. This assembly process begins before birth and continues after, as new structures come online. Thus, although "present at birth" is a poor gloss on "innate" in general, these very early-emerging characteristics are likely to be ones that are assembled nonpsychologically, because their growth parallels the growth of the newly built brain itself. It is therefore likely that many (though not all[10]) of these characteristics will be primitive, and hence innate, thus explaining why this conflation seems so natural.

Primitivism also has the advantage of accounting for the ubiquity of innateness claims. It is a familiar point, granted even by empiricists and other ardent anti-nativists (see Section 4.2.1), that everyone needs to posit some sort of innate structure or other. Even those who hold that almost all of the mind's contents and processes are learned must say that the basic initial stock of learning mechanisms themselves are innate; otherwise the mind would be an inert block, incapable of changing at all. This is just to say that some structures must be primitive on any theory of development, and thus that any such theory must be committed to positing a minimal stock of innate structures.

Finally, Fodor's argument for radical concept nativism seems grounded in primitivism, or something very close to it. It is the impossibility of learning concepts that entails their innateness, on his view, and since any rational process of getting a concept must ultimately amount to a form of learning

---

[10] "Not all" because there is evidence that children learn while in the womb; they become selectively sensitive to the phonological properties of their native language, for example.

by hypothesis confirmation, he concludes that there is no rational way to acquire concepts at all. From the fact that there is no such *rational* process, it is just a short step to the conclusion that there is no such *psychological* process as acquiring a concept at all.[11]

To see how this works, consider language acquisition again. It might at first seem that languages turn out not to be innate on primitivism, because many of the particular details of a language (e.g., its vocabulary and particular phonological profile) are clearly learned. Moreover, even acquiring syntactic competence seems to involve any number of psychological processes: the impoverished evidence needs to be compared against various candidate grammars, parameter settings need to be adjusted, and so on. These all involve settling on the right representation of an adequate grammar, given the input. However, the specific biases and domain-specific assumptions that underlie that process are not themselves acquired from experience, but rather are built into the structure of the learning system from the outset. The richly equipped learner's body of information is psychologically primitive (genetically specified or otherwise unlearned), which is what explains her ability to correctly go beyond the data.

However, primitivism faces a number of objections. One problem is that it overgeneralizes, counting too many things as innate. A somewhat fanciful example asks us to imagine a pill that, when ingested, rewires the brain in a way that confers upon the taker knowledge of Latin. The effect is achieved by directly rewiring the brain into the neural configuration that realizes this information. This is a nonpsychological way of producing a psychological structure, and hence this knowledge should count as innate. But this seems counterintuitive. The same goes for the effects of various brain lesions and diseases. Damage to area V4, at the junction of the lingual and the fusiform gyri, produces cerebral achromatopsia, the inability to perceive colors (Cowey & Heywood, 1997; Zeki, 1990). This damage involves a nonpsychological mechanism of action; hence the resulting trait (lack of color vision) should be innate. Acquired diseases such as Ross River fever can also cause unique and

---

[11] Fodor divides processes into those that are rational-causal and those that are brute-causal. Brute-causal processes are mere nonpsychological pushes and pulls, so to speak, whereas rational-causal processes constitute, on his view, the primary domain of psychology. Triggering of an innate structure is brute-causal because there is no rational or evidential relationship between the trigger and the emerging structure itself.

distressing psychological states involving visual hallucinations of collapsing buildings (Samuels, 2002, p. 258). And damage to ventromedial prefrontal cortex can cause people to lose their sensitivity to risk, resulting in radical personality changes, as the case of Phineas Gage demonstrates (Damasio, 1994). However, none of these physiological or neural interventions seems to produce anything innate.

In response, Samuels proposes that psychological primitives should be understood as structures that have their origin in nonpsychological processes *that occur in normal development*. That is, primitiveness is relativized to a set of normal conditions and processes. This can be seen as a third clause of primitivism:

(P3) That structure emerges as part of the normal developmental progression for the organism.

This move imports an element of invariance into primitivism, because primitives are now those structures that emerge across a normal (and presumably relatively wide) range of environments. Where acquisition of a trait results from some freakish or unlikely happening outside of the normal course of events, it fails to count as innate. Latin pills, if there were any, would presumably be outside of the normal developmental progression for most humans; similarly for brain lesions and neurodegenerative diseases.

The normal-invariance clause seems to deal with these problem cases. However, more objections immediately appear. First, "normal conditions" can change rather easily. Right now a Latin pill would be a serious oddity. But a world containing such things might also be a world in which people regularly indulge in "cosmetic neurology," dosing themselves with knowledge and skills for any occasion. In such a world where knowledge pills are dispensed by the corner vending machine, they form part of the normal background, and hence, what they convey is innate. Again, this seems unpalatable.

Second, congenital developmental disorders often produce abnormal cognitive phenotypes that would not emerge in the normal course of events. Autism sometimes presents with savant syndrome, defined as an island of extremely high functioning in a particular domain. Savant skills are focused on prodigious feats of calculation or perception. Similarly, synesthetes have unusual cross-modal perceptual experiences such as seeing a certain color when a number is presented, or having a certain taste when seeing a shape (Cytowic, 2002). Both savantism and synesthetic experience result from abnormally developing neural connectivity patterns. These traits simply emerge as psychological primitives during the affected person's development.

However, neither savant skills nor synesthesia are part of the "normal course of events" that humans undergo in development. By (P3), then, the characteristics that they produce cannot be innate. But this is strange. Savantism seems to be an innate trait of certain autistic individuals, and because it is grounded in abnormal neural development, there seems to be no answer to the question of how or by what psychological route it is acquired. And although there can be acquired synesthesia, the more normal form it takes is a congenital one. That is, it seems prima facie to be innate, contrary to the predictions of primitivism.

A brief diagnosis seems in order. Primitivism runs the risk of overgeneralizing and letting in many unlearned but not plausibly innate traits. The normality condition is supposed to rule this out, but it fails to do so, since normal environments for humans to develop in are highly malleable and may come to include a range of cosmetic neurological adjustments that we would not want to count as innate. Moreover, it also proves too restrictive, since it rules out abnormal traits as being innate. This stems from the fact that the normality condition ties innateness to what is normal for human beings – that is, to the idea that the innate endowment is in some sense part of general *human nature*. This idea plays a dominant role in much nativist thought, but trying to capture it by a combination of primitivism and invariance fails.

4.5 Informational impoverishment accounts

The last account of innateness that we will consider also focuses on the kinds of processes that produce innate characteristics. Rather than focusing strictly on the origins of these characteristics, as primitivism does, it compares the rich structure of the endstate with the relative lack of structure in the input. Some developmental processes require only the initiating presence of a simple feature to bring forth a complex product. It is the difference between the input and the output that constitutes a trait being innate.

This notion of informational impoverishment clearly lies behind the Chomskyan poverty of the stimulus argument, where the guiding idea is that normal linguistic competence could not be learned given what we know about the conditions of acquisition. If one assumes that learning is a process in which internal cognitive structures are constructed on the basis of information acquired from the environment, and that the informational content of these learned structures does not exceed what is in the data, then any additional information must be provided "by the organism" – that is, it must be innate. This notion of innateness is roughly the organism's contribution to the production of these traits.

Call this the *informational impoverishment* conception of nativism.[12] This conception has been developed in detail by Muhammad Ali Khalidi (2002, 2007). Khalidi's view is that:

> (II) A cognitive capacity is innate for an organism just in case it would become manifest in that organism as a result of environmental conditions that are impoverished relative to the endstate of the condition.

He refers to this as a "dispositional" account of innateness, since it claims that something is innate in a creature in the event that the creature is disposed to manifest it in certain circumstances. As with many other dispositional claims, there is an implicit reference here to normal background conditions: a fragile vase will shatter when dropped, but only under conditions that include standard gravity and the absence of any cushions underneath it; a neuron is disposed to fire an action potential when stimulated, but only so long as there are no inhibiting substances present; and so forth. As long as the conditions are normal with respect to allowing the organism's survival, then, innate traits are those informationally impoverished cognitive capacities that the organism is disposed to develop.

One virtue of treating innateness dispositionally is that a disposition may be present even though it never manifests. Many of the difficulties faced by invariance accounts thus disappear, since innate traits need not actually be present across any range of environments. All that is needed is that they *would* appear if the activating conditions were right.

The impoverishment account makes essential use of the idea that it makes sense to talk about the difference between the information in the input and that in the output. The notion that information can be quantified and subtracted in this way is controversial. In mathematical information theory as pioneered by Claude Shannon and Warren Weaver, it is possible to quantify

---

[12] Stich (1975) outlines an "Input-Output" view of nativism, which he ascribes to Chomsky and which is roughly equivalent to the informational impoverishment view discussed here.

the amount of information that a signal carries (Floridi, 2010). The information associated with an event's occurrence in this context corresponds, very roughly, to the likelihood of the event's occurrence. However, this communications-theoretic notion of information is not relevant for assessing the innateness of cognitive capacities. Here we may need something more like *semantic* information: this type of information comes packaged in propositional or other representational formats. Mental representations, at least those like beliefs and perceptions, have the function of informing us about the world. But, Khalidi suggests, it is too hard to quantify information if it is thought of in terms of sets of propositions (2007, pp. 103–104), and in any case it is not clear whether there is even a determinate answer to the question of how much semantic information is contained in a stretch of experience. Neither mathematical nor semantic information will do, then, in spelling out the sense in which cognitive endstates are impoverished relative to the input.

Khalidi's solution to the problem of defining impoverishment is to defer to the operational practices of scientists. Ethologists have at their disposal a variety of procedures for arranging different forms of impoverished conditions in which to raise animals, which vary in their duration, their severity, and the particular features that they manipulate. Ethical concerns prohibit such experimentation with humans, but "natural experiments" such as the case of Genie (Rymer, 1994) can provide some insight into extreme conditions of deprivation, although the more extreme they become the less likely it is that a single factor of interest is being manipulated. Even normal developmental environments can provide clues to innate capacities, however, since if an infant is exposed to roughly the same amount of various types of stimulation but one capacity develops faster than another (e.g., understanding of solid objects vs. understanding of gravity; see Spelke, 1991), then the infant may be thought of as being more richly equipped with respect to the faster-developing capacity.

An initial difficulty with the informational impoverishment view is that, as with other accounts, it does not cover all forms of nativist arguments equally well. Although impoverishment is more or less what arguments for linguistic nativism are designed around, it has little to do with the radical concept nativist's argument, which does not turn on the relationship between the input and the output in cases of concept learning, or on the sketchy nature of the data for making inductions to new concepts, but rather on the logical problem of how such learning could take place at all. An impossibility argument against concept learning does not turn on how much information is available to the learner, but rather on the fact that the output (a new concept) is necessarily presupposed by the input (a hypothesis), in the case of anything that can legitimately be called learning.

A deeper problem is that the informational impoverishment account also threatens to overgeneralize. To see this, consider the production of new structures by ampliative inference processes. Ampliative inferences are, by definition, those that produce conclusions that are logically stronger than the premises. A simple example would be numerical induction: from experience of a finite number of instances, a generalization is projected that covers innumerable unobserved instances as well. In a straightforward sense, this conclusion constitutes an increase in information over the premises. More sophisticated cases involve abductive inference. In abduction, one proposes a hypothesis that best explains some complex pattern of data. These explanatory hypotheses may make appeal to any number of unobserved causal laws, powers, and mechanisms. A conclusion about the causal structure of a domain and the way in which it explains a set of observations and experiments typically goes beyond those data. Both simple induction and abduction are central to everyday explanatory practices as well as scientific explanation. Creative insight in problem solving also constitutes a way of going beyond the data. Even if creative cognition is ultimately recombinative, the fact is that it nevertheless involves *new* combinations of concepts not given in previous experience.

These various ampliative cognitive capacities – induction, abduction, and insight – are all grounded in processes that involve going from relatively impoverished information to complex hypotheses and beliefs, all of which are logically stronger than, or at least distinct from, the data given. So by (II) these hypotheses and beliefs should count as innate. But this seems highly undesirable, since most of our cognition involves just such ampliative processes. There are clear echoes here of Plato's *Meno*: the fact that the slave boy could reach geometric conclusions that were never explicitly spelled out by his instructor Socrates was, indeed, the main reason for claiming that the knowledge he arrived at by "learning" was in fact merely being recollected. Unless we are willing, as Plato was, to embrace the anamnestic conclusion that all of this apparent creativity and learning is in fact the unfolding of some innate knowledge, we should reconsider the impoverishment account.[13]

An impoverishment theorist might reply by reminding us that the criterion for a capacity's having more information in its endstate than in its input is an operational one, defined by reference to the practices of ethologists, neurobiologists, and developmental psychologists themselves. These examples of ampliative inferences are not treated, by the relevant disciplines and practitioners, as cases in which learning involves making use of information beyond what is in the data. Hence they should not count as counterexamples to the proposed definition of innateness.

This reply, however, only highlights the fact that the proposed mark of informational impoverishment is an epistemic one. That is, it tells us something about how we normally spot capacities that are impoverished, but not about what it is to be such a capacity. This leaves it open that the normal taxonomy of impoverished capacities might be mistaken or misleading in any number of ways. Consider, just as an example, two cognitive devices, both of which are observed to take the same range of input conditions and produce the same psychological endstate (an ability, a body of knowledge, etc.). However, they achieve this end in different ways. One device contains a specialized learning system that comes richly equipped with the appropriate information and mechanisms; the other contains an inference engine that makes use of no specific information about the domain and no special-purpose logical, statistical, or abductive inference rules. From an "external" perspective, looked at from the point of view of all of the operational tests for detecting impoverished acquisition, both achieve an informationally richer endstate; hence in both cases we should say that the capacity or knowledge is innate. Although this seems plausible for the former device, it is not for the latter device.

---

[13] This problem is briefly raised by Khalidi (2002, pp. 267–8). However, he dismisses the point, noting that empiricists are also committed to innate mechanisms, and hence perhaps these general learning rules can themselves be thought of as innate. But we should distinguish between the learning rules or mechanisms being innate and their products being innate. Principle (II) says that a capacity produced as a result of being exposed to a range of input data is innate; hence the products of any ampliative inference rule will be innate by this criterion. This does not address the issue of whether the rules themselves are innate.

Of course, one could always refine these operational tests so that they can distinguish these two devices, perhaps by varying the learning environment, looking at differences in acquisition time, and so on. But making these adjustments just goes to show that the tests are only good ones if they are tracking the real characteristics that make one acquisition process genuinely impoverished relative to the input. What the example of the two devices shows is that this depends on the *internal structure* of these processes, not just whether it is ampliative (whether the total information in the endstate is greater than in the input). What matters instead is whether the process involves richly or minimally equipped learning rules. Richly equipped learning involves something more like unlocking or activating a capacity that is incipiently present in an organism – roughly the idea behind thinking of these dispositions as present but awaiting triggering. Minimally equipped learning involves using the input data as the basis for constructing a capacity. In both cases there are rules that can map the input onto the endstate, but the nature of the rules differs (though probably not in any sharp, noncontinuous way).

Informational impoverishment, then, does not seem to be fundamental to claims about innateness, at least not if it is understood just in terms of comparing input to output. One needs to consider the mechanism that implements this transition as well. Where the mechanism substantially embodies domain-specific assumptions, the resulting capacity or structure can be thought of as innate. Where, on the other hand, it comes from more general processes of ampliative inference, the result represents an innovation by the organism, not an innate endowment.

4.6 Fragmenting innateness

Of the three conceptions of innateness surveyed so far (invariantism, primitivism, and informational impoverishment), none are problem-free. Their problems mostly take the form of internal tensions, overgeneralization, and failure to account for the various uses of the concept of innateness in psychological argumentation. In light of this, it is hard not to speculate that something has gone badly wrong with appeals to innateness. Paul Griffiths argues just this, claiming that innateness is a mongrel concept that runs together three core properties that routinely dissociate from one another (Griffiths, 2002; Griffiths & Machery, 2008; Griffiths & Stotz, 2000). The notion of innateness prevalent in ethology and developmental biology typically connotes the following ideas (with their accompanying technical glosses):

(1) Developmental fixity: insensitivity to environmental factors in develop-
    ment
(2) Species nature: being either universal or typical of members of that species
(3) Intended outcome: being the product of adaptive evolution.

Griffiths also cites Bateson (1991), who adds that innateness in ethology has also been used to talk about traits that are present at birth, that are caused by genetic differences, or that are distinctly organized, internally driven behaviors.

The term "innate" is tossed about freely in all of these senses by differ-ent authors – and, at times, by one and the same author! However, these properties can come apart. Not everything that is developmentally insensi-tive is an adaptation, nor need it be typical of the species. Adaptive traits are not always universal in the species (they may take substantially different forms under the influence of different environmental conditions), nor are they necessarily environmentally insensitive. And species-typical traits need not be either environmentally insensitive or adaptations. The problem with lumping these properties together under the same heading is that it permits illicit inferences. It is much easier to fallaciously reason from something's being species-typical to its being an adaptation if both of these properties sometimes share the label "innate."

More seriously, conceiving of traits as being innate can actively impede research progress. As Griffiths and Machery (2008, p. 405) comment, "The con-cept of innateness is an anti-heuristic which encourages researchers to check the obvious sources of environmental input, and then to stop looking." This dynamic has played out numerous times in biology. For example, genetically different strains of laboratory rats display different species-typical person-alities, and especially strong differences in their behavioral and endocrine responses to stress. But raising rat pups from one strain with parents of another strain erases these differences, because it turns out that maternal behavior during rearing can activate genes that modify the brains of the devel-oping pups in ways that affect how they process stress in the environment. If this cross-rearing experiment had not been tried, these traits might have been assumed, by an over-hasty application of the innateness heuristic, to be under genetic control, and hence environmentally implastic. Something similar to this may have occurred in the language acquisition literature, where the early and widespread endorsement of stimulus poverty arguments arguably delayed close attention to the precise nature of the corpus of linguistic evidence that children have access to.[14]

The three analyses of nativism in psychology that we have surveyed only illustrate further the fragmentation of the innateness concept. The properties are clearly distinct: invariance focuses on the prevalence of a cognitive structure in a population, primitivism focuses on the origins of those structures in development, and informational impoverishment focuses on what the organism itself contributes to the structure's development. Not only are these properties distinct and dissociable, they do not clearly converge on the set of "pre-theoretically" innate characteristics. Of course, scientific terms may expand or contract their referential range with new discoveries, and we should not be tied to some sacrosanct pre-theoretical list of innate qualities, but these overgeneralizations only serve to strip the notion of innateness of its explanatory utility.[15]

Even if innateness does not pose the severe inferential and practical risks just outlined, the concept is clearly used to cover too many different properties to be useful. Philosophical attempts at semantic reform are valiant but ultimately better avoided, especially given the term's tendency to immediately trigger misleading associations in different audiences. Where a psychological feature is supposed to be typical or universal, to be present early in development, to be acquired on an impoverished inferential basis, to be nonpsychologically explained, and so on, it would be better to simply label it as such, rather than succumbing to temptation and reaching for the comforting but cloudy notion of innateness.

[14] However, we would add that in this case the delay was also due to the fact that gathering this evidence is difficult. Some early corpus databases of child-directed speech existed in the 1970s, but large corpora could only be gathered and analyzed once computing technology had advanced. So it may not be accurate to pin the blame here entirely on the concept of innateness.

[15] Griffiths, Machery, and Lindquist (2009) also present as further evidence for the fragmentation of innateness studies showing that subjects presented with miniature scientific vignettes will classify traits as innate when they fall under different properties, thus showing that the "pre-theoretical" concept of innateness is also a mongrel. We take no stand here on the status of the everyday concept of innateness, if there is such a thing, or on its relevance to the technical concept being explicated here. It is enough for our purposes to see that the concept fails to serve the explanatory ends for which theorists themselves posit it.

4.7 Conclusions

Explaining development will require appealing to a wide range of processes. Some aspects of cognition are assembled in a relatively fixed manner as part of the early growth of the nervous system itself, or as a product of mostly endogenous causal factors. Others emerge under the influence of environmental cues of varying complexity, where the processes of construction themselves may embody information and constraints that contribute to determining the form that the final structure takes. In many cases these constraints may be fairly open-ended, and something like relatively free construction of new representations and structures is possible. However, these construction processes also vary in how independent they are of environmental supports. Some proceed autonomously and treat the environment mainly as a source of input or evidence. Others depend on the existence of a structured environment where informational and task complexity is radically reduced by friendly adults and other experts. These heterogeneous developmental processes each have their own characteristics, and appreciating this multiplicity is the first step in moving beyond the theoretically sterile division of psychological structures into "innate" or "learned."

5   Beyond the brain and body

5.1 The four E's

So far we have been looking at the mind from the perspective of traditional cognitive science. In this chapter we discuss a set of new and purportedly revolutionary approaches to cognition that have been gathering force in the past decade or so. These approaches go under the headings of *Embedded*, *Embodied*, *Enactive*, and *Extended Cognition*. These "four E's" propose a radical re-examination of how cognition should be modeled by the sciences, and they encourage a metaphysical shift in our view of what cognition itself is. These views raise a fundamental challenge concerning the very nature of how cognitive processes are distinguished from noncognitive ones. An upshot of these discussions will be to highlight the need for the cognitive sciences to settle a major foundational question, namely what makes something a cognitive system in the first place – that is, what the "mark of the cognitive" might be.

Very briefly, the four E's are as follows:

Embedded cognition is the view that minds arise for the online solving of cognitive tasks in time-dependent situations, and minds should be studied in light of this situatedness.

Enactivism is the idea that minds are for action. Cognition should not be conceived of or studied independently of action, or as a process that takes place in the brain and exists independently of action. Rather, minds should be conceived of as existing "in" the acting or arising from the acting. Minds don't cause action so much as minds are enacted in the unfolding of our behavioral engagements with the world. Thinking isn't a cause of doing, it is a *kind* of doing on this view. Because enactivist views have largely been defended in the context of theories of perception, we will defer our discussion of them until Chapter 6 (Section 6.6).

Embodied cognition is the idea that thinking doesn't take place sandwiched between perceptual inputs and motor outputs. Rather, cognition takes place all across the sensory-motor divide in the brain. In fact, on the embodied view, cognition can take place within parts of the body outside the brain. Embodied approaches reject a functionalist vision of the mind that permits the possibility of minds like ours existing independently of bodies like ours. Minds like ours are metaphysically dependent on our kind of bodies.

Extended cognition is the view that cognition is not confined to processes of body or brain. The skin is no boundary for cognitive activity. If one thinks of cognition as a kind of symbolic operation that processes information, then where that processing takes place is of little or no consequence. It can take place within the brain, but there is no requirement that it do so. Hence, in principle, cognition can extend into the environment around us in the form of tools and the external symbolic manipulations we use to help us remember, solve problems, and act more effectively.

5.2 Embedded cognition

Embedded cognition is the view that minds arise in a dense network of causal interactions with their surroundings. Cognition is an evolutionary solution to the problem of dealing with changing environmental conditions. Organisms develop minds in order to maintain bodily integrity and permanence in the face of environmental change. Since minds arise out of the causal interaction with the environment and would not develop or function properly without that causal interaction, we cannot attempt to model their functions in abstraction from this environment. The "embedded" part of embedded cognition refers to the interaction with an environment that is often necessary for cognitive development (using the brain in real-time tasks as the brain develops prunes some neural connections and strengthens others) or for solving cognitive tasks (merely looking at the world in order to solve a cognitive task can be extremely important to solving that task – consider looking at a jigsaw puzzle to find where the piece in your hand may fit).

A central theoretical notion in embedded cognition is that of "off-loading." This is the idea that humans and other animals configure the environment in ways that aid or benefit cognition. So consider the use of road signs when driving a car. Their use is of enormous benefit so that we do not have to remember all the turns on a long-distance trip. Even maps or GPS devices, helpful though they are, would not be as helpful without the road signs that we post in order to make the environment more informative. What's more, as in the case of road signs or notes to ourselves on paper or on our smartphones, off-loading to the environment can free us up for other cognitive tasks (driving safely, planning other parts of a trip, balancing a checkbook). We don't have to store in memory or rehearse information that is off-loaded. We are experts at using the world to simplify or streamline our solutions to tasks that would otherwise swamp us.

Cognition for the purpose of dealing with interactions in real time and with online processing is "situated." Situated cognition consists of things like the cognition involved in driving a car, searching for food, or solving a puzzle. Although the origin of minds placed them in embedded contexts where cognition was situated, not all cognition now is situated. Indeed, the philosopher Michael Bratman (1987) has long drawn attention to the logic and rationality constraints on long-range planning, much of which involves offline, nonsituated processing until the time of action arises.

From the fact that cognition is embedded in countless real-time interactions with the environment, nothing more metaphysically follows about the nature of cognition. The causal interactions that are involved when minds are embedded and situated can be causally formative of cognitive capacities, can be supportive of cognitive operations and processing, or can partially constitute cognitive processing. But being causally supportive is distinct from being causally constitutive of cognitive processing. The former seems quite obvious. Minds don't arise or operate in a vacuum. Indeed, sensory deprivation seems to lead to hallucination, disorientation, and the destruction of normal thought and consciousness. So causal interaction with environment seems necessary for minds to develop and operate properly. However, a move to a view such as extended cognition takes the further step that since such causal interaction with the environment is necessary for cognitive development and deployment, such causal interaction must constitute cognitive processing. Although we endorse the claim that the mind is embedded, we will argue in Section 5.4 that taking this further step would be a mistake.

5.3 Embodied cognition

Embodied cognition comes in a strong and a weak version. The weak view is that bodily states make important causal contributions to cognition. This view is so clearly true as to be undeniable. The senses contribute information to beliefs and desires. The motor system does the mind's bidding in allowing us to configure the world to our liking. Emotions have bodily correlates in viscera, the adrenal system, and even blushing or gooseflesh. So the weak view is not controversial.

What is controversial is the strong claim that cognition takes place *within* the body but *outside* the brain. This view, if true, would genuinely revolutionize thinking about cognition and about the mind. Let's begin with a simple contrast of the classical view of cognition as compared to the revolutionary view of embodied cognition. Consider perceptual inputs and motor outputs. On the traditional view of cognition, these are what Margaret Wilson calls "peripheral plug-ins," much like keyboard inputs and printer outputs for computers. The senses provide information input to the mind – the raw materials from which the mind constructs sensory images and then generalizes to build concepts and ideas. Once there is a store of concepts, the mind can string them together to build thoughts. Finally, when we have ideas of things we want to do or changes we want to make to the world, the motor system sends signals to the body to move and do the mind's bidding. Cognition takes place in a functionally central region of the mind/brain, not in the sensory input or motor output systems.

However, on the embodied view of cognition there is no boundary within the brain (or body, for that matter) where cognition takes place. On this view it can and does take place all across the sensory-motor divide. Different researchers emphasize different regions. Some, such as Lawrence Barsalou, emphasize the role of perceptual areas in cognitive processing; others, such as Arthur Glenberg, emphasize the role of motor regions (Barsalou, 2010; Glenberg, 2010).[1]

5.3.1 Experimental evidence

Barsalou is a leading proponent of the *perceptual symbol system* hypothesis (PSS): that all mental representations have their origin in the perceptual system. A typical experiment used to support PSS is the property verification task. Participants are shown a word for a concept, such as "pony," followed by a word that either fits (is verified) such as "mane" or does not fit (is not

---

[1] For an excellent introduction to embodied cognition, see Shapiro (2010).

verified) such as "horn." The person is instructed to say as quickly as possible whether the property can be predicated of the concept: pony-mane (yes), pony-horn (no). The prediction is that perceptual symbols are used to do cognitive work. If the task is about something visual, then symbols in the visual area would be accessed. If the properties being verified are auditory, then auditory areas should be accessed. If another question is asked, but it changes sensory modalities (say, from visual to tactile or auditory) the response should be slower because perceptual symbols from different areas would be accessed. So apple-red would access visual areas, while apple-sweet would activate gustatory areas, and subjects should be slower to process the second after a series of visual property verifications.

Studies using this paradigm were performed by Kellenbach, Brett, and Patterson (2001). Judgments concerning different properties turn out to recruit neural regions that are specialized for the perception of those properties. Color judgments activated color processing areas in fusiform gyrus, sound judgments activated auditory areas of superior temporal gyrus, and size judgments activated parietal areas associated with processing spatial judgments. The predicted switching costs were also found (Pecher, Zeelenberg, & Barsalou, 2003, 2004; Marques, 2006): people were slower at property verification tasks when the modality switched across trials.

The favored explanation of these switching costs is that cognitive work is being done by perceptual symbols. People run simulations in the relevant modalities to solve the cognitive task. Switching modalities takes time and slows the task while symbols from a new modality are accessed. Barsalou (2008, p. 27) is aware of the possibility that the activation of modal areas may be merely "epiphenomenal" to the tasks at hand. However, he proposes that if the symbols involved in cognitive processes were amodal, there would be no switching cost. Because there is a cost, the modal symbols being accessed are constituents of the cognitive process of solving the property verification task.

The data indicate that something is going on in these tasks, but there are two competing hypotheses about *just what* is going on. On the PSS hypothesis, cognition itself involves the perceptual symbols being accessed as constituents of cognitive processing. There are switching costs because the cognitive process changes location (from visual areas to other areas). On a competing hypothesis, the property verification task requires a hypothesis to be tested: do ponies have manes? The person may retrieve the correct response from memory and then verify the answer by accessing stored memories of perceptual experiences, but the perceptual experiences themselves may be nonconceptual and hence noncognitive.

Here is an analogy. If I verify that a substance is an acid by seeing litmus paper turn pink, the observation is not itself cognitive. Seeing isn't thinking. But knowing what turning pink indicates lets me solve the cognitive task of telling that the liquid is an acid. Accessing a stored sensory memory of a prior sensory experience may be as perceptual and noncognitive as seeing pink litmus paper. Yet it takes time to access the stored image, and it may take more time to access stored images of a new modality after changing from one modality to another.

The mere fact that there is a temporal cost of switching modalities in the property verification task does not choose between these two quite different hypotheses. On the first hypothesis, cognition extends into the modality-specific systems. On the second hypothesis, cognition does not extend into the modality-specific systems and perceptual symbols themselves, though they may provide causal support for cognitive processing.

Evidence for embodied cognition also comes from other experimental paradigms. In an fMRI study, Pulvermueller (2008) found that visually-related versus action-related words activate different regions of the brain. Processing action words activates frontal areas, whereas perception words activate perceptual areas. The assumption is that action words refer to actions, and the neurons that process them are likely interwoven with neurons controlling action in specific areas of the body. Words for facial movements (such as smiling) activate motor neurons that control the face, words for leg-utilizing actions (such as kicking) activate motor neurons controlling the legs, and so on. The results indicate that specific motor representations are used in action word understanding, which is interpreted as evidence for the embodiment of some aspects of semantics.

However, these results may also reflect a post-understanding inference: these inferences would be activated by the comprehension of a word or sentence, but would not necessarily reflect processes intrinsic to language comprehension. The understanding would come first, followed by neural activation that is causally related to it, but not a part of it. But how to separate constitutive from causal support? This turns out to be a tricky question. Distinguishing them empirically is difficult at best.

Pulvermüller (2008) suggests that processes constitutive of cognition will be immediate, automatic, and functionally relevant. With respect to immediacy, he suggests that motor activation is constitutive of understanding if it takes place within 200 ms after the word itself can be identified. With respect to automaticity, he suggests that when seeing or hearing a word, it is hardly possible to avoid understanding its content. Hence, if we give subjects a distractor task and they still understand the words, the brain processes reflecting comprehension might be expected to persist, showing constitution. And with respect to functional relevance, if action word presentation automatically activates a specific brain region, a change in the functional state of that brain region should lead to a measurable effect on semantic processing. Altered brain function in perceptual or motor areas should alter cognition.

Hauk and Pulvermüller (2004) conducted experiments to test these properties. In an ERP study, when participants silently read face, arm, and leg words, activity in brain areas responsible for movements of those body parts was present about 200 ms after word onset. Testing for automaticity, they had participants watch a silent film while trying to ignore spoken language input including words referring to arm, leg, and face movement. The spread of neural activity in this task was consistent with fast propagation of information to sensorimotor areas, despite the fact that people were trying to ignore the words they were hearing. This supports the automaticity claim. Finally, findings of functional relevance involved transcranial magnetic stimulation (TMS) applied to arm motor areas in the left hemisphere. These magnetic pulses elicited muscle contractions in the right hand and led to faster processing of arm words relative to leg words, whereas the opposite pattern of responses emerged when TMS was applied to the cortical leg areas. So pre-activation of relevant cortical areas amped up the readiness for cognitive processing of language concerning actions that would be produced by these cortical motor areas. This is taken to show that activity in these areas constitutes linguistic understanding, rather than being epiphenomenal to the understanding itself.

Glenberg and colleagues believe that cognitive processing necessary to solve certain types of tasks extends into motor areas. Glenberg and Kaschak (2002) propose what they call the Indexical Hypothesis. This is the view that meaning is embodied and "consists in a set of affordances . . . a set of actions available to the animal" (p. 558). Words and phrases are indexed or mapped to perceptual and motor symbols. Like Barasalou, they contrast their view with one in which symbols in a central processing system are amodal, abstract, and arbitrary. Instead, affordances are derived from perceptual and motor systems, and the meanings of these symbols are grounded in the sensorimotor system.

Language comprehension appears to interact with motor behavior in some cases. Glenberg and Kaschak (2002) asked participants to read sentences and determine whether they are sensible or nonsense. A nonsensible sentence might be "boil the air" or "hang the coat on the coffee cup." A sensible sentence might be "boil the water" or "hang the coat on the vacuum cleaner." The task is to determine as quickly as possible whether the sentences are sensible or not and press a "yes" or "no" response button. They begin with their index finger on a neutral button. The "yes" button is either nearer to the person's body than the "no" button, or reversed and farther from the body than the neutral button. So the participants must move their finger either toward their body or away from their body to answer the questions.

These studies revealed an action sentence compatibility effect (ACE). People were either slower or faster to answer the sensibility questions depending upon whether the movement they made (toward or away from their bodies) matched or conflicted with the implied movement in the meaning of the sentence. So a "toward" sentence might be "open the drawer" or "put your finger under your nose." These imply movement toward the body. A typical "away" sentence might be "close the drawer" or "put your finger under the faucet." The prediction on the embodied view is that to answer the sensibility question, the participants run a simulation in the perceptual-motor system. If this simulation requires the same neural system as the planning and guidance of real action, understanding a toward sentence should interfere with making an away movement.

Similar connections exist between emotional expressions and comprehension (Havas, Glenberg, & Rinck, 2007). Participants were again asked to judge the sensibility of English sentences, but this time they had a pencil either held in their lips (producing a frown) or between their teeth (producing a smile). If understanding emotional language involves getting the body into the right emotional state, people with the pencil between their teeth should be faster to understand "pleasant" sentences, and those with the pencil between their lips should be faster to understand "sad" sentences. A pleasant sentence might be "the college president announces your name as you proudly step onto the stage," or "you and your lover embrace after a long separation." An unpleasant sentence might be "the police car rapidly pulls up behind you, siren blaring," or "your supervisor frowns as he hands you the sealed envelope." The striking results are that people who are smiling are faster to understand the pleasant sentences, while those who are frowning are faster to understand the unpleasant sentences.

These results are only a sample drawn from a rich body of studies (De Vega, Glenberg, & Graesser, 2008; Semin & Smith, 2008). The question is whether they support the strong embodied view that cognition occurs in the motor system (to explain ACE) or in the facial muscles (to explain the emotion results). One alternative hypothesis is that although cognition does not actually cross over into the motor system, the motor system *shadows* the cognitive system. As one understands the implied movement of the action sentences (toward or away), one may imagine making these movements, and this imagined accompaniment of understanding the sentences may account for the differences in reaction time discovered. And in the case of the facial contortions and differences in response times, the forced smiles or forced frowns from the location of the pencil may prime the understanding of pleasant or unpleasant sentences. So, interesting as the results are, they do not really demonstrate that the processing in the motor system or facial system constitutes a type of cognitive processing versus being causally relevant to cognitive processing. This alternative hypothesis is not ruled out by these experiments.

5.3.2 Evidence against embodiment

There are more direct arguments against the embodied view, however. A significant problem is that the very same bodily movements can accompany cognitively distinct actions (Caramazza & Mahon, 2006; Weiskopf, 2010b). If this is so, the meaning of a thought, or a sentence expressing the thought, cannot be tied exclusively to perceptual-motor activity, since a piece of behavior may be ambiguous, although the sentence itself is not. Consider the sentence "Fred takes a drink of water." Is this because he's nervous? Or is it because he's thirsty? Either cognitive state is compatible with the very same behavior. Deciding between these two possibilities relies on our background knowledge concerning Fred's state of mind. But this knowledge goes well beyond information about Fred's current sensorimotor state. So there must be something more going on when we understand this sentence than consulting activity in the perceptual and motor systems.[2]

Beyond problems of ambiguity, there are matters of motor deficiency. If perceptual and motor activity are *constitutive* of various processes of understanding, then it should be impossible to dissociate the two. Impairments in perceptual and motor systems should go hand-in-hand with deficiencies in understanding, since understanding essentially taps into those very same underlying systems. However, as Caramazza and Mahon (2006) point out, this does not always happen. The recognition of biological motion can occur without the ability to produce the relevant kinds of motion. Infants routinely recognize actions that they cannot themselves produce (walking, talking, and other specific types of actions). This holds for language as well: in children and in adults, sentence comprehension outruns production. Comprehension–production dissociations indicate that the processes involved in the two are not identical.

Conceptual knowledge may also survive even though modality-specific input and output processes are damaged. This indicates that higher cognitive knowledge is independent of these perceptual and motor systems. Calder, Keane, Cole, Campbell, and Young (2000) report on the performance of an individual, LP, who had bilateral paralysis of the face from infancy (Mobius syndrome). Despite this deficiency, LP was not impaired on a test of facial affect recognition. So the ability to recognize facial expressions of emotion can coexist with the inability to produce them. The same pattern holds for 13- to 16-year-old children with congenital motor disorders, who are capable of recognizing point-light displays corresponding to biological movements despite being unable to produce those movements themselves (Pavlova, Staudt, Sokolov, Birbaumer, & Krageloh-Mann, 2003). Similarly, patients may be able to name objects, and therefore to recognize them, but be not able to use them correctly because of apraxia (Ochipa, Rothi, & Heilman, 1989).

Finally, if sensorimotor processing is required for understanding action words, this processing should differ significantly between congenitally blind and sighted adults. This prediction was tested by Bedny, Caramazza, Pascual-Leone, and Saxe (2012). Their participants were asked to make semantic

---

[2] A very similar objection arises with respect to mirror neurons and action-based theories of understanding; see Section 8.4.

similarity judgments between pairs of verbs and nouns while undergoing fMRI. These judgments did not differ between blind and sighted individuals, suggesting that they did not find any differences in meaning despite the different perceptual associations that the words must have had. Moreover, the region of the brain that is commonly thought to process visual-motion features of actions, the inferior medial temporal gyrus, was active to the same degree in blind and sighted participants, and to the same degree for high- and low-motion verbs. Because the blind individuals had never had any visual experience, this region's activity cannot have been responsible for their judgments about the meanings of motion verbs and nouns. Although there are many changes to perceptual systems in the brains of blind individuals, these changes do not affect either their ability to comprehend language or many of the neural systems that they use to do so (Bedny & Saxe, 2012). These studies seem to indicate that there are at most causal correlations between perceptual-motor activity and cognition, but that such activity may not even be necessary for normal levels of competence.

5.3.3 The limits of embodied meaning

We now turn to the semantic claims made in support of embodiment. Glenberg and Kaschak (2002) suggest that "the sentence 'Hang the coat on the upright vacuum cleaner' is *sensible* because one can derive from the perceptual symbol of the vacuum cleaner the affordances that allow it to be used as a coat rack" (p. 559). In contrast, the sentence "Hang the coat on the upright cup" is *not sensible*, because cups cannot typically be effectively used as coat racks. What makes a sentence sensible, then, is whether it can be used to generate a coherent perceptual simulation: "language is made meaningful by cognitively simulating the actions implied by sentences" (p. 559) A sentence such as "Art stood on the can opener to change the bulb in the ceiling fixture" would be rejected as meaningless because it is hard to envision a scenario in which someone successfully performs the described action as a means to that goal (Glenberg, Gutierrez, Levin, Japunitch, & Kaschak, 2004, p. 426).

But how is the word "sensible" being used here? Does "sensible" mean "meaningful"? If so, then the claim is that the meaning of an English sentence *consists in* a set of sensorimotor simulations that one must perform to understand the sentence. But this claim is false, and demonstrably so (Weiskopf,

2010b, 2010c). Indeed, this would seem to be nothing more than an updated verificationist theory of meaning. Everyone knows what it would mean to attempt to hang the coat on the upright cup or to change the bulb in the ceiling fixture by standing on the can opener. Under normal circumstances with normal cups, coats, and can openers, one could not do these things. In fact, it is because one knows what these sentences *mean* that one can tell that they are false (or that one could not comply with the request). False things are not nonsensible. Everyone reading this knows what the sentence "Hang the coat on the upright cup" means. It is because you know what it means that it seems silly or ridiculous – something with which you cannot comply. The point is that we *know the truth (compliance) conditions*, and thereby understand the meaning, even if we find it tricky or impossible to carry out the perceptual simulation.

Now, on the other hand, if "sensible" does not mean "meaningful," then what does it mean? Imaginable? Perceptually simulable? If it means one of these, then the claims Glenberg and company are making are trivial. We are being told that subjects cannot perceptually simulate experiences that ground these sentences. Even if true, would that tell us that the sentences were not *meaningful*? No. They still have very clear and determinate truth conditions. Would it tell us that subjects who did not readily simulate perceptual-motor groundings for them did not understand them? Not necessarily. It may be that they are still quite understandable, even though subjects are faster on reaction times when there are perceptual groundings readily available.

Furthermore, if the Indexical Hypothesis amounts to a new verifiability theory of meaning, then it is likely to founder in the same place as the old one, namely on the meaning of the Indexical Hypothesis itself. It says that *a sentence is only sensible if an agent can perceptually simulate it using the relevant affordances.* Now: can one perceptually simulate IH itself? Hardly. (What are its affordances?) So just as the verifiability criterion of meaning was not itself empirically verifiable (Hempel, 1950), the Indexical Hypothesis may not itself offer affordances for sensorimotor simulation.

A related problem for embodied cognitivists is abstraction. Despite arguments that all abstract ideas can be traced to embodied perceptual representations (Barsalou, 1999, 2003), it is difficult to see how all human concepts can have perceptual or motor roots. Consider logical connectives: and, not, or, if-then (&, ~, ∨, →). These logico-mathematical concepts seem very clearly to be defined in terms of truth tables: if p is true, then ~p is false; p ∨ q is false if both p is false and q is false, and true otherwise; and so on. Recall Sheffer's discovery that all the connectives could be reduced to recursive instantiations of just one connective. This is not a matter of either perceptual or motor representations. It is strictly a matter of functions mapping sentence variables to values on truth tables and defining connectives for those mappings. It would be a heroic attempt to argue, as Barsalou seems to, that our concepts of such matters indeed are derived from running perceptual simulators. Supposedly, understanding truth is something like perceiving the cat is on the mat. Understanding falsity is something like perceiving the cat is off the mat (so "the cat is on the mat" is then false). This is heroic because although truth and falsity can be instantiated in actual real-world events, including perceptual episodes, the very concept surely is not restricted to perceptible events. Think of Cantor's proof that there are more numbers between 0 and 1 than there are natural numbers, or the consequent truth that there are orders of infinity. What perceivable situation do such truths represent?

So in addition to *truth* there are concepts such as *justice, courtly love, double-dip recession, modern art,* and *racial privilege,* to mention only a few. What perceptual or motor events are the groundings of such concepts? Indeed, even scientific concepts such as the periodic table of elements seem to be neither perceptual nor motor. What makes our concept of an element the concept that it is has to do with the atomic number of the element? What perceptual or motor interaction grounds our concept of atomic number? Someone might imagine atoms and electrons whizzing in orbits in the mind's eye. But does this mean if one were incapable of such imagery that one could not conceptualize the periodic table of elements? We strongly doubt it.

Concepts are about objects and properties, which are the contents of the concepts. How the mind gets in contact with those objects and properties is a daunting question (especially for mathematical concepts). Nonetheless, there can surely be empirical concepts that we form via the employment of sensory inputs. We may use a mental process of abstraction going from the particular (Fred's Doberman Raven) to the general (the concept of dogs, including Chihuahuas and Great Danes). For some empirical concepts, this may indeed involve something like running a perceptual "simulator." However, it is doubtful that this is the type of process involved in forming all human concepts. This remains a significant challenge for embodied cognitivists to overcome.

5.4 Extended cognition

Embodied cognition involves the attempt to locate cognition outside of the brain, but some theorists have wanted to go still further. In recent decades, the proposal that cognition spreads out beyond the brain *and body* has been gaining widespread acceptance. This *hypothesis of extended cognition* was most famously proposed by Andy Clark and David Chalmers (1998) in a short but enormously influential article, but similar versions of the thesis have shown up in many places. For example, it appears in van Gelder and Port (1995, p. ix), who say that "cognitive processes span the brain, the body, and the environment," and also in Rowlands (1999, p. 22), who says that "cognitive processes are not located exclusively inside the skin of cognizing organisms." Similar ideas had been considered by embodied cognitivists (Varela, Thompson, & Rosch, 1991) and earlier by some phenomenologists (Merleau-Ponty, 1962), but have not until now been widely discussed in mainstream cognitive science.[3]

It is easy to see the view that cognition extends beyond body and brain as a further consequence of the embodied or enactivist views. Susan Hurley (1998) coined the term "the sandwich model" to describe the classical view on which higher cognition is "sandwiched" between perception and motor systems. If one accepts that cognitive processing can escape being sandwiched between the perceptual regions and motor regions of the brain, it is not such a stretch to think that cognition may also expand its reach into other regions of body and beyond. Nonetheless, to maintain that cognition takes place beyond the boundaries of the body does seem surprising. If cognitive processing extends beyond the central processing areas of the brain, the processing in perceptual or motor areas of the brain is still taking place in neural structures. However, if cognition takes place outside of the body, then the medium of the processing is not neural, but includes segments of the environment, tools that we use to solve cognitive tasks, and other items.

Of course, the idea that cognition can take place in things that are not human brains is also not new. Proponents of artificial intelligence and

---

[3] Clark and Chalmers only argued for extension of cognitive states (thoughts, beliefs), not qualitative states (experiences). Chalmers' own view is that qualitative states do not reduce to brain states, but not for the reasons that he and Clark think cognitive states extend. Clark has also denied that conscious qualitative states extend, unlike purely cognitive states. We won't here go into the reasons behind either of these views but will limit our discussion to the arguments for cognitive extension.

functionalists in philosophy of mind have long argued that minds could be made out of almost any kind of material (see Chapter 2). What makes something a mind is not what it is made of, but what kind of processing it carries out. If something made of material other than a human brain had the same types of functional and causal properties, then that thing (computer, robot, other life form) would have a mind, too. Still, the question is whether physical systems such as an organism plus parts of its environment can support cognition. We turn now to arguments in support of the idea that cognition can or actually does extend outside of the brain and body.

5.4.1 Coupling and parity arguments

Nearly all the arguments for extended cognitive processing begin with a kind of coupling to the environment by a creature who is solving a cognitive task, the solution of which involves interacting with the environment in such a way that the processes used to deal with the task causally and informationally extend beyond the body and brain of the originating cognitive agent. Some examples include the following. In the process of putting together a jigsaw puzzle, one may pick up pieces and rotate them, similar to the process of rotating an image mentally to see if it matches an exemplar. Or in playing Scrabble, one may move the letters in the tray to discover possible words one can make with one's letters. These manipulations constitute a type of information processing that extends from brain to body to world. There is no reason in principle to think that the processing of information stops at the boundary of body or brain. It continues right out into the world we interact with.

Now consider solving a math problem. One might use an abacus and move the beads on the rows to keep track of digits. Or consider using paper and pencil to solve a long-division problem, finding it difficult to keep track of the digits in the hundreds, tens, and ones columns in your head. As one either moves the beads of the abacus or writes numerals with pencil and paper, one is moving symbolic representations in order to solve a cognitive task (finding the answer to the math problem). To theorists such as Raymond Gibbs, this process "is best understood as a distributed cognitive behavior involving a person, a device, and the environment" (Gibbs, 2001, p. 118).

The most widely discussed example from the original paper of Clark and Chalmers is a thought experiment about two characters, Inga and Otto. Let's say that they plan to meet at the Museum of Modern Art on 53rd Street in New

York City. Inga has normal memory, knows the route, and sets off to find her way there. Otto has early symptoms of Alzheimer's disease and cannot store in normal memory the route to MOMA. However, he has devised a system whereby he records maps and locations and routes to places he wants to visit and keeps them in a notebook that he keeps by his side and frequently consults as he travels the city. Inga and Otto meet at MOMA. Each get there by their own means. Otto's trajectory involves several stops to consult his notebook, drawings, directions, and comparing landmarks he can observe along the way. Inga's trajectory involves internally stored directions, maps, images, and comparison with landmarks she could observe along the way. Both Inga and Otto use information about the environment as they are progressing toward MOMA and both consult stored information about where MOMA is as opposed to where they are along the way. The only difference seems to be where the comparison of where they are versus where they want to be takes place. For Inga it is largely comparing what she sees with what she remembers. For Otto it also includes comparing where he is to his charts and maps of where he wants to be and how to get there that he has stored in his trusty notebook.

Clark and Chalmers make explicit the appeal to the agent's causal coupling to the environment and highlight the import of the contribution made by the environment in solving the cognitive task:

> In these cases, the human organism is linked with the external entity in a two-way interaction creating a *coupled system* that can be seen as a cognitive system in its own right. All the components in the system play an active causal role, and they jointly govern behavior in the same sort of way that cognition usually does. If we remove the external component the system's behavioral competence will drop, just as it would if we removed part of the brain. Our thesis is that this sort of coupled process counts equally well as a cognitive process, whether or not it is wholly in the head. (Clark & Chalmers, 1998, pp. 8–9)

Although there are subtle differences among the types of argument given to support extended cognition, the appeal to coupling is unmistakable in all of them. The appeal to *location* is significant here, because whether something is or is not a cognitive process cannot simply be a matter of geography (where something takes place). If cognitive processes are functionally defined, then they take place in whatever realizes that function, no matter *where* it is realized in space.

These examples of cognitive extension are meant to show that as long the right sort of environmental dependence relations are in place, facts about location simply drop out of the story. Without his notebook, for instance, Otto won't make it to MOMA. Inga might, but Otto won't. The informational contribution his notebook makes is absolutely essential to his cognitive success. In fact, Clark and Chalmers consider the relationship in which Otto stands to the information stored in his notebook to be *functionally equivalent* to that in which Inga stands to the information stored in her brain. Because location doesn't matter, Otto's notebook is playing the role of his memory. Indeed, Clark and Chalmers think of the sentences in Otto's notebook about how to get to MOMA as akin to dispositional beliefs of Inga's. Dispositional beliefs are ones that are present and potentially functionally relevant to our behavior even when we are not consciously aware of them or consciously accessing them. So we know that the square root of 16 is 4 even while asleep, and Inga knows 53rd street intersects Lexington Ave even when she isn't currently entertaining that thought. On their view, Otto knows this too, because he can consult his notebook-bound memories as easily as Inga can consult her brain-bound memories.

The reasoning here has come to be known in the literature as the parity principle. The principle states that if processes x and y are informationally and causally equivalent and yield solutions to the same cognitive tasks, then processes x and y are cognitively equivalent regardless of where x and y occur. Because geography does not matter, if x takes place at the interface of Inga's occurrent beliefs and memory storage areas inside Inga's head and y takes place at the interface between Otto's current beliefs and his dispositional beliefs stored in the sentences, maps, and directions inside his notebook, then x and y are cognitively equivalent processes.

We can divide these coupling arguments into two sorts. *Type I arguments* involve coupling a cognitive agent to an environmental process, resulting in the extension of some cognitive process that already existed in the agent before the coupling took place. *Type II arguments* involve coupling an agent to an environmental process, resulting in a *new* cognitive process that did not previously exist within the agent and which spans the boundary of the agent-world pair. This is sometimes called "cognitive integration" (Menary, 2010). In Type I, you have a cognitive process within an agent, and the agent then causally extends that process into the environment, with the extended portion becoming cognitive by being coupled to the agent and by being functionally equivalent to something that, were it done entirely in the agent's head, would be cognitive. In Type II, integrationists will maintain that there *is* no cognitive process until the agent is causally and informationally coupled to the environmental process that complements and completes the cognitive process. In this view, it is not as though cognition starts in the agent's head and "leaks out" via coupling. Rather, on this view, there is no cognition without first coupling to the extended causal and informational loop. Nonetheless, coupling is essential to Type II. Without coupling to a cognitive agent, there would be no extended cognitive processing, even on this view.

5.4.2 The coupling-constitution fallacy

Adams and Aizawa (2010) opened a paper with the following good-natured joke:

> *Question:* Why did the pencil think that $2 + 2 = 4$?
> *Clark's Answer:* Because it was coupled to the mathematician.

Although this is just a joke, it reveals an important conceptual point. Very early in the literature, Adams and Aizawa (2001) cried "foul" at Type I coupling arguments for extended cognition. Although some proponents (Menary, 2010) have objected that their own versions of the coupling arguments do not commit the fallacy Adams and Aizawa highlight, we will argue that Type II coupling commits a fallacy as well.

Is something cognitive just because it takes place *within or coupled to a cognitive system?* There are reasons to think not. Adams and Aizawa (2008) contend that both Type I and Type II arguments for extended cognition are fallacious. The fallacy has the following form. Begin with the premise that Y is a cognitive process. Add the fact that process X is causally coupled to cognitive process Y. The coupling can either be such that it is mere causal support for process Y, or it can even be necessary for the existence of process Y. The argument then attempts to conclude that in virtue of this coupling, X is thereby part of the cognitive process (or that there is some larger cognitive process Y∗ that includes both Y and X). But this does not in general follow. Consider that circulatory processes are causally coupled to cognitive processes; blood flow through the cerebral vasculature is essential for the survival of neurons, and without neurons there is no cognition. It hardly follows that circulation is a cognitive process – we don't think *in* our blood, not even the blood in our heads. The same is true for noncognitive processes. In older air conditioning systems, liquid Freon evaporated inside of the evaporation coil, and the coil was causally connected to the compressor and air conditioning ducts. But despite this coupling, evaporation only took place within the evaporation coil itself. No interaction with the environment would be sufficient to *extend* this process into its surroundings.

One simply cannot assume without further argument that causal coupling with a process of type Y is sufficient to render the process coupled to Y a Y-type process. Hence, one cannot reason from the fact that causal processes in the environment often serve as aids or tools to cognitive agents who are solving cognitive tasks to the fact that those processes are themselves cognitive processes. Of course, they may *be* cognitive processes, but whether they are or are not will not merely be due to their being causally coupled to a cognitive agent solving a cognitive task.

We are not denying that it is metaphysically possible for cognitive processes to extend beyond the boundaries of the body, but the arguments appealing to coupling do not demonstrate that this extension actually occurs. Some proponents of extended cognition reject the parity principle and claim that their Type II coupling arguments escapes the coupling-constitution fallacy. Here is Menary (2010, p. 234):

> Extended-mind-style arguments based on the parity principle have
> encouraged critics to think in terms of an internal cognitive system that is
> extended outward into the world. Hence, on one interpretation, it implicitly
> endorses a picture of a discrete cognitive agent some of whose cognitive
> processes get extended out into the world. It also argues for the cognitive role
> of the environment by claiming that such roles are functionally similar to (or
> the same as) the functions of neural processes. The main question of the
> extended mind would then be: "How do processes in the world get to function
> like processes in the brain."

Menary thus rejects the parity principle. He claims that an agent's manipulation of the world is a starting point, not something to be seen as where the processing bleeds out into the environment because it is functionally similar to something going on in the head. For Menary, there *is* no cognitive process to bleed outward without the appropriate sort of integration.

In this case, the inference looks like this: if a process X that extends into the environment is causally coupled to an agent Y that is a fully cognitive agent, then process X can become a cognitive process by virtue of being causally integrated into the processing of agent Y. This still seems to be a form of the coupling-constitution fallacy. It suggests that just because a causal process that extends beyond body and brain of a cognitive agent helps that cognitive agent solve a cognitive task, that process is thereby a cognitive process. However, it is still possible that that process only supplies information and causal support for a cognitive process that is taking place solely within the bounds of the cognitive agent. It might be otherwise, of course, with cognitive processing being a joint effort going on partly inside the agent and partly outside. But there is no guarantee that this is true, given only coupling and integration.

Pointing out this fallacy is only the first step; a more constructive way to settle the issue would be to have a mark of the cognitive. Without some independent criterion or way of drawing the cognitive/noncognitive distinction, arguments that causally coupled processes constitute cognitive ones are fallacious. So far we have noted that claims have been made for constitution based solely on coupling, but without appeal to any such mark. This does not imply that causal interactions with the environment *cannot* be constitutive of cognitive processes. Quite the contrary – this seems to be a legitimate, if contingent, possibility. But the issue cannot be settled by appeal to coupling alone. It is notable that theorists supporting extended cognition seldom offer criteria for what makes something a cognitive process. We will take up this challenge in Section 5.4.4.

5.4.3 Blocking cognitive bloat

In addition to the worries raised so far about causation and constitution, a further problem is cognitive bloat. This refers to the fact that once we allow the first few shoots of cognition to inch their way out into the world, it tends to spread like kudzu. Cognitive processing will start cropping up in places where it should not be, and prima facie would seem *not* to be. If cognition takes place in Otto's notebook, or in one's manipulation of beads on an abacus, or pieces of a jigsaw puzzle, why stop there? Why wouldn't cognition extend into one's calculator, laptop computer, or cell phone, or even to servers spread out across the Internet? How could we stop the spread, once we see all of these processes as contributing to our solving cognitive tasks?

The problem of bloat is yet another consequence of failing to draw the boundaries properly between causal influences and constitutive elements. Mark Sprevak (2009) has argued that this sort of bloat is inevitable. Sprevak notes, as we also did earlier, that functionalism seems to allow the possibility, at least in principle, of extended cognition. If cognition is functionally defined, and none of the functional criteria refer specifically to location or to seemingly arbitrary boundaries such as the skin, then cognitive functions can cross such boundaries freely. Creatures with exotic ways of realizing these functions are standard fare in the literature. Humans encode their memories and beliefs in neural connections, and artificially intelligent computers might store them in patterns on magnetic material. If the *storage* is all that matters, there could be creatures who store their beliefs in a mental filing system that makes use of actual scraps and scrolls of paper. And if paper as a medium for information storage is just as acceptable as neurons or ferromagnetic film, then it can hardly matter where this paper is kept. Libraries and archives are full of such frozen information. Just walking into such a building armed with the appropriate dispositions to access and make use of this stored textual information is enough to make it part of one's *beliefs*. So on a liberal conception of the kind of functional access required for belief, we will find that we believe everything in the library (or everything on the Internet) simply on the basis of being in the right sort of (potential) access relation to its contents.

The challenge for extended cognition is block the bloat by imposing some sort of constraints that will determine which causal influences on a system are properly part of it, and which are external influences operating on its behavior from the outside. Some critics of extended cognition who see bloat as an inevitable consequence of the view have argued that the best way to avoid bloat is not to adopt an extended perspective in the first place.

Extended cognition depends on there being extracranial or transcranial processes that actually realize cognitive functions. If there are no such functions, then ipso facto cognition is not extended, and the problem of cognitive bloat does not arise. One argument to this conclusion has been given by Rob Rupert (2004).[4] Rupert focuses on the example of memory, a capacity that is often cited as one that is especially easy to extend into the environment. Memory, after all, is merely storage. And literate, technology-using humans

---

[4] For a similar argument that focuses on the functional role of beliefs, see Weiskopf (2008b). The argument there equally emphasizes the functional asymmetries between internal and external information processing.

are experts at storing information in the world. We store more information than we know what do to with, and we have countless ways to interact with it. From an extended perspective, then, literacy is a technology of prosthetic memory.

But, according to Rupert, this move is too hasty. It glosses over significant differences in how we use our biological memory versus how we interact with environmental information. Rupert draws attention to the fact that human memory displays a cluster of characteristic phenomena that make it a particular distinctive object of study for psychologists. One example is the *generation effect*: being asked to generate a sentence rather than just read a sentence written by someone else can improve performance on a paired-associate completion task. If one group of participants reads a sentence such as "The cow chased the ball" while another group generates their own sentence involving the word "cow," the participants who generate their own sentences will typically be more accurate at completing pairs such as "cow – ???" More broadly, the effect refers to the fact that items that are self-generated are easier to recall than those that are generated by others. This effect appears using a variety of materials and testing procedures (see Bertsch, Pesta, Wiscott, & McDaniel, 2007). A second memory effect is *negative transfer*, also sometimes called proactive interference. In a typical experiment, participants are trained to memorize paired associates (A-B), and then trained on a new set of pairs, some of which have the same first member as the old pairs (e.g., A-C). Negative transfer refers to the fact that these new overlapping pairs are learned more slowly than the original list or a new list that contains no overlapping members. Having learned a pair that begins with A makes it harder to learn a different pair that starts with A. This is one of many forms of interference that occur in human memory (Kimball & Holyoak, 2000).

However, there is absolutely no reason to expect that extended forms of "memory" will be subject to the same sorts of effects. When one is manipulating information stored on paper or in a computer file, the processes that produce negative transfer are unlikely to operate. A new list on paper is just that: a separate entry that happens to share some entries with another list. There is no inherent mechanism involved in producing these lists by which the two could interfere with each other. Similarly, having read something and "stored" it in external memory just involves copying it there in the form of public symbols. These symbols will be just as available if the original sentence was generated by the person as they will if the person merely read the sentence. The phenomena that are distinctive of human memory processes do not occur in these cases of extended memory.

From this, Rupert concludes that it is overwhelmingly likely that biological memory processes and alleged extended memory processes will belong to different scientific kinds. They will produce different phenomena and operate according to different principles. But this fact is in tension with one argument that is often cited in support of extended cognition, namely that recognizing the reality of these extracranial cognitive processes will offer significant *explanatory* advantages. These advantages mainly take the form of theoretical unification. If extracranial processing were really functionally identical to intracranial processing, as the parity principle would seem to require, then we could simplify our overall account of cognition by folding them into a single theory covering both internal and external forms of memory. This is consistent with the goal of remaking cognitive science as an enterprise focused not solely on the bodies and nervous systems of living creatures, but on potentially all forms of cognitive systems, whether or not they are bounded by conventional bodies.

The debate between extended and classical cognitive science, then, depends on whether there is a common domain of phenomena and processes that cross bodily boundaries. Rupert is effectively proposing a type of *kind-splitting* argument (see Section 2.5): internal memory exhibits the characteristics of one scientific kind, whereas access to external information, whether it is properly thought of as memory or not, exhibits characteristics of a different kind. Accordingly, given the fine-grained differences between the two, there is no single unifying theory that covers them both. The argument that extended cognition will successfully unify these functionally distinct processes fails, since there is no set of functions that they share that is sufficiently deep or robust to support scientific inquiry. It is therefore a misnomer to think of embedded practices of interacting with information in the world as being *memory processes*, since that strongly suggests a commonality that we have reason to believe does not exist.

Rupert's argument rests on the assumption that phenomena such as those having to do with generation and interference are central to the kind *human memory*. Inasmuch as extended processes fail to exhibit these phenomena, they do not belong to that kind. However, as we noted in our earlier discussion of multiple realization, cognitive phenomena can be described at many different grains. In a highly fine-grained sense, human memory processing is indeed defined by the sorts of phenomena Rupert points out. It is not optional to mention these features if one is giving the complete story about how human memory works.

In response to this kind-splitting challenge, Clark (2008), has argued that "acceptable forms of unification need not require all systemic elements to behave according to the same laws" (p. 115). Legitimate sciences may deal with *hybrid* systems having components belonging to scientifically different kinds, charting the many interactions of those components without assigning them to any generic superordinate kind at all. On this view, the familiar philosophical dictum that the sciences deal only with unitary kinds is a form of mythological purity-mongering. For example, ecological inquiry may attempt to explain the behavior of systems made up of many different kinds of organisms and environments. The biomedical sciences include the study of neural prosthetics, which explicitly deals with designing mechanical systems that can interface with living tissue. It is hardly clear that these hybrid enterprises fail to be sciences in the absence of any single common kind for them to study. So Rupert may be right that intracranial and extracranial memory belong to distinct kinds, but this need not impugn the existence of a single scientific research program that embraces both of them, as well as their interactions.

Ultimately, then, whether some extracranial processes are cognitive is not settled by whether there is a scientific discipline that studies their interactions with humans' intracranial cognitive processing. In fact, there *is* such a science, known as human-centered or activity-centered design, that focuses on understanding the principles that underlie human use of technological supports and explaining how technology can succeed (or fail) to be effectively usable (Norman, 2013). Activity-centered design represents a robust merger of the psychology of perception, memory, and motor control with graphic design, software programming, and electrical engineering. The existence of such a hybrid field, however, tells us nothing about the relative distribution of cognitive activity within its domain. We turn now to some positive suggestions on how to draw boundaries around cognitive systems themselves.

5.4.4 The mark of the cognitive

Despite the fact that there has been an interdisciplinary study of mind called "cognitive science" for more than 30 years, and that in the science of psychology researchers have studied cognitive processing for more than a century, there is not currently an agreed-on theory of what makes something a cognitive process. This is part of the problem faced by both sides of the debate over extended cognition. If we are to know that causal processes coupled to and extending beyond the body and brain of an agent are themselves cognitive processes, then we need to understand what makes something cognitive in the first place.

As a first stab at saying what cognition is, we might appeal to the idea that it is a kind of information processing. However, this only takes us so far. Information processing takes place in the simplest pocket calculators, but these are not cognitive systems. Neither does the extensive literature on information that has developed in recent years help to settle questions about cognition on its own (Floridi, 2010, 2012).

To see what is special about cognitive information processing, we need to think about how minds differ from the other informationally sensitive systems in the world. In philosophy, much of this debate has centered on the topic of naturalized semantics, which aims to describe the conditions under which something becomes a *natural* representation. Many things in the world represent, of course, most notably words, diagrams, maps, paintings, graphs, and other public symbols. According to the conventions of English, the word "cat" represents cats, and by dabbing paint on a canvas, Géricault was able to represent the wreckage of the *Medusa*. But these representations are all created by human beings, and their representational powers derive from human purposes and intentions. In a courtroom, a prosecutor may re-create an accident using wooden blocks to represent cars, but this is not because of some intrinsic feature of the blocks. A blue block does not naturally mean *blue car*. Rather, it is her intention to use them to stand for something that gives them this representational function. Their representational properties are *derived* from our intentions and practices.

The representational powers of the mind, however, do not seem to be derived in this way. When you form a mental image of a pink cow, or wonder whether you left the stove on, you are mentally representing objects and events in the world by manipulating mental symbols that stand for those things. Unlike public, nonmental symbols, however, these mental symbols do not have their representational content derivatively. Rather, mental symbols are *original* (or nonderived) representations. Their ability to represent their content does not arise from anyone's assigning them that content. Minds are natural systems that have the function of representing the world, and their ability to do this is ultimately explained in causal, nonmental terms.

Once creatures have minds, they can create public representations that derive their content from the representational contents in the minds of the intentional agents. Once humans can think about water, they can develop a word for water: "water." But before having a word for water, they can still think about water. Some theorists accept the notion of a language of thought in which there are mental symbols prior to words that have meaning and are about the world. Such symbols in the language of thought would have nonderived meaning because there was no meaningful system that imposed content on these thought symbols from outside. Rather, the functioning brain had to develop these symbols on its own. Contrast this with things we invent to stand for other things (Roman numerals, Arabic numerals, binary arithmetic, and so on). These things have meaning *because* we can think and we employ these symbol systems to represent what we intend for them to represent. The meaning we intend comes first, and the meaning of the symbol systems we invent derives its content from the contents of our thoughts. But our thoughts themselves are "unmeant meaners." Meaning stops there as a first semantic cause, so to speak. Before the symbols in the language of thought developed their meanings, there were no meanings (at least not of the semantic kind).

In the naturalized semantics literature, there are many prominent accounts of how such underived meaning comes to exist. There are accounts by Dretske (1981, 1987), Fodor (1990), Cummins (1996), Millikan (1984, 2004), and many others.[5] The details of these theories won't matter here, because what is important is just that nonderived content requires that there be a set of natural causal conditions that, when met by creatures in their interactions with their natural environments, results in a set of symbols in their brains with which they think. These symbols have representational content, can express propositions, and can be true or false. Adams and Aizawa (2001; 2008) maintained that the presence of symbols such as these is a necessary condition for a process to be cognitive. Thus, cognitive processes have to have nonderived content.[6]

---

[5] See Adams and Aizawa's (2010) review essay in the *Stanford Encyclopedia of Philosophy* for more details.

[6] For a defense of nonderived content from objections that there really isn't any such thing, see Adams and Aizawa (2008, Chapter 3).

This requirement challenges the thesis of extended cognition because the bulk of the examples cited in its favor involve causal processes exploiting symbols with derived content. This suggests that these processes do not constitute cognitive processing itself. For instance, the symbols in Otto's notebook are symbols (words, maps, diagrams, directions) with derived content. He put them there with the intention that they help him navigate his environment. The meanings of the symbols all derive their content from his mind or from the minds of others. They have meaning by convention, whether consciously intended by Otto or socially transmitted through learning. Were it not for minded creatures with cognitive processing involving underived content, none of the symbols in Otto's notebook would have meaning or be useful to Otto. They seem to be the *products* of cognition, not the *medium* of cognition, functioning as tools to prompt or remind Otto of certain facts, with the actual mental grasp of those facts taking place inside Otto himself.

Another way of converging on this idea is to attend to the fact that cognitive systems, like other natural systems, seem to come with built-in boundaries and ways of maintaining their distinctiveness and integrity (Weiskopf, 2010d). In the case of minds, their natural boundaries are established by the presence of transducers and effectors. A *transducer* is a device that takes energy in the environment as its input and turns it into an output representation. For a simple example, consider sensory receptors such as the rods and cones in the eye, or Merkel cells within the skin. These receptors are sensitive to ambient light or pressure, and when exposed to this sort of stimulus they produce a distinctive train of neural responses that encodes the properties of the stimulus in a way that can be used by downstream processing. That is, their function is to represent the input signals to the nervous system so that it can formulate an overall sensory picture of the world. Sensory transducers are distributed within the traditional sense organs and also within the viscera, where they provide interoceptive awareness of bodily conditions. *Effectors*, on the other hand, are the output equivalents of transducers. Their job is to transform trains of neural firings into patterns of activation within muscle fibers. These outbound neural signals can be regarded as terminal motor commands, signaling how the organism intends its muscles to twitch in order to produce the behavior it is planning on executing. Every naturally evolved creature possesses some type of transducers and effectors, as do artificial creatures such as robots.

The salient point about both transducers and effectors is that they form the *representational boundaries* of a creature's mind. For something in the world outside to enter the mind, it must be represented. Anything that a creature cannot represent, it cannot think about either. And the natural channels through which the world is represented are the perceptual systems, which function by transducing stimuli (patterns of energy) into representations. Transducers, in other words, are the first contact points where representations with original content arise, and effectors are the point where representations "run out" and mere movement takes over.

Viewed in this light, the mind can be seen as a locus of nonderived representational content bounded by transducers and effectors. There is no clear notion of something's getting "into" or "out of" the mind unless there are such boundaries. Insofar as the mind is a representational system, an event in the world can affect the mind only if it can somehow affect it at the transducer layer.[7] Similarly, barring telekinesis, the mind can change the world only by changing the body it is embedded within, and these changes are restricted to the commands that can be carried out by its effectors. The interlocking back-and-forth causal chains between mind and world may involve many kinds of information flow, but the properly cognitive portion of this information flow occurs only within the transducer–effector boundary. Outside of that boundary there may be an environment filled with derived representations of all sorts, but for them to enter the mind their content, too, must somehow make an impact on the right transducers and be represented in the right way. Symbols and images must be seen and interpreted, marks and words must be read. All of these tasks involve transforming the inherently meaningless physical stimuli that fill the environment into naturally meaningful inner representations. Mere coupling and causal manipulation, no matter how complex, is not sufficient. The transducer–effector criterion gives us a further theoretical rationale for drawing the boundaries of the mind in approximately their traditional location.

5.5 Conclusions

Here we have defended two pillars of the classical view of cognition. First, against the claims of strong embodied cognition, we have sought to maintain

---

[7] We are ignoring the possibility of direct neural intervention here – for discussion of this and other complications, see Weiskopf (2010d).

a sharp distinction between the systems that implement higher cognitive processing and sensorimotor systems. Second, against the claims of extended cognition, we have sought to resist the spread of cognition into the environment, arguing that the boundaries of cognitive systems more or less coincide with the boundaries of the individual organisms that are the traditional subjects of psychological investigation.

However, none of this requires us to reject the insights of embedded or situated views of cognition. The empirical evidence reviewed here shows that embeddedness is absolutely pervasive. Central cognitive systems routinely call on processes in sensorimotor systems to solve various tasks. Perception and action are useful tools for cognitive processing to draw on, even if they do not constitute cognition. Similarly, extended cognitivists are correct to point out that many capacities that are traditionally assigned to the "bare mind" can only function if the correct environmental supports are in place. These contributions have heuristic value for psychology. They are a rich source of new hypotheses to investigate, as well as new experimental protocols and sources of evidence. Paying attention to embodied and environmental factors can only deepen our understanding of cognitive functioning. The mind may be shaped and marked by its entanglements with the body and the world while still being distinct from them.

6 Perception and action

6.1 Defining the senses

Psychologists have studied perception more deeply than any other of our cognitive capacities, and among the senses vision is by far the most closely scrutinized. Accordingly, although burgeoning philosophical attention has been paid in recent years to nociception (Aydede, 2006), audition (O'Callaghan, 2007), touch (Fulkerson, 2013), and olfaction (Batty, 2011), we mostly confine our attention here to vision. First, however, we address the more general question of how sensory systems are to be distinguished from the rest of cognition, as well as from each other.[1]

The traditional division that posits five separate senses goes back to Aristotle, at least in recorded Western philosophical thought. Dividing the senses into touch, smell, taste, hearing, and sight makes sense on two intuitive grounds. First, these senses correspond to manifestly different *sense organs*. The eyes, ears, nose, tongue, and skin are relatively salient parts of the body, and their role in mediating different types of sensory interaction with the environment is pre-scientifically manifest. Second, these sensory divisions seem to be associated with distinct *sensory phenomenology*. To see something is a different kind of experience than to touch it or hear it. On the basis of anatomy and sensory experience, then, the Aristotelian divisions have some support.

However, these criteria coincide only imperfectly. The phenomenology of smell and that of taste are intimately linked, and people often find it hard to tell which is producing a particular sensation. In extreme cases such as synesthesia, a single stimulus may simultaneously activate several different types

---

[1] Our discussion here is indebted to Fiona Macpherson's (2011) excellent taxonomy. See the other papers in that volume for further philosophical attempts to analyze the senses.

of sensory experience. A single Aristotelian sense organ can also produce several distinct kinds of experience. The skin mediates pressure, pain of various types, and temperature, all of which have distinct experienced qualities, and the ear mediates both audition and vestibular response, which is involved in the phenomenology of proprioception. And there are other sensory experiences that are associated with no particular organ, such as the feeling of movement or hunger. So types of sensory experience and sensory organs need not go together.

The idea of a sense organ is an anatomical structure that is specialized for carrying out a certain kind of perceptual task. In Aristotle's view, the task is the production of a kind of experience. The notion of a specialized sensory structure can be refined, however. Senses might be individuated according to what sorts of receptors they have. A *receptor* is a neuron that transduces a specific stimulus – a kind of energy such as electromagnetic radiation or pressure, or a kind of material such as volatile chemicals in the atmosphere – and turns it into neural signals that are processed downstream. Receptors are the basic components of sensory transducers, so sense receptors ultimately produce representations of stimulus conditions.

The receptor view of the senses has no intrinsic connection with experience, however, since there are dedicated neurons that track conditions that we do not directly experience at all. For an example, consider the chemoreceptors that monitor CO_2 content in the blood. We have complex bodily responses to spikes in blood CO_2 levels, but we are rarely conscious of them as such. Moreover, on the receptor view there are going to be many senses; indeed, possibly more than a dozen. The skin alone contains separate receptors that detect temperature, pressure, stretching, and various sorts of damage. The receptor view can also help to classify senses in different species, such as sharks that detect electrical current or pigeons that track the earth's magnetic field.

Receptors, though, are not capable by themselves either of producing sensations or of allowing an organism to process information in a sense modality. They are merely dedicated input channels tuned to a particular type of proximal stimulus. They function only in conjunction with *perceptual systems*: those parts of the neural or cognitive architecture that have the function of processing inputs from particular receptor types, transforming them into mental representations of the right type, and generating outputs that allow the organism to act appropriately on the information they carry. Rather than focusing on coarse-grained and anatomically obvious sense organs, we should refine our account to focus on sensory systems that take inputs from various receptor types. The senses are systems that have the function of turning inputs at various receptor surfaces into representations that are used by other cognitive systems.

A further way to distinguish one sense from another is in terms of the types of *distal properties* that each one represents. This representational approach posits that each sense is specialized for conveying information about a particular feature of the world. Vision, for instance, conveys information about the color and shape of objects; touch conveys information about their hardness and texture; hearing conveys information about the pitch and intensity of sounds; and so on. There are complicated questions to be sorted out here about just what the objects each sense detects actually are. The objects of olfaction and audition are difficult to pin down, for example. Moreover, some properties seem to be detected by more than one sense. An example of these "common sensibles" is shape, which is perceived both by vision and by touch. (It may be that visual and haptic shape are not exactly the same quality of an object, but this is debatable.)

Despite these difficulties, the notion that the senses are devices for representing distal properties has attractive features. The goal of perception is to do more than inform us about the world as it arrives at our receptors; rather, we want to know about the objects, events, and qualities that are in the environment (both external and internal). One way to arrange this is to sequester representations of these qualities in functionally distinct systems that take input from a relevant subset of receptors tuned to the local energy signal of those distal qualities.

Finally, if the senses were distinguished by their processing of information about distal qualities, this might help to explain the phenomenological differences among them. For although phenomenology may not be completely reducible to representation, differences in the kinds of perceptual experience that we have might track such representational differences. The experience of seeing color in space is different from the experience of tactile hardness in part because these involve representations of different properties.

We have several possible criteria for individuating our senses: (1) they are distinct systems for processing information; (2) they have receptors tuned to particular proximal stimuli; (3) they represent different distal properties of objects and events; and (4) they are associated with distinct phenomenology. Other possibilities have sometimes been raised. For instance, it might be claimed that the senses are *modular* systems. But as we have seen (Chapter 3), this fails in two ways: there may be central modular systems that are not sensory, or there may be few or no modular systems at all.

These qualities may not invariably coincide, however. Consider various examples of what might be called prosthetic vision. In one case, a person's damaged eyes are replaced with cameras that use the normal input channels of the optic nerve to send signals to the visual cortex. Here the receptors are no longer the same, but the rest of the system seems intact. This should plausibly be called a case of sight. Or consider experiments in sensory substitution such as those explored by Paul Bach-y-Rita (Bach-y-Rita & Kercel, 2003). In a typical case, the camera is wired to a device that turns the image on its sensor into a gridlike pattern of touch on the skin. The distribution of tactile pressure here corresponds with the intensity of light at various points in the image, making this "tactile image" a low-resolution mapping of what arrives at the sensor. But is this a form of vision? It isn't clear. The phenomenology will certainly be different at first, although people may adapt to this. The input modality is different (pressure vs. light), as is the neural system that responds to the stimulus at the receptors. In time, though, the information can be used by the subject to navigate the three-dimensional world.

Other individuating traits may also be removed or permuted. The clinical syndrome known as blindsight results from damage to primary visual cortex (V1). It is characterized by a lack of conscious visual perception with preserved visual discrimination abilities under certain circumstances. So patients report not being able to see anything in the parts of the visual field that correspond to the damaged region, but if they are shown a simple geometric figure (a cross or a circle) in the blind region of the field and asked to make a forced-choice decision as to which one is being displayed, they are right significantly more often than chance. So at least some visual information seems to be available for certain tasks. This is consistent with intact receptors and information processing by a somewhat damaged sensory system, but the phenomenology of normal vision is largely absent.

Ethology provides further cases that are difficult to classify. Pit vipers have small, thermally sensitive organs that allow them to track either sources of heat in the immediate environment or the recent traces of such sources. Is this a kind of "thermal vision"? The receptors are quite different from our visual receptors, and they respond to a very different part of the spectrum. Given the evolutionary distance between primates and snakes, the cognitive mechanisms are likely to be radically dissimilar. The qualities that these systems represent overlap only partially with vision: they track distance but not color or detailed shape, and they track temperature, a quality that our visual system ignores. Bat echolocation is equally puzzling. The modality here is pressure waves, and the receptors and sensory systems are acoustically tuned, but the system is used to navigate through space as vision is. Finally, there are animal perceptual modalities that are simply difficult to relate to human senses, such as pigeon magnetic field tracking and electric field detection in sharks. And in all of these cases it is difficult to determine what the associated phenomenology might be, or even if there is one.

Considering these cases of augmented, damaged, and animal (or alien) sensory systems, it seems clear that our own senses are not the only possible ones. Similarly, the criteria for individuating senses do not always point in the same direction, because features that cluster in human vision may dissociate in other types of vision. At the extremes, it may simply be unclear whether to call something a case of vision at all. For our purposes, we may take the prototypes of visual cognition to be given by the clustering that occurs in our own normal cases. We may, by a kind of analogical extension, also call systems visual when they have relevant similarities to the prototype of vision that we instantiate. In other cases it is just unclear whether something is visual (or tactile, or olfactory, etc.) at all. In these cases, all that we can do is note the characteristics that the sense has and attempt to treat it on its own terms. This allows for there to be a wide range of possible types of senses, but this seems an entirely reasonable conclusion. We should not allow an objective taxonomy of the senses to be beholden to the entrenched, folk-theoretic Aristotelian five (though see Nudds, 2004, for a contrary view).

6.2 The visual grand illusion

We begin by sketching some facts about the ordinary experience of seeing the world. Like all phenomenological descriptions these are disputable, and others may characterize their experience differently, but they may still have sufficient generality and plausibility to provide an initial basis for discussion.

First, our visual experience is richly detailed. Not only does the portion of the world that we are focusing on or attending to seem replete with visual details, but also this detail seems to extend in all directions more or less continuously, only beginning to fade out at the margins. If we imagine the visual field to be like a canvas, it is one that is painted with an equally fine brush and an equally rich palette across its whole expanse. This apparent richness of detail, which is there whether or not it is being attended to, is what underpins the sense that the whole visual environment is simultaneously present at every moment. Connected with this is the sense that this richness is continuously informative in a way that makes massive gaps or failures of visual accuracy unlikely. The continuous, vivid richness of visual experience gives us a sense of what might be called the presence of the visible world.

The sense of our visual experience, then, may be provisionally characterized as being rich in detail, continuous in extent, and broadly accurate in content. These all have to do with how our experience *seems* to us. We may ask, first, whether experience really is as it seems: do we really have visual experiences that have all of these qualities? If we ascribe to our experiences qualities that they do not have, this is one sort of gap that can open up that may well be regarded as a kind of mistake or illusion: we are systematically inaccurate about the character of our experiences themselves. A second question is whether, given that our experiences have these qualities, they are reflected somehow in the underlying representations that are processed by the visual system. That is, are these processes and representations themselves equally rich, continuous, and accurate? This has to do with the functioning of our cognitive systems rather than directly with experience itself.

There are two potential routes where illusions about vision can take hold: between the character of our experiences and the qualities we ascribe to those experiences, and between our experiences and the cognitive processes that underlie them. The idea that the visual world might be a *grand illusion* has been used to cover both of these ideas.[2]

Several lines of evidence seem to support the grand illusion hypothesis. One relies on the phenomenon known as *change blindness*: the widespread tendency of people not to notice large changes in the visual scene before them (Simons & Levin, 1997, 2003; Rensink, 2002). This occurs under a range of conditions. The eye is continually in motion, making saccadic motions several times per second as it targets various parts of the scene. If a change in the visual scene occurs during a saccade, it will often go overlooked. In one study, participants read passages of text written in AlTeRnAtInG cAsE. When they moved their eyes while reading, the case of the words switched

---

[2] The term "grand illusion" seems to originate with Noë, Pessoa, and Thompson (2000).

(lowercase letters became uppercase and vice versa); however, no participants seemed to notice the switch, nor did their reading time slow appre-
ciably (McConkie & Zola, 1979). This effect has been replicated with more
realistic images as well, in which changes to the features of houses, cars,
plants, and other ordinary objects routinely go unnoticed (McConkie & Currie,
1996).

Changes outside of saccadic motion also induce change blindness. In the
"flicker" paradigm, a scene and its modified variant flash back and forth with
a blank display between them (or some other interposed stimulus, such as a
mud splash that appears to cover part of the scene) (Rensink, O'Regan, & Clark,
1997). People can take a surprisingly long time to register major changes such
as a jet losing and gaining an engine across these flickers. Even changes to
highly realistic scenes can go unnoticed if they occur during the interposition
of an object. In one of the most striking examples, students were stopped on
campus by someone who claimed to be lost and in need of directions. During
the conversation, a pair of workers would walk between the two carrying a
large door. While the student's view was blocked, the lost questioner would
switch places with one of the workers, who then would take his place in the
conversation as if nothing had happened. Incredibly, many people failed to
notice after the switch that they were having a conversation with a completely
different person despite the fact that they differed in their clothes, hair, and
general appearance (Simons & Levin, 1998).

A second line of evidence comes from studies involving inattentional
blindness (Mack & Rock, 1998). As the name suggests, this refers to an inability
to detect features of the visual scene when normal attention is suppressed,
refocused, or otherwise disrupted. In one type of experiment, participants
were given the task of examining a visually presented cross and deciding
which of its arms was longer. The cross was shown only briefly, followed
by a masking stimulus. Given the small differences and the brief display
times, this task requires careful attention. On some of the trials, however,
an additional critical stimulus (a colored or moving bar or other geometric
shape, for example) was shown along with the cross. Participants were given
no warning that this additional object would also appear; however, they
often failed completely to notice its presence. When the cross was displayed
at the central fixation point with the critical stimulus off to the side, 25%
of participants didn't notice it; but, more surprisingly, when the cross was
displayed somewhat off-center from the central fixation point and the critical

stimulus was displayed directly at the fixation point itself, between 60% and 80% of participants failed to notice it.

Inattentional blindness has also been shown in surprising naturalistic contexts. In the famous "gorillas in our midst" experiments (Simons & Chabris, 1999), participants were again given an attentionally demanding task: they were shown a video of two teams of people, one wearing white shirts and the other wearing black shirts, each passing a basketball rapidly back and forth among themselves. The videos of the two teams were superimposed, making a complicated visual scene with overlapping and interpenetrating "ghosts" of both people and balls. Participants were required to count how many times one of the teams passed the ball. During the middle of this complex scene, a man in a gorilla suit strides out into the middle of the court, pauses for a moment, and then moves on. Seventy-three percent of the participants failed to report the gorilla walking across the middle of the display, and over half of the participants in several other studies failed to notice a woman carrying an open umbrella, despite the fact that these figures are completely obvious if one views the displays without attempting to do the task. Attentional demand, then, seems to result in selective blindness comparable to the blindness induced by various sorts of visual flickering and masking.

Do phenomena such as these support claims on behalf of the grand illusion? Once again, let's distinguish two possibilities: that we are subject to an *experiential grand illusion* (EGI) and that we are subject to a *representational grand illusion* (RGI). The former concerns a gap between how experiences are and how they appear to us, whereas the latter concerns a gap between experiences and their underlying representation and processing in the visual system. Consider the following representative statements of EGI:

> We have the subjective impression of great richness and "presence" of the visual world. But this richness and presence are actually an illusion, created by the fact that if we so much as faintly ask ourselves some question about the environment, an answer is immediately provided by the sensory information on the retina, possibly rendered available by an eye movement. (O'Regan, 1992)

> One of the most striking features of consciousness is its *discontinuity* – as revealed by the blind spot and saccadic gaps, to take the simplest examples. The discontinuity of consciousness is striking because of the *apparent* continuity of consciousness. (Dennett, 1991, p. 356)

In both of these cases, it is the subjective character of conscious experience itself that is called into question. On the other hand, consider this statement of RGI:

> If we do not have representations that are everywhere detailed and coherent, why do we have such a strong impression that these kinds of representations underlie our visual experience? (Rensink, 2000, p. 18)

Here we have a contrast between experience and the underlying representational machinery of perception. The impression that vision gives us is not matched by the structure of the system that produces those impressions. But does the evidence here support either EGI or RGI?

Let's begin by considering representational grand illusionism. Some have doubted whether these studies support RGI, because it doesn't seem prima facie credible that most people have *any* sort of beliefs about the representations that underlie their visual experience. These states and processes are introspectively invisible to us. On reflection, this is obvious: if introspection revealed how vision worked, we would hardly need experimental psychology to uncover such facts. And even the sort of psychological theory that could explain visual experience is largely unknown to nonexpert perceivers. Without this sort of governing metacognitive belief, though, how can we make sense of the claim that we are subject to an *illusion* here? The absence of any everyday beliefs about the representations that underlie our experience seems to preclude the possibility of illusion in the relevant sense.

This point is correct as far as it goes. Although we may have everyday beliefs about experience itself, representations and cognitive processes are in the domain of scientific psychology, not folk psychology. Non-theorists typically pay them no mind. However, there may still be an illusion here if we consider the sharp difference between the continuous, unified, detailed nature of our experience and the fragmentary, incomplete nature of the representations that underlie it. That is, perhaps the illusion involves a gap between experience *itself* and the underlying mechanisms that produce it.[3]

Not every such gap is an illusion, however. Consider ordinary cases in which we say that experiences are illusory. Typically these involve our perceiving something to have qualities that it does not actually have – to have

---

[3] This may be in the spirit of Rensink's quote, which refers to the "impression" that experience has a certain kind of representational support.

the wrong shape, size, surface contours, temperature, and so on. Roughly speaking, an experience is illusory when it presents something to us as having qualities that it does not have. Experiences do not, in this way, *present to us* any information about the mechanisms that underlie them. That would be a distraction from their main task of telling us about the world, rather than about themselves. Our experiences *depend* on these mechanisms, but they are not experiences *of* these mechanisms, whereas in the cases of genuine illusions they are experiences of the objects that are being systematically misperceived.

So it seems that there is no *illusion* at work here, although that is not to say that there is not an important or significant gap of any kind, or that there is nothing to be explained. If experience *does* have the relevant features of richness and continuity, we need to explain how this is possible given its sketchy representational underpinnings. This, however, only refocuses our attention on the claim concerning the nature of experience.

The experiential grand illusion makes a strong claim: that our metacognitive awareness of our experience simply gets its properties shockingly, massively wrong. Specifically, we take our experience to be rich in detail, continuous, and broadly accurate. Do these experiments show these claims to be false? Consider these claims one by one. If our experiences are, moment by moment, rich in details about the world, why is it that in the flicker paradigm it is so difficult for us to register large changes? Why do we not notice when our conversational partner turns into a different person after a brief occlusion? If our experiences are continuous, why do changes across saccades (which are themselves unnoticed) pass without our noticing? If experiences are broadly accurate, why is it surprising to learn that we have not registered an object displayed directly at our fixation point, or have overlooked a person in a gorilla suit walking directly across the screen?

Most people, when presented with reports of these studies, find them surprising and systematically underestimate how likely they and others are to being deceived in these ways (Levin, Momen, Drivdahl, & Simons, 2000). This seems to support experiential grand illusionism. Noë, Pessoa, and Thompson (2000) disagree, however, and propose not only that most of us not have the beliefs about experience that EGI ascribes to us, but also that a moment of close attention will confirm that they are false: "To say that we (ordinary perceivers) normally think we perceive all environmental detail with equal focus and clarity – as if we were looking at a fixed picture – is to misdescribe the character of perceptual experience" (p. 102). If we fix our gaze and stare out a window, they claim, we become aware that the visual field is graded in its acuity, rather than uniformly rich; perhaps as our gaze settles and becomes still, the experience of color and detail drains away from the periphery, leaving only a tiny foveated island in an indistinct sea. And being reminded of the tricks of artists and magicians should discourage us from finding our errors in these experimental contexts overly distressing.

All of these challenges rely on the principle that *experiences play functional roles*: if we ascribe to our conscious experiences properties such as richness, continuity, and accuracy, then these properties should be reflected in the kinds of behavior that experience enables. That is, the presence of such qualities can be used for experience-guided actions. If we assume that our conscious experience guides the kinds of visual judgments and behaviors elicited in these studies, they seem to show that experiences behave more as if they were impoverished, jumpy, and inaccurate, at least some of the time.

The message of the various grand illusion studies, then, is that there are several possibilities for the relationship between experience and behavior:

(1) Experiences are rich, but not causally responsible for much of our behavior.
(2) Experiences are rich, but their richness is not entirely accessible for causing behavior.
(3) Experiences are impoverished and causally responsible for our behavior.

The one possibility that seems decisively ruled out is that *both* experiences are richly textured and this richness is causally productive of behavior. If this were so, the gappiness of many of the experimental results would be hard to explain. That leaves these three as live options.

6.3 Dual visual systems and the role of experience

A different body of theories and experiments sheds a slightly different light on questions about the causal role of experiences. These studies focus on the large-scale organization of the human visual system. Here we begin with the well-known point that the visual system is not internally unitary. Rather, it is a complex system containing many interconnected subsystems, each of which is dedicated to its own proprietary processing domain. The evidence in favor of this claim has been accumulating for a century. Early neurological studies of visual deficits showed that it was possible to damage or destroy one aspect of visual functioning while leaving others largely intact. In 1909, Reszko Balint described a patient who, following bilateral parietal strokes, displayed a syndrome consisting of: (1) simultagnosia, or the inability to identify more than a single unified object in a scene at a single time; (2) gaze paralysis, or the inability to shift eye direction voluntarily to new target objects or locations; and (3) optic ataxia, or the inability to accurately reach for visually presented objects. These three deficits together constitute Balint's syndrome.

The dominant contemporary view about how the visual system is organized at its highest levels is that there are two "streams" of visual processing. Vision begins with a complicated cascade of processing at the retina, where incoming light is transduced and turned into neural signals. These signals then pass to the lateral geniculate nucleus of the thalamus, and then to V1. From V1, visual pathways move in two different directions. One stream of processing moves dorsally, the other ventrally. The dorsal stream passes through the middle temporal area (MT) and ends up in the posterior parietal cortex. The ventral stream passes through an area known as V4 and ends up in the inferotemporal cortex. These two streams are densely connected internally, but relatively sparsely connected to regions outside of themselves. Hence they are anatomically and functionally relatively autonomous units that have a common origin point.

The decisive identification of these two visual streams came with the work of Mishkin and Ungerleider. In a series of studies, monkeys were selectively lesioned in either the inferotemporal (IT) or the posterior parietal region. These lesions differentially affected their performance in visual tasks. The IT lesions disrupted performance on visual pattern recognition, whereas the parietal lesions disrupted performance in a spatial landmark discrimination task. The former task involved mainly identifying the type of object that was being visually perceived, whereas the latter, at least in the original interpretation of the experimental results, involved identifying where that object was located in space. They thus showed a double dissociation between two types of visual activity associated with each anatomical region. As a result of this pattern of deficits, they were dubbed the "what" (ventral) and "where" (dorsal) streams.

The description of these areas in terms of "what" and "where" is a difference in the kinds of properties these visual areas represent. However, this formerly standard interpretation of the two streams has been challenged by studies revealing a set of deficits that seem to suggest a different functional organization at work.

These studies, pioneered by Milner and Goodale, involve a patient known as DF. At age 34, DF suffered severe carbon monoxide poisoning, resulting in bilateral damage to areas of her lateral occipital cortex. These areas are ones that occur early in visual processing and feed into the ventral stream described earlier. The result of this damage is that DF has visual form agnosia: she cannot reliably identify geometric shapes, ordinary objects, or faces, no matter whether their outline is determined by color, motion, or depth cues. She can still perceive and experience colors, textures. motion, and depth, but only when they are assigned to neutral, non-objectlike stimuli; she can, for instance, identify natural scenes such as landscapes based on the broad distribution of colors they contain. She cannot perceive shapes and their orientation, however, because these involve integrating and organizing the visual stimulus into coherent wholes.

However, despite these form and object deficits, she can still perform surprisingly subtle visual tasks. If presented with a disc containing a slot oriented at various angles, she can extend her hand and pass a rigid plaque through the slot (a movement akin to posting a letter), even though she cannot make a correct identification of the angle that the slot is at. That is, although she at best appears to be guessing when asked the orientation of the slot, she can still visually guide her hand to it reliably. Similarly, she can reach out and pick up various smooth and rectangular objects normally – that is, she grips the object at the same opposing points that normal subjects do, indicating that she can use some visual information to detect the spots on the shape that will afford appropriate manipulation. However, when presented with these objects in pairs, she cannot make reliable same/different judgments about them. Her experience of these objects does not allow her to make a conscious judgment about their properties, even though her visually guided reaching seems controlled by those properties. This reaching behavior displays many of the features of normal sighted reaching and grasping; for example, she resizes her grip at the appropriate points in the act, and makes her grip more precise as it approaches the target. Moreover, even the accurate reaching responses she can make are limited in time and space: they do not persist if the target is displaced, or a blind delay is imposed between seeing the target and acting on it.

The phenomenon of accurate visually guided reaching and impaired visual object identification suggests an alternative hypothesis about the functions of the visual streams: the function of the ventral stream is *object and spatial perception*, rather than simply "what" an object is, whereas the function of the dorsal stream is the *visual guidance of action*, rather than "where" it is located. There is content shared between these two streams: spatial layout information, or "where" content, is used in both ventral and dorsal streams. However, this information is processed and used for different purposes in each stream. The ventral stream is about identifying and classifying the spatial layout around the perceiver. This information is used in a variety of processes, including reasoning and consciousness. The dorsal stream, on the other hand, is about a specific kind of task: the immediate control of action using primarily visual information. This need not rely on detailed knowledge or classification of the environment, and, crucially, it need not rely on consciousness. These functional differences have effects on how the visual information is encoded. The dorsal stream encodes information egocentrically: that is, it encodes the location and size of objects in a frame of reference that centers on the body of the perceiver. Knowing these relations is important for acting on objects effectively. The ventral stream, on the other hand, encodes information allocentrically: it ignores information about absolute size and focuses instead on the relations objects bear to one another in the world, independently of their relations to the perceiver. This information is most relevant for classification and reasoning tasks, which depend on what things are, not how they are related to the perceiver as such.

Milner and Goodale (2010) have dubbed these two streams "vision for action" and "vision for perception." Further support for this proposed functional dissociation comes from optic ataxia. Recall from the description of Balint's syndrome that optic ataxia involves an impairment in visuomotor coordination, specifically involving manual reaching and grasping for visual objects. Patients with optic ataxia have been shown to fail at the "mailbox slot" task that DF succeeds at readily. They also show grip abnormalities in picking objects up (although reaching and grasping abnormalities may also dissociate). This supports the notion that visuomotor processes may be disrupted independently of object recognition, which is largely intact in object ataxia. Finally, evidence for a dissociation of visuomotor coordination and perceptual awareness may be demonstrated even in intact subjects (Aglioti, DeSouza, & Goodale, 1995). The Ebbinghaus illusion is a visual illusion in which a central disc is surrounded by either a ring of small circles or a ring of much larger circles. When surrounded by the smaller circles, the central disc appears much larger than when surrounded by the larger ones. Participants reliably report this fact. However, when asked to reach out and pick up the central disc, the grip aperture that normal subjects use is automatically sized to accommodate the actual dimensions of the disc, not its perceived dimensions. This matching of grip aperture to the real target size rather than the perceived target size has been replicated in several other types of visual illusion (Goodale, 2008). This suggests that reaching and grasping is under the control of different visual processes than the ones responsible for conscious awareness, identification, and reporting.

A possible objection to the proposal that these functional streams are really distinct comes from the fact that DF is, surprisingly, sometimes capable of making *correct* same/different judgments about visually presented shapes. For instance, when presented with a square and a rectangle, DF can sometimes correctly pick up the square, despite being unable to verbally report which object is the square (Murphy, Racicot, & Goodale, 1996). This might imply that DF has some intact object identification skills localized within the dorsal stream. On closer inspection, however, DF's strategy appears to involve the use of kinesthetic or motor awareness: she is aware of how far apart her fingers are placed, and can use this information as a cue to whether she is reaching for the rectangle or the square. This strategic use of motor information is supported by the fact that she can even guess accurately which object is the square if she is allowed to make a grasping motion toward the object at the same time (Schenk & Milner, 2006). In both these cases, DF uses a width cue given by motor imagery or feedback from sensations of her fingers to make a correct object discrimination judgment.

Andy Clark (2001, 2007) has argued that this two-systems hypothesis calls into question the Assumption of Experience-Based Control (EBC):

> Conscious visual experience presents the world to a subject in a richly textured way, a way that presents fine detail (detail that may, perhaps, exceed our conceptual or propositional grasp) and that is, in virtue of this richness, especially apt for, and typically utilized in, the control and guidance of fine-tuned, real-world activity. (Clark, 2001, p. 496)

This assumption not only has an extensive philosophical pedigree, but also seems to make explanatory sense. As we have noted in the previous section, when we perceive the world, we seem to be aware of a kind of rich perceptual array of objects and qualities. It is precisely this awareness, which often exceeds our descriptive or conceptual resources, that enables us to act on the world in specific ways: to grasp and drink from a cup, to insert a coin into a vending machine, to intercept and catch a thrown object.

EBC seems to be challenged by the interpretation of the two visual systems presented here. Patients with impaired ventral stream processing appear to have damaged conscious experience of the visual world. They are subject to various forms of visual agnosia, including for forms, objects, and qualities, that prevent them from having normal awareness of and knowledge about what they are visually presented with. However, as in the case of DF, they can still often act on their environment in appropriate ways, at least where the actions in question are tied to the sorts of present interactions that require little sophisticated conceptual knowledge to execute. Action execution, then, seems to be potentially independent of experience.

If correct, this seems to strip experience of one central part of its functional role. If experiences are not for helping us get around in the world, what is their purpose? Clark proposes that we replace EBC with the Hypothesis of Experience-Based Selection (EBS):

> Conscious visual experience presents the world to a subject in a form appropriate for the reason-and-memory-based selection of actions. (Clark, 2001, p. 512)

According to EBS, experiences do play a role in guiding actions, but this role is at a much higher level than had previously been assumed. Their role is more like that of an executive than a direct, hands-on form of participation. Experiences function to aid us in determining the appropriate categorization of the visual scene so that we can bring to bear bodies of stored information about our situation, and on this basis formulate detailed plans of action. Experiences are the *inputs* to conceptually organized planning of intentional actions, not the *online controllers* of the actions that we produce. This view of the distribution of cognitive labor is something like the one that Milner and Goodale arrive at. They propose that the ventral stream is used for tasks such as identification and target selection, while the dorsal stream is used for online execution of behaviors directed at a particular target. The dorsal stream thus serves as a kind of remote controlled "tele-assistance" system for the ventral stream (2006, p. 232).

A final refinement needs to be added to this picture, having to do with the coordination of the activity in these two streams. Neither the dorsal nor the ventral stream by itself is capable of producing actions. That task requires higher cognitive abilities connected with reasoning and planning in order to choose appropriate goals and select available means. What the two visual systems provide is a set of resources for carrying out these vision-based tasks. It is clear that beyond these higher-level planning systems, there need to be more complex links between the two systems. Take one example (from Milner & Goodale, 2006, p. 229): picking up a knife or screwdriver requires not only closing one's grasp on it correctly, but also finding the right end – the handle – to pick it up by. This information cannot be derived from the dorsal stream alone, but requires semantic knowledge concerning what sort of object is at hand, and what its properties are. So even grasping actions involving everyday objects require some sort of collaboration between the two visual streams.

Although these studies do not directly help to settle the questions raised at the end of the previous section, they cast doubt on any picture that posits a *direct* causal role for conscious experience in causing behavior. Whether experiences themselves are rich or impoverished, they do not directly guide much of our visual action with respect to the environment.

6.4 Vision and imagery

We now widen our gaze slightly from vision itself to other forms of visual cognition. We not only have the ability to see the world and visually guide our actions, we also have the ability to imagine visual scenarios, creating scenes in our minds for the purpose of reasoning, planning, or simply entertainment. We now focus on one form of imagination in particular, namely the ability to form specifically visual images of objects, scenes, and events. There are other forms of imagination, of course. We may simply imagine something to be the case without this having any specifically visual component. We can imagine a world in which general relativity turned out to be false, or one in which Nixon clung to office rather than resigning, but these need involve nothing like visual experience. They are more like suppositions, or beliefs about how the world might have been. Following Currie and Ravenscroft (2002), we can call these *belief-like imaginings*.

On the other hand, many imaginative acts do involve vision, or perception more generally. Trying to move a piece of furniture into a new apartment often involves deciding whether it can be maneuvered through the door, which can involve visualizing how it would look turned one way or another (rather than the more exhausting strategy of arduously trying each possibility out). Call these *perception-like imaginings*. These states are often described as involving *imagery*, and we will use this term to refer to the phenomenon of perception-like imagining, and the term *image* to refer to the representations that we manipulate during imagery.

The contemporary revival of systematic work on imagery traces back to Roger Shepherd's studies of mental rotation in the 1970s. Shepard and Metzler (1971) presented people with pairs of line drawings of complex three-dimensional shapes and asked them to decide whether they depict the same shape or not. For some pairs, one shape was a rotated version of the other, whereas for the remainder there was no way to rotate the shapes into alignment. Finally, some of the objects could be determined to be the same by a simple rotation of the figure within the picture plane, whereas others correspond to rotations of the objects in three-dimensional space. The significant result is that across matching pairs, the response time to make correct judgments of sameness is a linear function of the degrees that the figure would need to be rotated to produce a matching view. Because there is no actual perceptual change in these studies, solving this task must be tapping into a capacity for visual imagery.

These studies provided the initial inspiration for the *picture theory* of mental imagery. This account comprises two claims about the representations and processes that underlie generating and using images. First, images appear to be encoded in a pictorial representational format. Images can be thought of as mental pictures in which the parts of the image are organized in a way that corresponds to the spatial distances among the parts of the pictured object or scene; that is, images preserve spatial metric information. So for each visible part of an imaged object, there is a representational part, and the distances between parts of objects are mirrored by the distances in the parts of the representation. Second, the operations over images make use of this spatial information. In the Shepard and Meltzer task, images are rotated at a constant rate, passing through each point in mental space in the same amount of time rather than either changing their rotational rate or flipping instantaneously into a new position. How images behave is a joint product of their format and their inherent processing characteristics.

Stephen Kosslyn has carried out studies that have provided extensive empirical and theoretical support for the picture theory (Kosslyn, 1980, 1994; Kosslyn, Thompson, & Ganis, 2006). Among these are studies using a mental scanning paradigm, in which a chronological effect akin to the rotation effect was found. Kosslyn, Ball, and Reiser (1978) asked people to memorize a simple map of an island containing a few marked locations (a beach, a church, a lighthouse, etc.). They then were asked to focus their attention on one such landmark within their image of the map, were given the name of a second landmark, and were asked to press a button when they could see the second landmark come into view as they panned across their image. The time to press the button in these studies varies linearly with the distance between the named landmarks in the original map (and hence, presumably, in people's image of the map). As with the rotation experiments, this is taken to license the claim that mental images preserve spatial information, and this information affects the kind of processes (scanning, rotating) that operate over images.[4]

Other behavioral results also support the depictive nature of mental images (Kosslyn, 1980). For example, an object may be imagined as being (or appearing) either small or large; when it is imaged as being small, it takes longer to confirm the presence of various properties of the object than if it is imaged as large. This too is consistent with the idea that images encode spatial information, since in a smaller image details will be more crowded together, and it will be harder to retrieve information, possibly require enlargement or "zooming in."

Although the rotation, scanning, and image size studies provide behavioral support for the picture view, further evidence has come from a battery of neuroscientific studies over the past two decades. Most crucially, forming mental images can produce activity in regions of the brain that are involved in visual perception (Kosslyn, Ganis, & Thompson, 2001). When people close their eyes and are asked to visualize objects of different sizes, this produces activity in primary visual cortex that varies with the size of the imaged object. These patterns of activity resemble those produced during ordinary visual object

---

[4] For an extensive review of the literature on image scanning, see Denis and Kosslyn (1999).

perception. Furthermore, interfering with this activity using transcranial magnetic stimulation (a magnetic pulse that noninvasively disrupts neural functioning in a specific brain region for a short time) produces degradation in people's performance in both imagery and perceptual tasks.

These neurobiological results are significant for the picture theory because early visual areas are topographically organized: distances between points in these areas correspond, roughly, to the distance between points on the original retinal image. The neurophysiological arrangement of these areas thus preserves spatial information in the way that the picture theory requires. These patterns of activation also covary with imaging performance, showing that they are actively involved in the task itself. Finally, they suggest a hypothesis about the cognitive architecture that underpins visual imagery, namely that it involves a kind of *simulation* of vision. One process is a simulation of another when the first process consists of a sequence of stages that correspond to those involved in the second process, and each step in this sequence resembles or duplicates the operations of the second process. For instance, seeing a three-dimensional figure (such as those used by Shepard and Metzler) rotate would produce a certain pattern of activity in the visual cortex. Imagining such a figure rotating through the same angle involves a series of representational transformations that correspond to the sequence of the perceptions themselves. Here, the simulation is achieved because a subset of the same neural and cognitive systems is used in both perceiving a rotating shape and generating an image of it. The mechanisms of perception are taken offline and reused in generating mental imagery. The processes and operations involved may be assumed to be similar, and so in this sense, imagery involves simulation of perception.[5]

The picture hypothesis says that mental imagery uses a pictorial (spatially organized) representational format and taps into specifically perceptual cognitive systems. This view, however, has been challenged, most prominently by Zenon Pylyshyn (2002, 2003a, 2003b). Pylyshyn has argued that the evidence for the picture hypothesis has been misinterpreted and that matters are at best inconclusive concerning the underlying format of the mental representations used in imagery. Instead, he proposes a null hypothesis that he dubs the *visual thinking hypothesis*. On this view, thoughts all have the same format,

---

[5] The notion of a simulation will become much more precise and theoretically prominent in Chapter 8.

no matter what they are about or how they are experienced. Thus, since generating imagery is a kind of thought, images are not mental pictures (or they are not more like mental pictures than other kinds of thoughts). If we generally think in a propositional or language-like code, then imagistic thought uses this as well. The experimental phenomena surrounding imagery are to be explained by how participants understand the experimenter's request to "imagine X." That is, it arises from the demands of the imagery task itself and from our general world knowledge, not from the underlying mental architecture. Mental imagery, in short, involves thinking about the visual properties of things using our ordinary reasoning mechanisms and the representational systems and resources that they provide.

Many of Pylyshyn's arguments turn on the fact that imagery is cognitively penetrable. That is to say, following the definition of cognitive penetrability given in Section 3.5.2, what we imagine is influenced strongly by what we know and believe about the things we are imagining. Pylyshyn illustrates this point using simple examples. For instance, imagine looking at a white wall through a yellow color gel, over which a blue gel is then superimposed. Within your image, what color appears in the region of overlap? The "correct" answer in this case depends on whether the mixing is additive or subtractive – an additive mixture produces white light, whereas the more familiar subtractive mixture produces green. Which one is imagined depends on the background knowledge you possess about these sorts of color interactions, but in the absence of such information, no particular color may appear in one's image. And in any case, it seems quite within one's own control to produce *any* color in the region of overlap. There is nothing that appears *mandatory* about the color that emerges. In both of these cases, the properties of the image seem unconstrained by the underlying visual architecture and responsive instead to more general beliefs about physical and optical interactions.

Similar comments may apply to the mental scanning results. The picture hypothesis explains these by positing that the imagistic representations encode spatial information, and the processes that access them require that this information be processed in a certain kind of way. But the nature of the experimental task may affect whether people scan when retrieving information from images or not. In one study, Pylyshyn (1981) asked participants to memorize maps like Kosslyn's island map, containing various named locations. They were then asked to judge the direction in which one landmark was located relative to a second landmark. Because this information is unlikely to have been encoded when people memorized the map, solving the problem requires retrieving both locations in the course of carrying out the computation. However, there is no effect of distance from the origin to the target on how long these judgments take – orientations of nearby objects are computed as quickly as those of distant objects. The picture hypothesis needs to account for why spatial metric information would impose temporal limits on image processing in one case, but not another. The visual thinking hypothesis, however, holds that there are no constraints on image processing that arise from the format of imagery. In cases where people do mentally scan across their image, they do so because their understanding of the task is that this is what it requires. The everyday way that they habitually solve these problems involves moving their "mind's eye" across a simulated visual landscape – as they would if they had a real map of the landscape in front of them. But this solution to the task is not imposed by the underlying architecture of imagery.

Other imagery results are similarly explained by the organization of general knowledge rather than inherent properties of the putative imagery system. For instance, mental paper-folding tasks often show a linear relationship between the number of folds one would need to imagine to solve the task and the time it takes to complete. Again, this seems to support the idea that we picture the folding taking place serially. But, Pylyshyn suggests, this result can be explained by the fact that we typically know in advance only what will happen when we make a single fold. The results of repeated folding accordingly need to be calculated one at a time. By analogy, we typically know only a letter or two ahead in the alphabet and would accordingly need to figure out by explicit counting what the fifth letter after "m" is. The letter-counting task relies on the organization of alphabetic knowledge, just as the folding task relies on the organization of geometric knowledge, but in neither case is any assumption made about the underlying format of that knowledge. The structure of knowledge plus processing demands can do all of the explanatory work.

Finally, Pylyshyn argues that the neurobiological results are at best inconclusive. A great deal of this evidence relies on the following inference: The neuroanatomical and physiological organization of visual cortex is topographic; therefore the mental representation of space in vision and imagery mirrors this topography. The regions of primary visual cortex that contain the structures used in imagery represent two-dimensional retinotopic arrays. However, images represent three-dimensional objects and scenes. Moreover, the objects and scenes in imagery are not necessarily egocentrically represented, nor are they restricted to the field of view given by the retina. They may extend panoramically in space in ways that retinal activations cannot capture. The retinotopic map in visual cortex receives predominantly foveal inputs, but images can occupy much more than the relatively small foveal region of space. Images, then, represent a vast array of spatial information that goes beyond what can be captured using the simple format of retinotopic patterns of activation, and thus those patterns of activation provide no direct support concerning the format of images.

The debate between the picture theory and the visual thinking hypothesis illustrates some of the difficulties in establishing firm claims about cognitive architecture. Deciding between them depends on settling both experimental questions, such as to what degree imagery is really cognitively penetrable (Borst, Kievit, Thompson, & Kosslyn, 2011) and whether cortical visual deficits are necessarily comorbid with imagery deficits (Bartolomeo, 2002), as well as interpretive questions, such as what activity in visual areas during imagery tasks might mean if it does not indicate the use of pictorial representations.

6.5 Perception as prediction

So far we have depicted visual perception mostly as a bottom-up process that is driven by causal inputs from the world, with higher-level cognitive processes being passive recipients and interpreters of these signals. This conforms to the classical notion of the senses as essentially receptive. However, this passive, input-driven view of perception has recently been challenged by a number of theorists who take their inspiration from a top-down view of perception espoused by German psychologist Hermann von Helmholtz (Clark, 2013; Friston & Stephan, 2007; Hohwy, 2013). In Helmholtz's view, perception is a form of *inference*. The mind starts out with access only to the proximal input signals from the world, and its job is to figure out what their most likely distal causal source is. This is the basic perceptual problem of constructing an accurate model of reality. But the relationship between signal and source is potentially many-many. A particular signal may have many possible sources (a flash of light in the sky may be lightning or a passing UFO), and a single source may present many different signals (Bruce Wayne in an expensive tuxedo strikes us as different from the menacing, caped Batman). The problem of determining what is actually occurring in the environment based only on local signals, then, is a challenging task that resembles other problems of causal inference.

To see how one kind of inferential approach proposes to solve this problem, consider the fact that the flow of information in perception is hierarchical, meaning that it can be divided into levels at which increasingly abstract and sophisticated features are processed. Early visual processing detects the presence of simple, local features such as the distribution, wavelength, and intensity of points of light. Higher levels extract features such as lines and their orientation, textures and shading of surfaces, and the discontinuities marking the edges and boundaries of objects. At the highest level, an image of the three-dimensional layout of space emerges, along with a conception of the type of overall visual scene it is and what kinds of objects it contains.

Inferentialism puts a new spin on this hierarchy, however, by proposing that the function of higher levels is not merely to passively receive inputs from lower levels, but rather to *predict* the signals that these levels will send them. In effect, each level contains a model of the one below it, and this model generates a set of hypotheses or expectations about how this lower level is going to perform. So level $n + 1$ will have a set of expectations about the kind of input that level n is likely to send it in the near future. These predictions percolate back via recurrent (downward) neural connections. If the incoming signal diverges from this expectation, an error signal is generated at level n, and level $n + 1$ will have to adjust its internal model to compensate. This reflects the fact that its hypothesis about level n's activity has been disconfirmed. Bottom-up perceptual signals have a dual role, then: they not only represent features of the environment, but also inform higher levels about the accuracy (or inaccuracy) of their predictions and the models that generate them. Perceptual processing is a cascade involving the (dis)confirmation of increasingly general expectations about present and future events.[6]

To get a sense for how hierarchical predictive models of perception work, consider an example: binocular rivalry (Hohwy, Roepstorff, & Friston, 2008). This phenomenon occurs when two wildly divergent images are presented to each eye independently. Suppose we present a picture of a

---

[6] Sorting out how these sorts of processes relate to the forms of cognitive penetrability discussed in Section 3.5.2 is a tricky issue. Attentional processes and those involved in establishing a "perceptual set" are usually not regarded as incompatible with the encapsulation of perception, but some predictive models go further than this. For discussion, see Clark (2013) and the following commentaries.

house to one eye and a face to the other. This can be achieved by using a stereoscope to separate out the images. What would one perceive in this circumstance – perhaps a wavering half-face/half-house? As it turns out, most participants report experiencing either a whole face or a whole house, with occasional switching back and forth between them. From time to time a mashed-up hybrid figure may appear, but this is the exception. The visual system seems to decide to treat one image as dominant, and ignore the other almost entirely.

Predictive models explain these results by supposing that there is a set of high-level expectations that the world contains faces and houses, but nothing that is (or looks like) a mashed-up hybrid of both of them. That would be a very low-probability, and hence extremely surprising, encounter. So the visual system chooses one of the two remaining high-probability alternatives instead; in fact, it alternates between the two, since the available evidence (the sensory input) is evenly balanced between them. Visual processing is not simply driven by the input to take things at face value; rather, the top-down signal drives processing so that the experience it generates is a function of what best *rationalizes* the input.

The same principles are intended to apply to everyday perceptual scenarios as well. Take a simplified example. Imagine you are scanning your eyes from right to left and you encounter a hint of a shape that resembles a lion's tail. That tiny bit of unexpected perceptual evidence percolates upward and, at a relatively high level of visual processing, produces the expectation that there is a lion in front of you. This generates a downward-cascading sequence of expectations at various lower levels, such as that there will be lion legs, a torso, forelegs and paws, and a head crested with a mane. These in turn all involve predictions about the precise spatial and temporal sequence in which these parts will be perceived, and the details of their appearance. Meanwhile, your eyes continue scanning. At each "stage" as they move leftward, low-level detectors make rapid predictions about the inputs that will result from panning a fraction of a degree over, which are then confirmed as the eyes move on. Each segment of the stream of visual input coheres with the low-level predictions concerning how a lion shaped like this would naturally continue.

This is how things work in the error-free case, at least. However, these expectations may fail. Suppose that the next visual segment reveals something shaped and textured not like a lion's torso, but more like the wing and feathers of an eagle. This mismatch would produce a lower-level error signal in visual processing that would percolate up the hierarchy. Not every such error will have far-reaching consequences. If the fur of this lion is just a little bit different from those seen previously, the result might be only a small, local error signal. But sufficiently discrepant low-level evidence such as the presence of a wing and feathers serves to disconfirm the guiding top-level hypothesis that this is a lion, since the probability that something is a lion given that it has eagle wings is effectively zero. It might, though, provide evidence in favor of the new hypothesis that this is a griffin.

What this example illustrates is that on the predictive model of perception, very low-level visual processing involves generating expectations on a fast temporal scale (under a few seconds) and in a restricted region of space (the next visual segment over). Higher levels deal with longer time scales and greater spatial extent, with the most abstract level of processing merely dealing with the kind of entity that is being perceived, without attending to any of the details of its particular shape, orientation, color, and so on. These high-level expectations are a kind of "fantasy" (Hohwy, 2013, p. 54) about what sensory input will be forthcoming. The goal of all of this perceptual activity is to *minimize surprise*: to achieve a state in which (by and large) the internal predictions of how the world will be are matched by how the sensory input says that it in fact is. Ultimately, perceptual representation "emerges in the ongoing predictive activity of the entire hierarchy of prediction error minimization mechanisms" (Hohwy, 2013, p. 54).

There is some evidence that neural populations in visual cortex are sensitive to factors such as surprise. More predictable visual inputs (e.g., regular patterns of motion) result in lowered average activation in V1 relative to unpredictable inputs (Alink, Schwiedrzik, Kohler, Singer, & Muckli, 2010). The hierarchical predictive model would lead us to expect this, because predictable inputs at lower levels should be "dialed down" by higher ones; only those surprising signals that indicate error are allowed to propagate upward. Similar results were found in more specialized neural regions. The fusiform face area has sometimes been conceived of as a simple "face detection" region, but the degree to which it becomes activated seems to depend as well on whether participants are led by the context to *expect* a face (Egner, Monti, & Summerfield, 2010). When faces are surprising, there is greater activation than when they are not, again consistent with the hierarchical predictive model.

Hierarchical predictive models have sometimes been developed as part of a more expansive theory of brain function. An example is Karl Friston's (2005, 2009, 2010; Friston & Stephan, 2007) free energy framework. Free energy is a concept from thermodynamics, but it has mathematical similarities with the notion of prediction error in statistics and probability theory.[7] Thermodynamically, the free energy principle states that the brain, like any other complex self-organizing system, has a tendency to resist disorder. The brain "tries" to stay in a certain narrow range of states that will ensure its continued existence, a tendency referred to as homeostasis. The safe states for the system to occupy are, collectively, low entropy (that is, they have high probability). In other words, biological systems such as the brain strive to remain in relatively *unsurprising* conditions. The mathematics that governs this thermodynamic behavior can be translated into inferentialist terms: to say that the brain tries to minimize its free energy is, roughly, to say that it attempts to minimize surprise, a quantity that is closely related to prediction error. Friston's bold proposal is that the hierarchical predictive model of perception actually applies at *all levels* of neural and cognitive functioning, as a consequence of the mathematics governing biological systems.

The free energy framework is an extremely ambitious attempt to capture all aspects of neural and cognitive functioning using a single, relatively simple type of process, namely the tendency of complex systems to minimize a specific informational quantity, their free energy. Assessing the free energy framework as a grand unified theory of brain functioning is well beyond our present scope, however. Others, such as Hohwy (2013), have followed Friston's lead and proposed that the prediction error minimization principle is an all-purpose tool that can account for action, attention, learning, mental disorders, and other broad types of psychological functioning. Although we have cited some evidence, both psychological and neurobiological, in favor of the predictive model of perception, its extension to other cognitive phenomena remains highly contentious. It is particularly unclear whether "minimizing surprise" in the technical sense developed here is a sufficient explanation of the whole complex range of human behavior, including most

---

[7] Our presentation here is, necessarily, extremely sketchy. Friston's papers provide ample technical details for readers interested in pursuing the mathematics of the free energy theory.

prominently our interest in pursuing projects whose interest lies precisely in the degree to which they surprise us.

6.6 From active to enactive vision

We have been converging on a critique of a standard picture of vision. The fundamentals of this critique were laid out by Churchland, Ramachandran, and Sejnowski (1994). They dubbed the orthodox view of vision "Pure Vision." Pure Vision assumes that the visual world is represented in a maximally detailed fashion at any moment, and that visual processing is exclusively hierarchical and bottom-up. This picture has the imprimatur not just of science, but also of common sense:

> From the vantage point of how things seem to be, there is no denying that at any given moment we seem to see the detailed array of whatever visible features of the world are in front of our eyes. Apparently, the world is there to be seen, and our brains do represent, essentially in all its glory, what is there to be seen. (p. 25)

In this view we can see shades of grand illusionism, as well as a perspective that places the production of experience front and center among the visual system's functions.

But the evidence has called both of these claims into doubt. Churchland, Ramachandran, and Sejnowski argued, along similar lines, that we should replace Pure Vision with an alternative conception of Interactive Vision. On this view, vision is fundamentally conceived of as a system that evolved in part to help facilitate effective action, not merely to present us with an experiential spectacle. It evolved under computational constraints that favor generating "visual semiworlds," or small-scale extractions of information from the environment, rather than all-encompassing representations. Moreover, rather than vision completing its work autonomously before passing information on to motor systems, there is continuous feed-forward of information to these systems, as well as feedback from higher levels of processing from layers that influence visual processing, including motor emulators, proprioceptive and kinesthetic systems, and conceptual regions. Interactive Vision thus denies that seeing is an exclusively bottom-up process. Rather, information spreads out in a range of directions to assist in completing visual tasks. Completing these tasks will rely on much less than a total representation of visual space and visual objects, making computationally cheap minimal representations the natural medium to employ.

A similar visual architecture was proposed by Ballard (1991) under the name "active vision." Active vision emphasizes the fact that mammalian visual systems are embodied and controllable and can engage in behaviors that simplify the computational task of extracting visual information from the world. Everyday seeing involves learning how to effectively reposition one's eyes, head, and body. This contrasts with many early attempts to simulate vision computationally, which attempted to solve visual problems from the standpoint of an immobile, monocular observer with access to all elements of the scene at equal resolution simultaneously. By contrast, systems with gaze control can quickly and effectively change their own view of an object, thus facilitating its rapid recognition. Sometimes the solution to a visual problem is to execute a series of visual behaviors, and the visual system is designed to rely on this ability. Seeing is not something passive or merely receptive, but rather is an activity: it takes place over time, under temporal constraints, and under the guidance of the organism.

We may contrast these approaches as follows:

	Pure Vision	Active Vision
Goal of vision	Produce internal model of the world	Successful guidance of action
Visual representations	Global and highly detailed	Local and sketchy
Visual processing	Bottom-up, hierarchical, autonomous	Recurrent and interactive with higher systems (including conceptual and motor systems)

Of course, these are broad descriptions of two research programs that need to be filled out in greater detail. With respect to the goal of vision, in particular, it is not clear that the two claims made are genuinely in conflict, since one way to guide action successfully may be to model the world internally, especially for complex or longer term actions. The balance of the evidence surveyed here supports an active rather than pure conception of vision.

Some have wanted to go still further than this. As noted in Chapter 5, a number of contemporary approaches to cognition treat it as a phenomenon that occurs not just within the brain, but also in the body and world. Proponents of *enactive* approaches to cognition have argued that psychological processes not only arise out of interactions between organisms and their environment, but also should be located in the interactions among body, brain, and environment. This is especially true for consciousness and perception. Thus Alva Noë, a leading enactivist, says: "Consciousness isn't something that happens inside us; it is something we do, actively in our dynamic interaction with the world" (2009, p. 24). It is not just the emphasis on action here that matters, since as we have seen this is shared with active vision approaches. Enactivism is distinguished by the further claim that the ability to act in the world, and to be acted on in turn, is *required* for consciousness and perception. This implies that perceiving is not just a matter of having the correct brain state. As Noë and O'Regan put it, "vision is not a process in the brain . . . [S]eeing is a skill-based activity of environmental exploration. Visual experience is not something that happens in individuals. It is something they *do*" (2002, p. 469).

Enactivists don't deny that a great deal happens in the brain during conscious perception; they simply assert that this activity is not sufficient for being in a perceptual state. Two structurally similar brains that were given similar stimulation would not necessarily have the same experience – it depends on how those brains are situated vis-à-vis their bodies and the world. This joint emphasis on embodiment and the environment distinguishes enactivism from mere activism. Active vision theorists hold that although vision is for guiding actions, and often depends on our being able to carry these actions out, it is not in any way *constituted* by these actions, or the environment that they relate us to. Vision may be a process that inherently involves interfacing with motor systems, but it remains a resolutely intracranial process, taking place exclusively within the nervous system.

The arguments for enactivism begin by pointing out that perceptual systems are tightly coupled to their environments. By moving around in one's environment, a subject learns to master a set of sensorimotor contingencies: one learns that moving *this* way causes *this* perceptual change, and moving *that* way causes another perceptual change. One thereby stores *sensorimotor knowledge* (SMK) of a vast array of such contingencies, which the system must integrate into its capacity to rationally guide action. Knowledgeable perceivers exercise these newly acquired capacities in actual online guidance in cases of situated cognition. This counts as a level of "basic perceptual sensitivity" to the world (Noë & O'Regan, 2002, p. 570). The argument here conforms to the familiar pattern: X is causally coupled to Y, and in virtue of this coupling, X navigates its environment; hence, the processes involved in the coupling constitute perceiving.

This general style of causal coupling argument has been criticized at length in Chapter 5 (see especially Section 5.4.2). Here we focus on the evidence for enactivism. The thesis has two forms. On *strong enactivism*, there is no perception without action – every occurrent perceptual process requires a concurrent act. As Noë puts it: "Perceptual awareness . . . is a state of interactive engagement with the world, not a state of picture-making" (2001, p. 51). This is one reading of the claim that perceptual processes are constituted by certain kinds of actions. On *weak enactivism*, it is only the exercise of sensorimotor knowledge derived from active exploration that is required for perception. For a representative statement, consider this by O'Regan and Noë: "We shall say that perceivers have sensations in a particular sense modality, when they *exercise their mastery of the sensorimotor laws* that govern the relation between possible actions and the resulting changes in incoming information in that sense modality" (2001b, p. 82). This maintains a strong connection between action and perception, because the knowledge of various sensory contingencies is acquired only through past action, but it does not require ongoing, occurrent action to constitute each perceptual episode.

Strong enactivism is challenged by a cluster of clinical examples: patients with locked-in syndrome, experimentally immobilized subjects, and inadequately anesthetized surgical patients (Aizawa, 2010). In all of these, there is little or no ongoing activity, yet conscious experience of one form or another seems preserved. Patients with locked-in syndrome often cannot move anything except their eyes, and even this final bit of function is eventually lost. However, this is enough function to allow them to communicate, and the reports they give are consistent with possession of conscious perceptual experiences.

In some studies this can be simulated, for example by administration of an immobilizing drug that affects the whole body except for one arm, thanks to the application of a tourniquet (Topulos, Lansing, & Banzett, 1993). The participants in this study were able, using their free arm, to report on their experiences, including many that were distressing or uncomfortable, such as the placement of an endotracheal tube. Although some movement in the free arm was possible, their conscious experience was widespread, normal, and unconnected with the sensorimotor contingencies having to do with that arm in particular. Finally, some patients who undergo surgery fail to be completely anesthetized, despite being unable to move due to the paralytic drugs that are also administered. In these horrible, and distressingly frequent, scenarios, patients have reported hearing sounds and voices, having visual perceptions, being touched, and even feeling moderate to severe pain. Often these recollections are corroborated by surgical staff present in the operating room.

There are various moves that strong enactivists might make to avoid these problematic cases. They might argue that some degree of residual motion is always present, and thus some form of active support for consciousness, but this is not true in the most extreme locked-in patients – and in any case, its relevance to the particular sensations experienced remains obscure. Or they might argue that consciousness in these cases is present, but minimal, abnormal, or highly disturbed. The experience of these patients may be abnormal, although any such alterations would seem to be fairly subtle and would need to be tested for specifically, but experience itself is undeniably present. This appears to flatly contradict the claim that perception is constituted by action of any ordinary overt kind.

On weak enactivism, overt action is not required for perception, only the employment of some form of sensorimotor knowledge, particularly knowledge of various contingencies holding between possible movements that could be made and perceptual states that would arise if they were. Although SMK is typically employed in exploration of the perceptual world, it can also be tapped in other contexts, which helps to account for why our perception of the world has some of its uniquely rich structure even when we are not engaged in these explorations. For example, Noë (2001) suggests that even when only part of an object is visible, we have the residual sense that the entire thing is somehow perceptually present to us. The phenomenological claim here is contestable, and we are not sure it is quite apt to say that objects are experienced as wholly perceptually present. The explanatory claim being made is that either actual exploratory action or skill-based knowledge of the results of such action explains the perceptual phenomenon in question.

The "knowledge" that we have when we possess SMK is sometimes described as a set of conditional propositions of this sort: if *this* type of act is performed, then *that* type of perception will result. It is also described as a kind of skill or expertise; this is often considered to depend on having knowledge-how. To be able to find your way perceptually around a surface or object is to know how to act on it in order to bring into view the feature that is currently relevant. The knowledge requirement faces several possible challenges. One comes from the cognitive impenetrability of various types of perceptual illusions. Knowing that you are subject to an illusion, even knowing a great deal about its mechanics and origins, does not make the illusion disappear. We know how to verify the length of the lines in the Müller-Lyer illusion; we also know how to scrutinize the Poggendorff illusion or the Herman grid illusion in any amount of detail we wish; but these illusions persist despite this knowledge.

Tying perception to the possession of knowledge also seems too strong. Indeed, it is not just possession that is required, but something stronger, namely *mastery*: "The sensation of red is the exercise of our mastery of the way red behaves as we do things" (O'Regan & Noë, 2001b, p. 85). This implies that we cannot even sense the presence of redness unless we have the relevant kind of mastery, a relatively sophisticated-seeming grasp of how surfaces behave under differing conditions of illumination, proximity, manipulation, and so on. Yet it also seems plausible to say that cognitively naïve subjects can readily sense redness – it is a perceptual capacity that psychologists frequently ascribe to young infants and animals, for example. However, according to weak enactivism, in that first moment when a child opens her eyes to receive the light from a red rattle, she does not yet sense its redness. Rather, she needs to master the relevant sensorimotor contingencies before this cognitive state is available to her. Before this, it is unclear whether she can be described as having any kind of sensations at all. Perhaps, prior to learning the right SMK, she senses and is conscious of nothing.

Whether this is plausible or not depends on exactly how much knowledge is needed for sensation to dawn, and how rapidly it may be acquired. One response would be to deflate the sophistication of the SMK itself, although this does not sit well with the concurrent emphasis on "mastery." Some knowledge might be so trivial as to be mastered at a glance, so to speak. Weak enactivists also need to say something about how this type of learning might work if there are no pre-existing sensory states that can be drawn on to guide the relevant learning processes. How does one learn a contingent relationship between movements and perceptions if one does not have any antecedent perceptions to work from?

Both forms of enactivism face difficulties: strong enactivism implausibly requires real bodily acts for perception, and weak enactivism must be squared with the cognitive impenetrability of perceptual illusions and the fact that perceiving seems to be possible in the absence of knowledge. A more modest active vision framework requires neither of these things, and it also squares more satisfyingly with the existing empirical evidence than does the pure vision framework. Theorizing about vision is likely to find its greatest successes when it forges a path between the two extreme poles of disembodied purity and embodied action.

6.7 Conclusions

The perspective we have sketched here is one in which vision, and perception generally, is an active enterprise, geared toward producing successful actions, often using no more resources than necessary for the job. Parts of it, such as the dorsal stream, are even spun off to be specialized for this purpose. Even in the parts of visual processing that contribute to reasoning and consciousness, the picture of the world that is formed comprises a handful of partial snapshots rather than a smooth, continuous, and rich panorama. These visual mechanisms contribute to other capacities such as our ability to form and manipulate imagery, although we have not taken a stand on the means by which it does so. Finally, picking up one of our themes from Chapter 5, we have argued that the slide into enactivism should be resisted. Vision is involved in exploring and acting on the world, but it is not constituted by such acts.

7   Attention and consciousness

7.1 The slipperiness of experience

Consciousness and attention are two of the most vexing, hard-to-define aspects of mentality. No wonder, then, that even the most brilliant and articulate theorists, such as William James, are reduced to merely gesturing at them, or to seeming platitudes ("Every one knows what attention is").[1] Our everyday language for describing experience seems impoverished compared to the richness and dynamic pulse of the thing itself. Thoughts and intentions, daydreams and vivid bursts of emotion, coils and snippets of language, sights, aches, and the whole of the sensory world: these conscious experiences are always simply there, like a constant buzz. Take them away and, as Descartes astutely observed, it is hard to see what would be left of our minds as we know them.

Attention, by contrast, is not merely there, but also there for us. It can be commanded, albeit sometimes unwillingly. Notice the shape of someone's hand. Now, without shifting your gaze, notice its color and the texture of their skin. Notice the web of tiny lines, the fine hairs, any nicks or scars. Focus on just one of them. We have no trouble focusing our attention in these ways. In doing so, the character of our conscious experience shifts also. Of course, attention can also be dragged away against our will, by the intrusive ping of a text message or a nagging itch. When this happens, our train of conscious thought is disrupted and the source of our distraction takes center stage. Here we chronicle some contemporary ways of modeling attention and explore the possibility that these links between attention and consciousness

---

[1] We say "seeming" platitudes, because James does go on to offer a more substantial account of what attention does. And it is not clear that our contemporary models do much better in escaping their metaphorical roots (Fernandez-Duque & Johnson, 1999).

are no coincidence but rather evidence for a deep theoretical connection between the two. In this way, perhaps two elusive mental phenomena can be grasped at once.

7.2 Theories of attention

One way to approach the problem of defining attention is to treat it as a partially theoretical term. Its meaning can then be extracted from the theories that psychologists have built to account for attentional phenomena.[2]

7.2.1 Filtering theories

Not long after the invention of the mathematical theory of information (Shannon & Weaver, 1949), psychologists started thinking of the mind itself as an information processor. Information was conceived as an abstract commodity that could flow through communication channels such as telephone wires or neurons. Perceiving, thinking, attention, and other psychological states were quickly reconceived along these lines as information-processing states of the mind or brain.

Applying concepts from information theory, Cherry (1953) devised an influential experiment resembling the phenomenon of a cocktail party, the so-called dichotic listening task. A participant hears different soundtracks played in each ear, and investigators determine how much information they are able to glean from each channel. Confident multitaskers might predict that they are perfectly good at absorbing information from multiple sources at once. These participants were asked to shadow (repeat out loud) the information coming into one of the two channels. When they could accurately repeat the information on that channel, this ensured that their full attention was being given to the information in that channel. After presenting the stimuli to both ears, Cherry tested to see how much information participants retained from the nonshadowed channel.

---

[2] This also leaves it open that attention might be more than one thing. Our overview here centers mostly on the literature in selective attention; for more on attention in general, see Pashler (1998).

Depressingly for self-styled multitaskers, participants were able to report almost nothing of the information from the other ear.[3] They knew they heard a voice speaking, and whether it was a man or woman, but they could not tell any of the content of the message or even what language the person was speaking. This proved to be the case even for words repeated many times. The interesting question is: why are people so poor at retaining the information presented to the nonattended channel?

To account for Cherry's results, Donald Broadbent (1958) introduced the *filter theory* of attention. Continuing in the information-processing framework, Broadbent suggested that sensory channels process incoming signals in a linear sequence of stages. The first stage is a preliminary scan of data in which very basic physical properties of the stimulus are extracted. These include basic elements such as the pitch and location of sounds. At the next stage the information is filtered, and the channel selected for attention is the one containing the information most promising for future processing. This is a limited-capacity process that extracts more abstract information such as the meaning and import of the incoming message.

On Broadbent's model, all perceptual information goes through these stages and is filtered prior to more extensive second-stage analysis and processing. Crucial to the filter theory and its explanation of why so little information is processed from the nonshadowed channel is the claim that the most intensive processing is allowed to go on only in the channel selected by the filter mechanism. Also important is the notion that once the filter selects one channel for intensive processing, the filter limits the processing of information from the other channel.

Because information is processed only at a relatively superficial level before being filtered by attention, this is known as an *early selection* model. Challenges to Broadbent's theory focused on finding effects of more abstract content presented in the unattended channel. Peters (1954) found that in dichotic listening experiments, if a message in the unattended ear is similar in content to that in the attended, it is more distracting than if it is dissimilar. So some processing of the unattended signal must be going on above the level that

---

[3] A caveat: this situation may not really be a good match for everyday multitasking scenarios. Whether performing multiple tasks at once results in a performance hit may depend on the timing of the tasks relative to one another and whether this timing is within the person's control (Pashler, Kang, & Ip, 2013).

Broadbent's theory would predict. Moray (1959) discovered that playing a person's name in the unattended channel draws attention to that channel. The explanation was that information about the participant has a higher priority or relevance than the information in the other channel, thereby drawing attention. These kinds of data challenge Broadbent's strict "filter" theory. There is more going on in the unattended channel than just a filtering of information.

Anne Treisman (1960) strengthened the case against Broadbent with a modification of the dichotic listening paradigm. In the shadowed ear was played a coherent story. In the nonshadowed ear was played a random string of words. Then, at some point, the channels were switched. What should happen? Let E1 stand for the channel with the coherent story and E2 the channel with the string of unrelated words. On the filter theory it seems that the prediction is that once the second stage of analysis has been reached, the filtering should be in place favoring channel E1 where the coherent story is being played. Switching to channel E2 should not focus attention on that channel because it has been "tuned out" by the filter. Treisman found that what actually happens is participants begin shadowing the coherent message now in channel E2 and stop tracking what is happening in E1. In order to make the switch, they had to have begun processing the information from the "filtered" channel.

Surveying these and other results, Deutsch and Deutsch (1963) concluded that "a message will reach the same perceptual and discriminatory mechanism whether attention is paid to it or not; and such information is then grouped or segregated by these mechanisms" (p. 83). They did not offer an explanation of how grouping takes place or by what rules, but suggested that all incoming signals must be rated on relative import weighted against other incoming signals. It is only at this point that attention can filter the information.

This led to the advent of *late-selection* theories, which propose that all information in all channels is processed in parallel to the highest and most abstract levels before being chosen for filtering. Attention and selection occur after perceptual inputs have activated semantic information in long-term memory (Norman, 1968). The debate between the early- and late-selection approaches concerns how much processing of incoming stimuli happens as part of the preattentional phase, which determines the effects that unattended stimuli can have on the rest of cognition.

7.2.2 Limited capacity and processing load theories

Over the years an accumulating body of conflicting results has made the early/late debate hard to settle.[4] Findings such as those just described led to rejection of simple filtering theories and to the alternative hypothesis that there are limited cognitive resources available for conscious attention and speculations about the principles for allocation of those resources. Within the limited resource approach, the appearance of early and late selection effects flows from the demands of different experimental tasks (Kahneman & Treisman, 1984).

Kahneman (1973) initially developed the idea that a limited pool of resources is available for attention. If the processing from multiple streams is not particularly taxing, people can allocate those resources to more than one stream. One might be able to watch a sporting event on television and read the scores that scroll across the bottom of the screen simultaneously with little difficulty. However, if one has to apply more effort to processing, then one may be unable to process two streams simultaneously. For example, trying to watch the game on ESPN while solving logic problem sets might prove much more challenging. So Kahneman's account does allow some significant semantic processing beyond where Broadbent's second-stage filter would have blocked such processing.

Nilli Lavie developed this context-sensitivity proposal into the centerpiece of the *load theory* of selective attention (Lavie & Tsal, 1994; Lavie, 1995, 2000). On this view, perceptual systems have an intrinsically limited capacity to process information. Before this capacity is reached, all incoming information is processed automatically to the highest degree possible. This assumption is in line with late selection theory. However, when this capacity is met or exceeded by the demands of the task, attention steps in to select information for further processing. This conforms to what early selection theory would predict. In the sorts of high-load conditions that were characteristic of many early selection tasks, the task difficulty makes filtering necessary. In lower demand tasks, there is a greater pool of resources to dedicate to processing multiple streams of information. Therefore, incoming information receives greater elaboration, as late selection predicts.

---

[4] See Driver (2001) for a review and Allport (1993) for criticisms of many theoretical presuppositions behind the debate itself.

To see how this works, consider a study by Lavie and Cox (1997). They asked participants to focus on the center of a visual display and signal the presence of a target letter. At the same time as the target was displayed, a distractor letter was flashed in the periphery of the display. The distractor was neutral, congruent, or incongruent with the target. Further, the target letter was either easy to pick out (appearing alone) or hard to pick out (surrounded by many easily confusable letters). In the easy condition, which is assumed to be one where perceptual load is light, participants were slower to report the presence of the target letter when it was accompanied by an incongruent distractor. In the hard condition (high load), however, they were just as fast to signal the target in both congruent and incongruent conditions. So it appears that *increasing* the perceptual load of a task makes it *easier* to ignore distractors. The explanation is that distractors do not appear to be processed when the task itself consumes more available resources. Where the task is resource-light, however, distracting stimuli intrude and slow down processing. This is consistent with the load theory's predictions.[5]

7.2.3 Spotlight theories

As we noted, attention is sometimes under voluntary control. It seems we can intentionally focus it as if shining a light on a location. This gives rise to the common metaphor of the attentional spotlight. At the same time, attention can be captured and oriented toward a target independently of our intending to direct it that way. The capture and orienting of attention have been studied extensively using the spatial cuing paradigm, an experimental setup popularized by Michael Posner. The task is similar to the one the eye doctor uses to test for loss of peripheral vision. A participant focuses on a fixation point on a screen. A cue is flashed some distance from the fixation point. Cues can be either direct markers of place or symbolic pointers to other places (e.g., an arrow). Some proportion of these cues are valid, others are invalid; a typical ratio might be 70% to 30%. After the cue presentation, the target itself is displayed either in the cued location or elsewhere in the display. The participant then presses a button recording having seen the target stimulus.

---

[5] For an up-to-date review of the ways in which different sorts of load and potentially interfering properties can affect processing, see Lavie (2005).

Posner and colleagues found that the presence of a valid cue will both speed up responses and increase accuracy in detecting the target (Posner, Snyder, & Davidson, 1980). These studies show that attention can be covertly directed by cues that are relevant to the task at hand, and that attention can be shifted in space independently of eye movements (Posner, 1980). You can test this yourself outside the lab. While having dinner with a friend, try to attend to someone's ludicrous hairstyle bobbing about elsewhere in your field of vision, or surreptitiously pay attention to another table's conversation. Both of these things can be accomplished without shifting your eyes or ears, although on the grounds of politeness neither is necessarily recommended.[6]

The finding that attention can be directed independently of physical reorientation gave rise to *attentional spotlight theories*. These are loosely defined by the claim that attention picks out targets for further processing based on restricted regions of space. What falls within the spotlight is selected and processed preferentially; what falls outside of it is at best minimally processed.

Other principles may be added to this basic idea (Cave & Bichot, 1999; Wright & Ward, 1998). A common claim early on was that to shift attention from one target to another requires traversing all of the intermediate points in space (Shepard, 1975). However, later studies have cast doubt on this. If attention is a spotlight, it seems capable of jumping around discretely from region to region (Yantis, 1988). Another recurring question has to do with whether the spotlight is unitary or multiple. There are arguments in favor of true division, meaning that several spatially distinct regions could be attended to simultaneously (Müller, Malinowski, Gruber, & Hillyard, 2003), and those that maintain that attention simply cycles rapidly among these locations, mimicking division through rapid shifting (VanRullen, Carlson, & Cavanagh, 2007). A related question has to do with the shape and size of the spotlight itself. Is it narrowly focused, or can it be distributed more broadly? LaBerge (1983) showed that narrow focus (on a single letter) and broad focus (on a whole word) are equally possible, though the question of whether there are costs to a wider spotlight remains open (Castiello & Umiltà, 1990).

There are also issues here having to do with the nature of the targets of attention. The spotlight model strongly implies that attention primarily selects *locations* or regions of space as its targets. Anything at that location

---

[6] For a review of work on covert attention, see Carrasco (2011).

would be attended and processed equally. Two alternative perspectives are that the main targets of attention are *objects* and *features* of objects. In favor of the location view, Tsal and Lavie (1988) found that when participants were asked to search for a target and then report all of the stimuli from the display that they could recall, they tended to report those that were closer to the target rather than those that merely shared features with the target. However, Duncan (1984) found evidence for object-based attention by presenting participants with two objects that overlapped with each other and asking them to report on their features. Switching to a different object imposed significant costs over reporting on multiple dimensions of a single object. And the Stroop effect (see Chapter 1) suggests that we may selectively attend, with difficulty, to the spoken pronunciation or the written color of a single word (Polk, Drake, Jonides, Smith, & Smith, 2008). This implies more flexibility than a purely spatial spotlight would predict.

7.2.4 The function of attention

Attention can be modeled as a filter on channels of information, as a limited resource that is allocated based on task demands, and as a spotlight that selects targets for further processing. What one thinks attention *is* will depend heavily on the experimental paradigm being used to investigate it. These conceptions have in common that they all treat attention as a process of *selection* among possible sources of information, a way to reduce the incoming perceptual signals to a cognitively manageable set. But this may still leave the need for attention slightly puzzling. The brain has massive parallel processing capacity. It constantly carries out innumerable cognitive tasks at once. Why should there be a need for a mechanism to reduce the complexity of the perceived situation in this way?

This mechanism may arise from the need to constrain *actions* in the appropriate way. At any point, the environment offers many objects for us to act on, and many possible ways to act on them. Consider the situation when one is faced with a table at the bar cluttered with glasses and snacks. One of these beers is yours, as is one of the many plates of nachos. All of them activate some mild tendency to action (eating or drinking). But these tendencies cannot all be acted on at the same time: this would result in attempting to drink from every glass and eat from every plate, with both hands at once. In a nutshell, "The problem is how to avoid the behavioral chaos that would result from an attempt to simultaneously perform all possible actions for which sufficient causes exist" (Neumann, 1987, p. 374).

The philosopher Wayne Wu (2011a) refers to this as the "Many-Many Problem": there are many possible behavioral inputs that a person can respond to at a time, and many possible outputs they can make in response. The need for actions to flow through a single body implies that the channels that control actions must be constrained somehow. By giving priority to one pathway, such mechanisms prevent other automatic response pathways from gaining control of behavior. Theories of selective attention require that there be an inhibitory function of consciousness, blocking the effects of information not selected for processing (Shallice, 1972; Tipper, 1992). In other words, successful action depends on a process of selection and inhibition. Attention itself is such a process, as we have seen. Hence it is nearly irresistible to conclude that the function of attention is the selection of targets for the purposes of action.

The *selection-for-action* theory of attention has gained prominence in recent years, among both psychologists (Allport, 1987; Hommel, 2010; Hommel, Müsseler, Aschersleben, & Prinz, 2001; Neumann, 1987; Norman & Shallice, 1986; Tipper, Howard, & Houghton, 1998) and philosophers (Wu, 2011a, 2011b, 2014).[7] On this view, the need to discard certain inputs comes not from any particular inherent capacity limitations in the brain's perceptual or cognitive systems themselves, but rather from the practical demands of control. Attention is the cognitive process of ensuring that situationally relevant inputs are paired with appropriate outputs in order to achieve the subject's most important goals.

This view has some claim to be a natural generalization of the standard models in the literature on selective attention. Even so, it requires some adjustments (Wu, 2014). For instance, sometimes we attend to something not to act immediately on it, but merely to think about it further. Directed thought of this kind need not lead to any overt behavior at all. A selection-for-action view needs to include both behavioral and *mental* actions. Selecting something for thought is a kind of internal action.

Selection-for-action and other views that identify attention with a type of functional process have been criticized by Mole (2011), who argues that it is

---

[7] For many contemporary viewpoints from across disciplines, see Mole, Smithies, and Wu (2011).

not *attending* that is the fundamental notion here, but rather *doing something attentively*. Paying attention (or attentiveness) is a manner of doing something, typically expressed adverbially. There is no such separate act as "attending." Mole develops a sophisticated position on which attentive doing involves the coordinated use of a whole ensemble of cognitive resources that he dubs "cognitive unison." Although more could be said on the debate between process theories and adverbial theories, we will have to leave the issue here.

7.3 Philosophical accounts of consciousness

7.3.1 Concepts of consciousness

The current study of consciousness is subdivided into a set of issues that (for better or worse) come with commonly recognized labels.[8] Consciousness can be the property of a whole person, as when one awakens from sleep or from anesthesia and regains consciousness, or falls into a drunken stupor and loses it. In this case, one is talking about a property of the person, namely whether they are alert and responsive to sensory input. Such a property is termed *creature consciousness*.

We might also ask whether a person was conscious *of* something. This is a *transitive* notion: Was she aware of his infidelity? Did he notice that his car scraped yours? Did the cat sense the opening of the tuna can? In such cases, we want to know whether there is some state of a person or creature that makes them aware of something in their environment.

The term "conscious" may also be used *intransitively* to talk not about the person, but rather about the particular cognitive state that they are in. The question is whether that state itself is something that is conscious. Take an example. During sleepwalking, one's eyes may be open and one may in some sense "see," but we would not regard the seeing as a conscious state of mind in the sleepwalker. The person is responding to visual input, but this visual processing is not itself conscious. By contrast, in a standard case of conscious perception (say, during a minor car accident), one has conscious visual, auditory, and tactile sensations of events (the blur of the oncoming vehicle, the crash of the impact, the bang of the airbag deploying). Not only do these perceptual states make one transitively conscious of the events of the accident, but also they themselves count as conscious states of the person. The experiences are intransitively conscious states, and through having them the person

[8] Our initial taxonomy here follows David Rosenthal's (1997).

may become transitively conscious of the sequence of events involved in the accident.

Following Ned Block (1995/1997), a further distinction can be made between *access* and *phenomenal* consciousness (A-consciousness and P-consciousness). Some state is A-conscious, in Block's words, if "it is poised for direct control of thought and action ... if it is poised for free use in reasoning and for direct 'rational' control of action and speech" (p. 382). Such states are often ones that a person can report on, though Block ultimately gives this condition little weight. A-conscious states are available for global use, which situates them at a central location within cognitive architecture, where they can guide online reasoning and planning.

P-consciousness is more elusive, but philosophers have developed elaborate ways of gesturing toward it. P-consciousness is "experience," specifically the sort of state that has a "what it's like" character (Farrell, 1950; Nagel, 1974). What it is like to smell turpentine is different from what it is like to smell acrylic paint, as comparing the two experiences reveals. Not every sensory registration automatically counts as P-conscious. Peripheral registration can occur without experience, as when a pin is driven into a finger that has been injected with a local anesthetic. The nociceptors register the damage, but no pain results. And visual stimuli flashed too fast for us to experience can be registered and have effects on behavior. By contrast, when we are P-conscious of the smell of burnt toast or the taste of coffee, there is a rich qualitative nature to such conscious experiences. Someone suffering from anosmia (loss of olfaction) can experience neither. The qualitative natures of such experiences are sometimes referred to as the "qualia" of conscious experience.

It should be clear that P-conscious states are intransitively conscious states. An (intransitively) conscious perception of the taste of coffee will be P-conscious. These two notions amount to the same thing. And it is this type of consciousness that philosophers have found most puzzling. What is the explanation of where the phenomenally conscious states come from? Is P-consciousness a complex neurophysiological property? Is it explained functionally or representationally, in information-processing terms? Explaining P-consciousness has come to be known as the "hard problem" of consciousness (Chalmers, 1996).[9]

[9] However, this term is wildly contentious. For fierce criticism of any overly simple division of problems into "easy" and "hard," see Churchland (1996) and Dennett (1996, 2001).

7.3.2 Gaps and mysteries

Before turning to positive theories, we should clear away some skeptical accounts that claim this is the sort of question that we simply cannot answer. "Mysterians" say that there is no way for human beings to achieve a satisfactory cognitive or explanatory grasp of the relation between P-consciousness and the brain. Colin McGinn (1989, 1999) exemplifies this mysterian point of view. McGinn is not a metaphysical dualist. He believes that there is a naturalistic property that accounts for consciousness in the brain, but "we are cut off by our very cognitive constitution from achieving a conception of that natural property of the brain (or of consciousness) that accounts for the psychophysical link" (1989, p. 350). He calls this being "cognitively closed" with respect to that property.

Let's call the property that links the brain and phenomenal consciousness M (for *Mediator*). M is whatever relates complex neural processes to conscious experience. To understand where P-consciousness comes from requires understanding the nature of M. But why might we be barred from ever gaining such understanding?

McGinn offers a dilemma. Either we must know about M through (1) introspective reflection on our own P-conscious states, or else we must know it through (2) the third-person methods of neuroscience. Against the first possibility, we cannot tell by introspection alone what property links P-consciousness and the brain. Even at its very best, introspection only tells us about P-consciousness itself, not in any direct way about its physical basis.

Against the second possibility, McGinn maintains that neuroscience cannot illuminate M either. Neuroscience, he says, ultimately tells us only about the spatial arrangement of states of the brain. But consciousness does not have spatial subparts. It simply does not make sense to talk about the spatial division of conscious experiences.[10] So information from neuroscience cannot help us to understand consciousness, because there is no "fit" between the kinds of structure displayed by the two relata. Further, we cannot grasp the nature of the relation M by an inference to the best explanation either, since any such inference made on the basis of neuroscientific evidence would necessarily only be able to introduce yet another purely neurobiological (i.e.,

[10] This idea has a Cartesian pedigree, since one of Descartes' own arguments for dualism was the alleged indivisibility of mental states as opposed (he thought) to the infinite divisibility of matter.

physical, nonconscious) property. And yet we know that M is fundamentally a kind of *mapping* between neurobiology and consciousness. Trying to understand the relation while only considering one side of it is doomed to failure.

As is so often true of philosophical dilemmas, McGinn's fails to consider all of the relevant possibilities. Take the claim that consciousness lacks spatial structure. Although we are not sure whether this is true, even if it were, we could still systematically map conscious states onto neural states. All that this kind of mapping requires is that the relevant structure in each domain be preserved, not that precisely the same elements and relations be present within each one.

As work by Austen Clark shows, the domain of color provides a nice example (Clark, 2000). Color space is organized by what sorts of hue combinations are possible and impossible, which hues are "warm" and "cool," and other similarity relations within the domain, such as which hues capture others. These provide a rich set of relations within the domain of sensory qualities. An explanation of why color experience has the qualities it does will involve finding neural states and processes that exhibit a similar set of relations. These physiological states may have properties, such as neural base firing rate or density of interregion connectivity, that are not shared by the space of color qualities themselves. But this is irrelevant to whether we have a successful explanatory mapping; here, only the common structure counts.

McGinn thinks that the usual scientific practice of using inference to the best explanation is no use here, because neuroscience provides only the third-person perspective, not the first-person perspective of consciousness. Just looking in the brain for some neurophysiological property is not going to tell one what consciousness is. But no one seriously proposes doing this. Rather, we begin with as much knowledge as we can gather concerning *both* sides of the relation, and pin it down by working our way inward. Thus, in the color space example, we gather all sorts of information – including introspective judgments, psychophysical measurements, and neurophysiological studies – and assemble a picture of the relation M by attempting to correlate them with each other systematically. McGinn's dilemma ignores the fact that bringing all of this evidence to bear at once puts us in a vastly stronger epistemic position. As discussed in Chapter 2, the method of discovering cross-domain relations depends on simultaneous modeling of the internal organization of each domain (here, the qualitative and the neural) and of their interrelations.

Another mysterian view is Joe Levine's (1983, 2001) explanatory gap argument. Levine's reasoning turns on a contrast between two different types of identity statements in science. If we suppose that P-conscious states are just states of the brain, then one could hold out hope in the future to be able to understand how the brain yields mental states and properties associated with identity statements of the form "pain = neural firing in the posterior insular cortex."[11] Levine contrasts this sort of identity statement with other well-known identity statements from science such as "heat = mean molecular kinetic energy." He maintains that we might understand and be able to explain what heat is by understanding the motion of molecules in a gas and how their motion might actually be heat. Thanks to this microstructural explanation, there is no gap here. We understand the mechanism by which heat in a gas is generated. It is generated in virtue of the motion of the molecules in the gas. As the kinetic energy of the molecules varies, so varies the heat in the gas. If we were to imagine an absence of molecular motion in the gas, we would understand an absence of heat in the gas to follow necessarily.

But he claims this understanding is unavailable in the identification of any qualitative state with neural events because we can *imagine* the possibility of someone's being in pain but there being (for instance) no posterior insular activation (PIA) occurring. If the occurrence of PIA truly explained the occurrence of pain, he thinks, we should not be able to imagine the former without the latter. A proper explanation shows in some way why the explanans makes the explanandum inevitable. Because this sense of inevitability is missing, we can dissociate the two in thought, leading to the explanatory gap.

The arguments of both McGinn and Levine may, in the end, amount to rubbing the noses of cognitive neuroscientists in the fact that we do not yet understand how neural activity produces painful experiences in humans. As a claim about the limits of our present understanding, this is fair enough. But we think that the gap itself can be explained, and ultimately perhaps overcome.

---

[11] Pain is actually so complicated that simple identity statements are impossible to come by. The traditional philosopher's example here involves identifying pain with "C-fiber firings." C-fibers are one type of sensory afferent that carries nociceptive information, but they are not part of the central "neuromatrix" that realizes the affective and sensory qualities of pain. Insular activation itself is neither necessary nor sufficient for experiencing pain. For more detail, see Aydede (2006) and Hardcastle (1999).

One possibility that has gained traction recently is that the explanatory gap might arise from the fact that we use different cognitive systems to think about conscious versus nonconscious systems in the physical world (Bloom, 2004; Fiala, Arico, & Nichols, 2011; Papineau, 2011; Robbins & Jack, 2006). When considering a human being, we can think about them either as a mechanistically described physical object, or else as a bearer of consciousness – a subjective locus of experience. But these two understandings are connected with distinct perspectives on the same object, and these may at times be in competition with each other. Paul Bloom (2004) calls this our "intuitive dualism," and Robbins and Jack (2006) capture it by distinguishing between the mechanistic stance and the phenomenal stance.[12]

The idea here is that the cognitive system that we use for understanding the movements of merely physical objects and simple machines may be partially independent of the system that we use for ascribing emotions, pains, and other conscious experiences. To understand or attribute a subjective experience of pain to someone, we may imaginatively project ourselves into their shoes, mimicking their experience. But to model their neurophysiological state we may use a different form of reasoning grounded in causal understanding. Normally, when we are interpreting people's behavior, we treat them as experiencing subjects. But when we engage in scientific reasoning, we also need to think of them as physical mechanisms. If mechanistic understanding can come apart from the ascription of consciousness, the *feeling* of an explanatory gap may arise as a by-product of the fact that we do not have any natural way of connecting these partially independent cognitive systems within our own minds.

On this account, the explanatory gap is a perfectly real, if accidental, consequence of our cognitive architecture. Overcoming it will require the construction of systematic, empirically supported mappings between the domain of P-conscious states and physical states. We turn now to some philosophical proposals about how this might be done.

7.3.3 Representational theories

Sense perception is a natural starting point for building a theory of consciousness. Perceptual systems, as we defined them in Section 6.1, are representational systems that have dedicated sets of receptors, particular distal

---

[12] This "stance" talk derives from Dennett's (1989) influential notion of the intentional stance.

properties that they function to detect, and distinctive phenomenological qualities. That is, they have as a matter of biological design the function of producing representations of properties in the world. Perhaps this is all (or *almost* all) that consciousness requires. This proposal forms the core of *representational theories* of consciousness.

Fred Dretske's view provides a nice example. Dretske (1993, 1995) claims that experiences may be identified with sensory states – that is, those that have the systematic function of indicating properties in the environment. So the outputs of sensory systems are conscious representations. When vision produces a representation of the look of the objects in one's surroundings, or olfaction delivers information about the intensity and character of a passing smell, those representations are conscious, and the sensory qualities of experience are just those that our sensory systems have the natural function of detecting. An experience of an object x is conscious "because, being a sort of representation, it makes one aware of the properties (of x) and objects (x itself) of which it is a (sensory) representation" (1993, p. 280). States are (intransitively) conscious when they function to make a person (transitively) conscious of something.

The elegance of this identification, however, is challenged by phenomena involving unconscious perceptual states. In a well-known example by Armstrong (1968), you may be driving for a long distance on "automatic pilot" and then suddenly realize that you have not been paying attention to the road. During this time you nevertheless have changed lanes, maintained (mostly) proper speed, avoided other cars, and so on. Yet the experiences themselves left no trace on your memory, and seemed even at the time to pass in a slight haze before you "came to" and took stock of your surroundings. It seems natural enough to describe this as a case of actions being guided by nonconscious perceptions.

But of course your actions were all along guided by the visual system, which was producing a constant stream of representations of the road. On Dretske's view, it seems these would all have to be conscious. And he endorses this conclusion, claiming that "coming to" amounts not to suddenly gaining conscious experiences of the road but rather merely to noticing something about your own perceptual states (1995, pp. 114–116). Visual representations make one aware of (i.e., *conscious* of) the road independently of whether one is aware of those perceptual states themselves. So for Dretske, one can have conscious experiences that one is *unaware* of, just as the driver on automatic pilot does.

A similar objection to representational views comes from neurological impairments such as blindsight. In patients with blindsight, there is extensive damage to the striate cortex (area V1), resulting in the presence of a large scotoma, or blind region in the person's visual field. Blindsight patients typically report that they can see nothing within this area – or at most, vague hints of sensations. Their conscious experience within the region seems largely or totally extinguished. However, when they are prompted by experimenters to make *guesses* about the content of the blind region, they can be amazingly accurate. They can distinguish between differently colored, oriented, or shaped objects; they can detect their direction of motion and can even point to them (Weiskrantz, 1997). Understandably, they report great surprise at their own accuracy in these cases, since to them it seems as if they have no idea what they are seeing at all. Despite the enormous damage to their early visual pathways, enough subsidiary connections remain to support all of these tasks, suggesting that the visual system is still succeeding in producing some representational outputs and that these can be recruited in behavior.

The blindsight patients report nothing in their visual field, and thus in one perfectly clear sense of the term seem not to be conscious of its contents. Yet as extensive studies show, they have some sort of visual processing going on that can actually guide their actions through the world under the right conditions. Blindsight raises a problem for representational theories that identify conscious experiences with the outputs of perceptual systems, because here the two seem to come apart (Carruthers, 2000, 2005; Pacherie, 2000).

The same point could also be made with neurologically intact subjects. Recall that according to the dominant understanding of how the visual system is organized, there are two major pathways that differ in their functional role (see Section 6.3). The ventral pathway is specialized for identifying objects in the environment, whereas the dorsal pathway is specialized for the visual guidance of actions such as reaching and grasping those objects. The operations of the dorsal visual pathway, though, seem largely unconscious even though they are responsible for the complex control of online behaviors. Even everyday actions may be guided by visual inputs without being guided by visual experience, just as in blindsight.

Representational theorists have responded to these cases by imposing further functional conditions on conscious states. Michael Tye (1995), for example, has proposed that it is only when perceptual states are appropriately *poised* to serve as direct inputs to belief-formation systems that they become conscious. It is not required that a subject actually form beliefs on the basis of those perceptual states, of course, only that they be ready to deliver information to higher conceptual systems. Dretske also endorses a version of this condition (1995, pp. 19–20). Conscious perceptions are those that are waiting in the wings, available to be taken up and consumed by other cognitive systems, especially conceptual thought.

This condition is met by the perceptions of Armstrong's distracted driver: given his visual input, he could at any time form beliefs about the conditions of the road, even if he does not do so. So those perceptions should count as conscious. In the cases of blindsight and action guidance by the dorsal pathway, Tye and Dretske might say that these states are *not* appropriately poised, because in neither case can the visual states that are guiding the responses serve as inputs to beliefs. Although blindsight patients can often guess correctly about what they see, they do not form beliefs about what they see in any sort of direct manner. So their visual states are not properly poised, and hence are not conscious.

7.3.4 Higher-order theories

Suppose, however, that sensory registration can occur without rising to the level of consciousness. The debate so far has centered on exactly what changes when a perceptual state (or a thought) becomes conscious. *Higher-order* theories say that the original percept or thought (call it a level one state, L1) becomes conscious when it becomes the representational target of a second mental state (call this a level two state, L2).[13] The term "higher order" here refers to the fact that a state's being conscious requires that it be *represented by* another state. Unlike on the simple representational theory, the outputs of perceptual systems are not intrinsically conscious; instead, they are conscious only when targeted by the right kind of higher-order state.

Higher-order theories come in at least two forms: *higher-order thought* (HOT) theories and *higher-order perception* (HOP) theories. These differ on the kind of higher-order state that produces consciousness. HOT theories say that L1 becomes conscious when there is another *thought* (L2) directed at it (Rosenthal,

[13] There is a difference between HO theorists who think that L1 must *actually* be the target of L2 and those who think it must be *disposed to be* the target of some L2 or other. We will largely ignore this distinction here; see Carruthers (2000, 2005) for extensive development of a dispositionalist HOT view.

2005; Lau & Rosenthal, 2011). Consider the pressure you are exerting on the seat you are sitting in. All along, your brain has been registering that information somewhere in your perceptual systems. You did not feel as though you were falling to the floor, but as though you were safely supported. But now you are thinking about that feeling, and it has become the target of your current thought. To put it a little pedantically, you might be thinking: *I am currently experiencing such-and-such pressure on my thighs.* Thinking about that experience is what makes it conscious. You are now aware of how it feels: the amount of pressure, whether the seat is hard or soft, and so on. When a perception (or thought) is accompanied by the thought that the subject is having such a perception (or thought), it thereby becomes conscious.

HOT captures one important idea concerning consciousness, namely that a state's being (intransitively) conscious is a matter of someone's being (transitively) conscious of *it*. This makes the crucial link between consciousness and awareness that was missing in representationalist accounts. Much of our ongoing cognitive and perceptual activity lies outside of the reach of our awareness and thus is unconscious. But there is debate over whether this awareness should be unpacked in terms of a cognitively sophisticated notion such as higher-order *thinking*. HOT demands that a conscious creature should be in command of a whole array of mentalistic concepts and be able to deploy them in acts of self-ascription. These concepts are the materials of higher-order thoughts themselves, such as the thought that *I am experiencing pressure on my thigh* or *I am having a visual experience of something red and rectangular*. In order for an L1 state to be the target of an L2 state, it needs to be described as a certain kind of perceptual or cognitive state, and this requires grasping concepts of those sorts of mental states.

This may be too much to ask, however. As we shall see (Chapter 8), understanding of mental states may be a somewhat late-developing skill in human beings, at least relative to the development of basic perceptual abilities. Some mental state attributions are not available until the ages of 3 and 4 years old. If HOT requires that we be able to self-attribute thoughts and experiences in order to be conscious, then consciousness itself may arise surprisingly late in human development.

Similarly, if consciousness requires some grasp of mental state concepts, this will mean that many nonhuman animals will not be conscious at all. Peter Carruthers, for example, argues that it is highly implausible that nonhuman animals have thoughts that take their own experiences as their content. They cannot think about such abstract topics as their own mental lives. Accordingly, they do not consciously experience pain or other qualitative states. Although Carruthers (2005) embraces this conclusion, many others have been sharply critical (Jamieson & Bekoff, 1992). It is unclear how far consciousness extends throughout the natural world, but it seems incredible that it might be restricted to intellectual sophisticates such as humans and possibly a few other primate species.

The demandingness of HOT has motivated a search for other higher-order accounts. Most prominent among these is the higher-order perception (HOP) view (Armstrong, 1968; Lycan, 1987, 1995). HOP resembles HOT with the exception that the consciousness-making higher-order state is a *perception*, not a thought. In Armstrong's formulation, "Introspective consciousness . . . is a perception-like awareness of current states and activities in our own mind" (1981, p. 61). On this view, consciousness arises as a form of "inner sensing": a state (L1) becomes conscious when it is the target of an internal perceptual state (L2).

Perhaps the biggest difference between HOT and HOP is the sophistication of the crucial second state. Perceptual states do not require concepts. Thus, in principle, even an infant could have an inner perception of an ongoing experience and bring it into consciousness, whereas if the higher-order state is a thought and thoughts require concepts, perhaps the infant could not yet conceptualize the experience as such. If the infant lacked the very concept of an experience, it would be unable to have the thought *I'm having an experience of such and such a kind*. HOP thus reduces the conceptual sophistication of conscious states and provides an answer to the problem of demandingness.

That is not to say that it is without problems of its own, however. One objection comes from its fellow travelers in the higher-order ranks. Thus Rosenthal (1997), an archetypal HOT theorist, has objected to HOP views on the grounds that perception is the wrong kind of higher-order relation to appeal to in explaining consciousness. His grounds for thinking this are that perceptual states always involve the occurrence of some sort of sensory quality. If inner sense models are literally meant to be perceptual, there must then be some specific type of sensation that occurs when we have second-order perception of our own psychological states. But there *is* no such sensory quality. If you are having a conscious experience of a cat's tongue rasping on your forearm, the only qualities you are aware of are the ones that are involved in the first-order perceptual state itself. There is no *further feel* that comes from the inner sensing of this state. Without such a special sensory quality, there is no perception, and thus HOP models fail.

A HOP theorist such as Lycan (2004) might reply by saying that inner sense should be counted as a kind of perception even if it is not maximally similar to the ordinary cases. He says: "No HOP theorist has contended that inner sense is like external-world perception in every single respect. Nor, in particular, should we expect inner sense to involve some distinctive sensory quality at its own level of operation" (p. 100). So perhaps inner sense is merely an unusual kind of perception. But this response downplays the number of dissimilarities between the two. As we argued in Section 6.1, sensory systems involve dedicated classes of receptors. But there are no receptors that trigger the operations of inner sense; there are no receptors of any kind in the brain. They also track a particular kind of distal object by means of a class of proximal stimuli. Both of these are missing in inner sense as well. Finally, they have a distinct phenomenology. Lycan himself admits the absence of any such thing for inner sense. What, then, is left of the idea of *perception*? Possibly very little.

7.4 Attention as the gatekeeper of consciousness

As should be clear from this review, discord has been the norm among theories of consciousness. Despite this, we may be in a position to arrive at some comity. In fact, the seeds of consensus can be found in the views discussed so far. For instance, although Tye's official position is that what matters to consciousness is whether a representation is poised to make an impact on our beliefs, he also points out that attention may play an important role here: perceptions can serve as inputs to belief "*if* attention is properly focused and the appropriate concepts are possessed. So, attentional deficits can preclude belief formation as can conceptual deficiencies" (1995, p. 138). Beliefs are what matters, for Tye, but attention may hold the keys to the kingdom of belief. And Lycan (2004), in stating his official version of the HOP theory, says that "consciousness is the functioning of internal *attention mechanisms* directed upon lower-order psychological states and events" (p. 100). Both simple representationalism and higher-order theorists seem to have flirted with the notion that attention is the inner illumination that produces P-consciousness.

The idea that attention is the gatekeeper of phenomenal consciousness forms the core of several prominent models. Among these are the Global Workspace Theory (GWT), developed by Bernard Baars and his collaborators

(Baars, 1988, 1997, 2002; Baars & Franklin, 2003; Dehaene & Naccache, 2001), and Jesse Prinz's Attended Intermediate Representations (AIR) theory (Prinz, 2012). Both of these in some way draw on the insight of William James, who proposed: "*My experience is what I agree to attend to.* Only those items which I *notice* shape my mind – without selective interest, experience is an utter chaos" (1890, p. 402).

First consider the architecture proposed by Global Workspace Theory. As we have seen (Chapter 3), the mind contains a vast set of cognitive systems, including the senses and many other reasoning and problem-solving devices. But these all need a way to coordinate their activities with one another and build up at least a semi-coherent overall representation of the world. To achieve this, the outputs of these systems are sent to *working memory*, a kind of temporary workspace where information that is (or may be) relevant to ongoing thinking and acting is collected. At any time, working memory may contain representations in many sense modalities, mental images, ideas and fragments of ongoing trains of thought, bit of language to be processed, and so on. Contemporary models of working memory treat it as having dissociable subcomponents dedicated to rehearsing inner speech, holding visuospatial information, and so on (Baddeley, 2007).

On GWT, all of the contents of working memory are *potentially* available to consciousness. But being in working memory by itself is not enough: a set of working memory representations become conscious when they are collectively attended to. Drawing on the spotlight metaphor, Baars proposes that attentional selection is a mechanism that broadcasts certain of these working memory representations widely across the brain, enabling them to gain more general access to and control over other cognitive systems. This amplifies their ability to play a role in the guidance of immediate behavior, in further inference processes, and in more complex forms of learning. Selective attention facilitates the movement of information through this cycle, promoting those representations that will be most useful in the current goal context. So conscious representations are those attended to, and thereby globally broadcast to other cognitive systems for the purpose of belief fixation, goal regulation, and the production of actions. This model captures some core properties of conscious states, such as the fact that they are often available for report and reasoning, and that when we are conscious of something we are often capable of thoughtful, planned action with respect to it.

Prinz also holds that attention is central to consciousness, though he gives it a slightly different role than does Baars. His own theory was developed by updating and extending an account of consciousness first presented by the psychologist and linguist Ray Jackendoff (1987, 2007). In Jackendoff's theory, consciousness arises from processing that takes place in a particular functional layer within perceptual systems. Following David Marr, we can distinguish among low-, intermediate-, and high-level perceptual processing. In the case of vision, low-level processing involves representing only the "bitmap" of the visual array: the pixel-by-pixel rendering of flat illumination across the visual scene. At the intermediate level, this array is processed slightly further. It becomes segmented into lines and edges, which define the initial boundaries of objects. These objects are also assigned visual qualities such as color, texture, and motion, and basic information about their distance from one another and from the perceived is encoded. Finally, at the highest levels, visual processing encodes an abstract and perspective-free three-dimensional model of the perceived object. This allows it to interface with stored information in memory about objects having similar geometric and spatial properties, and thereby support reasoning about categories of that type of thing generally.

Jackendoff's view holds that consciousness arises from intermediate-level representations (Prinz, 2007). He marshals a great deal of evidence for this claim, but note in particular that the description of the kinds of sensory qualities that are represented at the intermediate level correlates well with the content of our own apparent P-conscious states. These representations capture precisely the level of detail that consciousness possesses.[14] But intermediate-level processing by itself does not give rise to consciousness. Prinz suggests that, once again, what needs to be added is attention. When we direct our attention toward a part of the visual scene, we preferentially activate a subset of these intermediate-level representations and select them for further processing. Thus the name of his theory: Attended Intermediate Representations (AIR).

Like GWT, AIR posits a link between attention and working memory. However, Prinz denies that conscious representations are those that are

---

[14] This point is important in light of the strategy for overcoming mysterianism and the explanatory gap that we proposed in Section 7.3.2.

presently encoded in memory. Rather, the role of attention is to *allow* items into memory. Attention, he thinks, produces a change in the flow of information. It allows information to become "available for processes that are controlled and deliberative" (Prinz, 2012, p. 92). For GWT, it is only information that is already available in memory that can be attended to and broadcast. For AIR, information that is not yet in memory is made accessible to it by attention. Once in memory, however, it can be widely disseminated. Despite these subtle differences, both views maintain that attention is required for phenomenal consciousness. We turn now to evidence for and against these gatekeeper theories.

7.5 Assessing the gatekeeper theory

7.5.1 Blinks and blindness

Earlier, in our discussion of the experiential grand illusion (Section 6.2), we briefly introduced the phenomena of inattentional and change blindness. In a typical change blindness study, participants are shown a sequence of photos. The original photo will have everything intact (say, a head-on photo of a large passenger airplane). The next photo will have something missing (say, left engine missing, or less obviously, a passenger window missing). The participant is then asked if there is anything different or missing from the no-longer-visible first photo. In very many cases, people miss the change. They can't identify whether anything is different or what is different, though they can usually identify the change when both photos are seen side by side. In such experiments, the typical cues that tip off the fact that change is occurring are suppressed (Rensink, 2000a, 2000b; Rensink, O'Regan, & Clark, 1997, 2000). As a result of the suppression of normal change signals, attention is not directed to the change. Consequently, it fails to enter consciousness.

A few participants for whatever reason will instantly catch onto the change. Clearly they both *saw* the change and registered it in a *conscious* way. Moreover, when people are verbally cued to the possible location of the change, they detect it rapidly, a form of preparation that seems to establish the right attentional set. What about those who do not report the change? Some of them may have failed to pass their eyes across the right portion of the image. But given enough time to study the images, it seems unlikely that their inability to report comes from the mere failure to point their eyes in the right direction. In fact, Silverman and Mack (2001) found that the changed stimuli can actually facilitate performance on later recognition tasks: When subjects were shown changes to rows of letters, the changed letters primed subsequent completion of degraded figures. This indicates that information about the change has reached the perceptual systems but has not propagated to any higher-level comparison mechanisms. One possible reason for this is that the flicker between presentations disrupts the ability to selectively attend to portions of the scene. Because cueing attention to the change seems to reduce the occurrence of the phenomenon, it seems that the lack of conscious awareness in these cases ultimately traces to a lack of attention.

Inattentional blindness is the failure to consciously detect an unexpected stimulus when one's attention is occupied by another task (Mack & Rock, 1998). In experiments that are perhaps even more stunning than those associated with change blindness, those revealing the phenomenon of inattentional blindness provide further support for the view that without attending to something, conscious perception does not occur (Most, 2010; Most et al., 2001; Most, Scholl, Simons, & Clifford, 2005a; Simons & Chabris, 1999). In the classic "gorillas in our midst" demonstration, participants watch a video of students arranged in a circle and passing a basketball back and forth frequently among themselves. They are instructed to count the passes of the basketball, numbering as many as 20 or more. In the middle of this period, a person in a gorilla suit walks through the circle of players, beats its chest, and walks off. A majority of the participants report seeing nothing until they are reshown the video without counting passes. This remarkable demonstration illustrates the power of focused attention to screen off items in the visual field from entering consciousness.

How is this to be explained? One might expect that because participants' attention is directed to the basketball passes and away from the gorilla, the gaze of those who notice the gorilla versus those who don't notice it must be different. But eye-tracking studies show strong similarity of eye movements among those who notice and those who do not, making this unlikely (Most, 2010). Again, if a stimulus is being perceptually registered through gaze, but participants fail to report it, a candidate gatekeeper explanation is that attentional failures are blocking its entry into consciousness.

Finally, there is the so-called attentional blink. Though inattentional blindness (IB) and attentional blink (AB) are likely related, they are distinct phenomena.[15] Unlike IB, in AB there is no cognitive task participants perform that requires focused attention away from targets. In a typical AB experimental paradigm, participants are shown a rapid sequence of stimuli such as a series of photographs. The stream will include at least two targets to be identified from among nontarget stimuli. By systematically varying the time onset between targets T1 and T2, the temporal distance referred to as a "lag" between targets can be measured. After presentation of T1, when the targets are separated by up to a few hundred milliseconds, a "blink" occurs when participants fail to be able to notice or detect the second target in the sequence. Again, the existence of the blink is often based on self-report, but people often fail to identify or even detect the existence of T2. Some researchers argue that T2 is fully perceived even though it cannot be reported, suggesting that the blink occurs in a post-perceptual phase (Vogel & Luck, 2002).

There is some evidence that AB is related to attentional selection mechanisms. On reviewing literature investigating neurological correlates associated with AB, Martens and Wyble (2010) report that a T2 target elicits normal neural correlates of perceptual processing for the first 150 ms of processing even though the target fails to elicit an attentional selection response that would normally occur at about 200 ms after onset. It also fails to elicit an event-related potential (ERP) component normally associated with working memory consolidation. And this is true despite the fact that the so-called "blinked" T2 target activates some neural regions associated with semantic representation.

In addition, the attentional blink can be induced by putting an emotionally charged stimulus prior to T2 (McHugo, Olatunji, & Zald, 2013; Most, Chun, Widders, & Zald, 2005b). Steve Most and colleagues instructed participants to look for targets that were either rotated landscapes or architectural photos. Each photo was shown for 1 second. Into the visual stream they placed an emotional stimulus such as a gruesome wound or one person threatening another with a knife. This stimulus elicited AB significantly at lag 2 (when T2 comes two photos after the emotional stimulus), and disappeared 800 ms after emotional stimulus onset. Similar results have been found with non-aversive stimuli such as erotic images, with words rather than pictures, and with stimuli that have been aversively conditioned, suggesting that the

[15] Some researchers (Beanland & Pammer, 2012) have found that individuals susceptible to AB are also more likely to be susceptible to IB.

phenomenon is a general one involving emotional arousal regardless of presentation modality. Emotionally intense stimuli seem to capture attention,
temporarily blocking later presentations from becoming conscious.

7.5.2 Objections and open questions

Taken together, these phenomena suggest an intimate connection between
attention and consciousness, just as gatekeeper views like GWT and AIR would
predict. We now turn to some empirical and conceptual challenges facing the
view.

Consider change blindness. The standard view we have sketched is that
people do see the things that constitute the change, but lack consciousness
of the changes. An alternative perspective is that they see and are conscious
of the changes, but lack something else, namely the belief that the scene
has changed (Dretske, 2004, 2007). Lacking any further beliefs that would
more permanently record the existence of a change, people deny seeing one.
Dretske (2004) goes so far as to call the phenomenon "difference blindness,"
because he thinks the participants consciously experience the changed scenes,
but that without being able to compare the scenes one to the other, they
don't notice the difference. Blindness, Dretske insists, is the inability to see.
Difference blindness is not that. It is not the inability to see the things that
constitute the changes in the scenes, but it is the inability to form beliefs
about those changes, to record those changes *as changes*.

Dretske is relying here on the principle that one might *see* what constitutes a change without *seeing that* it constitutes the change; that is, one may
see an *a* which is now F without seeing *that a is now F*.[16] In many cases, we
can see and even consciously notice things and still not notice differences.
Suppose you have not seen someone for a long time and they have grown
a mustache. Talking with them for several minutes, you surely see (and *consciously* so!) the new mustache, but you have not attended to the fact that it is
new and have not formed a belief about the difference.

A similar challenge has been raised for inattentional blindness studies.
Jeremy Wolfe (1999) has proposed that these might better be seen as cases of
"inattentional amnesia." All of these studies involve presenting a stimulus

---

[16] Dretske (1993) calls the former "thing awareness" and the latter "fact awareness."
The former (seeing an *a* that is F) does not require employing the concept of F. The
latter (seeing that *a* is now F) does require employing the concept of F.

rapidly and then taking it away, sometimes to be replaced by another. It may be that the failure to report changes across these presentations is due to the fact that people are simply never conscious of them. This is the "blindness" interpretation. On the other hand, it might be that people are not only conscious of the two stimuli but also (potentially) conscious of some differences between them, but they simply do not retain this information in memory. As Wolfe puts it, "visual representation has no memory" (p. 74), so it is possible on this interpretation to have extraordinarily brief consciousness of changes that are not retained beyond the moment. He poses the central question in its sharpest form: "Can one be said to consciously see something if one cannot remember seeing it an instant later? I see no reason why not" (p. 89).[17]

This challenge has been pressed further by Block (2007, 2011), who argues that the contents of phenomenal consciousness are richer than what we can attend to and access at any particular moment. He refers to this as the "overflow" of phenomenal consciousness. Block's argument appeals to some famous results by George Sperling (1960). Sperling told participants that they were going to view a 3 by 4 grid of numbers and letters. After the grid was flashed for 50 ms, followed by a visual mask, a particular row of the symbols (top, middle, or bottom) was cued. The task was to report the contents of the cued row. Sperling found that participants could typically report all of the characters in a row accurately, even after such a brief presentation. However, when the array was flashed without any cue, they could at best recall three or so items. Because the row to be cued was only revealed after presentation, Sperling concluded that visual representations decay in an extremely short-term buffer that allows readout even after the stimulus disappears.

Most interestingly, participants also claim to be able to *see* all of the elements in the array, even though they could only recall a few of them later. That is, their phenomenal consciousness seemed to cover the entire grid at the time of its presentation. It did not appear to them as if they saw only a single row of symbols, even though that is all they could report. The fact that an arbitrary set of stimuli could be read back seems to support the idea of such short-lived richness. Access, on the other hand, is a much more limited-capacity affair. Attention may be able to rescue certain items from the short-term visual buffer and preserve them in working memory, but on

---

[17] However, see Most et al. (2005b) for studies that may defeat this explanation, and Simons (2000) for an explanation in terms of inattentional agnosia.

the overflow interpretation, these items are *all* conscious even before being selected. In terms of Block's earlier distinction, attention would be at most necessary for A-consciousness, but not P-consciousness.

7.6 Conclusions

Our discussion here has been an attempt to bridge the explanatory gap and bring some aspects of phenomenal consciousness within the purview of psychological explanation. Attention may prove to be key in achieving this unification. At the same time, theorists of attention have emphasized its central role in producing cogent behavioral responses. An intriguing and underexplored possibility here is that these two views might, taken together, provide insight into the basic role of consciousness in mental life. If attention is fundamentally for solving the problem of action selection, and consciousness is produced by attentional gatekeeping, then phenomenal consciousness itself might be functionally explained in terms of its role in generating rational action. But we will have to let these intriguing speculations rest for now.

Much remains to be done to settle these questions about how consciousness and attention are related. The problem of phenomenal overflow highlights just how difficult this work will be, because it is not even entirely clear how to correctly describe the phenomenology of the participants in experiments such as Sperling's. Anecdotes are plentiful, but even the best studies are hard to interpret. A troubling possibility is that this difficulty may derive from a more general inability of ours to adequately grasp our own consciousness. The philosopher Eric Schwitzgebel has argued that "we are prone to gross error, even in favorable circumstances of extended reflection, about our ongoing emotional, visual, and cognitive phenomenology" (2011, p. 129). If our experience proves inherently resistant to being conceptualized in a coherent, stable fashion, consciousness studies may face even greater challenges than those surveyed here.

8   The social mind

8.1 The minds of others

The term "folk psychology" was coined by philosophers to refer to the everyday capacities we have for predicting and explaining each other's behavior, as well as understanding each another as conscious, thinking, social beings. These capacities are also known as "commonsense psychology," "mindreading," or "everyday mentalizing." The term "folk," although it has a somewhat patronizing air, just refers to those of us who attempt to navigate the social world without appeal to the institutional apparatus of scientific psychology. At a minimum, folk psychology involves seeing others as having minds and attributing particular mental states and processes to them. Those that lack this capacity are said to be "mindblind": they may interpret the world as containing animate, biological creatures, but they do not under-stand these creatures' behaviors as *actions* driven by *reasons*, where reasons can include their perceptions, motives, and beliefs (Baron-Cohen, 1995). They may not even see the world as populated by persons who have inner lives of their own.

That we have such folk psychological skills from an early age is clear. However, folk psychology is not a transparent instrument. It cannot reliably be turned on itself to reveal its own inner workings. Although we often develop elaborate opinions about the operations of our own minds, they have at most prima facie standing as far as their accuracy is concerned. Our everyday perspective does not settle the question of how folk psychology itself operates: what sort of ability it is, what knowledge it draws on, and how it is situated vis-à-vis other cognitive systems. We turn now to some attempts to address these questions.

8.2 Folk psychology as a theory

The origin of contemporary research into folk psychology is arguably the work of Fritz Heider, particularly his 1958 book *The Psychology of Interpersonal Relations*. Heider inaugurated the study of the psychological processes underlying attributions (people's explanations for observed events in the physical and social world), and was arguably the first to take our commonsense psychological understanding as a primary object of study. Among social psychologists this work has continued within the fruitful research program of attribution theory (Malle, 2004, Chapter 1).

An early philosophical contribution is Wilfrid Sellars' influential essay "Empiricism and the Philosophy of Mind" (1956). Sellars proposed a kind of origin myth for our mentalistic language and concepts. He imagines the initial state of ancestral humans who possess a language for discussing publicly observable physical objects and describing the observable acts and speech of others, but who lack any vocabulary for talking about beliefs, desires, mental images, or thoughts. Thoughts, and the language to refer to them, had to be *discovered*, and for Sellars this discovery took the form of a theoretical insight, namely that for many behaviors, there exists a hidden, unobservable cause that can be conceptualized as being similar to an episode of inner speech. Inner speech is modeled on the observable speech that often accompanies behavior, with the exception that it precedes and explains such behavior. Various unobservable types of thoughts are then posited as part of an inference to the best explanation of why people act. Mythical attributes of this tale aside, Sellars clearly supposes that folk psychological discourse has the aim and structure of a theory.

A third origin is David Premack and Guy Woodruff's 1978 article, "Does the chimpanzee have a theory of mind?" (Premack & Woodruff, 1978). As its title suggests, the paper is concerned with the extent to which nonhuman primates share our abilities to comprehend and attribute mental states. It is also notably the first to explicitly coin the term "theory of mind" for this ability. This is not purely a lexical decision, since it implies a fairly specific type of organization for folk psychology, similar to the one proposed by Sellars. This is what has ultimately come to be known as the "Theory theory" of folk psychology (TT).[1]

---

[1] The term "Theory theory" itself derives from Adam Morton (1980). Despite giving the view its most popular name, Morton himself was opposed to it. We capitalize the somewhat awkward name to remind readers that it is not a typo.

The central construct of a *theory* needs further elaboration. Scientific theories provide one possible model for folk psychology. This seems to have been what Sellars had in mind: the activity of crafting mentalistic explanations is akin to the process of producing any other scientific account of the behavior of complex systems. The body of information that ordinary people possess should be thought of as similar in form and content to a scientific theory of human behavior, and the process of acquiring and applying this theory should similarly resemble the relevant scientific activities.

Few, however, believe that there is a strict parallel between people's everyday mentalizing and the activity of scientists as they try to theoretically model the causes of behavior (Faucher et al., 2002). Science is a collective, collaborative, technologically mediated endeavor. Scientists conduct carefully controlled experiments and make structured observations; they use recording and measurement devices; and they capture and analyze data, abstract away phenomena from the chaos of ordinary events, and share their results with others. These complex forms of activity have no echo in ordinary practice.

Naïve theories, then, are unlikely to resemble scientific theories in much detail. But at a more general level they may be similar. According to a prominent tradition in philosophy of science, theories are made up of laws (see Chapter 1). The core of a naïve theory, then, should be a body of lawlike generalizations. These laws are organized to serve the purposes of everyday mentalizing. These include explanation and prediction, both of which are causal notions. A naïve theory, whether of physics or psychology, is at a minimum a mentally represented body of lawlike causal generalizations that can be applied in a range of explanatory/predictive contexts. This set of generalizations is combined with the available behavioral evidence (actions and other movements, facial expressions, patterns of speech and gesture, etc.) in order to produce attributions, describe a person's inner mental dynamics, and link these dynamics with future behavior.

Attempts to articulate these theoretical principles have, unfortunately, not produced many viable candidates for folk psychological laws. Carruthers (1996b) lists as possible candidates such claims as "that someone who wants it to be the case that Q, and believes that if P then Q, and believes that P is in their power, will, other things being equal, form an intention to cause it to be the case that P; that someone who has formed an intention to bring it about that P when R, and who believes that R, will then act so as to bring it about that P" (p. 24). Armed with barely a handful of such principles, it is doubtful whether we could explicitly work our way through the simplest social interactions. Whereas folk psychological competence is obviously richly sophisticated, our articulation of it is impoverished. This highlights a typical feature of these theories, which is that they are *tacit* or *implicit*: their central principles are inaccessible to consciousness. Although they are represented in some mental system, and we can apply them fluently, we cannot introspect and verbalize their contents.

Not only are these theories implicit, however, they are often unspecific in various ways. This can be seen from the proliferation of hedging clauses ("all things being equal," "ceteris paribus," and so on) required to state them. Rather than giving the precise conditions under which each state they describe comes about, or giving exact and exceptionless dynamical accounts, they offer general descriptions of the kinds of interactions that are possible among perceptions, thoughts, and actions. They are what Henry Wellman (1990) refers to as *framework theories*: they define the broad causal principles that govern the entities within the domain of study, without giving a recipe for generating specific, local, individualized causal descriptions. These more particularized theories must be produced on a case-by-case basis, under the framework theory's guidance. As an example of this framework theory, Wellman (1990, p. 100) sketches a simplified scheme for belief–desire reasoning, describing beliefs as originating with perception and desires as originating with emotions and physiological states. Actions arise out of beliefs and desires, and affective reactions arise out of actions. More complex schemes include contributions from higher thought processes, intentions, different sorts of emotions, character traits, and so on. All of these types of states may be part of how we causally model actions. If our naïve psychology encodes theoretical principles, they are likely couched in terms of such high-level descriptions.

To summarize, then: for our purposes a *theory* is a tacitly known body of lawlike causal generalizations that provide the general framework for producing specific attributions, explanations, and predictions and for carrying out other tasks involving mentalistic understanding.

Several predictions flow from the Theory theory. The first is that folk psychology should exhibit an abstract explanatory structure in which our attributions and predictions have the form of causal hypotheses. Fundamentally, mindreading is a kind of *reasoning*, so confirming the theory will involve looking for the appropriate sorts of patterns in people's reasoning. The second prediction is that there should be characteristic types of *changes* in reasoning patterns in development. Theories in science change over time as new evidence accumulates, challenging previously held beliefs and forcing new ones to be adopted. We might expect mental theories both to be deployed in giving explanations and also to undergo such developmental processes. The third prediction derives from the fact that theories, especially naïve ones, need not be *accurate* depictions of their domains. Accordingly, there may be certain empirically distinctive ways that theory-based cognition goes wrong. (On the role of error patterns as evidence for theoretical reasoning, see Section 8.5.)

Here we briefly canvass some evidence for the first two predictions. First, do children make use of a causal theory of attitudes, emotions, and other mental states? One study that suggests so probed people's ability to generate action explanations (Bartsch & Wellman, 1989). The participants were three-year-olds, four-year-olds, and adults. They were given a short description of a character performing a single act and then asked why they might be doing that. The acts were either simple ("Jane is looking for her kitten under the piano"), anomalous with respect to beliefs ("Jane is looking for her kitten. The kitten is hiding under a chair, but Jane is looking for her kitten under the piano"), or anomalous with respect to desires ("Jane hates frogs, but Jane is looking for a frog under the piano"). Those who did not initially refer to beliefs or desires were given a follow-up prompt concerning what the actor thinks or wants.

The majority of all age groups spontaneously gave explanations that made some mention of psychological terms. Most of these psychological explanations made reference to beliefs and desires in particular, and almost all of the belief- and desire-based explanations were relevant to the action itself. A total of 37% of the explanations given by three-year-olds, 45% of those given by four-year-olds, and 53% of those given by adults involved relevant belief–desire pairs, and when participants were given some prompting, these numbers jumped to 67%, 75%, and 93%, respectively. So although there is improvement with age, all groups are capable of appealing to belief–desire pairs in explaining actions. Similar results hold for the anomalous cases. In anomalous belief cases, participants must explain the actor's behavior by positing ignorance or false belief. Belief-based explanations of anomalous actions were present in all groups: 74% of three-year-olds, 91% of four-year-olds, and 100% of adults gave at least one belief explanation for the anomalous cases, and all but one of these participants gave at least one relevant belief explanation.

These results indicate that children as young as three years old can explain actions by appealing to psychological states, including beliefs and desires, in both normal and abnormal cases. These states also function in predictions. In another study by Wellman and Bartsch (1988), three-year-olds and four-year-olds were given a brief description of a character's desires and beliefs and asked to predict his actions. The nature of the beliefs involved was systematically varied to see how children understand their role in producing behavior. For instance, suppose that the character Sam wants to find his puppy. In a *standard belief* condition, the child is simply told Sam's belief that the puppy is in the garage and asked whether he will look in the garage or under the porch. In the *not belief* condition, the child is told that Sam does *not* think that the puppy is in the garage, and then asked where he will look. This eliminates a simple response bias based on the earlier mention of a location. In the *not own belief* condition, the child is first asked where she herself thinks the puppy is, and is then told that Sam thinks the puppy is in the other location. The child must thus disregard her own belief in making an attribution. Finally, in the *changed belief* condition, the child makes a prediction about where Sam will look, then is told that Sam received new information and now thinks the puppy is in a different location. This requires suppression of an earlier belief attribution and an understanding that beliefs can change over time. These conditions thus cover a range of increasingly complicated tasks.

Both three- and four-year-old children pass these tests, averaging 85% and 89% correct across all tasks, respectively. This suggests that they are able to use the concept of belief to make correct attributions and predictions not merely in simple cases, but also in complex ones where beliefs change and conflict. They seem to understand many of the ways in which belief–desire pairs lead to action, and as the previous studies show, they can express this understanding in their spontaneous action explanations as well. This suggests a pattern of causal reasoning about the mental that is consistent with what theory-based approaches predict.[2] Adults also spontaneously generate similar

---

[2] Of course, these are all particular causal explanations. The evidence surveyed here, and elsewhere in the literature, does not directly show the general causal laws or principles that children and adults may know. But this is consistent with implicit theories in other domains (e.g., language and perception); we have experimental access at best to the output of those theories as they are applied in instances, and we must attempt to *infer* their structure.

explanations, positing belief–desire pairings that would rationalize actions directed toward target objects (Wertz & German, 2007).

Moreover, this pattern of reasoning develops over time. Theory theorists have appealed to these changes to bolster their view, though accounts differ of exactly how to characterize the various stages of development through which this theory moves (Gopnik, 1993; Gopnik & Wellman, 1992). On one view, advanced by Wellman and Woolley (1992), two-year-old children operate with a more impoverished psychological theory than three-year-olds. This early understanding makes reference to states such as desire, emotion, and perception, but full understanding of belief appears to be missing. So, for instance, a two-year-old might think that Jill wants an apple and might be aware that there is an apple in the kitchen, and on this basis predict that Jill will look in the kitchen for the apple. This "simple desire psychology" does not involve attributing belief or knowledge to Jill herself, but rather involves moving directly from Jill's desire plus the attributor's own knowledge of the apple's location to the prediction of Jill's action. On the simple view, desires are conceived of as being directly responsive to the state of the world, and as motivating action independently of representational states such as belief.

As Wellman and Woolley found, two-year-olds do have some understanding of desire. They judge that someone who desires an object will stop searching if they find it, but will keep searching if they find nothing or a different item, and that finding desired objects leads to happiness while failing to do so leads to sadness. However, they fail at certain tasks that require an understanding of belief, such as the not-own belief task described earlier, while passing analogous versions that involve desires. This suggests that the conceptual and theoretical resources of two-year-olds are lacking relative to their older peers. Either they do not have the concept of belief, or they have not yet integrated it into the rest of their theory to help them make predictions.[3]

There are many such changes in children's performance on related tasks throughout their development. Of course, the precise timing of these changes, as well as the correct way to describe them, is disputed. It is sometimes unclear whether failure on a particular task is evidence of lack of knowledge or folk

[3] We should add that it is not particularly credible to say that they lack the concept entirely. In these studies, correct responding on not-own-belief stories was 73% versus 93% on not-own-desire stories, and 45% of the children were correct on all three not-own-belief stories, versus 85% on all not-own-desire stories. This suggests poor belief task performance, but not total incomprehension.

psychological competence, or rather due to extraneous factors that make the task challenging. This problem arises in a sharp form for tasks that allegedly require an understanding of the causal role of false beliefs. As we noted in Chapter 1, many people have held that failures on various false-belief tasks show that this understanding appears at its earliest in four-year-olds (Wimmer & Perner, 1983). However, as we have seen, there is evidence that some understanding of belief is present in three-year-olds, and, moreover, several reasons why many versions of the false belief task are inherently difficult (Bloom & German, 2000). Task difficulties may be masking intact belief understanding.

A task difficulty explanation is bolstered by the fact that even 15-month-old children show the ability to make responses that indicate an understanding of false belief if the task is a nonverbal predictive one involving an implicit measure such as looking time (Onishi & Baillargeon, 2005). Consequently, a precise account of what changes in children's understanding of belief and other mental states requires consideration of many variations of the tasks and materials (Wellman, Cross, & Watson, 2001). Rather than delve into these complexities here, we simply note that Theory theorists take any such facts as potential support for their view, because these changes exhibit progressive modification of informational structures in response to their empirical deficiencies, with the result that later developmental stages are more predictively and explanatorily successful than earlier ones.

8.3 Simulation theory

Simulation theory (ST) holds that there is no need to suppose that we make use of implicit theory-driven reasoning mechanisms in order to account for our everyday mindreading. Instead, they propose that this can be explained by the reuse of our own cognitive mechanisms for generating attitudes, planning, and decision making. Different ways of stating this fundamental idea were proposed nearly simultaneously by Jane Heal (1986), Robert Gordon (1986), and Alvin Goldman (1989). Their accounts are similar in outline, though Heal calls the processes she is interested in "co-cognition," and Gordon has staked out a position he calls "radical simulationism." Here we lay out a general version of the view for purposes of discussion.

To see how simulation theory works, first consider where our own attitudes and actions come from. Seeing a bear can lead me to believe that there is a bear nearby (so long as I notice it and am capable of forming thoughts about bears). Seeing a snake, or hearing a noise when I am alone in a darkened house, may cause me to experience fear, and the sound of a dentist's drill causes me to want to flee. These attitudes lead to others: wanting some coffee and seeing where to get some causes the intention to pour a cup; thinking I am near a bear causes the intention to escape safely, followed by a cascade of planning how this might be done; fear of a possible intruder in the house may lead to either hiding or planning for self-defense. Finally, these intentions and plans often lead to behaviors such as creeping slowly back down the trail away from the bear, or taking a cup down from the cabinet and pouring some coffee from the carafe.

The causal pathways displayed here are familiar: perceptions lead to attitudes and emotions, which lead to further attitudes as well as plans and intentions, and these in turn lead to actions. All of this takes place using the complex systems that underlie attitude formation and decision making. The fundamental insight of simulation theory is that, given that we have these systems ourselves, they can be used not just in the production of our own mental states, but also in the attribution of those states to others, and to predict and explain their behavior.

To see how this works, suppose that the relevant systems can be taken "offline" by being decoupled from their normal inputs and outputs. New inputs can then be fed to them, and their outputs diverted and used for new purposes. Rather than beliefs having their ordinary causes in perception, we might generate imagined perceptual scenarios and see what they would cause us to believe and desire. If I imagine being confronted by a snake or a loud noise and feed this image into my attitude-formation systems, they may produce fears, beliefs, and desires just as they would if fed ordinary perceptual inputs. If I then feed these attitudes into my practical reasoning and decision-making systems, they may generate intentions to act in certain ways just as they would if I had the attitudes in question. This procedure is what is meant by the offline use of cognitive mechanisms.

However, the functional role of these offline attitudes differs on the output side as well as on the input side. When beliefs, desires, and emotions are generated by imagined perceptual inputs, we do not want them to "contaminate" our own actual attitudes. We do not, in every case, come to believe things formed on the basis of these imaginings. Similarly, when we generate behavioral intentions through this sort of imaginary routine, they do not cause us to act. The output side of their function is temporarily suspended. One way to capture this difference in functional role is to say that attitudes generated offline are *quarantined* in a separate memory workspace. This can be conceptualized as a temporary storage register that keeps them from being confused with the things that we ordinarily believe, feel, and intend.

It is not hard to see how this machinery might be turned to the purposes of folk psychology. In trying to decide what someone thinks, we imaginatively generate perceptual inputs corresponding to what we think their own perceptual situation is like. That is, we try to imagine how the world looks from their perspective. Then we run our attitude-generating mechanisms offline, quarantining the results in a mental workspace the contents of which are treated as if they belonged to our target. These attitudes are used to generate further intentions, which can then be treated as predictions of what the target will do in these circumstances. Finally, explaining observed actions can be treated as a sort of analysis-by-synthesis process in which we seek to imagine the right sorts of input conditions that would lead to attitudes which, in turn, produce the behavior in question. These are then hypothesized to be the explanation of the target's action.

The bones of the simulation procedure outlined here require three things: (1) the ability to take attitude-forming and decision-making systems offline and reroute their functional inputs and outputs, (2) the ability to appropriately quarantine the products of this offline processing, and (3) the ability to treat these quarantined products as if they belonged to a target individual. This is a basic model of how simulation theorists account for our folk psychological competence.

One way to capture the difference between the method of attribution used in simulation theory from that used in Theory theory is in terms of *informational richness* (Nichols & Stich, 2003, pp. 102–103). Theories are complex bodies of represented information about their target domain. On the other hand, the simulation process described here makes no such inherent appeal to informationally rich structures. Rather, it requires the ability to make use of certain mental mechanisms in novel ways. That isn't to say that simulation can take place without any information at all – in order for us to form beliefs and desires to use in attribution and prediction, a great deal of information might be required. But this information does not concern psychological states and processes, but rather the ordinary nonpsychological aspects of the world.

The key insight of simulation theory is that psychological *attribution* might not require a great deal of psychological *information*.

The notion of a mental simulation has been given a fairly precise specification by Goldman (2006). When we have any two mental processes, one of them, S, is a *simulation* of the target, T, when S duplicates, replicates, or resembles T in some significant respects, and performing this duplication is part of S's function (Goldman, 2006, p. 37). The resemblance clause of this definition captures the generic idea of one process being a simulation of another. Computer simulations of storm systems resemble, in a sufficiently abstract fashion, the meteorological processes that they model. A scale model of a plane may resemble the actual plane well enough to share its aerodynamic characteristics. These resemblances are non-accidental, the result of intentional human design in both cases. Resemblance alone is not sufficient for simulation, though. Notice that any two mass-produced objects will resemble one another to an arbitrary degree. If we both buy the same model chess computer, the processes that occur in mine will be identical to the ones in yours. Even so, neither one is simulating the gameplay of the other. The resemblances are not *explained* by the fact that my machine has the function of replicating the gameplay of yours. However, if my machine sometimes plays very similarly to Gary Kasparov or Bobby Fischer, this might be part of its intentional design function, and in doing so it might genuinely be simulating.

Evidence for simulation theory focuses on cases where mentalistic tasks involve this kind of duplication, rather than more detached theoretical understanding. One source of evidence comes from the existence of *paired deficits*. Where individuals show an inability to attribute a certain kind of mental state, and also a deficiency in experiencing that state themselves, this suggests that a common mechanism is at work, just as the offline simulation model predicts. And there are neuropsychological cases like this (Goldman, 2006, pp. 115–116). The patient known as SM suffers from a neurodegenerative disease that caused bilateral destruction of her amygdala. The amygdala is believed to play a significant role in, among other things, fear-based learning and memory. As a result of her condition, SM is impaired in the everyday experience of fear, and is unafraid when presented with scenes that induce fear in many people (such as scenes from horror movies). At the same time, when presented with slides of facial expressions corresponding to various types of emotions, SM is impaired at recognition of fearful faces, and to a lesser degree anger and surprise, but not other emotional expressions. A similar pattern is found in patient NM, who also suffered bilateral amygdala lesions. NM engaged in dangerous, even reckless behaviors without apparent fear and scored abnormally low in questionnaires that measure the subjective experience of fear. He also shows deficits in recognizing fear from photographs of faces and body postures.

This sort of pattern of paired deficits – impaired experience of a type of emotion plus impaired recognition of that emotion from facial or bodily cues – appears in many patient populations for the emotions of fear, anger, and disgust. The common-mechanism claim is bolstered by neuroimaging studies, which show some overlap in the neural regions activated when people observe facial expressions of disgust in others and when they experience disgusting stimuli themselves. Neural and cognitive reuse of mental systems is a hallmark of certain versions of simulation theory.[4]

A further source of evidence comes from *systematic misattributions* or biases that people are subject to in making attributions. A general finding in social psychology is that people are liable to attribute their own mental states to others, and they find it difficult to make attributions that diverge from their own thoughts, preferences, and feelings. This phenomenon goes by several names. It is sometimes called a form of "quarantine violation," meaning that people find it difficult to keep their own thoughts mentally penned off and separated from the attributed thoughts of others. It has also been dubbed the "curse of knowledge," indicating just how hard it can be to divest oneself of known information in taking another's perspective (Birch, 2005; Camerer, Loewenstein, & Weber, 1989). It is also related to a phenomenon known as the "illusion of transparency," which denotes people's habit of thinking that other people have a much easier time detecting their thoughts, emotions, and general mental state than they actually do.

The curse of knowledge can readily be demonstrated in young children. Birch and Bloom (2003) showed that if three- and four-year-old children were given a hollow toy and shown its contents, they were more likely to predict

---

[4] However, this prediction does not automatically follow from the very notion of a generic mental simulation process. Recall that the definition of simulation requires that there be resemblance or duplication of one process by another; but this is consistent with the target and the simulation sharing very different physical bases, as is the case with computer simulations of physical processes. Only in the case where the duplication results from the very same underlying physical basis are the paired deficits predicted.

that someone else would know what was in the toy than children of the same age who were not shown its contents. That is, they tended to assume that others would share the information they have. Adults also estimate how others will judge them based not on what is uncontroversially shared information, but on private information available only to them. For example, when deciding how strangers will assess them on some task, they will use their own self-assessments based on past performances that only they have access to (Chambers, Epley, Savitsky, & Windschitl, 2008). Difficulties in filtering out knowledge that we possess but others do not would be predicted on simulation accounts if the process of attribution makes use of our own belief-formation systems and memory stores, taking the default assignment to be one on which others believe more or less like us.

Illusory transparency, on simulation theory, also arises from the fact that attributions start from a default setting that corresponds to the attributor's own thoughts. In one set of studies, participants overestimated how likely others are to detect whether they are lying, or whether they are experiencing disgust as a result of drinking a foul-tasting beverage (Gilovich, Savitsky, & Medvec, 1998). The awareness of one's own lie or of the overpoweringly unpleasant gustatory sensations seem to "leak out" to observers, even though they are demonstrably less aware of these cues. Teachers and other public speakers are undoubtedly well acquainted with the phenomenon of feeling acute anxiety before a performance, only to discover that this felt anxiety on their part is largely invisible to the audience (Savitsky & Gilovich, 2003). People can be surprised to see how inexpressive they actually are on viewing videotapes of themselves (Barr & Kleck, 1995). Interestingly, this illusion seems cognitively penetrable: individuals in a greater position of social or economic power feel less transparent than subordinates or those in positions of lesser control, privilege, and authority (Garcia, 2002), and speakers who are briefed on the illusion of transparency before giving a speech subsequently judge that others perceived them to be less nervous (Savitsky & Gilovich, 2003).

Values and desires are also subject to quarantine violations. The endowment effect refers to the tendency of people to assign greater value to objects that they own. However, even though they are subject to the effect, people systematically misestimate how the endowment effect will affect people's valuations. Van Boven, Dunning, and Loewenstein (2000) showed that people who are given a mug as a gift will tend to assume that prospective buyers will have a higher maximum purchase price for the mug than they actually do, and prospective buyers who have not been given a mug tend to assume that mug owners will have a lower minimum selling price than they actually do. These paired misattributions arise because mug owners project their own endowment onto others, and mug buyers fail to take into account the endowment effect's influence on others. Similarly, after some moderately strenuous physical exercise, people tend to get thirsty. But they will be more likely to predict that a group of hikers lost in the woods without supplies will be extremely bothered by their own thirst and regretful over having not brought adequate water (Van Boven & Loewenstein, 2003). Again, the pattern is the same: self-experienced sensations, desires, and information are all attributed to others even when there is no particular evidence for these attributions, consistent with leakage of mental states into memory registers reserved for simulating others.

8.4 Mirror neurons, simulation, and action understanding

In the past decade and a half, a large number of studies involving both monkeys and humans has accumulated suggesting that there are neural systems dedicated to "mirroring" the observed actions of others. These mirror neurons and mirror systems have been cited as a major piece of evidence in support of ST. Sometimes even more ambitious claims are made on their behalf; for instance, mirror neurons have been mentioned as possible explanations for action understanding, the semantics of action verbs, speech processing and comprehension, nonverbal communication, shared emotion, and empathy. The neurologist V. S. Ramachandran (2000) has made perhaps the grandest and most wide-ranging claim on their behalf, saying that "mirror neurons will do for psychology what DNA did for biology: they will provide a unifying framework and help explain a host of mental abilities that have hitherto remained mysterious and inaccessible to experiments." We can't hope to tackle these exuberant claims in this limited space, but we will focus on explaining the core phenomenon of mirroring in the brain, and its possible role in underpinning mentalistic attributions.

In the brain of the macaque monkey there is a region known as F5, which was traditionally considered a "premotor" area: a part of the brain dedicated to producing particular orchestrated motor acts. Neurons in F5 fire when the monkey is about to perform various specific actions. Indeed, many cells seem to code for a particular sort of action such as grasping objects with a precision grip (between the fingertips) as opposed to an open grip. However, the classification of F5 as a purely motor region was called into doubt by the discovery that some neurons in F5 also respond to *visual* stimuli (Rizzolatti & Gentilucci, 1988). In one study by Murata et al. (1997), a monkey was shown a box in which various simple shaped objects were displayed one at a time. The monkey's task was either to grasp the object or simply to look at it. A large number of neurons fired both when the monkey moved to grasp the object and when the object itself was simply visually fixated. This suggests that they are coding not just for the movement that is specific to this object, but also to the presence of the object itself, whether the movement is made or not. These visuomotor neurons came to be known as *canonical* neurons.

Mirror neurons, like canonical neurons, were initially discovered in area F5. These cells discharge preferentially either when the monkey observes an action being performed by someone else, or when the monkey itself performs that action. They are thus a kind of visuomotor neuron that is sensitive to a particular type of action and that tends to fire during the production of that same action (di Pellegrino, Fadiga, Fogassi, Gallese, & Rizzolatti, 1992; Gallese, Fadiga, Fogassi, & Rizzolatti, 1996; Rizzolatti, Fadiga, Gallese, & Fogassi, 1996). For instance, they will fire when a monkey sees a person picking up something with a fine grasp and also when the monkey does so, and similarly for objects being placed, held, and manipulated. The match between observed and performed action can be strict or loose; about 70% of these neurons allow a fairly loose fit between the two, with the remainder requiring a more strict correspondence. The majority of hand-related mirror neurons are found in the dorsal region of F5, with the ventral region containing mainly those centered on mouth-related actions. Overall, the most common actions that mirror neurons respond to are ingestive actions involving placing food in the mouth and chewing it – 85% are dedicated to these types of acts.

These response properties are highly suggestive, but they do not by themselves tell us what mirror neurons are doing in the larger system. One proposal that has been widely influential is that they are "primarily involved in the *understanding of the meaning of 'motor events,' i.e. of the actions performed by others*" (Rizzolatti & Sinigaglia, 2008, p. 97). This is the *action understanding* hypothesis of mirror neuron function. "Understanding" here means the ability to recognize a particular type of action, to distinguish it from other actions, and to use this categorization to guide appropriate responses. This ability to recognize types of action on the basis of observed movements is clearly linked with interpreting others' behavior and attributing attitudes to them. Accordingly, on the action-understanding hypothesis, the discovery of mirror neurons constitutes a significant step forward in uncovering the neural basis of folk psychology.

In support of the action understanding hypothesis, it has been shown that some mirror neurons respond both to visually complete actions and also to visually incomplete ones that have the same goal state. Umiltà et al. (2001) recorded responses from cells in F5 that fire when the monkey performs and views acts involving grasping with the hand. A population of these same cells also fire when the monkey views a hand reaching toward an object that is blocked behind an occluding screen, so that the end of the action cannot be witnessed. Despite the act being visually incomplete, the neurons treat this display the same as in the original, unoccluded case. The presence of the object is essential: they do not respond to visually identical pantomimed acts that lack a target object. This phenomenon of completing visually incomplete actions suggests that they are being understood in terms of their entire planned course, from initiation to goal state.

The action understanding hypothesis fits naturally with a simulationist perspective on mentalizing. For here we have a set of neurons that are common both to action observation and to action execution. This suggests at least partial overlap between the motor system and the system of interpreting the motor acts of others. It is not too much of a stretch, then, to see action understanding as involving a process of action simulation: when the subject observes a target's act, patterns of motor activity are generated that would be involved in the subject's own production of the type of action observed in the target. These motor simulations resemble the motor commands produced in the target as they perform the action, and thus allow us to understand the organization and intentional goal of the target's behavior. Rizzolatti and Sinigaglia put this in the strongest possible terms: "motor knowledge of our own acts is a necessary and sufficient condition for an immediate understanding of the acts of others" (2008, p. 106).

Gallese and Goldman (1998) have fleshed this proposal out in some detail. On their view, internally generated mirror neuron activity represents a plan to carry out an action by means of a certain sequence of movements. When this same activity is produced externally – by the sight of the target performing an action, for example – these mirror neurons still represent the same action plan, but it is tagged as belonging to the target rather than the subject herself.

At the same time, the neurons are inhibited from having their normal effects on motor behavior, so the subject does not automatically start imitating the observed action. Still, the tagged representation of an action plan that the mirror neurons generate can be used as the input to simulation processes whose goal it is to generate the appropriate set of beliefs and desires that would lead to that particular action; in the simplest case, such as reaching into a refrigerator for a plum, these might be the belief that the fridge contains plums and the desire to eat one. So the primary role of mirror neurons is in understanding physical behaviors in terms of actions, or motor plans at the very least, that can be used to produce attributions of the mental states that lie behind them.

The results so far, however, have been confined to nonhuman primates, whose ability to understand mental states is widely believed to be limited (Call & Tomasello, 2008). More compelling evidence would be needed to show that these mechanisms are present and performing the proper functions in humans. Some evidence points toward the existence of mirror neuron systems in human beings (Iacoboni, 2008). In one study, human participants watched an experimenter grasping various objects with her hands while the participants were receiving transcranial magnetic stimulation to their motor cortex (Fadiga, Fogassi, Pavese, & Rizzolatti, 1995).[5] At the same time, electrical potentials were recorded from the participants' hands. While observing the experimenter's object manipulations, there was activation of the same hand muscles that the participants would use if they were to carry out that action themselves. Simple object observation elicited no muscle activity, although some was produced by observing undirected arm movements. This is a behavioral demonstration of the mirroring effect in which observation is paired with action.

Functional imaging studies of humans also hint at the existence of a mirroring system. In one study by Buccino et al. (2001), participants were shown videos of actions involving the hands, mouth, and feet, some which involved objects and some which didn't. Action observation alone resulted in activation in premotor areas as well as the inferior parietal lobule; moreover, these patterns varied with the type of action observed, in a way that suggests a somatotopic motor mapping in these regions.

---

[5] In this study, the role of TMS is to "amplify" the activity of the motor system so that its effects on the muscles themselves, if any, will be more measurable.

Further imaging studies show that observing actions in a variety of contexts also activates networks that seem to be selective not just for the particular motor pattern being observed, but also the *intention* behind that movement. In a widely cited fMRI study, Iacoboni et al. (2005) showed participants three different types of scene. In the Context condition, they were shown an object such as a teacup in one of two situations: an organized, well-stocked tea setting, or a dirty, used setting. In the Action condition, they were shown the teacup by itself being acted on in one of two ways: either being picked up with a whole-hand grasping motion, or being picked up with a precision finger grip. Finally, in the Intention condition, they were shown the cup being picked up using one of the two grips in either the before-tea context or the after-tea context. The idea here is that merely picking up a cup by itself may be interpreted differently if the surrounding context suggests that the action is aiming at different goals. In a messy tea setting, picking up the cup may be governed by the intention to put the cup away, whereas in a neat one it may be governed by the intention to take a drink. If people ascribe different intentions in each of these cases, that should show up in the underlying patterns of neural activity.

In line with this prediction, the activity in the Intention condition was different than that in the Context and Action conditions. In the case of the Context condition that is unsurprising, because no acts were shown in it, but the differences between Action and Intention suggest that the very same visual movement of the arm, the same corresponding series of motor commands, and the same resulting path of the object are all processed differently depending on the context in which they are observed. Not only was activity higher in the right inferior frontal cortex in the Intention condition (versus the Action condition), but the patterns of activity were different depending on the kind of grip used. This also suggests that this activity is sensitive to possible goals or uses of the cup.

The promise of mirror neurons, then, seems close to delivering crucial evidence in favor of simulation theory. They are a possible neural mechanism for automatic attributions of action plans to others, they may be present in humans, and their existence is unpredicted by rival accounts such as the Theory theory. However, questions have been raised both about the mirror neuron studies themselves and about their interpretation.

Greg Hickock has raised a number of difficulties for the action understanding hypothesis (Hickock, 2008). He notes that the literature tends to lump together neurophysiological and behavioral results from monkeys with those from humans. But these kinds of inferences demand caution. If we define mirror neurons purely in terms of the response profile of certain cells (as was originally done), it may be that they appear in both monkeys and humans. But this does not guarantee that they serve the same *functions* in both creatures. There are sharp differences between monkeys and humans in terms of their mentalistic capacities: human understanding of actions is much deeper and more complex, and this understanding can be tapped for capacities such as action imitation. But these further capacities (imitation in particular) are absent in monkeys. If mirror neurons alone were *sufficient* for the existence of these capacities, they should be shared across species. It remains to be seen to what extent any general form of "action understanding" is truly shared in this way, however, let alone whether the similarities that exist may be traced to the existence of a common mirroring system. If mirror neurons are not sufficient for the kind of robust action understanding present in humans, then they cannot *constitute* the neural basis for this capacity, even if they causally *contribute* to it in some way (Spaulding, 2012).

Second, it is possible to produce behavioral indicators that are usually assumed to show mirror system activity *without* involving action understanding. Catmur, Walsh, and Heyes (2007) carried out a study similar to that of Fadiga et al. (1995), in which participants watched videos of a hand moving either its index finger or its little finger. They were trained to make the opposite response to the movement observed: move the little finger in response to seeing the index finger move and vice versa. When they were simply shown the video and asked not to move, motor evoked potentials were greater in the finger that they had been *trained* to move, not the finger that they were *observing*. The existence of these evoked potentials was supposed to be evidence of mirror system activity, and therefore of action understanding. But in this case it is clear that the participants *understood* the movement that they saw perfectly well despite producing potentials that corresponded to a different motion. Thus, "mirror activity" does not necessarily coincide with action understanding – for what could it mean to understand the movement of one finger by simulating the movement of another?

Third, there are further dissociations between the activity in mirroring systems and action understanding. Three separate neuropsychological studies suggest that the ability to generate an action and the ability to understand it may come apart.[6] Pazzaglia, Smania, Corato, and Aglioti (2008) looked at 21 patients with limb apraxia (a centrally produced movement disorder), and found that 7 of them had no deficits for recognizing gestures produced by others even though they could not themselves produce them. Moreover, the ability to recognize actions can dissociate from the ability to use objects, and vice versa: this double dissociation was observed in two patients with left hemisphere lesions (Tessari, Canessa, Ukmar, & Rumiati, 2007). In these and other neuropsychological case studies (e.g., Negri et al., 2007), we find that action production and action recognition are not necessarily correlated, a prediction contrary to the simulation theory's view that they share a common neural substrate.

Hickock (2008) proposes an alternative interpretation of mirror neuron activity: the *sensorimotor association hypothesis*. On this view, mirror neurons serve to associatively link perceptions to possible motor activities. It is, after all, undeniable that they *are* associated, since that is testified to by the observed existence of mirror neurons themselves. Hickock points to the fact that these mappings can apparently be quickly changed as further support for this hypothesis. And Iacoboni et al. (1999) showed that there was mirror system activity present even in cases where human participants were viewing a non-action scene, such as a rectangle accompanied by a visual cue to which they had been trained to make a certain motor response. If the mirror system is active in these cases, perhaps it is simply reflecting the preplanned association between the perceived scene and the action.

None of this is to say that mirror neurons may not contribute *somehow* to understanding actions, because these sensorimotor associations may be quite useful to know. But they are not themselves causally responsible for or constitutive of such understanding. What is needed is a more subtle position on the possible role mirror neurons might play short of producing full-fledged action understanding, but pursuing this line further would take us too far afield (see Borg, 2007; Spaulding, 2012). For now, we simply note that although mirror neurons are an intriguing empirical discovery, and one that may turn out to be relevant to many aspects of mindreading, at this point we do not have enough evidence to show that they are the constitutive basis for action understanding, or that they provide decisive support for the simulation theory.

---

[6] Not coincidentally, these resemble the studies of similar dissociations we cited earlier in our discussion of embodied cognition (Section 5.3.2).

8.5 Hybrid approaches

As they have traditionally been developed, simulation and Theory theory are *monolithic* views: they are proposed as the single mechanism responsible for all (or nearly all) of our everyday mindreading competence. Evidence for one was therefore necessarily evidence against the other. However, a range of positions have emerged that attempt to integrate insights and mechanisms from both theories into a single framework. In contrast with their monolithic ancestors, these views are *hybrids* of simulation and theory (Adams, 2001; Stone & Davies, 1996). One of the most sophisticated hybrid models has been developed at length by Nichols and Stich (2003). To get the flavor of how such hybrids function, we now summarize how aspects of their model are motivated by shortcomings of both Theory theory and simulation theory taken individually.

First, we are capable not only of predicting others' behavior, but also the inferences they will make. On TT, these predictions requires having a theory of how people weigh evidence, draw conclusions, and move from one belief to the next. This theory of reasoning will coexist with the reasoning mechanisms that drive our own inferences. But this seems needlessly profligate. Why have both a reasoning mechanism and an inner model of how that reasoning mechanism functions? A theory of how humans reason is unnecessary for predictive purposes as long as they reason sufficiently like *us*. So when it comes to predicting others' inferences, Nichols and Stich suggest that we make use of our own inference mechanisms, simulation-style.

Some aspects of practical reasoning may also be explained by simulation. Achieving a goal, such as cooking a particular dish, often requires completing several subgoals: acquiring the ingredients and the cooking implements, preparing them appropriately (sometimes well in advance), and executing the steps of recipe in the right order. If we desire the end goal (cooking the dish), we also must desire all of the subgoals. In some cases, we may make use of our own goal-planning systems to attribute desires to others by assuming that they have a certain end goal and deriving plausible subgoals that they also have.

However, Nichols and Stich argue that there must be more to desire and goal attribution than simulation. Often, people are extremely bad at predicting the desires of others, including their own future selves. In studies of the endowment effect cited earlier (Section 8.3), people who are asked to *imagine*

receiving a mug as a gift fail to correctly predict the price that they themselves would ask for the mug if they were to receive it (Lowenstein & Adler,
1995). That is, they fail to predict that the endowment effect will occur *to
them*. This cannot simply be dismissed as an inability to recreate the appropriate inputs – how hard can it be to imagine receiving a mug? According
to Nichols and Stich, the fact that imagined responses to such simple scenarios do not correctly predict future desires is evidence that desire prediction
does not employ simulation, but rather an (inaccurate) theoretical reasoning
process.

Belief attributions, too, exhibit inaccuracies that seem inconsistent with
the use of simulation. Consider a phenomenon such as belief perseveration
(Nichols & Stich, 2003, pp. 140–142). Often, experimental psychologists will
manipulate participants into holding a particular belief about themselves.
For example, they might be given feedback indicating that they are extremely
good at distinguishing fake suicide notes from real ones. Once they come to
hold this belief, however, it becomes extremely hard to dislodge, even when
the participants are assured that the evidence for it is totally fraudulent. The
belief perseveration effect came as a surprise to researchers when it was discovered, but it seems a safe bet that it is also surprising to most people. Most
of us would likely predict that we would discard a belief once we had been
shown that it was based on fabricated evidence – or at least we would before
knowing about the perseveration effect itself. Yet this effect should not be surprising if we make these predictions using simulation, because simulating the
appropriate input circumstances should lead us to simulate perseveration
as well.

On a hybrid view such as that of Nichols and Stich, then, mindreading
employs a motley set of processes. For tracking others' inferences and the
structure of their high-level plans and goals, we can make offline use of our
own inference and planning mechanisms, just as simulation theory would
counsel. These also seem to be circumstances where we are likely to make
effortlessly correct predictions. On the other hand, information-rich processes
are needed where simulations fall short, such as predicting discrepant beliefs
and desires. Where we systematically fail to attribute the attitudes that we
ourselves would hold, theory-based processes are likely to blame. That is not
to say that theory-based attribution is always inaccurate, however; in general,
theory may function as both a curse and a corrective. Simulation alone is
often impossible or impractical to use in making many kinds of attributions,

such as simulating the attitudes and behavior of people whose tastes and preferences differ sharply from our own.[7]

In addition to these virtues, the model developed by Nichols and Stich also provides unified explanations of phenomena that are closely related to folk psychology, such as pretense and pretend play in children (Nichols & Stich, 2000). On their view, some of the same cognitive mechanisms are employed in pretense as are used in mental state attribution, particularly the ability to manipulate propositions without actually believing them. They ascribe this function to a mental system called the "Possible World Box," which is also involved in quarantining the propositions being ascribed to the target from the subject's own beliefs. The presence of this common mechanism can also help to explain the comorbidity of mentalizing and pretend play in certain developmental disorders such as autism.

8.6 Minimalism, narrative, and mindshaping

It is often assumed that the practice of folk psychology must essentially rest on the use of a high-powered cognitive mechanism such as theory or simulation. This assumption is common even to hybrid views. But this assumption can also be challenged. Some *minimalists* contend that much of our social life can be negotiated without any sophisticated appeal to mental concepts at all. For example, consider routine interactions in which people play stable social roles (Bermúdez, 2003). In buying coffee or ordering a meal at a restaurant, a customer understands that the barista or waiter is someone whose job it is to fill an order in a certain kind of way. There are culturally normal ways in which such interactions are supposed to go, and normally do go as long as people conform to the behaviors associated with their role. To understand how to handle these situations, it may be necessary only to have in mind an "ordering coffee" script for such stereotypical situations. This script tells each participant what to do next, so engaging in complex mindreading is usually beside the point. Reasoning in terms of scripts and social roles requires matching the situation at hand to the appropriate scenario in memory. This may itself involve subtle detection of similarities and differences (as when one tries to figure out how to apply a domestic script for bartender interactions

---

[7] A similar point concerning the attribution of discrepant tastes is developed as an objection to Gordon's radical simulation theory in Weiskopf (2005).

to ordering drinks in a foreign country), but this is a matter of matching roles and behaviors rather than mindreading. Of course, the strategy of making use of scripted interactions will apply only where social life follows such familiar and routine patterns. But it may do so more often than we think.

Moreover, a widely noted problem for both theory and simulation is that they seem ill suited to constrain the range of possible explanations of behavior (Hutto, 2008, Chapter 1; Zawidzki, 2013, Chapter 3). Having observed someone produce a particular behavior, how is an interpreter to come up with a single most likely mental cause of that behavior? Actions never have single, unique, obvious explanations; any act, even the most commonplace, can be rationalized by indefinitely many sets of beliefs and desires. The cat who chases down the mouse may wish to eat it; or she may not be hungry, but merely amusing herself by terrifying rodents; or she may wish to please her owner by eliminating pests; and so on. A person who chases down a mouse is unlikely to want to eat it, but may wish just to get it out of the house. The behavior of mouse-chasing itself does not tell in favor of any of these hypotheses, let alone more exotic possibilities (perhaps the person is hoping to capture the mouse for her rodent circus). Without any other constraints of plausibility, possible explanations proliferate wildly. In principle, with sufficient imagination, any of these might serve as states that might be simulated to account for the observed behavior. And abstract theoretical schemata seem to fare no better in telling us which of these explanations to prefer.

Such arguments have motivated theorists such as Dan Hutto to suggest that folk psychological explanations do not centrally rely on either theory or simulation. According to Hutto's Narrative Practice Hypothesis (NPH), we should understand folk psychology primarily as an intersubjective practice of producing and interpreting narratives. A narrative is a bit of text or a dialogue delivered in such a way that it can become the object of joint discussion and attention. This might be as part of a conversation, or delivered by one speaker to an audience, such as when parents lead their children through a storybook. These narratives involve causally and temporally related sequences of thought and behavior on the part of various intentional agents. Most importantly, a narrative presents a segment of the mental life of some particular individuals as they reflect, argue, reason, and attempt to carry out their plans. Among the constituents of such a narrative will be the mental states of these participating characters, and the story itself is driven not merely by external events that impinge on them, but by their own drives and motives. These mental states are further contextualized by being framed in a way that makes them part of the characters' larger life story.

Storytelling is a ubiquitous part of childrearing, at least in many Western societies. According to the NPH, this practice of telling and explaining stories plays a central role in our developing mentalistic understanding. A story can be thought of as an exemplar that demonstrates the range of possible things that typically serve as reasons for people's actions, as well as providing a structural template for how these reasons are related to each other. From listening to narratives, children can acquire an inventory of the kinds of beliefs and motives that people are commonly driven by, as well as the ways that they are likely to act under the influence of such reasons. Parents often sensitize children to these facts by asking questions intended to elicit reason-giving explanations, such as "Why do you think she did that?" Children's answers to such questions show where their attention needs to be directed so that they pick up on the correct factors. Narrative practices can thus convey both the "forms and norms" of reason-explanations.

As Hutto puts it, then, stories are "not bare descriptions of current beliefs and desires of idealized rational agents – they are snapshots of the adventures of situated persons, presented in the kinds of settings in which all of the important factors needed for understanding reasons are described" (2007, p. 63). By attending to the narratives given by their caregivers, children come to develop a sense for what motives are commonplace, and for what sorts of behavioral explanations are acceptable. Because the sorts of things that can motivate people are highly variable from one human culture to another, this involves an active process of nudging the child's expectations to line up with prevailing sociocultural norms.

It is possible that narrative practices play a role in shaping children's expectations not only about how others are likely to act, but also about how they *themselves* will act. Storytelling and other folk psychological practices might not just be about training us to be better mindreaders, but also about *mindshaping* (Mameli, 2001; Zawidzki, 2013). Consider that familiarizing children with people's patterns of reason-guided behavior will only be effective in getting them to predict that behavior if those patterns are really the ones that their social cohort exemplifies. Perhaps the very act of highlighting these examples, along with other sociocultural practices, might reshape the cognitive and behavioral dispositions of developing minds, actually bringing them into conformity with prevailing norms.

This is the fundamental idea of a mindshaping mechanism: "one that aims to make a target's *behavioral dispositions* match, in relevant respects, some model" (Zawidzki, 2013, p. 32). The models may be other members of the community, or the fictional characters in a story. There are a number of candidates for such mechanisms. For example, human habits of unconscious imitation and behavioral conformity such as the "chameleon effect" show that people tend to spontaneously take on even the incidental mannerisms of those with whom they are socially engaged (Chartrand & Bargh, 1999). But there are also deeper phenomena such as natural pedagogy, an early-emerging procedure that facilitates transmission of knowledge from experts to novices in development (Csibra & Gergely, 2006, 2009; Gergely & Csibra, 2013).

The need for pedagogy arises because certain types of knowledge and skill are important for children to acquire early, but are unlikely to be acquired if the child is left to learn by solo observation. These typically have three characteristics. First, they are cognitively opaque, meaning that their purpose, function, or causal structure is not obvious to naïve observation. Complex tool use, multiply embedded chains of instrumental actions where the immediate goal is not perceivable, and many normative conventions or social rules fit this description. Second, they involve knowledge concerning the properties of objects and events that generalize beyond particular situations, individuals, or uses. Third, they involve culturally shared knowledge, the acquisition of which is taken for granted for all group members or that is regarded as criterial for proper membership in the group.

Pedagogy involves the teacher explicitly indicating that she is manifesting knowledge for the learner to receive. These signals take many forms, one of the strongest of which is eye contact. Infants can detect upright faces from an early age and attempt to meet the gaze of potential teachers; such eye contact is a signal that indicates the initiation of a pedagogical event. Other resources for marking the pedagogical situation include sensitivity to the temporal signature of turn-taking, such as silence when the infant is acting followed by signaling when the action ceases. Infant gaze-tracking then functions to establish joint attention on the object or event about which the teacher is trying to communicate information; once an object is established as salient, infants tend to keep track of it. Finally, once joint attention has been achieved in what is taken to be a pedagogical situation, infants need to discern the most relevant information being conveyed in the situation. This might be the appropriate way to use an unfamiliar object, the right way to interact with another person, the right thing to call a certain object, and so on.

When infants are cued that a situation is pedagogical, they will imitate an unusual action precisely (e.g., touching a box with one's forehead to make it light up), whereas without these cues they will later only keep track of the goal of the action (touching the box somehow), rather than the specific means used. Similarly, when pedagogical cues are given, children will generalize the emotional attitude a teacher displays toward an object to other people, whereas without these cues they will take them to apply only to that person. Pedagogical cues that children track appear to signify that actions have general application and that their fine-grained structure is important. Developing the skills to use this information relies crucially on the formation of these intersubjective pedagogical bonds.

Pedagogy and other mindshaping mechanisms may help to ensure that humans raised in the same groups have similar behavioral dispositions as well as similar underlying patterns of reasoning. By imposing a kind of cognitive homogeneity, they help to make members of such groups more mutually intelligible, thus making their minds more easily legible to each other. There may even be more widespread cognitive effects from such interactions. Autobiographical memory provides a striking example of how cognitive skills develop in response to sociocultural interactions involving narrative (Nelson & Fivush, 2004). Certain social interactions seem to significantly structure the development of autobiographical memory. Style of maternal interaction is one important factor (Reese, Haden, & Fivush, 1993). Some mothers use a "highly elaborative" way of speaking to children, prompting them to recall more details, embellishing narrative structure, and treating remembering as a social event. Children of highly elaborative mothers tended to contribute more pieces of information when engaging in autobiographical recall. This ability develops over time, so early maternal style predicts how good children become at remembering personal life events over a year later. Children of low-elaboration mothers, by contrast, tended to be able to recall fewer details. The effects of high-elaboration interaction persist even after children's nonverbal memory and language skills are factored out (Harley & Reese, 1999). These effects may be long-lasting: cross-culturally, differences in how much elaborative autobiographical recall takes place in development are also correlated with how many early-life memories adults report (Mullen & Yi, 1995). This suggests that not only can narrative practices help to winnow down the range of possible behavioral explanations, they also help to shape the structure of memory itself.

8.7 Conclusions

Our account of social cognition has necessarily been brief and partial. We have mostly discussed attribution of mental states to others, leaving aside theories of how we come to know our *own* minds (Carruthers, 2011; Gertler, 2011; Wilson, 2002). We have not discussed how mindreading capacities relate to language (Astington & Baird, 2005), nor how evidence from disorders such as autism may bear on the normal functioning of mindreading (Frith & Hill, 2004). Nor have we examined the scope of mindreading in nonhumans, or its phylogenetic origins (Tomasello, 2014).

However, even within our purview there are complexities enough. A full account of mindreading, although it may rely on components of theory and simulation, will necessarily be more expansive than either one taken individually. This is because the phenomena of folk psychology in a broad sense are so heterogeneous. Human sociality includes cooperation and competition, symbolic communication, the transmission of culture, justifying and regulating behavior, attributing character and other personal traits, and moral praise and blame. The explanatory and predictive roles that have been emphasized here are part of the story, but cannot give a full explanation for all of these practices. In the end, a more fine-grained dissection of these sociocognitive phenomena may reveal that folk psychological practices are not a singular thing and need to be accounted for by a plurality of different mechanisms (Andrews, 2012; Morton, 2007).

9 Thought and language

9.1 On wordless minds

Which comes first, thought or language? Do thoughts about the world take shape and then become expressed in a language? Or does one acquire a language first, and only later, or simultaneously by virtue of the very tools of language, gain the ability to think about the world? Descartes notoriously took one of the hardest lines on this question. Speechless animals, he claimed, did not think at all. He may have even meant to imply by this that they lack experience of any kind. The ability to use language in a productive and creative way, for Descartes, was the only sure sign of mentality because it was a performance that could not be duplicated by a mere physical machine. Language is an infinite resource and one that is endlessly adaptable to new contexts. By contrast, the grunts of pigs and the cunning life-and-death dance of wolves hunting sheep are all purely material acts produced by mindless neural machinery.

To modern ears, this may sound peculiar. Language itself is an evolutionarily recent innovation, one that builds on a complex and extensive foundation of behavioral and cognitive processes. Once we adopt an evolutionary perspective, the phylogeny of cognition appears as a series of increasingly elaborate minds, and the Cartesian attempt to draw a bright line marking out the simultaneous emergence of thought and language seems fruitless (Dennett, 1997).

Debates over how and where to draw these lines draw on anecdotes and introspection as well as more systematic data. In her autobiography, Helen Keller said that before she learned sign language, she could not think and was not aware of the world – though her teacher Annie Sullivan denied this. And we may feel that our own experience gives us evidence of thought preceding language. Everyone knows the tip-of-the-tongue phenomenon, in which an idea frustrates us by hovering just beyond our verbal grasp (Schwartz & Metcalfe, 2011). If the idea were couched in words, how could we fail to find words for it? And extensive psycholinguistic data suggest that we remember the gist, not the letter of the message we read or hear (Bransford & Franks, 1971; Gernsbacher, 1985). People often have poor memories for the exact sentences that they hear or read. This does not prevent them from acquiring the content of what is said, but it does lend credence to the view that we store this content at a level of abstraction above that of the natural-language sentence.

As we will see, however, there are substantial philosophical arguments favoring the "language first" view. This view maintains that before the development of language, the mind is not yet furnished with words or concepts and lacks the tools for thinking about the world. Even if some forms of thought precede language, language may still be a major force in *shaping* thought. There may be an early stock of basic, universal concepts necessary for thought to originate. However, the process of learning a language may build new capacities that reshape one's conceptual repertoire, ways of thinking, and overall worldview. This position has been defended by linguistic anthropologists impressed with the range of human linguistic and cultural diversity. If it is correct, there should be evidence of the variation in cognitive capacities of a single language learner over time and between learners of different languages. We chronicle part of the hunt for this evidence in the remainder of this chapter.

9.2 Language–thought relations

For present purposes, mental states that take propositions as their content will count as thoughts. A proposition is a structured entity that consists of something in the subject position (*George Washington*) and predicate position (*was the first US president*). A thought is always a thought *that* such-and-such is the case, for example that Washington was the first US president. Similarly for hopes (that there will be global nuclear disarmament) or fears (that there will be another recession). Hence, thoughts come in a wide range of types but have in common that they relate a subject's mental state M to a propositional content *that p*. Thought in this sense is primarily *conceptualized* thought.

What about language? Here we focus mainly on public or natural languages such as English, Russian, Hindi, Welsh, or Mandarin. Language has unique properties that distinguish it from other signaling systems. It is often casually said that dogs have a language, since they bark, growl, and whimper, or that the songs of dolphins and whales are languages. Or consider the cries of vervet monkeys, who signal the presence of predators and vary their signal according to whether the predator is in the trees, on the ground, or overhead (Seyfarth, Cheney, & Marler, 1980). These animals are able to convey information about the world and about themselves via an array of different sounds and signals. Yet, these signals, informative though they are, do not have the properties that make something a language for the purposes of this debate.

Languages are governed by structured set of rules for the formation of sentences. These rules are productive, meaning that there are infinitely many sentences of each natural language. So in English not only is "The man kicked the table" a sentence, but so are these:

> "The man kicked the wooden table."
> "The man in the bowler hat kicked the cheap wooden table."
> "The recently divorced man in the bowler hat kicked the cheap wooden table, scattering peanut brittle and scaring the children."

And so on. By inserting further phrases and conjoining other sentences, infinitely many new and distinct sentences can be formed. This productivity is possible because languages have a phonology (sound system), syntax (formal structure system), and semantics (system of meaning), and these generate a discrete infinity of well-formed sentences using only a finite set of lexical elements (words and affixes).

The standard explanation for the productivity of language is that it is compositional. Compositionality means that the properties of complex expressions are determined in a rule-governed fashion by the properties of the expressions that make them up, plus the way in which they are combined. So the meaning of "red barn" is determined by that of "red" and "barn," plus the way they are put together. Mere signal systems, however, are not compositional. A natural language can express the thought that the same predator that was in the trees is now on the ground and coming this way. The vervets may let out a call that first lets one know there is a predator in the trees and later lets one know there is a predator on the ground. But because the signals have no decomposition into repeatable parts, there is no way to signal its being the same predator. The signals are not compositional in phonology, syntax, or semantics. They operate more or less as whole unanalyzed units.

Perhaps dolphins or whales have systems of communication that are compositional and productive – we don't yet know. But unless they do, these won't count as language in the debate we are sketching here.

Finally, language is multifunctional. The rules of language allow it to represent complex propositions. Sometimes we simply want to communicate these propositions to others. But languages are not restricted to communicative uses. They can also be used to command, to cajole or persuade, to inquire, to convey something nonliteral (as in metaphorical, sarcastic, or ironic uses), or simply to entertain (as in fiction, poetry, and song). They may do many of these things at once. Honeybee dances are sometimes called a language because they possess a complex structure and are used to convey information. But these signals, like others in the animal kingdom, may not be governed by any communicative intentions on the bees' part. And even where animal signals are used with the intention to communicate, they are rarely capable of being used in this potentially open-ended fashion. Were animals able to bring such calls under voluntary control, this might allow them to use the calls for their own purposes (Adams & Beighley, 2013). The calls would then take on the functional properties associated with language.

The languages of the world offer an amazing array of resources for carrying out these purposes. They differ widely in properties such as their phonological structure, syntax, lexicon, and semantic properties. *Linguistic diversity* is the post-Babel human condition. The anthropologist Franz Boas noted this in his landmark survey of Native American languages: "It is perfectly conceivable that this variety of ideas, each of which is expressed by a single independent term in English, might be expressed in other languages by derivations from the same term" (1911, p. 21). Therefore, he continued, "what appears as a single simple idea in one language may be characterized by a series of distinct phonetic groups in another" (p. 22).

Linguists debate about whether these differences are deep or superficial, but that languages have different formal patterns seems beyond dispute. As anyone who has learned several languages knows, these patterns can sometimes seem extremely strange. Not only do languages differ in the sorts of things named by their basic lexical inventory, they often draw distinctions or mark qualities that can seem bizarre from the point of view of one's native language. For example, paying attention to the evidential source of a piece of information is optional for English speakers, but in Turkish it is obligatory for speakers to mark whether an event in the past was observed by the speaker or not observed. It can be difficult to see why this information should be part of the very grammar of the language itself.

Given such diversity, it may seem tempting to posit the idea that speakers of other languages are not merely using a different expressive medium to convey the same basic underlying thoughts, but also thinking about the world (and perhaps even perceiving it) in different ways. The philosopher and linguist Wilhelm von Humboldt held this view, famously saying:

> Language is the formative organ of thought. Intellectual activity, entirely mental, entirely internal, and to some extent passing without trace, becomes through sound, externalized in speech and perceptible to the senses. Thought and language are therefore one and inseparable from each other. (von Humboldt, 1836/1988, p. 54)

This is the thesis of *linguistic determinism*: the formal patterning of language has systematic psychological consequences. Language is not just an adjunct or servant of thought, it actually shapes the form and content of thought itself. There is a clear implied direction of causation in linguistic determinism. The properties of language *cause* thought to be shaped in various ways.

Linguistic diversity and linguistic determinism, when combined, entail the thesis of *linguistic relativity*: speakers of different languages are psychologically different *as a result of* speaking those languages. As the linguist Edward Sapir put the point: "This is the relativity of concepts or, as it might be called, the relativity of the form of thought" (1924, p. 159). However, linguistic determinism and relativity only posit a direction of causation between the properties of language and those of thought. This leaves open *which* properties may be involved on both sides of the equation, as well as how strong this influence is.

Ultrastrong determinism is the claim that language is needed for the very existence of thought. There is no such thing as thinking without some language, either because language is the seed from which higher thought grows, or because language is the inner medium that constitutes such thought. Ordinary *strong* determinism says that certain *types* of thought are only possible given the possession of a certain type of language. Here we should distinguish between determinism about the form and content of thought and determinism about thought processes. The former has to do with the kinds of concepts that we can entertain and the propositions we may formulate using them, whereas the latter has to do with the mechanisms by which thinking operates. On strong determinism, the influence of language leads certain thought contents to become accessible or certain patterns of thought to become mandatory, while others become inaccessible or impossible.

Sapir seems to have held the strong thesis: "Language and our thought-grooves are inextricably interrelated, are, in a sense, one and the same" (1921, p. 218). Benjamin Lee Whorf, a student of Sapir, added that the grammar of a language "is not merely a reproducing instrument for voicing ideas but rather is itself a shaper of ideas, the program and guide for the individual's mental activity, for his analysis of impressions, for his synthesis of his mental stock in trade" (1940, p. 212). There is no such thing as a world that is grasped conceptually prior to the acquisition of language. Thus the thesis of linguistic determinism, particularly in its strong form, is sometimes called the *Sapir–Whorf hypothesis*.[1]

Finally, there are various forms of *weak* determinism. Whereas (ultra)strong determinism says that language is in some way necessary for thought, weak determinism only holds that language *influences* thought in some way. Most frequently, weak determinism involves the claim that language affects "habitual thought" (Whorf's term) by biasing attention, memory, or preferences. We will discuss several forms of weak determinism in Section 9.4.

9.3 Strong linguistic determinism

Obviously, some thoughts can only be entertained if one has learned a language – for example, thoughts about language itself, such as the thought that "red" means *red*, or the thought that "i" comes before "e" except after "c." A related area where the strong thesis may be true is certain types of technical or mathematical and logical reasoning. It is unlikely that one could do sophisticated mathematics without any system of numerals at all. And surely Gödel would not have been able to discover an incompleteness proof for mathematics or Cantor the diagonal proof of orders of infinite numbers, without the necessary human-made formal symbolic systems that made these proofs possible.[2] But the strong thesis is not usually aimed at these topics. It

[1] For extensive reviews of the history and recent anthropological, linguistic, and experimental literature on linguistic relativity and determinism, see Hill and Mannheim (1992), Hunt and Agnoli (1991), Koerner (1992), and Lucy (1997).
[2] Our claim here is both tentative and restricted to advanced reasoning in the formal sciences, not elementary geometry, arithmetic, or basic deductive logic; as we will see in Section 9.5, there are good reasons to think that these are intact even when language itself is impaired.

is normally focused on more humdrum kinds of thoughts had by ordinary speakers of natural languages, not users of these specialized symbol systems.

Arguments in favor of the strong and ultrastrong theses have been given by philosophers such as W. V. Quine (1960), Jonathan Bennett (1988), and Donald Davidson (1975/1984, 1982/2001). Quine thinks it is unlikely that we can properly attribute thoughts to languageless animals. In such attributions, he would say that we are indulging in an essentially "dramatic idiom," putting ourselves in their place and imagining what we would be inclined to think or say (Quine, 1960, p. 219). But these acts of attribution are merely projective and somewhat fanciful exercises.

Quine extends this line of thought to the cognitive development of prelinguistic children. He famously argues that without mastery of the difference between count nouns and mass nouns, the child fails to draw certain ontological distinctions. Understanding the difference in what these terms refer to depends on mastering the terms themselves:

> We in our maturity have come to look upon the child's mother as an integral body who, in an irregular closed orbit, revisits the child from time to time: and to look upon red in a radically different way, viz., as scattered about. Water, for us, is rather like red, but not quite; things are red, stuff alone is water. But then mother, red, and water are for the infant all of a type; each is just a history of sporadic encounter, a scattered portion of what goes on. His first learning of the three words is uniformly a matter of learning how much of what goes on about him counts as the mother, or as red, or as water. It is not for the child to say in the first case 'Hello! Mama again', in the second case 'Hello! another red thing', and in the third case 'Hello! more water'. They are all on a par: Hello! more mama, more red, more water. (1960, p. 92)

So it is clear for Quine that the child, in these first instances, is not using "Mama" as a count term, rather than a mass term, and therefore is not able to distinguish in thought among individuals, properties, and substances. In Quine's view, the thoughts cannot come prior to the words – prior to understanding the meaning of what he calls "divided reference."

Quine appears committed to a principle of the manifestability of thought – that the capacity for thought requires the capacity to manifest these thoughts (Glock, 2003). The idea is that ascribing thoughts makes sense only where there are means of publicly identifying those thoughts, and for Quine this requires identification via behavior or speech. Of course, this may be a restriction not on what kinds of thoughts creatures actually have, but only on what thoughts we are justified in ascribing. It may also mean that some thoughts need not be manifest in linguistic behavior. Behavior of the nonlinguistic kind may be sufficient for justifying ascriptions of some thoughts. So Quine's restriction of manifestability may be more about limiting languageless creatures to simple thoughts rather than a claim that no thought can be possessed by them.

In a similar spirit, Jonathan Bennett (1964/1989; 1988) argued not that there could not be thought without language, but that there could not be thoughts of certain types without language. Specifically, Bennett claims that without language, animal thoughts are locked into the present and the particular. Only language allows thoughts about the distant past or the future. And only words for quantification allow general thoughts about *many*, *most*, or even *all* or *no* events or objects of certain kinds. Animals, he allows, may have beliefs that are *shaped* by past events, but they do not have beliefs about those past events themselves. Nor, even if they respond similarly to every object of a certain kind, do they have general thoughts about all objects of that kind. Without language, there is no decisive evidence that would manifest possession of such beliefs by an animal.[3]

Where Bennett is skeptical that animals or languageless creatures could have thoughts of certain kinds without language, Donald Davidson questions whether they could have thoughts at all. Although Davidson's conclusions put him on the same page as Descartes, his reasons for this controversial position differ. Davidson rests his arguments on the claims that (1) thoughts are intensional, (2) they are holistic, and (3) they require the concept of belief itself.

Consider intensionality first. If a dog thinks a cat went up a tree, and the tree is the oldest oak tree in town, does the dog think the cat went up the oldest oak tree in town? This hardly follows. Even if $a = b$, to believe that a is F need not imply that one believes that b is F. This is the intensionality of thought: it is possible to have differing attitudes toward one and the same thing if one does not *grasp* that they are the same. Davidson appeals to language to account for this phenomenon: "the intensionality we make so much of in attributing thoughts is very hard to make much of when speech is not present. The dog, we say, knows that its master is at home. But does it know that Mr. Smith

---

[3] However, in later work Bennett significantly criticized and modified his earlier positions on what sorts of thoughts languageless animals can have (see Bennett, 1976/1990, pp. 96–123).

(who is his master)... is home? We have no real idea how to settle, or to make sense of, these questions" (1975/1984, p. 163).

Like Quine, Davidson maintains that we can only ascribe thoughts to others, including animals, against a background of complex patterns of behavior. This is not to identify thinking with behaving or dispositions to behave, but it does require the proper evidential basis in behavior to ascribe thoughts. As he puts it:

> My thesis is not, then, that thought depends for its existence on the existence of a sentence that expresses that thought. My thesis is rather that a creature cannot have a thought unless it has a language. In order to be a thinking, rational creature, the creature must be able to express many thoughts, and above all, be able to interpret the speech and thoughts of others. (1982/2001, p. 100)

For Davidson, rationality, thought, and language (including the ability to interpret the language of others) are co-dependent and occur at the same time. Why does he think this? For one, he is a holist about beliefs. Nobody can have just one. Returning to our previous example, to believe the cat went up the oak tree, the dog would need the concept of a tree, of an oak, and of all that goes along with being an oak tree. But this may require endlessly many beliefs. Does the dog know what a cat is, or what a tree is? Does it know trees are alive? Does it know trees need water to live? Does it have a general supply of truths about trees, or about cats for that matter? Davidson thinks the dog does not, disqualifying it from thinking about trees or cats or anything. It doesn't have the appropriate general concepts necessary for these kinds of thoughts. Only in a language can one acquire these general beliefs.

Davidson realizes he needs a further step in his argument from the lack of general beliefs about kinds of things to the view that animals can't think at all. So he turns to the question of what the capacity for language supplies that makes it essential for thought. His argument has two steps: (1) in order to have a belief, it is necessary to have the concept of belief; and (2) in order to have the concept of a belief, one must have language.

Were these true, Davidson would have a powerful argument. To defend premise (1), Davidson turns to the state of being surprised. He says that to be surprised requires having the concept of belief. The idea is that if I am surprised that a is not F then I must know that I expected a to be F. I must be aware of my state of belief to see the world does not fit my expectation.

So I need to have the concept of the way the world is according to me – but that just is to have a concept of belief. To be surprised is to be aware that the world is not as you believed it to be. Davidson completes his argument by saying that the only way one could acquire this notion of a subjective-objective contrast (the world as it seemed to me vs. the world as it really is) requires language and linguistic interaction between persons. "Our sense of objectivity is the consequence of another sort of triangulation, one that requires two creatures" (1982/2001, p. 105).

In reply to Davidson, it may turn out that there is a kind of intensionality even for creatures like dogs. Consider the sniffer-dog at the airport. It believes that the white powder it smells is the target it has been trained on, namely cocaine. But in an airtight bag, the same substance may get no response from the dog. It is the smell, not the sight of the drug that alerts the dog to its presence. It believes that the substance that smells like *this* is the target (cocaine). The target looks like *that* in an airtight pouch. But the dog does not believe that the target looks like *that*. The dog does not connect the substance that has *this* particular smell with the substance that has *that* particular look. This is a plausible manifestation of intensionality by a languageless creature.

In regard to the nature of general concepts, Davidson's requirements of holism are so stringent that a baby could not believe it was being held by its mother, if it did not hold many general beliefs about the biological and cultural functions of maternity. Nor is it clear that there is any way of deter-mining which such beliefs must be possessed in order for the child to have that concept. This has seemed to many to be a reductio of such a strong requirement on having thoughts (Fodor & Lepore, 1992).

In regard to Davidson's notion that one needs the concept of belief to have beliefs and to be capable of surprise, we have good reason to think he is wrong. Just as it seems infants can have beliefs without need-ing the concept of belief (or, anyway, without a sophisticated concept of belief), infants display surprise without needing the concept of surprise. This is a presupposition of research in developmental psychology that uses a dishabituation paradigm. For example, infants show surprise (they look longer and with more intensity) when only one object appears where there appeared to be two or when one object appears in a location where it would have appeared to have to pass through another (Baillargeon, 1995; Spelke, 1990).

To be surprised is to have the world turn out other than as one expects. But that does not require that one have the concept of expectation (or belief). It requires only that one be capable of having expectations (or beliefs). Davidson would be correct if he were giving an argument about thought ascriptions to others. But if, as it seems, his argument is intended only to cover necessary conditions for having thoughts at all, it seems to fall short. One does not need the concept of cancer to acquire cancer, or the concept of thought to have a thought. No strong conclusions about the nature of thought itself follow from the epistemic conditions under which we *attribute* thoughts.[4]

9.4 From strong to weak determinism

The philosophical arguments for strong linguistic determinism are contentious. But in recent decades there has been a tremendous "neo-Whorfian" revival in psychology, centered on finding linguistic effects on thought in many cognitive domains, including color, number, and theory of mind. Here we focus on three of these: basic ontology, space, and grammatical gender.

9.4.1 Ontology

Recall that Quine held that mastering the ontological distinction between objects and substances depended on mastering the linguistic distinction between count nouns and mass nouns. Soja, Carey, and Spelke (1991) devised a behavioral test of this claim. They presented two-year old children who had not yet mastered count versus mass nouns with unfamiliar objects such as a curved copper tubing pipe or a curved stream of pink hair gel. These items were paired with words, such as "This is my tulver" for the curved tubing. They then showed the children two test items, one of the same shape, but a different substance, the other of the same substance, but a different shape, and asked the children to point to the "tulver." When the word was first paired with the copper tubing, the children pointed to an object of the same shape, but a different substance, such as a curved plastic pipe. When the word was paired with a substance such as the hair gel, they pointed to the same substance, regardless of its shape. Children thus distinguish

---

[4] Of course, we should add that Davidson's arguments here are extraordinarily complicated, and we have only sketched them in the barest outlines. For much more discussion and critical analysis, see Lepore and Ludwig (2005, Chapter 22).

individual objects from types of stuff (not differentiated as individuals), prior to acquiring distinct count versus mass terms. These results suggest that the conceptual ability precedes the acquisition of the terms that mark the distinction exhibited by our use of count nouns and mass nouns.

This point is further supported by cross-linguistic studies. In a series of careful investigations, John Lucy and his collaborators compared English speakers with Mayan speakers of Yucatec. There are a few salient differences between the languages (Lucy, 1992). First, English has a strong count/mass noun distinction, meaning that many nouns are obligatorily given plural marking; hence the difference between "two cats" versus *"two sands," and "a badger" versus *"a mud." In Yucatec, pluralization is optional and applies to relatively few nouns. Second, English numeral quantifiers directly modify plural nouns ("one candle"), whereas in Yucatec numerals must be conjoined with a separate term known as a numeral *classifier*. These classifiers usually indicate the shape or composition of the noun's referent, so to talk about "two candles" requires a construction that can be paraphrased as "two *long thin* candles" (the shape classifiers are italicized). Indeed, Lucy suggests the quantificationally unmarked nature of bare nouns in Yucatec makes them more like terms for "unformed substances," so this expression might better be translated as "two long thin *waxes*" (Lucy & Gaskins, 2001, p. 261).

From these linguistic differences, a cognitive prediction follows: because attention to shape is habitually required for correct application of nouns in English, speakers of English will tend to be more focused on that quality, whereas speakers of Yucatec will tend to focus on facts about material composition, since that is more relevant to applying nouns in that language. Lucy (1992) showed adult speakers of each language a standard object and two comparison objects, one of which matched the standard in shape and the other which matched it in material. The participants were then asked to decide which of the two was most similar to the standard. The majority of English speakers matched by shape, whereas the majority of Yucatec speakers matched by material, a result consistent with the predicted focus each language places on these different characteristics.

Early patterns of word use turn out to diverge in language-specific ways. Imai and Gentner (1993, 1997) compared English- and Japanese-speaking children (two year olds and four year olds) and adults. Japanese, like Yucatec, is a numeral classifier language. Each participant was shown three standards: a simple object, a complex object, and a sample of a substance. The standard was named, and participants were shown a target that matched the standard either in shape or in material composition and asked to extend the label to one of the two new objects. For the complex objects, all age groups within both languages generalized the new word to the object with the same shape. For the substances, the Japanese participants of all ages preferred to generalize according to material; the youngest English-speaking participants share this preference, although older English speakers are more ambivalent. For simple objects, however, the linguistic groups diverge sharply. English speakers always prefer to generalize by shape. Japanese speakers show no preference until adulthood, when they show a slight preference to generalize on the basis of material.

These studies point toward two conclusions. First, contra Quine, the individual/substance distinction is in place early in childhood no matter what the linguistic environment is. Second, though, language may influence certain habits of classification later in development. When some objects are labeled, it is not clear whether the label they are given attaches to the kind of stuff they are made of or the type of coherent, countable entity they are. The situation is ambiguous. In such unclear cases, the boundary of classification can be nudged one way or another by language. Speaking English may encourage people to conceptualize potentially ambiguous entities as *objects*, whereas speaking Japanese may encourage conceptualizing them as *substances*. This type of influence is consistent with, at most, a form of weak determinism.

9.4.2 Space

Languages differ not only in their ontological preferences but also in how they divide up and refer to space (Bowerman, 1996; Choi & Bowerman, 1991). In English, the prepositions "on" and "in" can be used to designate a range of spatial relations: (1) the apple is *in* the bowl, (2) the cassette tape is *in* its case, (3) the lid is *on* the bowl, (4) the cup is *on* the table. Here (1) and (2) include any sort of spatial containment relation, while (3) and (4) include any relation of spatial support. In Korean, however, there are no precise equivalents to these relations. Rather, there are spatial verbs that carve events involving these relations along different dimensions. Korean ignores the English "in" and "on" as distinctions for containment, but pays close attention to whether the containment is "tight" (a cap going on a pen) or "loose" (apples in an open bowl). So an apple being put in a bowl (loose containment) would be referred to using *nehta*, a tape being put in its case or a lid closed on a bowl (tight containment) would be referred to using *kkita*, and a cup being placed on a table (loose support) is designated by *nohta*.

If languages cross-classify space with respect to one another, these linguistic differences may direct children's developing spatial attention. Children between the ages of 1.5 and 2 years old are only starting to grasp how their language represents space. When presented with visual scenes that illustrate different types of containment and support, they seem to show no particular preferences in which ones they look at. However, when these scenes are accompanied by a verbal label, they stare longer at the scene that exemplifies the relation encoded by their language (Choi, McDonough, Bowerman, & Mandler, 1999; Casasola, 2005). Although these language-guided looking preferences emerge early, they come out of a prelinguistic background in which neither set of spatial contrasts is privileged. Infants as young as 9 months old seem to be able to distinguish between tight fit and loose fit no matter whether they are reared in an English- or a Korean-speaking household. Before language takes hold, then, *both* relations are equally available. English-speaking adults, however, have a more difficult time perceiving differences in these scenes compared to Korean-speaking adults (McDonough, Choi, & Mandler, 2003). In some studies, infants even detect the tight fit/loose fit contrast as young as 5 months old (Hespos & Spelke, 2004). Language learners may start out being indifferent among the many ways human languages can categorize space, only coming to prefer one framework as they become fluent.

Languages also differ in their built-in spatial reference systems. These systems are employed in describing a scene or giving directions. In English, objects are commonly related to one another using a body-centered (or egocentric) reference scheme. The cup can be said to be *to your left*, or the man *to the left* of the tree. Left and right are defined in terms of a reference body, either one's own or that of a target. However, other languages do not lexicalize the left-right distinction, instead using geocentric reference schemes. In the Mayan language Tzeltal, for example, objects are described as being either "uphill" or "downhill" of one another. This distinction arises from the fact that Tzeltal-speaking inhabitants of Tenejapa live on inclined terrain, with highlands in the south and lowlands in the north. The slope of the land is a highly salient directional marker. Consequently, using geocentric references will have nearly universal utility within the community (Levinson & Brown, 1994). Geocentric reference systems occur in other languages as well, such as Longgu, which characterizes objects as being "inland" or "toward the sea."

If language constrains the way people can talk about space because it is geocentric or egocentric, and if language biases cognition, we would expect to find significant differences and possibly even deficiencies where a cognitive task required a type of spatial reasoning not captured by one's language. Using a nonlinguistic task, Pederson and collaborators found such differences across languages that differ in their preferred spatial reference frame (Pederson et al., 1998). They asked participants to face a table containing a set of toy objects placed in a line running transversely. Their task was to memorize the arrangement of the objects. Participants were then turned around to face an empty table and asked to recreate the arrangement of the objects (specifically, they were told to "make it the same"). As linguistic determinism would predict, speakers of geocentric languages and egocentric languages recreated these arrangements in opposite ways, suggesting that the object locations are coded and remembered in terms of the language's preferred orientation even in a nonlinguistic task.

However, these results were challenged by Li and Gleitman (2002). They replicated the table rotation memory task using monolingual English speakers, but varied the visible environmental conditions of the scenario. One group worked in a featureless room, a second group worked in a room with the windows open, and a third group worked in an open space on campus surrounded by buildings. These different scenarios were intended to mimic the naturalistic field conditions used to test many of the geocentric speakers, and the relatively austere laboratory conditions used to test the egocentric speakers. The results were that in conditions offering more obvious landmarks, participants preferred to arrange objects in a geocentric fashion. Where there were no such cues, they resorted to egocentric arrangements. Since the task itself is open-ended and ambiguous, speakers will make a "pragmatically sensible guess" (Li & Gleitman, 2002, p. 286) about how to proceed. And which guess is appropriate depends on the circumstances, not the language.

In fact, when the task context is changed so that there is an unambiguously *correct* solution, even speakers of geocentric languages can successfully adopt egocentric strategies (Li, Abarbanell, Gleitman, & Papafragou, 2011). Speakers of Tzeltal were given a series of spatial disorientation tasks that could be solved geocentrically or egocentrically. In one, they were seated in a spinning office chair and a coin was placed in one of two boxes. In the egocentric condition, the boxes were affixed to the chair itself; in the geocentric condition, they were placed on the floor. Participants were then blindfolded, spun around, and asked to point to the box containing the coin. In the egocentric condition, no matter how much the chair was spun around, participants found it easy to point to its location afterward. Because the box moved with the chair, this is a fairly trivial task. In the geocentric condition, however, the more they were aimed away from the starting position, the worse their performance. This is inconsistent with the idea that their language leads them to habitually encode geocentric mappings and much more in line with a task-sensitive recruitment of egocentric resources.

These results, like all others, are suggestive rather than definitive. Certainly they may be contested (see, e.g., Levinson, Kita, Haun, & Rasch, 2002; Majid, Bowerman, Kita, Haun, & Levinson, 2004). But they are consistent with a view on which languages may encode many different spatial relations and reference frames without these encodings exerting a strong determining effect on spatial cognition itself. Infants appear flexible in their ability to attend to spatial categories, and adult speakers may adopt spatial reasoning strategies that make sense in the context, even when this conflicts with the habitual cues provided by their language. Perception and thought about space seems only weakly Whorfian.

9.4.3 Gender

Many languages possess gender systems. These may seem to be mere superficial curiosities. Are pens really feminine? Perhaps they were in the days of quill and feather – thus, *la plume* in French. Maybe not now, in the day of Paper Mate ball pens (*le stylo à bille*). Still, grammatical gender may influence thought. Genders are a way of marking noun classes in order to impose agreement between nouns and other words, such as pronouns and adjectives. Although the terms "masculine" and "feminine" are arbitrary labels assigned by linguistic theorists, they also coincide with sociocultural stereotypes about males and females. These gender markers may actually influence how speakers of the language think about objects, so that mere things may have gendered properties.

In one study aimed at testing the influence of gendered nouns, Boroditsky, Schmidt, and Phillips (2003) found that objects named by masculine nouns were judged to be more "potent" than those named by nouns grammatically feminine – even though the objects named (inanimate objects, places, events, abstract entities) had no biological gender. They also paired male or female names with objects that either matched or mismatched feminine nouns in Spanish and German (e.g., apple–Patricia vs. apple–Patrick). The prediction was that whether it was easier to recall the pairs would depend on whether the pairs matched (apple is masculine in German and feminine in Spanish). Memory for these pairs was better when the gender of the name coincided with the grammatical gender of the word for the object in the speaker's native language.

They found similar effects on the choices people make in English description of objects that would vary by gender in their home languages of German or Spanish. Speakers of languages with gendered nouns carry those gender categorizations over to the objects themselves. The suggestion is that if the noun is masculine, then the speaker may look for some property of the object associated with stereotypes of masculinity, and if the noun is feminine, they will look for some property of the object typically associated with femininity. The word "key" is masculine in German and feminine in Spanish. German speakers described keys as "hard, heavy, jagged, metal, serrated, and useful" while Spanish speakers described them as "golden, intricate, little, lovely, shiny, and tiny." On the other hand "bridge" is feminine in German and masculine in Spanish. German speakers typically characterize them as "beautiful, elegant, fragile, peaceful, pretty, and slender" while Spanish speakers say they are "big, dangerous, long, strong, sturdy, and towering." Similar attributions of qualities are found even when objects are presented without accompanying labels (Sera, Berge, & del Castillo Pintado, 1994).

These results are surely startling. But it is unclear how widespread or deep they are. For instance, in some studies the effects of gender on object stereotypes is weaker in German than in French or Spanish, possibly because German has three genders rather than two, suggesting that the effects may be limited in scope (Sera et al., 2002). In fact, most studies of gender have used a highly limited sampling of languages. Languages such as Dyirbal have four genders, and Proto-Bantu has 14. In Tamil, the genders approximate a distinction between rational and nonrational entities; in Dyirbal there is a gender that seems to mean "non-flesh food" (Dixon, 1972). What sorts of stereotypical properties should we expect to be generated in these languages? This is a perennial problem with attempts to draw large-scale conclusions about the effect of general properties such as gender on thought: the range of linguistic diversity is vastly greater than has been experimentally sampled, and the determinism hypothesis generates no clear predictions for much of the space of this variation.

9.5 Dissociating language and thought

The studies reviewed so far argue indicate that language may influence thought in subtle ways, by directing our attention to certain features of the environment rather than others, or by providing a certain default way of reasoning about how to solve a problem or to encode items in memory. But although these patterns of habitual thinking may exist, we can be nudged out of them given the right circumstances. These patterns themselves emerge out of a prelinguistic state in which many possible ways of representing and reasoning about the world are already available. Language, then, neither creates nor strongly determines thought content or processes. It is merely one source of information among many.

For an example of just how easy it can be to reshape these language-inflected thought processes, consider a study by Casasanto, Fotakopoulou, Pita, and Boroditsky (unpublished manuscript), which compared speakers of English and Greek. In English, it is customary to use distance terms ("long") to refer to quantities of time, whereas Greek uses amount terms ("more"). These linguistic differences are mirrored by cognitive ones: there is interference on tasks that require distance and time estimation for English speakers, and amount and time estimation for Greek speakers. So far, so Whorfian. However, English speakers can easily be induced to perform like Greek speakers. After only a brief training session in which they were encouraged to talk about time in terms of amounts rather than distances, English speakers also show Greek-like patterns of interference on the same estimation task. This rapidly induced plasticity suggests that language-driven effects may be shallow ones.

Evidence from stroke or trauma patients indicates that language deficits can be accompanied by otherwise normal intelligence. Rosemary Varley and her collaborators have shown this in an impressive battery of studies with profoundly aphasic patients. In aphasia, damage to the frontal lobe of the left hemisphere results in impaired syntactic production and comprehension, dysfluent speech, and difficulty in word finding. If language were an essential component of cognitive tasks, such a profound disorder should produce widespread intellectual impairments.

These aphasic patients, however, succeed on many cognitive tasks despite their grammatical impairment. They are able to solve a range of elementary arithmetic problems (even those involving grouping of operations), showing an intact competence with precise numbers as well as approximate magnitudes (Varley, Klessinger, Romanowski, & Siegal, 2005).[5] They are able to solve elementary theory of mind tasks such as the simple false belief task, showing a grasp of mental states and their causal interactions (Siegal, Varley, & Want, 2001). Their mindreading facility is further demonstrated by the fact that they are able to successfully communicate messages to one another in a nonverbal sender-receiver task, showing a grasp of the basic notion of a communicative intention (Willems, Benn, Hagoort, Toni, & Varley, 2011). Some patients were even able to solve deductive reasoning problems requiring long chains of inferences, despite not having the ability to verbally formulate the premises (Varley, 2010). This converges nicely with studies suggesting that language and deductive reasoning do not share a substantial neural basis (Monti & Osherson, 2012). Taken together, these results suggest that massive damage to the neural systems underlying language is compatible with preserved cognitive function in many domains. Although aphasic patients suffer from serious (and extremely frustrating) social and communicative challenges, their inner mental lives may be substantially unchanged.

Similar independence shows up in so-called split-brain patients. These individuals have undergone a radical surgical procedure known as commissurotomy, in which the two hemispheres of the brain, which are normally connected through a thick connective bundle known as the corpus callosum, are separated from one another. Among the functions of the corpus callosum is to transfer and integrate neural information across the hemispheric boundaries. Commissurotomy has been performed only in rare cases in which patients suffer from severe, untreatable epilepsy. With the corpus callosum severed, seizures are less prone to spread in the brain, and the

---

[5] Other evidence also suggests that basic mathematical skills, both in arithmetic and geometry, are largely language-independent. Language and algebraic reasoning seem to have different neural foundations (Monti, Parsons, & Osherson, 2012). Children and adult members of the Mundurukú, an indigenous Amazonian group, can recognize squares, trapezoids, and other geometric figures even though their language lacks a wide array of geometrical terms (Dehaene, Izard, Pica, & Spelke, 2006). And the Pirahã of Brazil lack precise number words but have no trouble matching large sets with respect to their cardinality, implying that they nevertheless grasp numerical equivalence (Frank, Everett, Fedorenko, & Gibson, 2008).

patients' symptoms usually lessen. However, the procedure also dissociates normal cognitive activity taking place in the two hemispheres. This produces a range of phenomena that are among the most striking in all of neuroscience, but here we focus just on the implications of these cases for language and thought.

As we saw in the case of aphasia, language processing is often (though not always) localized in the left hemisphere. But in split-brain patients we can examine the cognitive performance of the right hemisphere in almost total isolation from linguistic influence. The overwhelming pattern is that there are significant nonverbal spatial and visual reasoning skills associated with activity in the right hemisphere. Gazzaniga (1988), for instance, reports the case of DR, a 38-year-old woman who had nearly complete resection of the corpus callosum. Postoperatively she was able to carry out picture matching, matching target to sample of everyday objects such as apples, books, and bicycles, and other cognitive tasks with her right hemisphere. In another case, when patient JW was presented with a stimulus of the name of a state sent to his right hemisphere, he was unable to name it (as he was able when the stimulus was sent to his left hemisphere), but he was quite able to point out the position of the state on a map and to draw its correct shape. Patients whose languageless right hemispheres were presented with pictures of pets and family members as well as famous and infamous faces (Churchill, Stalin) were able to signal their opinion by giving a thumbs up/thumbs down response (Sperry, Zaidel, & Zaidel, 1979). Memory, classification, and emotional response integration all seem available in the absence of language.

Finally, there are dissociations of language and thought even in ordinary, neurologically intact people. In one cross-linguistic study, speakers of English, Chinese, and Spanish were asked to do two sorts of categorization tasks (Malt, Sloman, Gennari, Shi, & Wang, 1999). The first involved giving the appropriate names to a set of everyday containers. As would be expected, the languages divide these objects up quite differently. Chinese speakers lumped most of the objects into a single large category with several outlying minor categories, English speakers used three common nouns to cover most of the objects, and Argentinian Spanish speakers used up to 15 different terms. In a second set of tasks, the speakers were asked to make various judgments of similarity (physical, functional, and overall) among the items. Although the similarity ratings, particularly the perceived overall similarity of the items, were highly correlated across linguistic groups, they did not correlate well with the patterns of naming. This suggests that these artifacts appear similar cross-linguistically, even though the languages themselves impose divisions among them.

How objects are named in language, then, is not a simple reflection of the prelinguistically perceived similarities among objects. This is a bit of an embarrassment to certain simple theories of naming that assume that words exist to group together objects by perceived similarity. But by the same token, naming itself does not exert a strong "downward" effect on perceived similarity. The two cognitive processes of judging similarity and deciding what something should be called seem to be largely independent. And this is just what we might predict, because the two processes are subject to different demands. Naming is sensitive to sociocultural and communicative constraints, whereas similarity judgments and categorization are sensitive to the perceived characteristics of objects and our beliefs about the ontological organization of the world.

Dan Slobin (1996) famously introduced the idea that we should replace the abstract terms *language* and *thought* with *speaking* and *thinking*. This shifts the focus from vague abstract entities to concrete activities and processes. In particular, it lets us focus on the phenomenon of what Slobin calls "thinking for speaking." This is the process of organizing one's thoughts in order to verbalize them: to tell a story, to give a command, to present one's justifications, or to sway someone's emotions. Thinking for speaking is a specific kind of mixed activity. A thinker preparing to speak must organize and worry about word order, subject–verb agreement, subject gender, and so on in some languages, but not in others. Resources of attention, memory, and categorization will be mobilized for this particular task in language-specific ways. This may reflect the nature of constraints on communicating in a particular language, rather than anything about the underlying processes of thinking themselves.

9.6 Arguments for the priority of thought

So far we have argued that the experimental evidence linking language and thought points to at most a weak form of linguistic determinism. The constant use of certain formal patterns tends to direct our attention to certain features of the world and shapes our habits of classification and recall. It is hard to see how there could fail to be such effects, in fact. Over time, all tools tend to reshape their users. The speaking-for-thinking hypothesis proposes that the forms of thought that are recruited for the online use of language may vary depending on the demands that the language makes on our cognitive resources. But this would still leave untouched those parts of cognition that do not make active use of language. Dissociation studies show that the two faculties are distinct, though of course they must interface at some level. We now turn to some arguments that thought must be prior to language.

9.6.1 Arguments from learning

Arguments from learning have often been deployed to show that fairly robust forms of thought precede language. This is the basis of Fodor's famous claim that there exists a "language of thought," or Mentalese, in which most of our conceptual thinking is conducted (Fodor, 1975). The argument runs as follows. To acquire language, infants must already be able to identify and think about both the linguistic labels themselves and also the things paired with them in the learning process. Learning that "cat" refers to cats involves learning the pairing of a sound with a category. To successfully arrive at the communally appropriate meaning, the child needs to represent *both* of these to-be-associated elements. This can be put in the form of a general principle: for any distinction that is made in the language itself, the child must be able to make that distinction in thought in order to successfully learn the language. Learning the language is, in a sense, just learning this system of differences. And from this it follows that language learners must arrive at their task cognitively prepared with mechanisms that allow them to make *any* distinction that could be expressed in *any* humanly learnable language, because an infant can have no foreknowledge of the language community into which it will be placed.

In its strongest form, the argument from learning concludes that children come pre-equipped with every concept that can be expressed in their language (and every other humanly speakable language). Radical concept nativism follows. This was, indeed, the use to which Fodor himself originally put the argument (see Section 4.2.2). Here we have stated the argument somewhat more cagily, however. We have not said that the prelinguistic child *already* possesses the concepts that will be expressed in what will eventually be her language. We have said, rather, that she must be prepared to acquire those concepts, or that there must be cognitive mechanisms that will allow her to make those distinctions.

This preparedness might take many forms, of which radical nativism is only one. The radical nativist will argue that the child must have the concept *cat* in order to successfully arrive at the pairing of "cat" with its appropriate reference. A somewhat weaker, intermediate claim would be that the child possesses some set of concepts that will allow her to construct the concept *cat*. For example, she might be able to assemble that concept out of other ones that she possesses. This still requires that the child possess some concepts or other. The weakest possible claim would be that the child need not possess any concepts before learning the language, but only preconceptual or nonconceptual mechanisms that, when provided with perceptual and linguistic inputs, produce concepts that capture the meanings of the to-be-learned words themselves.

The skeptics will argue that whatever cognition goes on before language is acquired, it does not involve the full apparatus of propositional conceptual thinking itself. Grasping and manipulating propositions only come onboard with the productive and compositional apparatus of language, so the capacities the language learner possesses are at the outset nonconceptual. However, some evidence indicates that even prelinguistic thought is richly organized. For example, Susan Goldin-Meadow (2003) has for years studied individuals who have had no exposure to any conventional language whatsoever. On the view that thought is not possible without conventional language, such people should not be able to think at all. But her results show that they are capable of communication using regular patterns that mirror those present in language itself.

The participants in these studies are deaf children born to hearing parents who are not exposed to sign language until adolescence. Such children sometimes invent gestures that have syntactic, morphologic, and lexical structure in order to communicate. In these invented sign systems they distinguish actor-patient roles (John hit Sam) and introduce pronouns (he hit him). But do they have stable structural preferences? In English, the subject of transitive and intransitive verbs are placed at the beginning of the sentence, thus "John hit Carl" and "John ran." Despite its impoverished case system, this shows that English displays what is called *accusative* ordering. Other languages treat these constructions differently. In languages such as Basque, subjects of intransitive verbs occupy the position held by the direct object of transitive verbs, which would be glossed as "Ran John." These languages display what is known as an *ergative* ordering.

Goldin-Meadow wanted to know if the deaf children would have a bias for the accusative form or the ergative form. She found that in general, the languageless deaf children overwhelmingly tended to treat the actors (subjects) of intransitive verbs identically to the patients (objects) of transitive verbs. This pattern occurs not only in American deaf children, but also in Chinese deaf children. Surprisingly, English-speaking adults asked to create an unspoken sign system to express themselves also settle on using ergative patterns similar to those used by the deaf children, rather than the ones encoded in English syntax. The prevalence of ergative constructions in these disparate populations is some evidence that spontaneous nonlinguistic thinking itself has ergative characteristics, even in people whose native language uses accusative forms.

These nonlinguistic patterns may not only precede language, but also explain some of its more puzzling features. Steven Pinker (2007) argues that explanation of certain syntactic facts depends on pre-existing conceptual structures. Many locative verbs permit alternation: consider the similarities between "Jason sprayed water on the roses" and "Jason sprayed the roses with water" or between "Betsy splashed paint on the wall" and "Betsy splashed the wall with paint." These sentences express subtly distinct perspectives on the same event. Some sentences do not alternate, however. One can say "Amy poured water into the glass" but not *"Amy poured the glass with water." The first member of each of these pairs is known as a content locative, whereas the second is known as a container locative. The two constructions are clearly related, but as the last pair of examples shows, we cannot always shift freely between content and container senses. What explains this distinction?

According to Pinker, the meaning of the content locative is "A causes B to go to C." The meaning of the container locative is "A causes C to change state by means of causing B to go to C." Loading hay onto the wagon is something you do to the hay. Loading the wagon with hay is something you do to the wagon (cause it to be loaded with hay). The former can be done with a few pitchforks full. The latter is done only when the wagon is full. But not every verb allows this kind of transformation:

> Now take the verb fill. To fill something means to cause it to become full (it is no coincidence that full and fill sound alike). It's all about the state of the container. No fullness, no filling. But fill is apathetic about how the container became full. You can fill a glass by pouring water into it ... That's why fill is

the syntactic mirror image of pour; by specifying the change of state of a container, it is compatible with a construction that is about a state-change, and thereby allows us to say fill the glass with water. But because it says nothing about a cause or manner of motion of the container, it isn't compatible with a construction that is all about a motion, and thereby doesn't allow us to say fill water into the glass. (2007, p. 50)

Pinker identifies a set of verbs that allow alternation (brush, dab, daub, plaster, rub, slather, smear, smudge, spread, streak, swab) and a set that do not (dribble, drip, drop, dump, funnel, ladle, pour, shake, siphon, slop, slosh, spill, spoon). The difference between these classes arises because our concepts are sensitive to the physics of the situations described. In the first, the agent applies force to the substance and the surface simultaneously. In the second, the agent allows gravity to do the work. The two classes encode a difference between *causing* and *letting happen*. What this implies is that underlying the linguistic patterns is a more general and abstract conceptual grasp of how these scenarios differ.

The challenge raised for the skeptic by the argument from learning is to explain how language acquisition is possible if there is not some sort of conceptual apparatus, even of an impoverished sort, already present. The examples discussed here are meant to show the existence of such conceptual resources. The burden of the argument is thus on the language-first proponent to show how nonconceptual cognition could give rise to these patterns of behavior.

9.6.2 Arguments from misalignment

A further reason to think that thought comes first is that the languages that we speak are in many ways badly suited to serve as the medium of thinking. They contain both too much and too little information. A spoken sentence contains information that only makes sense if it is being used as a vehicle for auditory communication: word order, intonational contours, tempo and pacing, and other devices of emphasis that serve the needs of the hearer, rather than the underlying meaning. Public language sentences are also ambiguous in many ways. A string of words such as "Flying planes can be dangerous" can be syntactically parsed in several ways, and hence have several different readings. Sentences can contain polysemous terms that map onto many underlying meanings. It is unclear whether thought can be similarly ambiguous (Pinker, 1994, pp. 78–80). These considerations point to the conclusion that language and thought are systematically *mismatched* and hence should not be identified.

Taking this idea a step further transforms it into an argument for the priority of thought. Jerry Fodor (2001) offers such an argument, which turns on the fact that sentences typically express richer content than is present in their surface constituents. In particular, what one says by uttering a sentence in a particular context often goes beyond the content that is encoded just in the words of the sentence itself. Recall from Section 9.2 that *compositionality* is the property whereby the semantic content of a complex expression is inherited from the semantic content of its constituents. Fodor proposes that the way to decide whether language or thought is explanatorily prior is to see which one is fully compositional:

> If, as between thought and language, only one of them can plausibly be supposed to be compositional, then that is, *ipso facto*, the one that comes first in order of explanation of content; the other has only such secondary content as it "derives" from the first. But, as a matter of empirical fact, language is pretty clearly *not* compositional; so it can't have content in the first instance. (2001, pp. 10–11)

The idea here is that if, in speaking, we express more content than is compositionally packed into the sentences themselves, that "extra" content must come from somewhere. Since the only plausible place that it can come from is thought itself, it must be thought that comes before language.

What support is there for Fodor's empirical premise about the content of language? He offers two examples, both intended to show that language is "strikingly elliptical and inexplicit about the thoughts it expresses" (p. 11), too much so for language itself to be strictly compositional.[6] First example: you ask me the time, and I reply "It's 3 o'clock." I haven't bothered to tell you whether I mean AM or PM, because it would be a waste of words. Nevertheless, despite this omission, the truth conditions of my utterance are quite determinate. What I said is in fact true in the event that it is 3:00 PM, and

[6] We ought to note that it is a very odd historical fact that the philosopher who over the years has probably done the most to draw our attention to the crucial theoretical role of the compositionality of language is also the one who is here denying that language itself is compositional. But we will put aside questions about the overall coherence of Fodor's views on this issue and stick to the argument at hand.

false if it's 3:00 AM. Putting the point another way, the sentence does not state everything that I say in uttering it.

Second example: if you ask me "Where is the book?" I might reply with "The book is on the table." On Russell's famous analysis of definite descriptions, my reply is equivalent to the claim that there is one and only one book and it is on the table. But of course neither you nor I mean to be saying that there is exactly one book in the world and it is on the table. Rather, both participants in the conversation have singled out a unique book to be discussed using contextual indicators. These indicators have come to be taken for granted in the conversation so far and need not be explicitly repeated in their full, logical dress every time mention of the book is made.

Further examples could be analyzed, but Fodor's general point is clear enough.[7] In speaking, our utterances often express much more than we say in words. If this is possible, the remaining content must be expressed somewhere, and the only plausible location for this content is in the thoughts of the speakers and hearers themselves. In response to this argument, some language-first advocates have responded by trying to narrow the gap between the two. For example, in response to the problems of ambiguity and polysemy, they say that the mistake is to take strings of spoken words to be the vehicles of inner thought. Rather, we think in more complex, annotated structures. Instead of thinking in the bare and unmarked string of words "Hitchhikers may be escaping convicts," we might make use of one of these disambiguated, bracketed sentences (Gauker, 2011, p. 262):

[[Hitchhikers] [may [be [[escaping] [convicts]]]]]
[[Hitchhikers] [may [[be escaping] [convicts]]]]

Thus at the level of thought, the sentences we use are appropriately marked so that we do not "think ambiguously" in an inner analogue of spoken words, but instead use an enriched form of representation. A similar strategy can be applied to the case of polysemy. Rather than using a simple unmarked term like "bank," we use distinct lexical items that carry unpronounced markers: "$bank_1$" and "$bank_2$." This move can also be applied to the case of context-sensitive utterances such as the ones highlighted by Fodor. In all of these cases, our outer speech is backed by an inner sentence that fleshes

---

[7] For discussion of the merits of the linguistic side of Fodor's argument, see Elugardo (2005), Pagin (2005), and Szabo (2010).

out and expresses more completely the thought that we publicly express elliptically.

If this hypothesis is correct, every time we speak ambiguously or elliptically, our spoken sentences are backed by a clear, determinate, and complete inner sentence. Inner speech is invariably perfectly articulate as compared with its flawed, worldly cousin. This is a strong claim that we will not be able to address completely here, though it has been criticized extensively elsewhere (Stainton, 2005, 2006). We will make only two points in response.

First, this reply effectively doubles down on the centrality of language to higher thought. But, as we have surveyed, there are sound empirical reasons to believe that much of our thinking can be carried out even in the absence of language.

Second, this reply may push language-first theorists perilously close to their opponents' position. Theorists who believe in the existence of conceptual thought hold that it takes place in an internal representational system that is more abstract than spoken language, capable of making distinctions that go beyond spoken language, and richer in content. But all of these things are true of these "enriched" linguistic representations. The empirical pressures that lead us to posit all manner of abstract enrichments to spoken language are the very same ones that also lead us to posit nonlinguistic conceptual representations as well. In other words, if the enriched inner sentence proposal is appealing, this is only because it duplicates the appeal of the thought-first proposal. It would be a Pyrrhic victory indeed to posit linguistic representations that turn out to fulfill the exact same causal and explanatory role as conceptual representations.

9.7 Conclusions

The issues discussed here are subtle ones, and much more could be added on all sides of the debate. We have been attempting to deflate the intellectual appeal of the Sapir–Whorf hypothesis, nudging the reader instead toward the view that fairly rich forms of thought may precede the emergence of language, which may influence certain habitual patterns of thinking without strongly determining them. Despite its marvelous cognitive and social benefits, language remains a tool from which we, its creators and users, stand somewhat apart.

Throughout this book, we have heard at length from the philosophers and the scientists. We cede the final word on our subject to the late novelist David Foster Wallace:

> This is another paradox, that many of the most important impressions and thoughts in a person's life are ones that flash through your head so fast that *fast* isn't even the right word, they seem totally different from or outside of the regular sequential clock time we all live by, and they have so little relation to the sort of linear, one-word-after-another-word English we all communicate with each other with that it could easily take a whole lifetime just to spell out the contents of one split-second's flash of thoughts and connections ... What goes on inside is just too fast and huge and all interconnected for words to do more than barely sketch the outlines of at most one tiny little part of any of it at any given instant.[8]

[8] From "Good Old Neon," reprinted in *Oblivion* (2004).

References

Adams, F. (2001). Empathy, neural imaging, and the theory versus simulation debate. *Mind and Language, 16*, 368–392.

Adams, F., & Aizawa, K. (2001). The bounds of cognition. *Philosophical Psychology, 14*, 43–64.

Adams, F., & Aizawa, K. (2008). *The bounds of cognition.* Oxford: Blackwell.

Adams, F., & Aizawa, K. (2010). Defending the bounds of cognition. In R. Menary (Ed.), *The extended mind* (pp. 67–80). Cambridge, MA: MIT Press.

Adams, F., & Beighley, S. (2013). Information, meaning, and animal communication. In U. Stegmann (Ed.), *Animal communication theory: Information and influence* (pp. 399–418). Cambridge, England: Cambridge University Press.

Aglioti, S., DeSouza, J. E. X., & Goodale, M. A. (1995). Size-contrast illusions deceive the eye but not the hand. *Current Biology, 5*, 679–685.

Aizawa, K. (2010). Consciousness: Don't give up on the brain. *Royal Institute of Philosophy Supplement, 67*, 263–284.

Alink, A., Schwiedrzik, C. M., Kohler, A., Singer, W., & Muckli, L. (2010). Stimulus predictability reduces responses in primary visual cortex. *Journal of Neuroscience, 30*(8), 2960–2966.

Allport, A. (1987). Selection for action: Some behavioral and neurophysiological considerations of attention and action. In H. Heuer & A. F. Sanders (Eds.), *Perspectives on perception and action* (pp. 395–419). Hillsdale, NJ: Lawrence Erlbaum.

Allport, A. (1993). Attention and control: Have we been asking the wrong questions? A critical review of twenty-five years. In D. E. Meyer & S. Kornblum (Eds.), *Attention and performance XIV* (pp. 183–218). Cambridge, MA: MIT Press.

Anderson, J. R. (1978). Arguments concerning representation for mental imagery. *Psychological Review, 85*, 249–277.

Anderson, M. (2007). The massive redeployment hypothesis and the functional topography of the brain. *Philosophical Psychology, 21*, 143–174.

Anderson, M. (2010). Neural reuse: A fundamental organizational principle of the brain. *Behavioral and Brain Sciences, 33*, 245–313.

Andrews, K. (2012). *Do apes read minds?* Cambridge, MA: MIT Press.

Ariew, A. (1996). Innateness and canalization. *Philosophy of Science, 63,* S19–S27.

Ariew, A. (1999). Innateness is canalization: In defense of a developmental account of innateness. In V. Hardcastle (Ed.), *Biology meets psychology: Conjectures, connections, constraints.* Cambridge, MA: MIT Press.

Armstrong, D. M. (1968). *A materialist theory of the mind.* New York, NY: Routledge and Kegan Paul.

Armstrong, D. M. (1981). What is consciousness? In D. M. Armstrong, *The nature of mind and other essays* (pp. 56–67). Ithaca, NY: Cornell University Press.

Astington, J. W., & Baird, J. A. (Eds.). (2005). *Why language matters for theory of mind.* Oxford, England: Oxford University Press.

Aydede, M. (Ed.). (2006). *Pain: New essays on its nature and the methodology of its study.* Cambridge, MA: MIT Press.

Baars, B. J. (1988). *A cognitive theory of consciousness.* Cambridge, England: Cambridge University Press.

Baars, B. J. (1997). *In the theater of consciousness.* Oxford, England: Oxford University Press.

Baars, B. J. (2002). The conscious access hypothesis: Origins and recent evidence. *Trends in Cognitive Sciences, 6,* 47–52.

Baars, B. J., & Franklin, S. (2003). How conscious experience and working memory interact. *Trends in Cognitive Science, 7,* 166–172.

Bach-y-Rita, P., & Kercel, S. W. (2003). Sensory substitution and the human-machine interface. *Trends in Cognitive Science, 7,* 541–546.

Baddeley, A. D. (2007). *Working memory, thought and action.* Oxford, England: Oxford University Press.

Baillargeon, R. (1995). Physical reasoning in infancy. In M. S. Gazzaniga (Ed.), *The cognitive neurosciences* (pp. 181–204). Cambridge, MA: MIT Press.

Balcetis, E., & Dunning, D. (2010). Wishful seeing: Desired objects are seen as closer. *Psychological Science, 21,* 147–152.

Ballard, D. H. (1991). Animate vision. *Artificial Intelligence, 48,* 57–86.

Baron-Cohen, S. (1995). *Mindblindness.* Cambridge, MA: MIT Press.

Barr, C. L., & Kleck, R. E. (1995). Self-other perception of the intensity of facial expressions of emotion: Do we know what we show? *Journal of Personality and Social Psychology, 68,* 608–618.

Barsalou, L. W. (1999). Perceptual symbol systems. *Behavioral and Brain Sciences, 22,* 577–660.

Barsalou, L. W. (2003). Abstraction in perceptual symbol systems. *Philosophical Transactions of the Royal Society of London: Biological Sciences, 358,* 1177–1187.

Barsalou, L. W. (2008). Cognitive and neural contributions to understanding the conceptual system. *Current Directions in Psychological Science, 17,* 91–95.

Barsalou, L. W. (2010). Grounded cognition: Past, present, and future. *Topics in Cognitive Science, 2*, 716–724.

Bartolomeo, P. (2002). The relationship between visual perception and visual mental imagery: A reappraisal of the neuropsychological evidence. *Cortex,* 357–378.

Bartsch, K., & Wellman, H. (1989). Young children's attribution of actions to beliefs and desires. *Child Development, 60*, 946–964.

Bateson, P. (1991). Are there principles of behavioural development? In P. Bateson (Ed.), *The development and integration of behaviour: Essays in honour of Robert Hinde* (pp. 19–40). Cambridge, England: Cambridge University Press.

Batty, C. (2011). Smelling lessons. *Philosophical Studies, 153*, 161–174.

Beanland, V., & Pammer, K. (2012). Minds on the blink: The relationship between inattentional blindness and attentional blink. *Attention, Perception, & Psychophysics, 74*, 322–333.

Bechtel, W. (2003). Modules, brain parts, and evolutionary psychology. In S. J. Scher & F. Rauscher (Eds.), *Evolutionary psychology: Alternative approaches* (pp. 211–227). Dordrecht, The Netherlands: Kluwer.

Bechtel, W. (2008). *Mental mechanisms*. London, England: Routledge.

Bechtel, W., & Abrahamsen, A. (2005). Explanation: A mechanistic alternative. *Studies in History and Philosophy of the Biological and Biomedical Sciences, 36*, 421–441.

Bechtel, W., & Mundale, J. (1999). Multiple realizability revisited: Linking cognitive and neural states. *Philosophy of Science, 66*, 175–207.

Bechtel, W., & Richardson, R. C. (1993). *Discovering complexity: Decomposition and localization as strategies in scientific research*. Princeton, NJ: Princeton University Press.

Bedny, M., Caramazza, A., Pascual-Leone, A., & Saxe, R. (2012). Typical neural representations of action verbs develop without vision. *Cerebral Cortex, 22*, 286–293.

Bedny, M., & Saxe, R. (2012). Insights into the origins of knowledge from the cognitive neuroscience of blindness. *Cognitive Neuropsychology, 29*, 56–84.

Bennett, J. (1964/1989). *Rationality: An essay towards an analysis*. New York, NY: Hackett.

Bennett, J. (1976/1990). *Linguistic behaviour*. Cambridge, England: Cambridge University Press.

Bennett, J. (1988). Thoughtful brutes. *Proceedings and Addresses of the American Philosophical Association, 62*, 197–210.

Bermúdez, J. L. (2003). The domain of folk psychology. In A. O'Hear (Ed.), *Minds and persons* (25–48). Cambridge, England: Cambridge University Press.

Bertsch, S., Pesta, B. J., Wiscott, R., & McDaniel, M. A. (2007). The generation effect: a meta-analytic review. *Memory & Cognition, 34*, 201–210.

Bhalla, M., & Proffitt, D. R. (1999). Visual-motor recalibration in geographical slant perception. *Journal of Experimental Psychology: Human Perception and Performance*, *25*, 1076–1096.

Bickle, J. (2003). *Philosophy and neuroscience: A ruthlessly reductive account*. Norwell, MA: Kluwer.

Bickle, J. (2006). Reducing mind to molecular pathways: Explicating the reductionism implicit in current cellular and molecular neuroscience. *Synthese*, *151*, 411–434.

Birch, S. A. J. (2005). When knowledge is a curse. *Current Directions in Psychological Science*, *14*, 25–29.

Birch, S. A. J., & Bloom, P. (2003). The curse of knowledge in reasoning about false beliefs. *Psychological Science*, *18*, 382–386.

Block, N. (1995/1997). On a confusion about a function of consciousness. In N. Block, O. Flanagan, & G. Guzeldere (Eds.), *The nature of consciousness* (pp. 375–415). Cambridge, MA: MIT Press.

Block, N. (2007). Consciousness, accessibility, and the mesh between psychology and neuroscience. *Behavioral and Brain Sciences*, *30*, 418–499.

Block, N. (2011). Perceptual consciousness overflows cognitive access. *Trends in Cognitive Science*, *15*, 567–575.

Block, N., & Fodor, J. A. (1972). What psychological states are not. *Philosophical Review*, *81*, 159–181.

Bloom, P. (2004). *Descartes' baby*. New York, NY: Basic Books.

Bloom, P., & German, T. (2000). Two reasons to abandon the false belief task as a test of theory of mind. *Cognition*, *77*, B25–B31.

Boas, F. (1911). *Handbook of American Indian languages*. Washington, DC: Government Printing Office.

Boden, M. (2006). *Mind as machine: A history of cognitive science*. Oxford, England: Oxford University Press.

Bogen, J., & Woodward. J. (1988). Saving the phenomena. *Philosophical Review*, *97*, 303–352.

Borg, E. (2007). If mirror neurons are the answer, what was the question? *Journal of Consciousness Studies*, *14*, 5–19.

Boroditsky, L., Schmidt, L., & Phillips, W. (2003). Sex, syntax, and semantics. In D. Gentner & S. Goldin-Meadow (Eds.), (pp. 61–79). Cambridge, MA: MIT Press.

Borst, G., Kievit, R. A., Thompson, W. L., & Kosslyn, S. M. (2011). Mental rotation is not easily cognitively penetrable. *Journal of Cognitive Psychology*, *23*, 60–75.

Bowerman, M. (1996). The origins of children's spatial semantic categories: Cognitive vs. linguistic determinants. In J. J. Gumperz & S. C. Levinson (Eds.),

Rethinking linguistic relativity (pp. 145–176). Cambridge, England: Cambridge University Press.

Boysson-Bardies, B. (1999). *How language comes to children: From birth to two years.* Cambridge, MA: MIT Press.

Bransford, J. D., & Franks, J. J. (1971). The abstraction of linguistic ideas. *Cognitive Psychology, 2,* 331–350.

Bratman, M. (1987). *Intention, plans, and practical reason.* Cambridge, MA: Harvard University Press.

Broadbent, D. (1958). *Perception and communication.* London, England: Pergamon Press.

Buccino, G., Binkofski, F., Fink, G. R., Fadiga, L., Fogassi, L., Gallese, V., ... Freund, H. J. (2001). Action observation activates premotor and parietal areas in a somatotopic manner: An fMRI study. *European Journal of Neuroscience, 13,* 400–404.

Buller, D. (2005). *Adapting minds.* Cambridge, MA: MIT Press.

Bush, R. R., & Mosteller, F. (1951). A mathematical model for simple learning. *Psychological Review, 58,* 313–323.

Buss, D. (1995). Evolutionary psychology: A new paradigm for psychological science. *Psychological Inquiry, 6,* 1–30.

Buttelman, D., Carpenter, M., & Tomasello, M. (2009). Eighteen-month-old infants show false belief understanding in an active helping paradigm. *Cognition, 112,* 337–342.

Calder, A. J., Keane, J., Cole, J., Campbell, R., & Young, A. W. (2000). Facial expression recognition by people with Mobius syndrome. *Cognitive Neuropsychology, 17,* 73–87.

Call, J., & Tomasello, M. (2008). Does the chimpanzee have a theory of mind? 30 years later. *Trends in Cognitive Science, 12,* 187–192.

Calvin, W. (1996). *The cerebral code.* Cambridge, MA: MIT Press.

Camerer, C., Loewenstein, G., & Weber, M. (1989). The curse of knowledge in experimental settings: An experimental analysis. *Journal of Political Economy, 97,* 1232–1254.

Caramazza, A., & Mahon, B. Z. (2006). The organisation of conceptual knowledge in the brain: The future's past and some future directions. *Cognitive Neuropsychology, 23,* 13–38.

Carrasco. M. (2011). Visual attention: The past 25 years. *Vision Research, 51,* 1484–1525.

Carruthers, P. (1986). Brute experience. *Journal of Philosophy, 86,* 258–269.

Carruthers, P. (1996a). *Language, thought, and consciousness.* Cambridge, England: Cambridge University Press.

Carruthers, P. (1996b). Simulation and self-knowledge: A defence of theory-theory. In P. Carruthers & P. Smith (Eds.), *Theories of theories of mind* (pp. 22–38). Cambridge, England: Cambridge University Press.

Carruthers, P. (2000). *Phenomenal consciousness.* Cambridge, England: Cambridge University Press.

Carruthers, P. (2004). Practical reasoning in a modular mind. *Mind and Language, 19,* 259–278.

Carruthers, P. (2005). *Consciousness: Essays from a higher-order perspective.* Oxford, England: Oxford University Press.

Carruthers, P. (2006). *The architecture of the mind.* Oxford, England: Oxford University Press.

Carruthers, P. (2011). *The opacity of mind.* Oxford, England: Oxford University Press.

Casasanto, D., Fotakopoulou, O., Pita, R., & Boroditsky, L. (N.d.). How deep are effects of language on thought? Time estimation in speakers of English and Greek. Unpublished manuscript.

Casasola, M. (2005). Can language do the driving? The effect of linguistic input on infants' categorization of support spatial relations. *Developmental Psychology, 41,* 183–192.

Castiello, U., & Umiltà, C. (1990). Size of attentional focus and the efficiency of processing. *Acta Psychologica, 73,* 195–209.

Catmur, C., Walsh, V., & Heyes, C. (2007). Sensorimotor learning configures the human mirror system. *Current Biology, 17,* 1527–1531.

Cave, K. R., & Bichot, N. P. (1999). Visuo-spatial attention: Beyond a spotlight model. *Psychonomic Bulletin & Review, 6,* 204–223.

Chalmers, D. (1966). *The conscious mind.* Oxford, England: Oxford University Press.

Chalmers, D. (2003). Consciousness and its place in nature. In S. Stich & T. Warfield (Eds.), *Blackwell guide to philosophy of mind* (pp. 102–142). Malden, MA: Blackwell.

Chambers, J. R., Epley, N., Savitsky, K., & Windschitl, P. D. (2008). Knowing too much: Using private knowledge to predict how one is viewed by others. *Psychological Science, 19,* 542–548.

Chartrand, T. L., & Bargh, J. A. (1999). The chameleon effect: The perception-behavior link and social interaction. *Journal of Personality and Social Psychology, 76,* 893–910.

Cherry, E. C. (1953). Some experiments on the recognition of speech, with one and two ears. *Journal of the Acoustical Society of America, 25,* 975–979.

Choi, S., & Bowerman, M. (1991). Learning to express motion events in English and Korean: The influence of language-specific lexicalization patterns. *Cognition, 41,* 83–121.

Choi, S., McDonough, L., Bowerman, M., & Mandler, J. M. (1999). Early sensitivity to language-specific spatial categories in English and Korean. *Cognitive Development, 14*, 241–268.

Chomsky, N. (1980). *Rules and representations*. New York, NY: Columbia University Press.

Chomsky, N. (1986). *Knowledge of language: Its nature, origins and use*. New York, NY: Praeger.

Churchland, P. M. (1981). Eliminative materialism and the propositional attitudes. *Journal of Philosophy, 78*, 67–90.

Churchland, P. M. (1988). Perceptual plasticity and theoretical neutrality. *Philosophy of Science, 55*, 167–87.

Churchland, P. S. (1986). *Neurophilosophy*. Cambridge, MA: MIT Press.

Churchland, P. S. (1996). The hornswoggle problem. *Journal of Consciousness Studies, 3*, 402–408.

Churchland, P. S., Ramachandran, V. S., & Sejnowski, T. J. (1994). A critique of pure vision. In C. Koch & J. L. Davis (Eds.), *Large-scale neuronal theories of the brain* (pp. 23–60). Cambridge, MA: MIT Press.

Clark, Al., & Lappin, S. (2011). *Linguistic nativism and the poverty of the stimulus*. London, England: Wiley-Blackwell.

Clark, An. (2001). Visual experience and motor action: Are the bonds too tight? *Philosophical Review, 110*, 495–519.

Clark, An. (2007). What reaching teaches: Consciousness, control, and the inner zombie. *British Journal for the Philosophy of Science, 58*, 563–594.

Clark, An. (2008). *Supersizing the mind*. Oxford, England: Oxford University Press.

Clark, An. (2013). Whatever next? Predictive brains, situated agents, and the future of cognitive science. *Behavioral and Brain Sciences, 36*(3), 181–204.

Clark, An., & Chalmers, D. J. (1998). The extended mind. *Analysis, 58*, 7–19.

Clark, Au. (2000). *A theory of sentience*. Oxford, England: Oxford University Press.

Coltheart, M. (1999). Modularity and cognition. *Trends in Cognitive Science, 3*, 115–120.

Coltheart, M., Curtis, B., Atkins, P., & Haller, M. (1993). Models of reading aloud: Dual route and parallel distributed processing approaches. *Psychological Review, 100*, 589–608.

Cosmides, L., & Tooby, J. (1992). Cognitive adaptations for social exchange. In J. Barkow, L. Cosmides, & J. Tooby (Eds.), *The adapted mind: Evolutionary psychology and the generation of culture* (pp. 163–228). New York, NY: Oxford University Press.

Cosmides, L., & Tooby, J. (1994). Origins of domain-specificity: The evolution of functional organization. In L. Hirschfeld & S. Gelman (Eds.), *Mapping the mind* (pp. 85–116). Cambridge, England: Cambridge University Press.

Cowey, A., & Heywood, C. A. (1997). Cerebral achromatopsia: Color blindness despite wavelength processing. *Trends in Cognitive Science, 1*, 133–139.

Cowie, F. (1999). *What's within? Nativism reconsidered.* Oxford, England: Oxford University Press.

Craver, C. F. (2007) *Explaining the brain: Mechanisms and the mosaic unity of neuroscience.* Oxford, England: Oxford University Press.

Csibra, G., & Gergely, G. (2006). Social learning and social cognition: The case for pedagogy. In Y. Munakata & M. H. Johnson (Eds.), *Attention and performance XXI* (pp. 249–274). Oxford, England: Oxford University Press

Csibra, G., & Gergely, G. (2009). Natural pedagogy. *Trends in Cognitive Science, 13*, 148–153.

Cummins, R. (1975). Functional analysis. *Journal of Philosophy, 72*, 741–765.

Cummins, R. (1996). *Representations, targets, and attitudes.* Cambridge, MA: MIT Press.

Cummins, R. (2000) "How does it work" versus "what are the laws?": Two conceptions of psychological explanation. In F. Keil & R. A. Wilson (Eds.), *Explanation and cognition* (pp. 117–145). Cambridge, MA: MIT Press.

Currie, G., & Ravenscroft, I. (2002). *Recreative minds: Imagination in philosophy and psychology.* Oxford, England: Oxford University Press.

Cytowic, R. (2002). *Synesthesia: A union of the senses* (2nd ed.). Cambridge, MA: MIT Press.

Damasio, A. (1994). *Descartes' error.* New York, NY: Penguin.

Davidson, D. (1975/1984). Thought and talk. In *Inquiries into truth and interpretation* (pp. 155–170). Oxford, England: Oxford University Press.

Davidson, D. (1982/2001). Rational animals. In *Subjective, intersubjective, objective* (pp. 95–105). Oxford, England: Oxford University Press.

de Vega, M., Glenberg, A. M., & Graesser, A. C. (Eds.). (2008). *Symbols and embodiment: Debates on meaning and cognition.* Oxford, England: Oxford University Press.

Dehaene, S., Izard, V., Pica, P., & Spelke, E. (2006). Core knowledge of geometry in an Amazonian indigene group. *Science, 311*, 381–384.

Dehaene, S., & Naccache, L. (2001). Towards a cognitive neuroscience of consciousness: Basic evidence and a workspace framework. *Cognition, 79*, 1–37.

Denis, M., & Kosslyn, S. M. (1999). Scanning visual mental images: A window on the mind. *Cahiers de Psychologie Cognitive, 18*, 409–465

Dennett, D. C. (1978). Intentional systems. In *Brainstorms* (pp. 3–22). Cambridge, MA: MIT Press.

Dennett, D. C. (1989). *The intentional stance.* Cambridge, MA: MIT Press.

Dennett, D. C. (1991). *Consciousness explained.* New York, NY: Back Bay Books.

Dennett, D. C. (1996). Facing backwards on the problem of consciousness. *Journal of Consciousness Studies, 3*, 4–6.

Dennett, D. C. (1997). *Kinds of minds*. New York, NY: Basic Books.

Dennett, D. C. (2001). Are we explaining consciousness yet? *Cognition, 79*, 221–237.

Deutsch, J. A., & Deutsch, D. (1963). Attention: Some theoretical considerations. *Psychological Review, 70*, 80–90.

di Pellegrino, G., Fadiga, L., Fogassi, L., Gallese, V., & Rizzolatti, G. (1992). Understanding motor events: A neurophysiological study. *Experimental Brain Research, 91*, 176–180.

Dixon, R. W. (1972). *The Dyirbal language of North Queensland*. Cambridge, England: Cambridge University Press.

Dretske, F. (1981). *Knowledge and the flow of information*. Cambridge, MA: MIT Press.

Dretske, F. (1987). *Explaining behavior*. Cambridge, MA: MIT Press.

Dretske, F. (1993). Conscious experience. *Mind, 102*, 263–283.

Dretske, F. (1995). *Naturalizing the mind*. Cambridge, MA: MIT Press.

Dretske, F. (2004). Change blindness. *Philosophical Studies, 120*, 1–18.

Dretske, F. (2007). What change blindness teaches about experiences. *Philosophical Perspectives, 21*, 215–220.

Driver, J. (2001). A selective review of selective attention research from the past century. *British Journal of Psychology, 92*, 53–78.

Driver, J., & Spence, C. (2000). Multisensory perception: Beyond modularity and convergence. *Current Biology, 10*, 731–35.

Duncan, J. (1984). Selective attention and the organization of visual information. *Journal of Experimental Psychology: General, 113*, 501–517.

Earman, J., & Roberts, J. T. (1999). Ceteris paribus, there is no problem of provisos. *Synthese, 118*, 439–478.

Earman, J., Roberts, J. T., & Smith, S. (2002). Ceteris paribus lost. *Erkenntnis, 57*, 281–301.

Ebbinghaus, H. (1964). *Memory: A contribution to experimental psychology* (H. A. Ruber & C. E. Bussenius, Trans.). New York, NY: Dover.

Edelman, G. (1987). *Neural Darwinism*. New York, NY: Basic Books.

Egner, T., Monti, J. M., & Summerfield, C. (2010). Expectation and surprise determine neural population responses in the ventral visual stream. *Journal of Neuroscience, 30*, 16601–16608.

Elugardo, R. (2005). Fodor's inexplicitness argument. In E. Machery, G. Schurz, & M. Werning (Eds.), *The compositionality of concepts and meanings: Vol. 1. Foundational issues* (pp. 59–85). Frankfurt, Germany: Ontos Verlag.

Fadiga, L., Fogassi, L., Pavese, G., & Rizzolatti, G. (1995). Motor facilitation during action observation: A magnetic stimulation study. *Journal of Neurophysiology, 73*, 2608–2611.

Farrell, B. A. (1950). Experience. *Mind, 59*, 170–198.

Faucher, L., Mallon, R., Nazer, D. Nichols, S., Ruby, A., Stich, S., & Weinberg, J. (2002). The baby in the lab-coat: Why child development is not an adequate model for understanding the development of science. In P. Carruthers, S. Stich, & M. Siegal (Eds.), *The cognitive basis of science* (pp. 335–362). Cambridge, England: Cambridge University Press.

Fechner, G. T. (1860). *Elemente der Psychophysik*. Leipzig, Germany: Breitkopf und Härtel.

Fernandez-Duque, D., & Johnson, M. L. (1999). Attention metaphors: How metaphors guide the cognitive psychology of attention. *Cognitive Science, 23*, 83–116.

Feyerabend, P. K. (1963). Materialism and the mind-body problem. *Review of Metaphysics, 17*, 49–66.

Fiala, B., Arico, A., & Nichols, S. (2011). On the psychological origins of dualism: Dual-process cognition and the explanatory gap. In M. Collard & E. Slingerland (Eds.), *Creating consilience: Integrating science and the humanities* (pp. 88–110). Oxford, England: Oxford University Press.

Floridi, L. (2010). *Information: A very short introduction*. Oxford, England: Oxford University Press.

Floridi, L. (2011). *The philosophy of information*. Oxford, England: Oxford University Press.

Fodor, J. A. (1965). Explanations in psychology. In M. Black (Ed.), *Philosophy in America*. Ithaca, NY: Cornell University Press.

Fodor, J. A. (1968). *Psychological explanation*. New York, NY: Random House.

Fodor, J. A. (1975). *The language of thought*. Cambridge, MA: Harvard University Press.

Fodor, J. A. (1981). The present status of the innateness controversy. In J. A. Fodor, *Representations* (pp. 265–273). Cambridge, MA: MIT Press.

Fodor, J. A. (1983). *The modularity of mind*. Cambridge, MA: MIT Press.

Fodor, J. A. (1984). Observation reconsidered. *Philosophy of Science, 51*, 23–43.

Fodor, J. A. (1990). *A theory of content and other essays*. Cambridge, MA: MIT Press.

Fodor, J. A. (1991). You can fool some people all of the time, everything else being equal: Hedged laws and psychological explanations. *Mind, 100*, 19–34.

Fodor, J. A. (1994). *The elm and the expert*. Cambridge, MA: MIT Press.

Fodor, J. A. (1998). *Concepts: Where cognitive science went wrong*. Oxford, England: Oxford University Press.

Fodor, J. A. (2000). *The mind doesn't work that way*. Cambridge, MA: MIT Press.

Fodor, J. A. (2001). Language, thought, and compositionality. *Mind and Language, 16*, 1–15.

Fodor, J. A. (2008). *LOT 2: The language of thought revisited*. Oxford, England: Oxford University Press.

Fodor, J. A., & Lepore, E. (1992). *Holism: A shopper's guide*. Cambridge, England: Blackwell.

Frank, M. C., Everett, D. L., Fedorenko, E., & Gibson, E. (2008). Number as a cognitive technology: Evidence from Pirahã language and cognition. *Cognition, 108,* 819–824.

Friston, K. J. (2005). A theory of cortical responses. *Philosophical Transactions of the Royal Society of London, Series B, 360,* 815–836.

Friston, K. J. (2009). The free-energy principle: A rough guide to the brain? *Trends in Cognitive Sciences, 13,* 293–301.

Friston, K. J. (2010). The free-energy principle: A unified brain theory? *Nature Reviews. Neuroscience, 11,* 127–138.

Friston, K. J., & Stephan, K. E. (2007). Free-energy and the brain. *Synthese, 159,* 417–458.

Frith, U., & Hill, E. (2004). *Autism: Mind and brain*. Oxford, England: Oxford University Press.

Fulkerson, M. (2013). *The first sense: A philosophical study of human touch*. Cambridge, MA: MIT Press.

Funnell, E. (1983). Phonological processing in reading: new evidence from acquired dyslexia. *British Journal of Psychology, 74,* 159–180.

Gallese, V., Fadiga, L., Fogassi, L., & Rizzolatti, G. (1996). Action recognition in the premotor cortex. *Brain, 119,* 593–609.

Gallese, V., & Goldman, A. I. (1998). Mirror neurons and the simulation theory of mind-reading. *Trends in Cognitive Science, 2,* 493–501.

Gallistel, C. R. (1990). *The organization of learning*. Cambridge, MA: MIT Press.

Garcia, S. M. (2002). Power and the illusion of transparency in negotiations. *Journal of Business and Psychology, 17,* 133–144.

Gauker, C. (2011). *Words and images*. Oxford, England: Oxford University Press.

Gazzaniga, M. S. (1988). The dynamics of cerebral specialization and modular interactions. In L. Weiskrantz (Ed.), *Thought without language* (pp. 430–450). Oxford, England: Oxford University Press.

Gentner, D. (1998). Analogy. In W. Bechtel & G. Graham (Eds.), *A companion to cognitive science* (pp. 107–113). Oxford, England: Blackwell.

Gentner, D., & Markman, A. B. (1997). Structure mapping in analogy and similarity. *American Psychologist, 52,* 45–56.

Gergely, G., & Csibra, G. (2013). Natural pedagogy. In M. R. Banaji & S. A. Gelman (Eds.), *Navigating the social world: What infants, children, and other species can teach us* (pp. 127–132). Oxford, England: Oxford University Press.

Gernsbacher, M. A. (1985). Surface information loss in comprehension. *Cognitive Psychology, 17,* 324–363.

Gertler, B. (2011). *Self-knowledge*. New York, NY: Routledge.

Gescheider, G. A. (1988). Psychophysical scaling. *Annual Review of Psychology, 39*, 169–200

Gibbs, R. W. (2001). Intentions as emergent products of social interactions. In B. F. Malle, L. J. Moses, & D. A. Baldwin (Eds.), *Intentions and intentionality: Foundations of social cognition* (pp. 105–122). Cambridge, MA: MIT Press.

Gigerenzer, G. (2008). Why heuristics work. *Perspectives on Psychological Science, 3*, 20–29.

Gilovich, T., Savitsky, K., & Medvec, V. H. (1998). The illusion of transparency: biased assessments of others' ability to read one's emotional states. *Journal of Personality and Social Psychology, 75*, 332–346.

Glenberg, A. M. (2010). Embodiment as a unifying perspective for psychology. *Wiley Interdisciplinary Reviews: Cognitive Science, 1*, 586–596.

Glenberg, A. M., Gutierrez, T., Levin, J. R., Japuntich, S., & Kaschak, M. P. (2004). Activity and imagined activity can enhance young children's reading comprehension. *Journal of Educational Psychology, 96*, 424–436.

Glenberg, A. M., & Kaschak, M. P. (2002). Grounding language in action. *Psychonomic Bulletin & Review, 9*, 558–565.

Glennan, S. (1996). Mechanisms and the nature of causation. *Erkenntnis, 44*, 49–71.

Glennan, S. (2002). Rethinking mechanistic explanation. *Philosophy of Science, 69*, S342–S353.

Glock, H-J. (2003). *Quine and Davidson on language, thought and reality*. Cambridge, England: Cambridge University Press.

Goldin-Meadow, S. (2003). Thought before language: Do we think ergative? In D. Gentner & S. Goldin-Meadow (Eds.), *Language in mind: Advances in the study of language and thought* (pp. 493–522). Cambridge, MA: MIT Press.

Goldman, A. I. (1989). Interpretation psychologized. *Mind and Language, 4*, 161–185.

Goldman, A. I. (2006). *Simulating Minds*. Oxford, England: Oxford University Press.

Goodale, M. A. (2008) Action without perception in human vision. *Cognitive Neuropsychology, 25*, 891–919.

Gopnik, A. (1993). How we know our minds: The illusion of first-person knowledge of intentionality. *Behavioral and Brain Sciences, 16*, 1–15.

Gopnik, A., & Wellman, H. (1992). Why the child's theory of mind really is a theory. *Mind and Language, 7*, 145–171.

Gordon, R. (1986). Folk psychology as simulation. *Mind and Language, 1*, 158–171.

Griffiths, P. E. (2002). What is innateness? *The Monist, 85*, 70–85.

Griffiths, P. E., & Machery, E. (2008). Innateness, canalization and "biologicizing the mind." *Philosophical Psychology, 21*, 397–414.

Griffiths, P. E., Machery, E., & Lindquist, S. (2009). The vernacular concept of innateness. *Mind and Language*, *24*, 605–630.

Griffiths, P. E., & Stotz, K. (2000). How the mind grows: A developmental perspective on the biology of cognition. *Synthese*, *122*, 29–51.

Hacking, I. (1983). *Representing and intervening*. Cambridge, England: Cambridge University Press.

Hardcastle, V. G. (1999). *The myth of pain*. Cambridge, MA: MIT Press.

Harley, K., & Reese, E. (1999). Origins of autobiographical memory. *Developmental Psychology*, *35*, 1338–1348.

Hauk, O., & Pulvermüller, F. (2004). Neurophysiological distinction of action words in the fronto-central cortex. *Human Brain Mapping*, *21*, 191–201.

Havas, D. A., Glenberg, A. M., & Rinck, M. (2007). Emotion simulation during language comprehension. *Psychonomic Bulletin & Review*, *14*, 436–441.

Hawkins, R. D. (1984). A cellular mechanism of classical conditioning in *Aplysia*. *Journal of Experimental Biology*, *112*, 113–128.

Hawkins, R. D., & Kandel, E. (1984). Is there a cell-biological alphabet for simple forms of learning? *Psychological Review*, *91*, 375–391.

Heal, J. (1986). Replication and functionalism. In J. Butterfield (Ed.), *Language, mind, and logic* (pp. 135–150). Cambridge, England: Cambridge University Press.

Heider, F. (1958). *The psychology of interpersonal relations*. New York, NY: Wiley & Sons.

Hempel, C. (1950). Problems and changes in the empiricist criterion of meaning. *Revue Internationale de Philosophie*, *41*, 41–63.

Hempel, C. (1965). *Aspects of scientific explanation and other essays in the philosophy of science*. New York, NY: Free Press.

Hempel, C., & Oppenheim, P. (1948). Studies in the logic of explanation. *Philosophy of Science*, *15*, 135–175.

Hespos, S. J., & Spelke, E. (2004). Conceptual precursors to language. *Nature*, *430*, 453–456.

Hickock, G. (2008). Eight problems for the mirror neuron theory of action understanding in monkeys and humans. *Journal of Cognitive Neuroscience*, *21*, 1229–1243.

Hill, J. H., & Mannheim, B. (1992). Language and world view. *Annual Review of Anthropology*, *21*, 381–404.

Hoffman, D. D. (1998). *Visual intelligence*. New York, NY: W. W. Norton.

Hommel, B. (2010). Grounding attention in action control: The intentional control of selection. In B. J. Bruya (Ed.), *Effortless attention* (pp. 121–140). Cambridge, MA: MIT Press.

Hommel, B., Müsseler, J., Aschersleben, G., & Prinz, W. (2001). The theory of event coding (TEC): A framework for perception and action planning. *Behavioral and Brain Sciences, 24*, 849–878.

Hohwy, J. (2013). *The predictive mind*. Oxford, England: Oxford University Press.

Hohwy, J., Roepstorff, A., & Friston, K. J. (2008). Predictive coding explains binocular rivalry: An epistemological review. *Cognition, 108*, 687–701.

Hull, C. L. (1943). *Principles of behavior*. New York, NY: Appleton-Century-Crofts.

Hunt, E., & Agnoli, F. (1991). The Whorfian hypothesis: A cognitive psychology perspective. *Psychological Review, 98*, 377–389.

Hurley, S. L. (1998). *Consciousness in action*. Cambridge, MA: Harvard University Press.

Hutto, D. (2007). The narrative practice hypothesis: Origins and applications of folk psychology. *Royal Institute of Philosophy Supplements, 82*, 43–68.

Hutto, D. (2008). *Folk psychological narratives*. Cambridge, MA: MIT Press.

Iacoboni, M. (2008). *Mirroring people*. New York, NY: Farrar, Straus & Giroux.

Iacoboni, M., Molnar-Szakacs, I., Gallese, V., Buccino, G., Mazziotta, J. C., & Rizzolatti, G. (2005). Grasping the intentions of others with one's own mirror neuron system. *PLoS Biology, 3*, e79.

Iacoboni, M., Woods, R. P., Brass, M., Bekkering, H., Mazziotta, J. C., & Rizzolatti, G. (1999). Cortical mechanisms of human imitation. *Science, 286*, 2526–2528.

Imai, M., & Gentner, D. (1993). Linguistic relativity vs. universal ontology: Cross-linguistic studies of the object/substance distinction. *Proceedings of the Chicago Linguistic Society*. Retrieved from http://groups.psych.northwestern.edu/gentner/newpdfpapers/ImaiGentner93.pdf

Imai, M., & Gentner, D. (1997). A crosslinguistic study of early word meaning: Universal ontology and linguistic influence. *Cognition, 62*, 169–200.

Jackendoff, R. (1987). *Consciousness and the computational mind*. Cambridge, MA: MIT Press.

Jackendoff, R. (2007). *Language, consciousness, and culture*. Cambridge, MA: MIT Press.

James, W. (1890). *The principles of psychology* (Vol. 1). New York, NY: Henry Holt.

Jamieson, D., & Bekoff, M. (1992). Carruthers on non-conscious experience, *Analysis, 52*, 23–28.

Kahneman, D. (1973). *Attention and effort*. Englewood Cliffs, NJ: Prentice-Hall.

Kahneman, D., & Treisman, A. (1984). Changing views of attention and automaticity. In R. Parasuraman, D. R. Davies, & J. Beatty (Eds.), *Variants of attention* (pp. 29–61). New York, NY: Academic Press.

Kamin, L. J. (1969). Predictability, surprise, attention, and conditioning. In B. A. Campbell & R. M. Church (Eds.), *Punishment and aversive behavior* (pp. 279–296). New York, NY: Appleton-Century-Crofts.

Kellenbach, M. L., Brett, M., & Patterson, K. (2001). Large, colorful, or noisy? Attribute- and modality-specific activations during retrieval of perceptual attribute knowledge. *Cognitive, Affective, & Behavioral Neuroscience, 1*, 207–221.

Khalidi, M. A. (2002). Nature and nurture in cognition. *British Journal for the Philosophy of Science, 53*, 251–272

Khalidi, M. A. (2007). Innate cognitive capacities. *Mind and Language, 22*, 92–115.

Kim, J. (1993). *Supervenience and mind.* Cambridge, England: Cambridge University Press.

Kim, K. H., Relkin, N. R., Lee, K. M., & Hirsch, J. (1997). Distinct cortical areas associated with native and second languages. *Nature, 388*, 171–174.

Kimball, D. R., & Holyoak, K. J. (2000). Transfer and expertise. In E. Tulving & F. I. M. Craik (Eds.), *The Oxford handbook of memory* (pp. 109–122). New York, NY: Oxford University Press.

Koerner, E. F. K. (1992). The Sapir-Whorf hypothesis: A preliminary history and a bibliographical essay. *Journal of Linguistic Anthropology, 2*, 173–198.

Kosslyn, S. M. (1980). *Image and mind.* Cambridge, MA: Harvard University Press.

Kosslyn, S. M. (1994). *Image and brain: The resolution of the imagery debate.* Cambridge, MA: MIT Press.

Kosslyn, S. M., Ball, T. M., & Reiser, B. J. (1978). Visual images preserve metric spatial information: Evidence from studies of image scanning. *Journal of Experimental Psychology: Human Perception & Performance, 4*, 47–60.

Kosslyn, S. M., Ganis, G., & Thompson, W. L. (2001). Neural foundations of imagery. *Nature Reviews Neuroscience, 2*, 635–642.

Kosslyn, S. M., Thompson, W. L., & Ganis, G. (2006). *The case for mental imagery.* Oxford, England: Oxford University Press.

LaBerge, D. (1983). Spatial extent of attention to letters and words. *Journal of Experimental Psychology: Human Perception & Performance, 9*, 371–379.

Land, M. F., & Nilsson, D. (2002). *Animal eyes.* Oxford, England: Oxford University Press.

Lau, H., & Rosenthal, D. (2011). Empirical support for higher-order theories of conscious awareness. *Trends in Cognitive Sciences, 15*, 365–373.

Laurence, S., & Margolis, E. (2001). The poverty of the stimulus argument. *British Journal for the Philosophy of Science, 52*, 217–276.

Laurence, S., & Margolis, E. (2002). Radical concept nativism. *Cognition, 86*, 25–55.

Lavie, N. (1995). Perceptual load as a necessary condition for selective attention. *Journal of Experimental Psychology: Human Perception and Performance, 21*, 451–468.

Lavie, N. (2000). Selective attention and cognitive control: Dissociating attentional functions through different types of load. In S. Monsell & J. Driver (Eds.), *Attention and performance XVIII* (pp. 175–194). Cambridge: MIT Press.

Lavie, N. (2005). Distracted and confused? Selective attention under load. *Trends in Cognitive Sciences, 9,* 75–82.

Lavie, N., & Cox, S. (1997). On the efficiency of attentional selection: Efficient visual search results in inefficient rejection of distraction. *Psychological Science, 8,* 395–398.

Lavie, N., & Tsal, Y. (1994). Perceptual load as a major determinant of the locus of selection in visual attention. *Perception & Psychophysics, 56,* 183–197.

Leibniz, G. (1765/1996). *New essays on human understanding* (P. Remnant & J. Bennett, Eds.). Cambridge, England: Cambridge University Press.

Lepore, E., & Ludwig, K. (2005). *Donald Davidson: Meaning, truth, language, and reality.* Oxford, England: Oxford University Press.

Levin, D. T., Momen, N., Drivdahl, S. B., & Simons, D. J. (2000). Change blindness blindness: The metacognitive error of overestimating change-detection ability. *Visual Cognition, 7,* 397–412.

Levin, D. T., & Simons, D. J. (1997). Failure to detect changes to attended objects in motion pictures. *Psychonomic Bulletin and Review, 4,* 501–506.

Levine, J. (1983). Materialism and qualia: The explanatory gap. *Pacific Philosophical Quarterly, 64,* 354–361.

Levine, J. (2001). *Purple haze.* Oxford, England: Oxford University Press.

Levinson, S. C., & Brown, P. (1994). Immanuel Kant among the Tenejapans: Anthropology as empirical philosophy. *Ethos, 22,* 3–41.

Levinson, S. C., Kita, S., Haun, D. B. M., & Rasch, B. H. (2002). Returning the tables: Language affects spatial reasoning. *Cognition, 84,* 155–188.

Li, P., Abarbanell, L., Gleitman, L., & Papafragou, A. (2011). Spatial reasoning in Tenejapan Mayans. *Cognition, 120,* 33–53.

Li, P., & Gleitman, L. (2002). Turning the tables: Language and spatial reasoning. *Cognition, 83,* 265–294.

Lowenstein, G., & Adler, D. (1995). A bias in the prediction of tastes. *The Economic Journal, 105,* 929–937.

Lucy, J. (1992). *Grammatical categories and cognition: A case study of the linguistic relativity hypothesis.* Cambridge, England: Cambridge University Press.

Lucy, J. (1997). Linguistic relativity. *Annual Review of Anthropology, 26,* 291–312.

Lucy, J., & Gaskins, S. (2001). Grammatical categories and the development of classification preferences: A comparative approach. In S. Levinson & M. Bowerman (Eds.), *Language acquisition and conceptual development* (pp. 257–283). Cambridge, England: Cambridge University Press.

Lycan, W. G. (1981). Form, function, and feel. *Journal of Philosophy, 78,* 24–50.

Lycan, W. G. (1987). *Consciousness.* Cambridge, MA: MIT Press.

Lycan, W. G. (1995). Consciousness as internal monitoring: I. *Philosophical Perspectives, 9,* 1–14.

Lycan, W. G. (2004). The superiority of HOP to HOT. In R. Gennaro (Ed.), *Higher-order theories of consciousness* (pp. 93–114). Amsterdam, The Netherlands: John Benjamins.

Machamer, P. K., Darden, L., & Craver, C. F. (2000). Thinking about mechanisms. *Philosophy of Science, 67,* 1–25.

Mack, A., & Rock, I. (1998). *Inattentional blindness.* Cambridge, MA: MIT Press.

MacLeod, C. M. (1991). Half a century of research on the Stroop effect: An integrative review. *Psychological Bulletin, 109,* 163–203.

Macpherson, F. (2011). Individuating the senses. In F. Macpherson (Ed.), *The senses: Classic and contemporary philosophical perspectives* (pp. 3–43). Oxford, England: Oxford University Press.

Majid, A., Bowerman, M., Kita, S., Haun, D. B. M., & Levinson, S. C. (2004). Can language restructure cognition? The case for space. *Trends in Cognitive Sciences, 8,* 108–114.

Malle, B. (2004). *How the mind explains behavior.* Cambridge, MA: MIT Press.

Mallon, R., & Weinberg, J. (2006). Innateness as closed process invariance. *Philosophy of Science, 73,* 323–344.

Malt, B. C., Sloman, S. A., Gennari, S., Shi, M., & Wang, Y. (1999). Knowing versus naming: Similarity and the linguistic categorization of artifacts. *Journal of Memory and Language, 40,* 230–262.

Mameli, M. (2001). Mindreading, mindshaping, and evolution. *Biology and Philosophy, 16,* 597–628.

Margolis, E. (1998). How to acquire a concept. *Mind and Language, 13,* 347–369.

Marques, J. F. (2006). Specialization and semantic organization: Evidence for multiple semantics linked to sensory modalities. *Memory & Cognition, 34,* 60–67.

Marr, D. (1982). *Vision.* San Francisco, CA: W. H. Freeman.

Marshall, J. C., & Newcombe, F. (1973). Patterns of paralexia: A psychological approach. *Journal of Psycholinguistic Research, 2,* 175–199.

Martens, S., & Wyble, B. (2010). The attentional blink: Past, present, and future of a blind spot in perceptual awareness. *Neuroscience Biobehavioral Review, 34,* 947–957.

McCarthy, J., & Hayes, P. (1969). Some philosophical problems from the standpoint of artificial intelligence. In B. Meltzer & D. Michie (Eds.), *Machine Intelligence 4* (pp. 463–502). Edinburgh, Scotland: Edinburgh University Press.

McCarthy, R., & Warrington, E. K. (1986). Phonological reading: Phenomena and paradoxes. *Cortex, 22,* 359–380.

McConkie, G. W., & Currie, C. B. (1996). Visual stability across saccades while viewing complex pictures. *Journal of Experimental Psychology: Human Perception & Performance, 22,* 563–581.

McConkie, G. W., & Zola, D. (1979). Is visual information integrated across successive fixations in reading? *Perception & Psychophysics, 25,* 221–224.

McDonough, L., Choi, S., & Mandler, J. M. (2003). Understanding spatial relations: Flexible infants, lexical adults. *Cognitive Psychology, 46,* 229–259.

McGinn, C. (1989). Can we solve the mind-body problem? *Mind, 98,* 349–366.

McGinn, C. (1999). *The mysterious flame.* New York, NY: Basic Books.

McGurk, H., & MacDonald, J. (1976). Hearing lips and seeing voices. *Nature, 264,* 746–748.

McHugo, M., Olatunji, B. O., & Zald, D. H. (2013). The emotional attentional blink: What we know so far. *Frontiers in Human Neuroscience, 7,* 1–9.

Menary, R. (Ed.). (2010). *The extended mind.* Cambridge, MA: MIT Press.

Merleau-Ponty, M. (1962). *Phenomenology of perception.* (C. Smith, Trans.). New York, NY: Routledge.

Miller, R. R., Barnet, R. C., & Grahame, N. J. (1995). Assessment of the Rescorla-Wagner model. *Psychological Bulletin, 117,* 363–386.

Millikan, R. G. (1984). *Language, thought, and other biological categories.* Cambridge, MA: MIT Press.

Millikan, R. G. (2004). *Varieties of meaning.* Cambridge, MA: MIT Press.

Milner, A. D., & Goodale, M. A. (2006). *The visual brain in action* (2nd ed.). Oxford, England: Oxford University Press.

Milner, A. D., & Goodale, M. A. (2010). Cortical visual systems for perception and action. In N. Gangopadhyay, M. Madary, & F. Spicer (Eds.), *Perception, action, consciousness: Sensorimotor dynamics and two visual systems* (pp. 71–94). Oxford, England: Oxford University Press.

Mole, C. (2011). *Attention is cognitive unison.* Oxford, England: Oxford University Press.

Mole, C., Smithies, D., & Wu, W. (Eds.). (2011). *Attention: Philosophical and psychological essays.* Oxford, England: Oxford University Press.

Monti M. M., & Osherson D. N. (2012). Language, logic and the brain. *Brain Research, 1428,* 33–42.

Monti, M. M., Parsons, L. M., & Osherson D. N. (2012). Thought beyond language: Neural dissociation of arithmetic and natural language. *Psychological Science, 23,* 914–922.

Moray, N. (1959). Attention in dichotic listening: Affective cues and influence of instructions. *Quarterly Journal of Experimental Psychology, 11,* 56–60.

Morton, A. (1980). *Frames of mind.* Oxford, England: Oxford University Press.

Morton, A. (2007). Folk psychology does not exist. In D. Hutto & M. Ratcliffe (Eds.), *Folk psychology re-assessed* (pp. 211–221). Dordrecht, The Netherlands: Springer.

Morton, J., & Patterson, K. (1980). A new attempt at an interpretation, or, an attempt at a new interpretation. In M. Coltheart, K. Patterson, & J. C. Marshall (Eds.), *Deep dyslexia*. London, England: Routledge and Kegan Paul.

Most, S. B. (2010). What's "inattentional" about inattentional blindness? *Consciousness and Cognition, 19*, 1102–1104.

Most, S. B., Chun, M. M., Widders, D. M., & Zald, D. H. (2005b). Attentional rubbernecking: Cognitive control and personality in emotion-induced blindness. *Psychonomic Bulletin & Review, 12*, 654–661.

Most, S. B., Scholl, B. J., Simons, D. J., & Clifford, E. (2005a). What you see is what you get: Sustained inattentional blindness and the capture of awareness. *Psychological Review, 112*, 217–242.

Most, S. B., Simons, D. J., Scholl, B. J., Jimenez, R., Clifford, E., & Chabris, C. F. (2001). How not to be seen: The contribution of similarity and selective ignoring to sustained inattentional blindness. *Psychological Science, 12*, 9–17.

Mullen, M., & Yi, S. (1995). The cultural context of talk about the past: Implications for the development of autobiographical memory. *Cognitive Development, 10*, 407–419.

Müller, M. M., Malinowski, P., Gruber, T., & Hillyard, S. A. (2003). Sustained division of the attentional spotlight. *Nature, 424*, 309–312.

Murata, A., Fadiga, L., Fogassi, L., Gallese, V., Raos, V., & Rizzolatti, G. (1997). Object representation in the ventral premotor cortex (area F5) of the monkey. *Journal of Neurophysiology, 78*, 2226–2230.

Murphy, K. J., Racicot, C. I., & Goodale, M. A. (1996). The use of visuomotor cues as a strategy for making perceptual judgments in a patient with visual form agnosia. *Neuropsychology, 10*, 396–401.

Nagel, E. (1961). *The structure of science: Problems in the logic of scientific explanation.* New York, NY: Harcourt, Brace and World.

Nagel, T. (1974). What is it like to be a bat? *Philosophical Review, 83*, 435–450.

Negri, G. A., Rumiati, R. I., Zadini, A., Ukmar, M., Mahon, B. Z., & Caramazza, A. (2007). What is the role of motor simulation in action and object recognition? Evidence from apraxia. *Cognitive Neuropsychology, 24*, 795–816.

Nelson, K., & Fivush, R. (2004). The emergence of autobiographical memory: A social cultural developmental theory. *Psychological Review, 111*, 486–511.

Neumann, O. (1987). Beyond capacity: A functional view of attention. In H. Heuer & A. F. Sanders (Eds.), *Perspectives on perception and action* (pp. 361–394). Hillsdale, NJ: Lawrence Erlbaum.

Newell, A. (1980). Physical symbol systems. *Cognitive Science, 4*, 135–183.

Nichols, S., & Stich, S. (2000). A cognitive theory of pretense. *Cognition*, 115–147.

Nichols, S., & Stich, S. (2003). *Mindreading*. Oxford, England: Oxford University Press.

Noë, A. (2001). Experience and the active mind. *Synthese*, *29*, 41–60.

Noë, A. (2009). *Out of our heads*. New York, NY: Hill and Wang.

Noë, A., & O'Regan, J. K. (2002). On the brain-basis of visual consciousness: A sensorimotor account. In A. Noë & E. Thompson (Eds.), *Vision and mind: Selected readings in the philosophy of perception* (pp. 567–598). Cambridge, MA: MIT Press.

Noë, A., Pessoa, L., & Thompson, E. (2000). Beyond the grand illusion: What change blindness really teaches us about vision. *Visual Cognition*, *7*, 93–106.

Norman, D. (1968). Toward a theory of memory and attention. *Psychological Review*, *75*, 522–536.

Norman, D. (2013). *The design of everyday things* (Rev. ed.). New York, NY: Basic Books.

Norman, D., & Shallice, T. (1986). Attention to action: Willed and automatic control of behavior. In R. Davidson, R. Schwartz, & D. Shapiro (Eds.), *Consciousness and self-regulation: Advances in research and theory IV* (pp. 1–18). New York, NY: Plenum Press.

Nudds, M. (2004). The significance of the senses. *Proceedings of the Aristotelian Society*, *104*, 31–51.

O'Callaghan, C. (2007). *Sounds: A philosophical theory*. Oxford, England: Oxford University Press.

Ochipa, C., Rothi, L. J. G., & Heilman, K. M. (1989). Ideational apraxia: A deficit in tool selection and use. *Annals of Neurology*, *25*, 190–193.

Onishi, K. H., & Baillargeon, R. (2005). Do 15-month-old infants understand false beliefs? *Science*, *308*, 255–258.

Oppenheim, P., & Putnam, H. (1958). The unity of science as a working hypothesis. In H. Feigl, M. Scriven, & G. Maxwell (Eds.), *Minnesota studies in the philosophy of science* (Vol. 2, pp. 3–36). Minneapolis: Minnesota University Press.

O'Regan, J. K. (1992). Solving the "real" mysteries of visual perception: The world as an outside memory. *Canadian Journal of Psychology*, *46*, 461–488.

O'Regan, J. K., & Noë, A. (2001a). A sensorimotor account of vision and visual consciousness. *Behavioral and Brain Sciences*, *24*, 939–1031.

O'Regan, J. K., & Noë, A. (2001b). What it is like to see: A sensorimotor theory of visual experience. *Synthese*, *129*, 79–103.

Pacherie, E. (2000). Conscious experience and concept forming abilities. *Acta Analytica*, *26*, 45–52.

Pagin, P. (2005). Compositionality and context. In G. Preyer & G. Peter (Eds.), *Contextualism in philosophy* (pp. 303–348). Oxford, England: Oxford University Press.

Papineau, D. (2011). What exactly is the explanatory gap? *Philosophia*, *39*, 5–19.

Pashler, H. (1998). *The psychology of attention*. Cambridge, MA: MIT Press.

Pashler, H., Kang, S. H. K., & Ip, R. (2013). Does multitasking impair studying? Depends on timing. *Applied Cognitive Psychology, 27*, 593–599.

Patterson, K., & Morton, J. (1985). From orthography to phonology: An attempt at an old interpretation. In K. Patterson, J. C. Marshall, & M. Coltheart (Eds.), *Surface dyslexia: Neuropsychological and cognitive studies of phonological reading* (pp. 335–359). London, England: Lawrence Erlbaum.

Pavlova, M., Staudt, M., Sokolov, A., Birbaumer, N., & Krageloh-Mann, I. (2003). Perception and production of biological movement in patients with early periventricular brain lesions. *Brain, 126*, 692–701.

Pazzaglia, M., Smania, N., Corato, E., & Aglioti, S. M. (2008). Neural underpinnings of gesture discrimination in patients with limb apraxia. *Journal of Neuroscience, 28*, 3030–3041.

Pecher, D., Zeelenberg, R., & Barsalou, L.W. (2003). Verifying properties from different modalities for concepts produces switching costs. *Psychological Science, 14*, 119–124.

Pecher, D., Zeelenberg, R., & Barsalou, L. W. (2004). Sensorimotor simulations underlie conceptual representations: Modality-specific effects of prior activation. *Psychonomic Bulletin & Review, 11*, 164–167.

Pederson, E., Danziger, E., Wilkins, D. G., Levinson, S. C., Kita, S., & Senft, G. (1998). Semantic typology and spatial conceptualization. *Language, 74*, 557–589.

Peters, R. W. (1954). Competing messages: The effect of interfering messages upon the reception of primary messages. *USN Sch. Aviat. Med. Res. Rep.*, 1954, Project No. NM 001 064.01.27.

Pietroski, P., & Rey, G. (1995). When other things aren't equal: Saving ceteris paribus laws from vacuity. *British Journal for the Philosophy of Science, 46*, 81–110.

Pinker, S. (1994). *The language instinct*. New York, NY: Harper Perennial.

Pinker, S. (2007). *The stuff of thought*. New York, NY: Viking.

Pinto-Correia, C. (1997). *The ovary of Eve*. Chicago, IL: University of Chicago Press.

Place, U. T. (1956). Is consciousness a brain process? *British Journal of Psychology, 47*, 44–50.

Place, U. T. (1960) Materialism as a scientific hypothesis. *Philosophical Review, 69*, 101–104.

Polk, T. A., Drake, R. M., Jonides, J., Smith, M. R., & Smith, E. E. (2008). Attention enhances the neural processing of attended features and suppresses the neural processing of unattended features in humans: An fMRI study of the Stroop task. *Journal of Neuroscience, 28*, 13786–13792.

Polk, T. A., & Seifert, C. M. (Eds.). (2002). *Cognitive modeling*. Cambridge, MA: MIT Press.

Posner, M. I. (1980). Orienting of attention. *Quarterly Journal of Experimental Psychology, 32,* 3–25.

Posner, M. I., Snyder, C. R., & Davidson, B. J. (1980). Attention and the detection of signals. *Journal of Experimental Psychology, 109,* 160–174.

Premack, D., & Woodruff, G. (1978). Does the chimpanzee have a theory of mind? *Behavioral and Brain Sciences, 1,* 515–526.

Prinz, J. J. (2007). The intermediate-level theory of consciousness. In M. Velmans & S. Schneider (Eds.), *Blackwell companion to consciousness* (pp. 247–260). Malden, MA: Blackwell.

Prinz, J. J. (2012). *The conscious brain.* Oxford, England: Oxford University Press.

Proffitt, D. R., Bhalla, M., Gossweiler, R., & Midgett, J. (1995). Perceiving geographical slant. *Psychonomic Bulletin & Review, 2,* 409–428.

Proffitt, D. R., Stefanucci, J., Banton, T., & Epstein, W. (2003). The role of effort in perceiving distance. *Psychological Science, 14,* 106–112.

Pullum, G. K., & Scholz, B. C. (2002). Empirical assessment of stimulus poverty arguments. *The Linguistic Review, 19,* 9–50.

Pulvermüller, F. (2008). Grounding language in the brain. In M. de Vega, A. Graesser, & A. M. Glenberg (Eds.), *Symbols, embodiment, and meaning* (pp. 85–116). Oxford, England: Oxford University Press.

Putnam, H. (1967/1975). Psychological predicates. Reprinted as "The nature of mental states" in *Mind, language, and reality* (pp. 429–440). Cambridge, England: Cambridge University Press.

Putnam, H. (1975). Philosophy and our mental life. In *Mind, language, and reality* (pp. 291–303). Cambridge, England: Cambridge University Press.

Pylyshyn, Z. W. (1981). The imagery debate: Analogue media versus tacit knowledge. *Psychological Review, 88,* 16–45.

Pylyshyn, Z. (1984). *Computation and cognition: Towards a foundation for cognitive science.* Cambridge, MA: MIT Press.

Pylyshyn, Z. (Ed.). (1987). *The robot's dilemma: The frame problem in artificial intelligence.* Norwood, NJ: Ablex.

Pylyshyn, Z. W. (2002). Mental imagery: In search of a theory. *Behavioral and Brain Sciences, 25,* 157–237.

Pylyshyn, Z. W. (2003a). Return of the mental image: Are there really pictures in the head? *Trends in Cognitive Science, 7,* 113–118

Pylyshyn, Z. W. (2003b). *Seeing and visualizing: It's not what you think.* Cambridge, MA: MIT Press.

Quine, W. V. O. (1953/1980). Two dogmas of empiricism. In *From a logical point of view* (Rev. ed., pp. 20–46). Cambridge, MA: Harvard University Press.

Quine, W. V. O. (1960). *Word and object.* Cambridge, MA: MIT Press.

Ramachandran, V. S. (2000). Mirror neurons and imitation learning as the driving force behind "the great leap forward" in human evolution. Retrieved from http://www.edge.org/3rd_culture/ramachandran/ramachandran_p1.html

Ramachandran, V. S., & Hirstein, W. (1998). The perception of phantom limbs: The D. O. Hebb lecture. *Brain, 121*, 1603–1630.

Ramachandran, V. S., & Rogers-Ramachandran, D. (1996). Synaesthesia in phantom limbs induced with mirrors. *Proceedings: Biological Sciences, 263*, 377–386.

Reese, E., Haden, C. A., & Fivush, R. (1993). Mother-child conversations about the past: Relationships of style and memory over time. *Cognitive Development, 8*, 403–430.

Rensink, R. A. (2000a). Seeing, sensing, and scrutinizing. *Vision Research, 40*, 1469–1487.

Rensink, R. A. (2000b). The dynamic representation of scenes. *Visual Cognition, 7*, 17–42.

Rensink, R. A. (2002). Change detection. *Annual Review of Psychology, 53*, 245–277.

Rensink, R. A., O'Regan, J. K., & Clark, J. J. (1997). To see or not to see: The need for attention to perceive changes in scenes. *Psychological Science, 8*, 368–373.

Rensink, R. A., O'Regan, J. K., & Clark, J. J. (2000). On the failure to detect changes in scenes across brief interruptions. *Visual Cognition, 7*, 127–145.

Rescorla, R. A. (1988). Pavlovian conditioning: It's not what you think it is. *American Psychologist, 43*, 151–160.

Rescorla, R. A., & Wagner, A. R. (1972) A theory of Pavlovian conditioning: Variations in the effectiveness of reinforcement and nonreinforcement. In A. H. Black & W. F. Prokasy (Eds.), *Classical conditioning II* (pp. 64–99). New York, NY: Appleton-Century-Crofts.

Rizzolatti, G., Fadiga, L., Gallese, V., & Fogassi, L. (1996). Premotor cortex and the recognition of motor actions. *Brain Research/Cognitive Brain Research, 3*, 131–141.

Rizzolatti, G., & Gentilucci, M. (1988). Motor and visual-motor functions of the premotor cortex. In P. Rakic & W. Singer (Eds.), *Neurobiology of neocortex* (pp. 269–284). New York, NY: Wiley.

Rizzolatti, G., & Sinigaglia, C. (2008). *Mirrors in the brain*. Oxford, England: Oxford University Press.

Robbins, P., & Jack, A. I. (2006). The phenomenal stance. *Philosophical Studies, 127*, 59–85.

Roediger, H. L. (1985). Remembering Ebbinghaus. *Contemporary Psychology, 30*, 519–523.

Rorty, R. (1965). Mind-body identity, privacy, and categories. *Review of Metaphysics, 19*, 24–54.

Rosenthal, D. M. (1997). A theory of consciousness. In N. Block, O. Flanagan, & G. Güzuldere (Eds.), *The nature of consciousness* (pp. 729–754). Cambridge, MA: MIT Press.

Rosenthal, D. M. (2005). *Consciousness and mind.* Oxford, England: Oxford University Press.

Rowlands, M. (1999). *The body in mind.* Cambridge, England: Cambridge University Press.

Rupert, R. (2004). Challenges to the hypothesis of extended cognition. *Journal of Philosophy, 101,* 389–428.

Rymer, R. (1994). *Genie.* New York, NY: Harper.

Salmon, W. (1989). *Four decades of scientific explanation.* Minneapolis: University of Minnesota Press.

Sampson, G. (2005). *The 'language instinct' debate.* London, England: Continuum.

Samuels, R. (1998). Evolutionary psychology and the massive modularity hypothesis. *British Journal for the Philosophy of Science, 49,* 575–602.

Samuels, R. (2002). Nativism in cognitive science. *Mind and Language, 17,* 233–265.

Sapir, E. (1921). *Language: An introduction to the study of speech.* New York, NY: Harcourt Brace.

Sapir, E. (1924, February). The grammarian and his language. *The American Mercury,* 149–155.

Savitsky, K., & Gilovich, T. (2003). The illusion of transparency and the alleviation of speech anxiety. *Journal of Experimental Social Psychology, 39,* 618–625.

Schenk, T., & Milner, A. D. (2006). Concurrent visuomotor behaviour improves form discrimination in a patient with visual form agnosia. *European Journal of Neuroscience, 24,* 1495–1503.

Schiffer, S. (1991) Ceteris paribus laws. *Mind, 100,* 1–17.

Schmidt M., & Lipson H. (2009). Distilling free-form natural laws from experimental data. *Science, 324,* 81–85.

Scholz, B. C., & Pullum, G. K. (2002) Searching for arguments to support linguistic nativism. *The Linguistic Review, 19,* 185–224.

Schwartz, B. L., & Metcalfe, J. (2011). Tip-of-the-tongue (TOT) states: Retrieval, behavior, and experience. *Memory & Cognition, 39,* 737–749.

Schwitzgebel, E. (2011). *Perplexities of consciousness.* Cambridge, MA: MIT Press.

Segal, G. (1996). The modularity of theory of mind. In P. Carruthers & P. K. Smith (Eds.), *Theories of theories of mind* (pp. 141–158). Cambridge, England: Cambridge University Press.

Seidenberg, M. S., & McClelland, J. L. (1989). A distributed developmental model of word recognition and naming. *Psychological Review, 96,* 523–568.

Sekuler, R., Sekuler, A. B., & Lau, R. (1997). Sound alters visual motion perception. *Nature, 385,* 308.

Sellars, W. (1956). Empiricism and the philosophy of mind. In H. Feigl & M. Scriven (Eds.), *Minnesota studies in the philosophy of science* (Vol. 1, pp. 253–329). Minneapolis: University of Minnesota Press.

Semendeferi, K., Armstrong, E., Schleicher, A., Zilles, K., & Van Hoesen, G. W. (2001). Prefrontal cortex in humans and apes: A comparative study of area 10. *American Journal of Physical Anthropology, 114,* 223–241.

Semin, G. R., & Smith, E. R. (Eds.). (2008). *Embodied grounding: Social, cognitive, affective, and neuroscientific approaches.* Cambridge, England: Cambridge University Press.

Sera, M. D., Berge, C., & del Castillo Pintado, J. (1994). Grammatical and conceptual forces in the attribution of gender by English and Spanish speakers. *Cognitive Development, 6,* 119–142.

Sera, M. D., Elieff, C., Forbes, J., Burch, M. C., Rodriguez, W., & Dubois, D. P. (2002). When language affects cognition and when it does not: An analysis of grammatical gender and classification. *Journal of Experimental Psychology: General, 131,* 377–397.

Seyfarth, R. M., Cheney, D. L., & Marler, P. (1980). Monkey responses to three different alarm calls: Evidence for predator classification and semantic communication. *Science, 210,* 801–803.

Shallice, T. (1972). Dual functions of consciousness. *Psychological Review, 79,* 383–393.

Shallice, T. (1988). *From neuropsychology to mental structure.* Cambridge, England: Cambridge University Press.

Shams, L., & Kim, R. (2010). Crossmodal influences on visual perception. *Physics of Life Reviews, 7,* 269–284.

Shannon, C. E., & Weaver, W. (1949). *The mathematical theory of communication.* Urbana: The University of Illinois Press.

Shapiro, L. (2000). Multiple realizations. *Journal of Philosophy, 97,* 635–664.

Shapiro, L. (2004). *The mind incarnate.* Cambridge, MA: MIT Press.

Shapiro, L. (2010). *Embodied cognition.* New York, NY: Routledge.

Shepard, R. N. (1975). Form, formation and transformation of internal representations. In R. L. Solso (Ed.), *Information processing and cognition: The Loyola Symposium* (pp. 87–122). Hillsdale, NJ: Lawrence Erlbaum.

Shepard, R. N. (1978). On the status of "direct" psychophysical measurement. In C. W. Savage (Ed.), *Minnesota studies in the philosophy of science* (Vol. IX, pp. 441–490). Minneapolis: University of Minnesota Press.

Shepard, R. N., & Metzler, J. (1971). Mental rotation of three-dimensional objects. *Science, 171*, 701–703.

Shimojo, S., & Shams, L. (2001). Sensory modalities are not separate modalities: Plasticity and interactions. *Current Opinion in Neurobiology, 11*, 505–509.

Siegal, M., Varley, R., & Want, S. C. (2001). Mind over grammar: Reasoning in aphasia and development. *Trends in Cognitive Sciences, 5*, 296–301.

Silva, A. J. (2003). Molecular and cellular cognitive studies of the role of synaptic plasticity in memory. *Journal of Neurobiology, 54*, 224–237.

Silverman, M. E., & Mack, A. (2001). Change blindness and priming: When it does and does not occur. *Consciousness and Cognition, 15*, 409–422.

Simons, D. J. (2000). Current approaches to change blindness. *Visual Cognition, 7*, 1–15.

Simons, D. J., & Chabris, C. F. (1999). Gorillas in our midst: Sustained inattentional blindness for dynamic events. *Perception, 28*, 1059–1074.

Simons, D. J., & Levin, D. T. (1997). Change blindness. *Trends in Cognitive Science, 1*, 261–267.

Simons, D. J., & Levin, D. T. (1998). Failure to detect changes to people during a real-world interaction. *Psychonomic Bulletin & Review, 5*, 644–649.

Simons, D. J., & Levin, D. T. (2003). What makes change blindness interesting? In D. E. Irwin & B. H. Ross (Eds.), *Cognitive vision* (pp. 295–322). San Diego, CA: Academic Press.

Simons, D. J., & Rensink, R. A. (2005). Change blindness: Past, present, and future. *Trends in Cognitive Science, 9*, 16–20.

Skinner, B. F. (1965). *Science and human behavior*. New York, NY: The Free Press.

Slobin, D. (1996). From "thought and language" to "thinking for speaking." In J. J. Gumperz & S. C. Levinson (Eds.), *Rethinking linguistic relativity* (pp. 70–96). Cambridge, England: Cambridge University Press.

Smart, J. J. C. (1963). Materialism. *Journal of Philosophy, 60*, 651–662.

Smart, J. J. C. (1959). Sensations and brain processes. *Philosophical Review, 68*, 141–156.

Smith, S., Most, S., Newsome, L., & Zald, D. (2006). An emotion-induced attentional blink elicited by aversively conditioned stimuli. *Emotion, 6*, 523–527.

Sober, E. (1999a). The multiple realizability argument against reductionism. *Philosophy of Science, 66*, 542–564.

Sober, E. (1999b). Innate knowledge. In E. Craig (Ed.), *Routledge encyclopedia of philosophy* (Vol. 4, pp. 794–797). New York, NY: Routledge.

Soja, N., Carey, S., & Spelke, E. (1991). Ontological categories guide young children's inductions of word meaning: Object terms and substance terms. *Cognition, 38*, 179–211.

Spaulding, S. (2012). Mirror neurons are not evidence for the simulation theory. *Synthese*, *189*, 515–534.

Spelke, E. (1990). Principles of object perception. *Cognitive Science*, *14*, 29–56.

Spelke, E. (1991). Physical knowledge in infancy: Reflections on Piaget's theory. In S. Carey & R. Gelman (Eds.), *Epigenesis of mind: Studies in biology and cognition* (pp. 133–169). Hillsdale, NJ: Lawrence Erlbaum.

Sperling, G. (1960). The information available in brief visual presentations. *Psychological Monographs: General and Applied*, *74*, 1–29.

Sperry, R. W., Zaidel, E., & Zaidel, D. (1979). Self-recognition and social awareness in the disconnected minor hemisphere. *Neuropsychologia*, *17*, 153–166.

Sprevak, M. (2009). Extended cognition and functionalism. *Journal of Philosophy*, *106*, 503–527.

Squire, L. R. (2004). Memory systems of the brain: A brief history and current perspective. *Neurobiology of Learning & Memory*, *82*, 171–177.

Stainton, R. J. (2005). In defense of non-sentential assertion. In Z. Szabó (Ed.), *Semantics versus pragmatics* (pp 383–457). Oxford, England: Oxford University Press.

Stainton, R. J. (2006). *Words and thoughts: Subsentences, ellipsis, and the philosophy of language*. Oxford, England: Oxford University Press.

Stefanucci, J. K., & Proffitt, D. R. (2009). The roles of altitude and fear in the perception of heights. *Journal of Experimental Psychology: Human Perception & Performance*, *35*, 424–438.

Stefanucci, J. K., Proffitt, D. R., Clore, G., & Parekh, N. (2008). Skating down a steeper slope: Fear influences the perception of geographical slant. *Perception*, *37*, 321–323.

Stevens, S. S. (1957). On the psychophysical law. *Psychological Review*, *64*, 153–181.

Stevens, S. S. (1975). *Psychophysics*. New York, NY: Wiley.

Stich, S. (Ed.). (1975). *Innate Ideas*. Berkeley: University of California Press.

Stone, T., & Davies, M. (1996). The mental simulation debate: A progress report. In P. Carruthers & P. K. Smith (Eds.), *Theories of theories of mind* (pp. 119–137). Cambridge, England: Cambridge University Press.

Stroop, J. R. (1935). Studies of interference in serial verbal reactions. *Journal of Experimental Psychology*, *18*, 643–662.

Szabo, Z. (2010). The determination of content. *Philosophical Studies*, *148*, 253–272

Tessari, A., Canessa, N., Ukmar, M., & Rumiati, R. I. (2007). Neuropsychological evidence for a strategic control of multiple routes in imitation. *Brain*, *130*, 1111–1126.

Tipper, S. P. (1992). Selection for action: The role of inhibitory mechanisms. *Current Directions in Psychological Science*, *1*, 105–109.

Tipper, S. P., Howard. L. A., & Houghton, G. (1998). Action-based mechanisms of attention. *Philosophical Transactions of the Royal Society of London, Series B, 353,* 1385–1393.

Tomasello, M. (2014). *A natural history of human thinking.* Cambridge, MA: Harvard University Press.

Topulos, G. P., Lansing, R. W., & Banzett, R. B. (1993). The experience of complete neuromuscular blockade in awake humans. *Journal of Clinical Anesthesia, 5,* 369–374.

Treisman, A. (1960). Contextual cues in selective listening. *Quarterly Journal of Experimental Pyschology, 12,* 242–248.

Treisman, A. (1988). Features and objects: The fourteenth Bartlett Memorial Lecture. *Quarterly Journal of Experimental Psychology, 40A,* 201–236.

Tsal, Y., & Lavie, N. (1988). Attending to color and shape: The special role of location in selective visual processing. *Perception & Psychophysics, 44,* 15–21.

Tye, M. (1995). *Ten problems of consciousness.* Cambridge, MA: MIT Press.

Umiltà, M. A., Kohler, E., Gallese, V., Fogassi, L., Fadiga, L., Keysers, C., & Rizzolatti, G. (2001). I know what you are doing: A neurophysiological study. *Neuron, 31,* 155–165.

Van Boven, L., Dunning, D., & Loewenstein, G. (2000). Egocentric empathy gaps between owners and buyers: Misperceptions of the endowment effect. *Journal of Personality and Social Psychology, 79,* 66–76.

Van Boven, L., & Loewenstein, G. (2003). Projection of transient drive states. *Personality and Social Psychology Bulletin, 29,* 1159–1168.

Van Essen, D. C., & DeYoe, E. A. (1994) Concurrent processing in the primate visual cortex. In M. S. Gazzaniga (Ed.), *The cognitive neurosciences* (pp. 383–400). Cambridge, MA: MIT Press.

van Gelder, T., & Port, R. (1995). It's about time: Overview of the dynamical approach to cognition. In R. Port and T. van Gelder (Eds.), *Mind as motion: Explorations in the dynamics of cognition* (pp. 1–43). Cambridge, MA: MIT Press.

VanRullen, R., Carlson, T., & Cavanagh, P. (2007). The blinking spotlight of attention. *Proceedings of the National Academy of Sciences, 104,* 19204–19209.

van Ulzen, N. R., Semin, G. R., Oudejans, R. R. D., & Beek, P. J. (2008). Affective stimulus properties influence size perception and the Ebbinghaus illusion. *Psychological Research, 72,* 304–310.

Varela, J., Thompson, E., & Rosch, E. (1991). *The embodied mind: Cognitive science and human experience.* Cambridge, MA: MIT Press.

Varley, R. A. (2010). *Language and thinking: The evidence from severe aphasia* (Full Research Report ESRC End of Award Report, RES-051-27-0189). Swindon, England: ESRC.

Varley, R. A., Klessinger, N. J., Romanowski, C. A., & Siegal, M. (2005). Agrammatic but numerate. *Proceedings of the National Academy of Sciences, 102*, 3519–3524.

Vogel, E. K., & Luck, S. J. (2002). Delayed working memory consolidation during the attentional blink. *Psychonomic Bulletin & Review, 4*, 739–743.

von Humboldt, W. (1836/1988). *On language: The diversity of human language-structure and its influence on the mental development of mankind.* Cambridge, England: Cambridge University Press.

von Melchner, L., Pallas, S. L., & Sur, M. (2000). Visual behavior induced by retinal projections directed to the auditory pathway. *Nature, 404*, 871–875.

Watson, J. (1913). Psychology as the behaviorist views it. *Psychological Review, 20*, 158–177.

Weber, E. H. (1834). De pulsu, resorptione, auditu et tactu. *Annotationes anatomicae et physiologicae.* Leipzig, Germany: Koehler.

Weiskopf, D. A. (2005). Mental mirroring as the origin of attributions. *Mind and Language, 20*, 495–520.

Weiskopf, D. A. (2008a). The origins of concepts. *Philosophical Studies, 140*, 359–384.

Weiskopf, D. A. (2008b). Patrolling the bounds of cognition. *Erkenntnis, 68*, 265–276.

Weiskopf, D. A. (2010a). Concepts and the modularity of thought. *Dialectica, 64*, 107–130.

Weiskopf, D. A. (2010b). Embodied cognition and linguistic comprehension. *Studies in History and Philosophy of Science, 41*, 294–304.

Weiskopf, D. A. (2010c). Understanding is not simulating: A reply to Gibbs and Perlman. (2010). *Studies in History and Philosophy of Science, 41*, 309–312.

Weiskopf, D. A. (2010d). The Goldilocks problem and extended cognition. *Cognitive Systems Research, 11*, 313–323.

Weiskrantz, L. (1997). *Consciousness lost and found.* Oxford, England: Oxford University Press.

Weiskrantz, L. (Ed.). (1988). *Thought without language.* Oxford, England: Clarendon Press.

Wellman, H. (1990). *The child's theory of mind.* Cambridge, MA: MIT Press.

Wellman, H., & Bartsch, K. (1988). Young children's reasoning about beliefs. *Cognition, 30*, 239–277.

Wellman, H., & Woolley, J. D. (1992). From simple desires to ordinary beliefs: The early development of everyday psychology. *Cognition, 35*, 245–275.

Wellman, H. M., Cross, D., & Watson, J. (2001). Meta-analysis of theory-of-mind development: The truth about false belief. *Child Development, 72*, 655–684.

Wertz, A. E., & German, T. C. (2007). Belief-desire reasoning in the explanation of behavior: Do actions speak louder than words? *Cognition, 105*, 184–194.

Whorf, B. L. (1940). Science and linguistics. *MIT Technology Review, 42*, 229–231.

Willems, R. M., Benn, Y., Hagoort, I., Toni, I., & Varley, R. A. (2011). Communicating without a functioning language system: Implications for the role of language in mentalizing. *Neuropsychologia*, *49*, 3130–3135.

Wilson, D., & Sperber, D. (2012). *Meaning and relevance*. Cambridge, England: Cambridge University Press.

Wilson, T. (2002). *Strangers to ourselves*. New York, NY: Belknap Press.

Wimmer H., & Perner, J. (1983). Beliefs about beliefs: Representation and constraining function of wrong beliefs in young children's understanding of deception. *Cognition*, *13*, 103–128.

Witt, J. K., Linkenauger, S. A., Bakdash, J. Z., & Proffitt, D. R. (2008). Putting to a bigger hole: Golf performance relates to perceived size. *Psychonomic Bulletin & Review*, *15*, 581–585.

Wolfe, J. (1999). Inattentional amnesia. In V. Coltheart (Ed.), *Fleeting memories* (pp. 71–94). Cambridge, MA: MIT Press.

Woodward, J. (2002a). What is a mechanism? A counterfactual account. *Philosophy of Science*, *69*, S366–S377.

Woodward, J. (2002b). There is no such thing as a ceteris paribus law. *Erkenntnis*, *57*, 303–328.

Wright, R. D., & Ward, L. M. (1998). The control of visual attention. In R. D. Wright (Ed.), *Visual attention* (pp. 132–186). Oxford, England: Oxford University Press.

Wu, W. (2011a). Confronting many-many problems: Attention and agentive control. *Nous*, *45*, 50–76.

Wu, W. (2011b). Attention as selection for action. In C. Mole, D. Smithies, & W. Wu (Eds.), *Attention: Philosophical and psychological essays* (pp. 97–116). Oxford, England: Oxford University Press.

Wu, W. (2014). *Attention*. New York, NY: Routledge.

Yantis, S. (1988). On analog movements of visual attention. *Perception & Psychophysics*, *43*, 203–206.

Young, L., Dodell-Feder, D., & Saxe, R. What gets the attention of the temporoparietal junction? An fMRI investigation of attention and theory of mind. *Neuropsychologia*, *48*, 2658–2664.

Zawidzki, T. (2013). *Mindshaping*. Cambridge, MA: MIT Press.

Zeki, S. (1990). A century of cerebral achromatopsia. *Brain*, *113*, 1721–1777.

Index